TRUST

THE FREE PRESS

New York   London   Toronto   Sydney   Tokyo   Singapore

FRANCIS FUKUYAMA

TRUST

The Social Virtues and the Creation
of Prosperity

The Free Press
A Division of Simon & Schuster Inc.
1230 Avenue of the Americas
New York, N.Y. 10020

Printed in the United States of America

printing number

1 2 3 4 5 6 7 8 9 10

Text design by Carla Bolte

Library of Congress Cataloging-in-Publication Data

Fukuyama, Francis.
    Trust : The social virtues and the creation of prosperity / Francis Fukuyama.
      p. cm.
    Includes bibliographical references and index.
    ISBN 0-02-910976-0
    1. Economics—Moral and ethical aspects. 2. Trust (Psychology). 3. Virtue.
4. Economic history—1945. I. Title.
HB72.F85   1992
306.3—dc20   95-19320
                                                 CIP

For Laura, one and only

A society composed of an infinite number of unorganized individuals, that a hypertrophied State is forced to oppress and contain, constitutes a veritable sociological monstrosity. . . . Moreover, the State is too remote from individuals; its relations with them too external and intermittent to penetrate deeply into individual consciences and socialize them within. . . . A nation can be maintained only if, between the State and the individual, there is interposed a whole series of secondary groups near enough to the individuals to attract them strongly in their sphere of action and drag them, in this way, into the general torrent of social life. . . . Occupational groups are suited to fill this role, and that is their destiny.

—Emile Durkheim
The Division of Labor in Society

The art of association then becomes, as I have said before, the mother of action, studied and applied by all.

Alexis de Tocqueville, *Democracy in America*

CONTENTS

PART II

Low-Trust Societies and the Paradox of Family Values

PART III

High-Trust Societies and the Challenge of Sustaining Sociability

PART IV

American Society and the Crisis of Trust

PART V

*Enriching Trust: Combining Traditional Culture and
Modern Institutions in the Twenty-first Century*

PREFACE

When Alexander Kojève, the twentieth century's preeminent interpreter of Hegel, concluded at mid-century that the latter was essentially correct in declaring that history had ended, he decided as well that philosophers like himself had no further useful work to do. Relegating the study of philosophy to weekends, he became a full-time bureaucrat in the Commission of the newly formed European Economic Community, where he remained until his death in 1968. In the light of this progression, it seemed only natural that I also should follow my own *The End of History and the Last Man* with a book about economics.

It seems to me that the emphasis on economics is almost inevitable. There has, of course, been a great deal of *Sturm und Drang* following the collapse of communism, with apparent instability and much pessimism in Europe concerning that continent's political prospects. But virtually all political questions today revolve around economic ones; security problems themselves are shaped by issues welling up from within fragile civil societies, East and West. But economics is not what it appears to be either; it is grounded in social life and cannot be understood separately from the larger question of how modern societies organize themselves. It is the arena in which modern recognition struggles play themselves out. This book, then, is not a cookbook in the "competitiveness" genre, explaining how to create a winning economy or how Americans ought to imitate the Japanese or Germans. It is, rather, the story of how economic life reflects, shapes, and underpins modern life itself.

A study that tries to compare and contrast different cultures with respect to economic performance is an open invitation to insult virtually everyone it touches upon. I have covered a great deal of ground in this book, and I am sure that people more knowledgeable than I about the particular societies under discussion will be able to think of countless objections, exceptions, and contradictory pieces of evidence to the different generalizations contained here. To those who feel I have misunderstood *their* culture or, worse yet, said something slighting or belittling about it, I apologize in advance.

I owe a debt of gratitude to many people. Three editors influenced the book greatly: Erwin Glikes, who signed the book prior to his untimely death in 1994; Adam Bellow of the Free Press, who saw it to completion; and Peter Dougherty, who labored long hours to put the manuscript into final shape. I also thank, for their help at various points along the way, Michael Novak, Peter Berger, Seymour Martin Lipset, Amitai Etzioni, Ezra Vogel, Atsushi Seike, Chie Nakane, Takeshi Ishida, Noritake Kobayashi, Saburo Shiroyama, Steven Rhoads, Reiko Kinoshita, Mancur Olson, Michael Kennedy, Henry S. Rowen, Clare Wolfowitz, Robert D. Putnam, George Holmgren, Lawrence Harrison, David Hale, Wellington K. K. Chan, Kongdan Oh, Richard Rosecrance, Bruce Porter, Mark Cordover, Jonathan Pollack, Michael Swaine, Aaron Friedberg, Tamara Hareven, and Michael Mochizuki. Abram Shulsky, as usual, contributed greatly to the book's conceptualization.

Once again, I am grateful to James Thomson and the RAND Corporation, which tolerated my presence as I was writing this book. I owe a long-standing debt of gratitude to my literary agents, Esther Newberg and Heather Schroder, who made both this and the volume that preceded it possible. Much of the material covered in this book would never have come to my attention but for the hard work of my research assistants, Denise Quigley, Tenzing Donyo, and especially Chris Swenson, who was of invaluable assistance through all phases of this study.

My wife, Laura, to whom the book is dedicated, has always been a careful reader and critic, and helped enormously. She was a source of great support throughout this effort.

Yoshia Fukuyama, my father, was a sociologist of religion, and passed down to me several years ago his library of social science classics. After resisting this perspective for many years, I think I now more fully understand his own interest in it. He read and commented on the manuscript, but passed away before the book could be published. I hope he understood how much his own life's interests are reflected here.

As previously , in lieu of thanks to a typist, I must express gratitude to all of those ever-curious and inventive tinkerers and designers—many of them immigrants—who made possible all of the software, computers, and networking equipment on which production of this book depended.

I

THE IDEA OF TRUST

The Improbable Power of Culture in the
Making of Economic Society

CHAPTER I

On the Human Situation at the End of History

As we approach the twenty-first century, a remarkable convergence of political and economic institutions has taken place around the world. Earlier in this century, deep ideological cleavages divided the world's societies. Monarchy, fascism, liberal democracy, and communism were bitter competitors for political supremacy, while different countries chose the divergent economic paths of protectionism, corporatism, the free market, and socialist centralized planning. Today virtually all advanced countries have adopted, or are trying to adopt, liberal democratic political institutions, and a great number have simultaneously moved in the direction of market-oriented economies and integration into the global capitalist division of labor.

As I have argued elsewhere, this movement constitutes an "end of history," in the Marxist-Hegelian sense of History as a broad evolution of human societies advancing toward a final goal.[1] As modern technology unfolds, it shapes national economies in a coherent fashion, interlocking them in a vast global economy. The increasing complexity and information intensity of modern life at the same time renders centralized economic planning extremely difficult. The enormous prosperity created by technology-driven capitalism, in turn, serves as an incubator for a liberal regime of universal and equal rights, in which the struggle for recognition of human dignity culminates. While many countries have had trouble creating the institutions of democracy and free markets, and others, especially in parts of the former communist world, have slid backward into fascism or anarchy, the world's advanced countries have no alternative model of political and economic organization other than democratic capitalism to which they can aspire.

This convergence of institutions around the model of democratic capitalism, however, has not meant an end to society's challenges. Within a given institutional framework, societies can be richer or poorer, or have more or less satisfying social and spiritual lives. But a corollary to the convergence of institutions at the "end of history" is the widespread acknowledgment that in postindustrial societies, further improvements cannot be achieved through ambitious social engineering. We no longer have realistic hopes that we can create a "great society" through large government programs. The Clinton administration's difficulties in promoting health care reform in 1994 indicated that Americans remained skeptical about the workability of large-scale government management of an important sector of their economy. In Europe, almost no one argues that the continent's major concerns today, such as a high continuing rate of unemployment or immigration, can be fixed through expansion of the welfare state. If anything, the reform agenda consists of cutting back the welfare state to make European industry more competitive on a global basis. Even Keynesian deficit spending, once widely used by industrial democracies after the Great Depression to manage the business cycle, is today regarded by most economists as self-defeating in the long run. These days, the highest ambition of most governments in their macroeconomic policy is to do no harm, by ensuring a stable money supply and controlling large budget deficits.

Today, having abandoned the promise of social engineering, virtually all serious observers understand that liberal political and economic institutions depend on a healthy and dynamic civil society for their vitality.[2] "Civil society"—a complex welter of intermediate institutions, including businesses, voluntary associations, educational institutions, clubs, unions, media, charities, and churches—builds, in turn, on the family, the primary instrument by which people are socialized into their culture and given the skills that allow them to live in broader society and through which the values and knowledge of that society are transmitted across the generations.

A strong and stable family structure and durable social institutions cannot be legislated into existence the way a government can create a central bank or an army. A thriving civil society depends on a people's habits, customs, and ethics—attributes that can be shaped only indirectly through conscious political action and must otherwise be nourished through an increased awareness and respect for culture.

Beyond the boundaries of specific nations, this heightened significance of culture extends into the realms of the global economy and international order. Indeed, one of the ironies of the convergence of larger institutions since the end of the cold war is that people around the world are now even more conscious of the cultural differences that separate them. For example, over the past decade, Americans have become much more aware of the fact that Japan, an erstwhile member of the "free world" during the cold war, practices both democracy and capitalism according to a different set of cultural norms than does the United States. These differences have led to considerable friction at times, as when the members of a Japanese business network known as a *keiretsu* buy from one another rather than from a foreign company that might offer better price or quality. For their part, many Asians are troubled by certain aspects of American culture, such as its litigiousness and the readiness of Americans to insist upon their individual rights at the expense of the greater good. Increasingly, Asians point to superior aspects of their own cultural inheritance, such as deference to authority, emphasis on education, and family values, as sources of social vitality.[3]

The increasing salience of culture in the global order is such that Samuel Huntington has argued that the world is moving into a period of "civilizational clash," in which the primary identification of people will not be ideological, as during the cold war, but cultural.[4] Accordingly, conflict is likely to arise not among fascism, socialism, and democracy but among the world's major cultural groups: Western, Islamic, Confucian, Japanese, Hindu, and so on.

Huntington is clearly correct that cultural differences will loom larger from now on and that all societies will have to pay more attention to culture as they deal not only with internal problems but with the outside world. Where Huntington's argument is less convincing, however, is that cultural differences will necessarily be the source of conflict. On the contrary, the rivalry arising from the interaction of different cultures can frequently lead to creative change, and there are numerous cases of such cultural cross-stimulation. Japan's confrontation with Western culture after the arrival of Commodore Perry's "black ships" in 1853 paved the way for the Meiji Restoration and Japan's subsequent industrialization. In the past generation, techniques like lean manufacturing—the process of eliminating buffers from the manufacturing process to facilitate feedback from the factory floor—have made their way from Japan to the United States, to the latter's benefit. Whether the confrontation of cultures leads to conflict or to adaptation and progress, it is now vitally important to develop a deeper understanding of what makes these cultures distinctive and functional, since the issues surrounding international competition, political and economic, increasingly will be cast in cultural terms.

Perhaps the most crucial area of modern life in which culture exercises a direct influence on domestic well-being and international order is the economy. Although economic activity is inextricably linked with social and political life, there is a mistaken tendency, encouraged by contemporary economic discourse, to regard the economy as a facet of life with its own laws, separate from the rest of society. Seen this way, the economy is a realm in which individuals come together only to satisfy their selfish needs and desires before retreating back into their "real" social lives. But in any modern society, the economy constitutes one of the most fundamental and dynamic arenas of human sociability. There is scarcely any form of economic activity, from running a dry-cleaning business to fabricating large-scale integrated circuits, that does not require the social collaboration of human beings. And while people work in organizations to satisfy their individual needs, the workplace also draws people out of their private lives and connects them to a wider social world. That connectedness is not just a means to the end of earning a paycheck but an important end of human life itself. For just as people are selfish, a side of the human personality craves being part of larger communities. Human beings feel an acute sense of unease—what Emile Durkheim labeled *anomie*—in the absence of norms and rules binding them to others, an unease that the modern workplace serves to moderate and overcome.[5]

The satisfaction we derive from being connected to others in the workplace grows out of a fundamental human desire for recognition. As I argued in *The End of History and the Last Man,* every human being seeks to have his or her dignity recognized (i.e., evaluated at its proper worth) by other human beings. Indeed, this drive is so deep and fundamental that it is one of the chief motors of the entire human historical process. In earlier periods, this desire for recognition played itself out in the military arena as kings and princes fought bloody battles with one another for primacy. In modern times, this struggle for recognition has shifted from the military to the economic realm, where it has the socially beneficial effect of creating rather than destroying wealth. Beyond subsistence levels, economic activity is frequently undertaken for the sake of recognition rather than merely as a means of satisfying natural material needs.[6] The latter are, as Adam Smith pointed out, few in number and relatively easily satisfied. Work and money are much more important as sources of identity, status, and dignity, whether one has created a multinational media empire or been promoted to foreman. This kind of recognition cannot be achieved by individuals; it can come about only in a social context.

Thus, economic activity represents a crucial part of social life and is knit together by a wide variety of norms, rules, moral obligations, and other habits that together shape the society. As this book will show, one of the most important lessons we can learn from an examination of economic life is that a nation's well-being, as well as its ability to compete, is conditioned by a single, pervasive cultural characteristic: the level of trust inherent in the society.

Consider the following vignettes from twentieth-century economic life:

- During the oil crisis of the early 1970s, two automakers on opposite sides of the world, Mazda and Daimler-Benz (maker of Mercedes-Benz luxury cars), were both hit with declining sales and the prospect of bankruptcy. In both cases, they were bailed out by a coalition of companies with which they had traditionally done business, led by a large bank: Sumitomo Trust, in the instances of Mazda, and the Deutsche Bank, in the case of Daimler. In both cases, immediate profitability was sacrificed for the sake of saving the institution—in the German case, to prevent it from being bought out by a group of Arab investors.
- The recession of 1983–1984 that ravaged America's industrial heartland also hit the Nucor Corporation very hard. Nucor had just entered the steelmaking business by building mini-mills using a new German continuous-casting technology. Its mills were built in places like Crawfordsville, Indiana, outside the traditional rust belt, and were operated

by nonunionized workers, many of them former farmers. To deal with the drop in revenues, Nucor put its employees—from the CEO to the lowliest maintenance worker—on a two- or three-day workweek, with a corresponding cut in pay. No workers were fired, however, and when the economy and the company recovered, it enjoyed a tremendous esprit de corps that contributed to its becoming a major force in the American steel industry.[7]

- In the Toyota Motor Company's Takaoka assembly plant, any of the thousands of assembly line workers who work there can bring the entire plant to a halt by pulling on a cord at his or her workstation. They seldom do. By contrast, workers at the great Ford auto plants like Highland Park or River Rouge—plants that virtually defined the nature of modern industrial production for three generations—were never trusted with this kind of power. Today, Ford workers, having adopted Japanese techniques, are trusted with similar powers, and have greater control over their workplace and machines.

- In Germany, shop foremen on the floor of a typical factory know how to do the jobs of those who work under them and frequently take their place if the need arises. The foreman can move workers from one job to another and evaluates them based on face-to-face dealings. There is great flexibility in promotion: a blue-collar worker can obtain credentials as an engineer by attending an extensive in-company training program rather than going to a university.

The common thread that runs through these four apparently unrelated vignettes is that in each case, economic actors supported one another because they believed that they formed a community based on mutual trust. The banks and suppliers that engineered the Mazda and Daimler-Benz rescues felt an obligation to support these auto companies because the latter had supported them in the past and would do so again in the future. In the German case, moreover, there was a nationalistic feeling that such an important trademark German name as Mercedes-Benz should not fall into non-German hands. Workers at Nucor were willing to accept severe cuts in their weekly pay because they believed that the managers who devised the pay cut plan were hurting as well and were committed to not laying them off. The workers at the Toyota plant were given immense power to stop the entire assembly line because management trusted them not to abuse that power, and they repaid this trust by using that power responsibly to improve the line's overall productivity.

Finally, the workplace in Germany is flexible and egalitarian because workers trust their managers and fellow workers to a higher degree than in other European countries.

The community in each of these cases was a cultural one, formed not on the basis of explicit rules and regulations but out of a set of ethical habits and reciprocal moral obligations internalized by each of the community's members. These rules or habits gave members of the community grounds for trusting one another. Decisions to support the community were not based on narrow economic self-interest. The Nucor management could have decided to award themselves bonuses while laying off workers, as many other American corporations did at the time, and Sumitomo Trust and Deutsche Bank could perhaps have maximized their profits by selling off their failing assets. Solidarity within the economic community in question may have had beneficial consequences over the long run for the bottom line; certainly Nucor's workers were motivated to give their company an extra measure of effort once the recession was over, as was the German foreman whose company helped him to become an engineer. But the reason that these economic actors behaved as they did was not necessarily because they had calculated these economic consequences in advance; rather, solidarity within their economic community had become an end in itself. Each was motivated, in other words, by something broader than individual self-interest. As we will see, in all successful economic societies these communities are united by trust.

By contrast, consider situations in which the absence of trust has led to poor economic performance and its attendant social implications:

- In a small town in southern Italy during the 1950s, Edward Banfield noted that the wealthy citizens were unwilling to come together to found either a school or hospital, which the town needed badly, or to build a factory, despite an abundance of capital and labor, because they believed it was the obligation of the state to undertake such activities.
- In contrast to German practice, the French shop foreman's relations with his or her workers are regulated by a thicket of rules established by a ministry in Paris. This comes about because the French tend not to trust superiors to make honest personal evaluations of their workers. The formal rules prevent the foreman from moving workers from one job to another, inhibiting development of a sense of workplace solidarity and making very difficult the introduction of innovations like the Japanese lean manufacturing system.

- Small businesses in American inner cities are seldom owned by African-Americans; they tend to be controlled by other ethnic groups, like the Jews earlier in this century and Koreans today. One reason is an absence of strong community and mutual trust among the contemporary African-American "underclass." Korean businesses are organized around stable families and benefit from rotating credit associations within the broader ethnnic community; inner-city African-American families are weak and credit associations virtually nonexistent.

These three cases reveal the absence of a proclivity for community that inhibits people from exploiting economic opportunities that are available to them. The problem is one of a deficit of what the sociologist James Coleman has called "social capital": the ability of people to work together for common purposes in groups and organizations.[8] The concept of human capital, widely used and understood among economists, starts from the premise that capital today is embodied less in land, factories, tools, and machines than, increasingly, in the knowledge and skills of human beings.[9] Coleman argued that in addition to skills and knowledge, a distinct portion of human capital has to do with people's ability to associate with each other, that is critical not only to economic life but to virtually every other aspect of social existence as well. The ability to associate depends, in turn, on the degree to which communities share norms and values and are able to subordinate individual interests to those of larger groups. Out of such shared values comes trust, and trust, as we will see, has a large and measurable economic value.

With regard to the ability to form spontaneous communities such as those detailed above, the United States has had more in common with Japan and Germany than any of these three has with Chinese societies like Hong Kong and Taiwan, on the one hand, and Italy and France on the other. The United States, like Japan and Germany, has historically been a high-trust, group-oriented society, despite the fact that Americans believe themselves to be rugged individualists.

But the United States has been changing rather dramatically over the past couple of generations with respect to its art of association. In many ways, American society is becoming as individualistic as Americans have always believed it was: the inherent tendency of rights-based liberalism to expand and multiply those rights against the authority of virtually all existing communities has been pushed toward its logical conclusion. The decline of trust and sociability in the United States is also evident in any number of changes in American society: the rise of violent crime and civil litigation; the breakdown of family structure; the decline of a wide range of intermediate social structures like neighborhoods, churches, unions, clubs, and charities; and the general sense among Americans of a lack of shared values and community with those around them.

This decline of sociability has important implications for American democracy, perhaps even more so than for the economy. Already the United States pays significantly more than other industrialized countries for police protection and keeps more than 1 percent of its total population in prison. The United States also pays substantially more than does Europe or Japan to its lawyers, so that its citizens can sue one another. Both of these costs, which amount to a measurable percentage of gross domestic product annually, constitute a direct tax imposed by the breakdown of trust in the society. In the future, the economic effects may be more far-reaching; the ability of Americans to start and work within a wide variety of new organizations may begin to deteriorate as its very diversity lowers trust and creates new barriers to cooperation. In addition to its physical capital, the United States has been living off a fund of social capital. Just as its savings rate has been too low to replace physical plant and infrastructure adequately, so its replenishment of social capital has lagged in recent decades. The accumulation of social capital, however, is a complicated and in many ways mysterious cultural process. While governments can enact policies that have the effect of depleting social capital, they have great difficulties understanding how to build it up again.

The liberal democracy that emerges at the end of history is therefore not entirely "modern." If the institutions of democracy and capitalism are to work properly, they must coexist with certain premodern cultural habits that ensure their proper functioning. Law, contract, and economic rationality provide a necessary but not sufficient basis for both the stability and prosperity of postindustrial societies; they must as well be leavened with reciprocity, moral obligation, duty toward community, and trust, which are based in habit rather than rational calculation. The latter are not anachronisms in a modern society but rather the sine qua non of the latter's success.

The American problem starts with a failure of Americans to perceive their own society, and its historical communitarian orientation, correctly. Part I addresses this failure, beginning with a discussion of why recent arguments among certain thinkers miss a critical point about the cultural dimension of economic life. The remainder of this part will define more precisely what is meant by culture, trust, and social capital. It will explain how trust is related to industrial structure and the creation of those large-scale organizations vital to economic well-being and competitiveness.

Parts II and III deal with two major bridges to sociability, the family and nonkinship-based communities, respectively. There are four "familistic" societies detailed in part II: China, France, Italy, and South Korea. In each, the family constitutes the basic unit of economic organization; each has experienced difficulties in creating large organizations that go beyond the family, and in each, consequently, the state has had to step in to promote durable, globally competitive firms. Part III examines Japan and Germany, both high-trust societies, which, in contrast to the familistic societies of part II, have had a much easier time spawning large-scale firms not based on kinship. Not only did such societies move early to modern professional management, but they have been able to create more efficient and satisfying workplace relationships on the factory floor. Lean manufacturing, invented by the Toyota Motor Corporation, will be considered as one example of the organizational innovations possible in a high-trust society.

Part IV discusses the complicated problem of where to locate the United States in the spectrum of low- and high-trust societies. Where the American art of association came from, and why it has been weakening, are the chief issues taken up in this part of the book. Finally, part V will draw some general conclusions concerning the future of global society and the role of economic life in the broader scope of human activity.

CHAPTER 2

The Twenty Percent Solution

Over the past generation, economic thought has been dominated by neoclassical or free market economists, associated with names like Milton Friedman, Gary Becker, and George Stigler. The rise of the neoclassical perspective constitutes a vast improvement from earlier decades in this century, when Marxists and Keynesians held sway. We can think of neoclassical economics as being, say, eighty percent correct: it has uncovered important truths about the nature of money and markets because its fundamental model of rational, self-interested human behavior is correct about eighty percent of the time. But there is a missing twenty percent of human behavior about which neoclassical economics can give only a poor account. As Adam Smith well understood, economic life is deeply embedded in social life, and it cannot be understood apart from the customs, morals, and habits of the society in which it occurs. In short, it cannot be divorced from culture.[1]

Consequently, we have been ill served by contemporary economic debates that fail to take account of these cultural factors. An example is the argument that has taken place in the United States between free market economists and the so-called neomercantilists over the past decade. Proponents of the latter perspective—including people like Chalmers Johnson, James Fallows, Clyde Prestowitz, John Zysman, Karl van Wolferen, Alice Amsden, and Laura Tyson—have argued that the dynamic and fast-growing economies of East Asia have succeeded not by following but by violating the rules of neoclassical economics.[2] The Asian fast developers have achieved such astoundingly high growth rates, the neomercantilists argue, not because of the untrammeled working of free markets but because governments in each case stepped in to promote development through industrial policies. For all of their awareness of the distinctiveness of Asia, however, many neomercantilists argue their policy conclusions in the same abstract and universal terms as the neoclassical economists. They argue that Asia is different not because of culture, but because societies there, reacting to their situation as "late developers" trying to catch up to Europe and North America, chose a different set of economic institutions. This fails, however, to take into account the degree to which the ability to create certain institutions and run them effectively is itself culture bound.

James Fallows has made perhaps the most sweeping indictment of neoclassical economics in his book, *Looking at the Sun*.[3] Fallows argues that the Anglo-American preoccupation with market-oriented economics has blinded Americans to the critical role played by governments and that much of the world outside the United States operates on assumptions very much at variance with the rules of neoclassical economics. Asian governments, for example, have protected domestic industries through enacting high tariffs, restricting foreign investment, promoting exports through cheap credits or outright subsidies, granting licenses to favored companies, organizing cartels to share research and development costs and to allocate market shares, or else funding cutting-edge R&D directly.[4] Chalmers Johnson was one of the first to argue that it was Japan's Ministry of International Trade and Industry (MITI) rather than the market that was responsible for guiding the postwar Japanese economy to its extraordinarily high growth rates. Virtually all neomercantilists have charged that the United States has fallen behind in the economic competition with Japan and other Asian states because the free market orientation of successive U.S. administrations has allowed key industries to fall victim to foreign competition. They have promoted the American equivalent of a MITI that would subsidize, coordinate, and otherwise promote American high-tech industries in the global marketplace, and argued for a far more confrontational trade policy that would protect American industries faced with "unfair" foreign competitors.

The debate the neomercantilists have stirred up has centered on whether industrial policies were in fact responsible for Asia's high rates of growth and whether governments are capable of guiding economic development better than markets.[5] The neomercantilists, however, neglect the role of culture in shaping industrial policy itself. For even if we accept the hypothesis that the wise guidance of technocrats was responsible for Asian progress, it is clear that there are sharp differences in the relative capabilities of states to plan and carry out industrial policies. These differences are shaped by culture, as well as by the nature of political institutions and historical circumstances of different countries. The French and Japanese have long statist traditions, while the United States has an equally long history of antistatism, and there is a world of difference in the training and general quality of human beings that go into their respective national bureaucracies. That there is a great difference in the quality of policies and management that result should not be surprising.

There are also clearly major cultural differences with respect to the nature and prevalence of corruption. One of the chief problems with any industrial policy is that it invites the corruption of public officials, which in turn vitiates any possible beneficial effects of the policy. Clearly industrial policies work better in societies with long traditions of honest and competent civil service. Although the corruption of Japanese politicians has become a national scandal, few accusations of a similar nature have ever been leveled against MITI or Finance Ministry bureaucrats. The same is very unlikely to be the case with bureaucrats in Latin America, not to speak of other parts of the Third World.

Other cultural considerations are likely to affect the success of an industrial policy as well. Attitudes toward authority in Asia may have helped countries there implement industrial policies in ways that would not be possible elsewhere in the world. Consider the question of government help for sunrise versus sunset industries. It may be possible in theory for technocrats in countries not at the leading edge of technology to pick industries or sectors for promotion, but political factors usually intervene to skew government policy in the wrong direction. By definition, sunrise industries do not yet exist and therefore have no interest groups promoting them. Sunset industries, on the other hand, are often big employers and usually have vocal and politically powerful proponents. One of the distinctive features of the industrial policies carried out by many Asian governments has been their ability to dismantle older industries with large numbers of employees in an orderly way. In Japan, for example, employment in the textile industry fell from 1.2 million to 655,000 between the early 1960s and 1981, employment in the coal industry sank from 407,000 to 31,000 between 1950 and 1981, and shipbuilding underwent a similarly dramatic reduction in the 1970s.[6] In each case, the state intervened not to prop up employment in these sectors but *to assist in their demise.* Governments in Taiwan and South Korea have presided over similar reductions in employment in older labor-intensive industries.

In Europe and Latin America, by contrast, governments have found it almost impossible politically to dismantle sunset industries. Rather than helping to accelerate their decline, European governments nationalized failing industries like coal, steel, and automobiles, in the vain hope that state subsidies would make them internationally competitive. While paying lip-service to the need to shift resources into more modern sectors, the very democratic character of European governments led them to give in to political pressures to direct government subsidies to older industries, often at tremendous cost to taxpayers. There is no doubt that something similar would happen in the United States if the government got into the business of handing out "competitiveness" subsidies. Congress, responding to interest group pressure, could be relied on to declare that industries like shoes and textiles, rather than aerospace and semiconductors, were "strategic" and thus worthy of government subsidization. Even in the high-tech area, older technologies are likely to carry more political clout than ones under development. Thus, the most compelling argument against an industrial policy for the United States is not an economic one at all but is related to the character of American democracy.

As this book will show, the significance of the state sector varies enormously by culture. In familistic societies such as China or Italy, state intervention is often the only avenue by which a nation can build large-scale industries and is therefore relatively important if the country is to play in global economic sectors demanding large scale. On the other hand, societies with a high degree of trust and social capital like Japan and Germany can create large organizations without state support. In other words, in calculating comparative advantage, economists need to take into account relative endowments of social capital, as well as more conventional forms of capital and resources. When there is a deficit in social capital, the shortfall can often be made good by the state, just as the state can rectify a deficit in human capital by building more schools and universities. But the need for state intervention will depend very much on the particular culture and social structure of the society over which it presides.

The other pole of the current industrial policy debate is represented by neoclassical economists, who today dominate the economics profession. Neoclassical economics is a far more serious and sustained intellectual enterprise than neomercantilism. Substantial empirical evidence confirms that markets are indeed efficient allocators of resources and that giving free rein to self-interest promotes growth. The edifice of free market economics is, to repeat, about eighty percent right, which is not bad for a social science and substantially better than its rivals as the basis for public policy.

But the totality of the intellectual victory of free market economic theory in recent years has been accompanied by a considerable degree of hubris. Not being content to rest on their laurels, many neoclassical economists have come to believe that the economic method they have discovered provides them with the tools for constructing something approaching a universal science of man. The laws of economics, they argue, apply everywhere: they are equally valid in Russia as the United States, Japan, Burundi, or the Papua New Guinea highlands, and do not admit significant cultural variations in their application. These economists believe that they are right in a deeper epistemological sense as well: through their economic methodology, they have unlocked a fundamental truth about human nature that will allow them to explain virtually all aspects of human behavior. Two of the most prolific and renowned contemporary neoclassical economists, Gary Becker of the University of Chicago and James Buchanan of George Mason University (both of whom won Nobel Prizes for their work), have built careers extending economic methodology to what are usually regarded as noneconomic phenomena like politics, bureaucracy, racism, the family, and fertility.[7] The political science departments of many major universities are now filled with followers of so-called rational choice theory, which attempts to explain politics using an essentially economic methodology.[8]

The problem with neoclassical economics is that it has forgotten certain key foundations on which classical economics was based. Adam Smith, the premier classical economist, believed that people are driven by a selfish desire to "better their condition," but he would never have subscribed to the notion that economic activity could be reduced to rational utility maximization. Indeed, his other major work besides *The Wealth of Nations* was *The Theory of Moral Sentiments,* which portrays economic motivation as highly complex and embedded in broader social habits and mores. The very change in the name of the discipline from "political economy" to "economics" between the eighteenth and late nineteenth centuries reflects the narrowing of the model of human behavior at its core. Current economic discourse needs to recover some of the richness of classical, as opposed to neoclassical, economics, by taking account of how culture shapes all aspects of human behavior, including economic behavior, in a number of critical ways. Not only is the neoclassical economic perspective insufficient to explain political life, with its dominant emotions of indignation, pride, and shame, but it is not sufficient to explain many aspects of economic life either.[9] Not all economic action arises out of what are traditionally thought of as economic motives.

The entire imposing edifice of contemporary neoclassical economic theory rests on a relatively simple model of human nature: that human beings are "rational utility-maximizing individuals." That is, human beings seek to acquire the largest possible amount of the things they think are useful to themselves, they do this in a rational way, and they make these calculations as individuals seeking to maximize the benefit to themselves before they seek the benefit of any of the larger groups of which they are part. In short, neoclassical economics postulates that human beings are essentially rational but selfish individuals who seek to maximize their material well-being.[10] Economists, to a much greater extent than philosophers, poets, clergy, or politicians, preach the virtues of the pursuit of narrow self-interest because they believe that the greatest good to society as a whole can be achieved by allowing these individuals to pursue their self-interest through the market. In one social experiment, a large group of people at a university were given tokens that they could exchange for money that they would receive personally or for money that the group as a whole would have to share. It turned out that between forty and sixty percent of those in the experiment contributed altruistically to the group's well-being. The only exception was a group of entering graduate students in economics.[11] In the words of one economist, "The first principle of Economics is that every agent is actuated only by self-interest."[12]

The power of neoclassical theory rests on the fact that its model of humanity is accurate a good deal of the time: people can indeed be relied on to pursue their own selfish interests more often than they pursue some kind of common good. Rational self-interested calculation transcends cultural borders. Every first-year economics student reads of studies that show that when the price of wheat goes up relative to corn, peasants shift their output from corn to wheat regardless of whether they live in China, France, India, or Iran.

But every one of the terms of the neoclassical premise that human beings are rational utility-maximizing individuals is subject to significant qualification or exception.[13] Take the assertion that people pursue utility. The most basic definition of utility is the narrow one associated with the nineteenth-century utilitarian, Jeremy Bentham: that utility is the pursuit of pleasure or the avoidance of pain. Such a definition is straightforward and corresponds to a commonsense understanding of economic motivation: people want to be able to consume the largest possible quantity of the good things of life. But there are numerous occasions when people pursue goals other than utility.[14] They have been known to run into burning houses to save others, die in battle, or throw away lucrative careers so that they can commune with nature somewhere in the mountains. People do not simply vote their pocketbooks: they also have ideas that certain things are just or unjust, and they make important choices accordingly.[15] There would not be nearly as many wars if the latter were fought simply over economic resources; unfortunately, they usually involve nonutilitarian goals like recognition, religion, justice, prestige, and honor.

Some economists try to get around this problem by broadening the definition of utility beyond pleasure or money to take account of other motivations such as the "psychic pleasure" one receives for "doing the right thing," or the "pleasure" people can take in other people's consumption.[16] Economists assert that one can know what is useful only by what people reveal to be useful by their choices—hence their concept of "revealed preference."[17] The abolitionist dying to end slavery and the investment banker speculating on interest rates are both said to be pursuing "utility," the only difference being that the abolitionist's utility is of a psychic sort. At its most extreme, "utility" becomes a purely formal concept used to describe whatever ends or preferences people pursue. But this type of formal definition of utility reduces the fundamental premise of economics to an assertion that people maximize whatever it is they choose to maximize, a tautology that robs the model of any interest or explanatory power. By contrast, to assert that people prefer their selfish material interests over other kinds of interests is to make a strong statement about human nature.

It should also be quite evident that people do not always pursue utility, however defined, in a "rational" way, that is, by considering available alternatives and choosing the one that maximizes utility in the long run. Indeed, it is possible to argue that people are usually not rational in this sense.[18] The Chinese, Korean, and Italian preference for family, Japanese attitudes toward adoption of nonkin, the French reluctance to enter into face-to-face relationships, the German emphasis on training, the sectarian temper of American social life: all come about as the result not of rational calculation but from inherited ethical habit.

Most neoclassical economists would respond to these examples by saying that they are cases not of irrational behavior but of imperfect information. Information about relative prices and product quality is often unavailable or requires considerable time and effort to acquire. People will make seemingly irrational choices because the costs of acquiring better information outweigh the benefits they expect from it. It is not rational for people to be "rational" about every single choice they make in life; if this were true, their lives would be consumed in decisions over the smallest matters.[19] People in traditional cultures will follow the dictates of tradition and act very differently from people in industrialized societies, but that is because traditional culture contains embedded rules of behavior that are rational for that culture.[20]

But while habits can be economically rational or may once have had rational causes, many are not, or else take on a life of their own in situations when they are no longer appropriate. It may have been rational, in the context of traditional Chinese peasant society, to seek to have many sons, since sons are their elders' only source of support. But why, then, does this preference persist when Chinese immigrate to the United States or Canada, which have state-sponsored social security systems? The French preference for centralized bureaucratic authority may have been a reasonable reaction to centralized absolutism, but why do the French continue to have such difficulties at self-organization even when contemporary central governments deliberately devolve power to them? It may be rational for a mother on welfare not to marry the father of her child, given the economic incentives established by the welfare system, but why does that habit persist even when the benefits are taken away, and in the light of the clear long-run economic disadvantages to single parenthood? It is impossible to maintain that all cultures embed rules that are totally rational in their own terms. The simple variety of cultures that exist in the world, and the enormous range of cultural adaptations to similar economic situations, suggest that not all of them can be equally rational.

Finally, it is very questionable whether human beings act as individual utility maximizers rather than seeing themselves as parts of larger social groups. In Mark Granovetter's phrase, people are embedded in a variety of social groups—families, neighborhoods, networks, businesses, churches, and nations—against whose interests they have to balance their own.[21] The obligations one feels toward one's family do not arise out of a simple cost-benefit calculation, even if that family is running a business; rather, it is the character of the business that is shaped by preexisting family relationships. Workers are never merely counters in a company's table of organization; they develop solidarity, loyalties, and dislikes that shape the nature of economic activity. In other words, social, and therefore moral, behavior coexists with self-interested utility-maximizing behavior on a number of levels. The greatest economic efficiency was not necessarily achieved by rational self-interested individuals but rather by groups of individuals who, because of a preexisting moral community, are able to work together effectively.

To say that there is an important side of the human personality that does not correspond to the rational utility maximizer of neoclassical economics does not undermine the basic structure of the neoclassical edifice. That is, people will act as self-interested individuals often enough for the "laws" of economics to be a useful guide for making predictions and formulating public policy. In questioning the neoclassical model, we do not have to resort to the Marxist premise man is a "species being," giving priority to society over self-interest as a matter of course. But human beings act for nonutilitarian ends in arational, group-oriented ways sufficiently often that the neoclassical model presents us with an incomplete picture of human nature.

The long-standing debates between free market economists and neomercantilists over whether and how the government ought to intervene in the economy sidestep an important issue. Certainly macroeconomic policy is important, but it must be applied within a particular political, historical, and cultural context. Policy prescriptions arising from either perspective may not be generalizable: the same industrial policy that leads to utter disaster in Latin America may prove effective, or at least not do any harm, in Asia. Some societies can shield their technocrats from day-to-day popular pressures to keep plant X open or to subsidize industry Y more effectively.[22] The important variable is not industrial policy per se but culture.

CHAPTER 3

Scale and Trust

The early 1990s saw a flood of writing about the information revolution and the transformation that will be brought to everyone's doorstep as a result of the information superhighway. One of the most consistent and widely heralded themes of information age futurologists is that this technological revolution will spell the end of hierarchy of all sorts—political, economic, and social. As the story goes, information is power, and those at the top of traditional hierarchies maintained their dominance by controlling access to information. Modern communications technologies—telephones, fax machines, copiers, cassettes, VCRs, and the centrally important networked personal computer—have broken this stranglehold on information. The result, according to information age gurus from Alvin and Heidi Toffler and George Gilder to Vice President Al Gore and House Speaker Newt Gingrich, will be a devolution of power downward to the people and a liberation of everyone from the constraints of the centralized, tyrannical organizations in which they once worked.[1]

Information technology has indeed contributed to many of the decentralizing and democratizing tendencies of the past generation. It has been widely remarked that the electronic media have contributed to the fall of tyrannical regimes, including the Marcos dictatorship in the Philippines and communist rule in East Germany and the former Soviet Union.[2] But information age theorists argue that technology is deadly to all forms of hierarchy, including the giant corporations that employ the vast majority of American workers. The dislodging of IBM from its once-legendary dominance of the computer industry by upstarts like Sun Microsystems and Compaq during the 1980s is often presented as a morality play, where small, flexible, innovative entrepreneurship challenges large, centralized, bureaucratized tradition and is handsomely rewarded. A variety of authors have argued that as a result of the telecommunications revolution, all of us will someday be working in small, networked "virtual" corporations. That is, firms will ruthlessly downsize until they have stripped out all activities but their "core competence," contracting out through glass telephone lines to other small firms for everything from supplies and raw materials to accounting and marketing services.[3] Some argue that networks of small organizations, rather than large hierarchies or chaotic markets, will be the wave of the future, all driven by the relentless advance of electronic technology. Spontaneous community, not chaos and anarchy, will emerge only if society is freed from the centralized authority of large organizations, from the federal government to IBM and AT&T. With technologically powered communications, good information will drive out bad information, the honest and industrious will shun the fraudulent and parasitic, and people will come together voluntarily for beneficial common purposes.[4]

Clearly broad changes will be brought about by the information revolution, but the age of large, hierarchical organizations is far from over. Many information age futurologists overgeneralize from the computer industry, whose fast-changing technology does in fact tend to reward small and flexible firms. But many other areas of economic life, from building airliners and automobiles to fabricating silicon wafers, require ever-increasing amounts of capital, technology, and people to master. Even within the communications industry, fiber optic transmission favors a single, giant long-distance company, and it is no accident that by 1995

AT&T had grown back to the size it was in 1984, when eighty-five percent of the firm was divested into local telephone companies.[5] Information technology will help some small firms do large tasks better but will not eliminate the need for scale.

More important, when the information age's most enthusiastic apostles celebrate the breakdown of hierarchy and authority, they neglect one critical factor: trust, and the shared ethical norms that underlie it. Communities depend on mutual trust and will not arise spontaneously without it. Hierarchies are necessary because not all people within a community can be relied upon to live by tacit ethical rules alone. A small number may be actively asocial, seeking to undermine or exploit the group through fraud or simple mischievousness. A much larger number will tend to be free riders, willing to benefit from membership in the group while contributing as little as possible to the common cause. Hierarchies are necessary because all people cannot be trusted at all times to live by internalized ethical rules and do their fair share. They must ultimately be coerced by explicit rules and sanctions in the event they do not live up to them. This is true in the economy as well as in society more broadly: large corporations have their origins in the fact that it is very costly to contract out for goods or services with people one does not know well or trust. Consequently, firms found it more economical to bring outside contractors into their own organization, where they could be supervised directly.

Trust does not reside in integrated circuits or fiber optic cables. Although it involves an exchange of information, trust is not reducible to information. A "virtual" firm can have abundant information coming through network wires about its suppliers and contractors. But if they are all crooks or frauds, dealing with them will remain a costly process involving complex contracts and time-consuming enforcement. Without trust, there will be a strong incentive to bring these activities in-house and restore the old hierarchies.

Thus, it is far from clear that the information revolution makes large, hierarchical organizations obsolete or that spontaneous community will emerge once hierarchy has been undermined. Since community depends on trust, and trust in turn is culturally determined, it follows that spontaneous community will emerge in differing degrees in different cultures. The ability of companies to move from large hierarchies to flexible networks of smaller firms will depend, in other words, on the degree of trust and social capital present in the broader society. A high-trust society like Japan created networks well before the information revolution got into high gear; a low-trust society may never be able to take advantage of the efficiencies that information technology offers.

Trust is the expectation that arises within a community of regular, honest, and cooperative behavior, based on commonly shared norms, on the part of other members of that community.[6] Those norms can be about deep "value" questions like the nature of God or justice, but they also encompass secular norms like professional standards and codes of behavior. That is, we trust a doctor not to do us deliberate injury because we expect him or her to live by the Hippocratic oath and the standards of the medical profession.

Social capital is a capability that arises from the prevalence of trust in a society or in certain parts of it. It can be embodied in the smallest and most basic social group, the family, as well as the largest of all groups, the nation, and in all the other groups in between. Social capital differs from other forms of human capital insofar as it is usually created and transmitted through cultural mechanisms like religion, tradition, or historical habit. Economists typically argue that the formation of social groups can be explained as the result of voluntary contract between individuals who have made the rational calculation that cooperation is in their long-term self-interest. By this account, trust is not necessary for cooperation: enlightened self-interest, together with legal mechanisms like contracts, can compensate for an absence of trust and allow strangers jointly to create an organization that will work for a common purpose. Groups can be formed at any time based on self-interest, and group formation is not culture-dependent.

But while contract and self-interest are important sources of association, the most effective organizations are based on communities of shared ethical values. These communities do not require extensive contract and legal regulation of their relations because prior moral consensus gives members of the group a basis for mutual trust.

The social capital needed to create this kind of moral community cannot be acquired, as in the case of other forms of human capital, through a rational investment decision. That is, an individual can decide to "invest" in conventional human capital like a college education, or training to become a machinist or computer programmer, simply by going to the appropriate school. Acquisition of social capital, by contrast, requires habituation to the moral norms of a community and, in its context, the acquisition of virtues like loyalty, honesty, and dependability. The group, moreover, has to adopt common norms as a whole before trust can become generalized among its members. In other words, social capital cannot be acquired simply by individuals acting on their own. It is based on the prevalence of social, rather than individual virtues. The proclivity for sociability is much harder to acquire than other forms of human capital, but because it is based on ethical habit, it is also harder to modify or destroy.

Another term that I will use widely throughout this book is *spontaneous sociability*, which constitutes a subset of social capital. In any modern society, organizations are being constantly created, destroyed, and modified. The most useful kind of social capital is often not the ability to work under the authority of a traditional community or group, but the capacity to form new associations and to cooperate within the terms of reference they establish. This type of group, spawned by industrial society's complex division of labor and yet based on shared values rather than contract, falls under the general rubric of what Durkheim labeled "organic solidarity."[7] Spontaneous sociability, moreover, refers to that wide range of intermediate communities distinct from the family or those deliberately established by governments. Governments often have to step in to promote community when there is a deficit of spontaneous sociability. But state intervention poses distinct risks, since it can all too easily undermine the spontaneous communities established in civil society.

Social capital has major consequences for the nature of the industrial economy that society will be able to create. If people who have to work together in an enterprise trust one another because they are all operating according to a common set of ethical norms, doing business costs less. Such a society will be better able to innovate organizationally, since the high degree of trust will permit a wide variety of social relationships to emerge. Hence highly sociable Americans pioneered the development of the modern corporation in the late nineteenth and early twentieth centuries, just as the Japanese have explored the possibilities of network organizations in the twentieth.

By contrast, people who do not trust one another will end up cooperating only under a system of formal rules and regulations, which have to be negotiated, agreed to, litigated, and enforced, sometimes by coercive means. This legal apparatus, serving as a substitute for trust, entails what economists call "transaction costs." Widespread distrust in a society, in other words, imposes a kind of tax on all forms of economic activity, a tax that high-trust societies do not have to pay.

Social capital is not distributed uniformly among societies. Some show a markedly greater proclivity for association than others, and the preferred forms of association differ. In some, family and kinship constitute the primary form of association; in others, voluntary associations are much stronger and serve to draw people out of their families. In the United States, for example, religious conversion often induced people to leave their families to follow the call of a new religious sect, or at least enjoined on them new duties that were in competition with duty to their families. In China, by contrast, Buddhist priests were less often successful, and frequently castigated, for seducing children away from their families. The same society may acquire social capital over time, or lose it. France at the end of the Middle Ages had a dense network of civil associations, but the French capacity for spontaneous sociability was effectively destroyed beginning in the sixteenth and seventeenth centuries by a victorious centralizing monarchy.

Conventional wisdom maintains that Germany and Japan are group-oriented societies. Traditionally prizing obedience to authority, they both practice what Lester Thurow labels "communitarian capitalism."[8] Much of the literature of the past decade or so on competitiveness makes a similar assumption: Japan is a "group-oriented" society; the United States lies at the other extreme as the epitome of an individualistic society, in which people do not readily work together or support one another. According to the Japanologist Ronald Dore, all societies can be located somewhere along a continuum that stretches from the individualistic Anglo-Saxon countries like the United States and Britain at one extreme to the group-oriented Japan at the other.[9]

This dichotomy, however, represents a great distortion of the way social capital is distributed around the globe, and it represents as well a profound misunderstanding of Japan and, particularly, the United States. There are indeed truly individualistic societies with little capacity for association. In such a society, both families and voluntary associations are weak; it often happens that the strongest organizations are criminal gangs. Russia and certain other former communist countries come to mind, as well as inner-city neighborhoods in the United States.

At a higher level of sociability than contemporary Russia are familistic societies, in which the primary (and often only) avenue to sociability is family and broader forms of kinship, like clans or tribes. Familistic societies frequently have weak voluntary associations because unrelated people have no basis for trusting one another. Chinese societies like Taiwan, Hong Kong, and the People's Republic of China itself are examples; the essence of Chinese Confucianism is the elevation of family bonds above all other social loyalties. But France and parts of Italy also share this characteristic. Although familism is not as pronounced in either society as in China, there is a deficit of trust among people not related to one another, and therefore weakness in voluntary community.

In contrast to familistic societies are ones with a high degree of generalized social trust and, consequently, a strong propensity for spontaneous sociability. Japan and Germany do indeed fall into this category. But from the time of its founding, the United States has never been the individualistic society that most Americans believe it to be; rather, it has always possessed a rich network of voluntary associations and community structures to which individuals have subordinated their narrow interests. It is true that Americans have been traditionally much more antistatist when compared to Germans or Japanese, but strong community can emerge in the absence of a strong state.

Social capital and the proclivity for spontaneous sociability have important economic consequences. If we look at the size of the largest firms in a series of national economies (excluding those that are owned and/or heavily subsidized by the state, or else by foreign multinationals), we notice some interesting results.[10] In Europe and North America, private sector firms in the United States and Germany are significantly larger than those in Italy and France. In Asia, the contrast is even sharper between Japan and Korea, on the one hand, which have large firms and highly concentrated industries, and Taiwan and Hong Kong, on the other, whose firms tend to be much smaller.

One might think at first that the ability to spawn large-scale firms is related simply to the absolute size of a nation's economy. For obvious reasons, Andorra and Liechtenstein are not likely to be seedbeds for giant multinationals on the scale of Shell or General Motors. On the other hand, there is no necessary correlation between absolute gross domestic product and large corporations for much of the industrialized world. Three of Europe's smaller economies—Holland, Sweden, and Switzerland—are host to gigantic private corporations; by most measures, Holland is the most industrially concentrated nation in the world. In Asia, the economies of Taiwan and South Korea have been roughly comparable in size over the past generation, yet Korea's firms are much larger than those of Taiwan.

Although there are other factors accounting for firm size, including tax policy, antitrust, and other forms of regulatory law, there is a relationship between high-trust societies with plentiful social capital—Germany, Japan, and the United States—and the ability to create large, private business organizations.[11] These three societies were the first—both on an absolute time scale and relative to their own development histories—to develop large, modern, professionally managed hierarchical corporations. The economies of relatively low-trust societies like Taiwan, Hong Kong, France, and Italy, by contrast, have traditionally been populated by family businesses. In these countries, the reluctance of nonkin to trust one another delayed and in some cases prevented the emergence of modern, professionally managed corporations.

If a low-trust, familistic society wants to have large-scale businesses, the state must step in to help create them through subsidies, guidance, or even outright ownership. The result will be a saddle-shaped distribution of enterprises, with a large number of relatively small family firms at one end of the scale, a small number of large state-owned enterprises at the other, and relatively little in between. State sponsorship has enabled countries like France to develop large-scale, capital-intensive industrial sectors, but at a cost: state-owned companies are inevitably less efficient and well managed than their private sector counterparts.

The prevalence of trust does not simply facilitate the growth of large-scale organizations. If large hierarchies are able to evolve into networks of smaller companies through modern information technology, trust will help in this transition as well. Societies well supplied with social capital will be able to adopt new organizational forms more readily than those with less, as technology and markets change.

At least at an early stage of economic development, firm size and scale do not appear to have serious consequences for a society's ability to grow and prosper. Although the absence of trust in a society may encourage small enterprises and imposes a tax on economic activity, these deficiencies may be more than compensated for by advantages that small companies often have over large ones. They are easier to establish, more flexible, and adjust more quickly to changing markets than large corporations. And in fact, countries with relatively small firms on average—Italy within the European Community, for example, and Taiwan and Hong Kong in Asia—have grown faster in recent years than their neighbors with large firms.

But firm size does affect the sectors of the global economy that a nation can participate in and may in the long run affect overall competitiveness. Small firms are associated with relatively labor-intensive goods destined for segmented, fast-changing markets, such as apparel, textiles, plastics, electronics components, and furniture. Large firms are required to master complicated manufacturing processes requiring large amounts of capital, such as aerospace, semiconductors, and automobiles. They are also necessary to create the marketing organizations that stand behind brand names, and it is no accident that the world's best-known brand names—Kodak, Ford, Siemens, AEG, Mitsubishi, Hitachi—come from countries that are also good at creating large organizations. By contrast, it is much harder to think of brand names from small-scale Chinese firms.

In classical liberal trade theory, the global division of labor is determined by comparative advantage, usually measured by different nations' relative endowments of capital, labor, and natural resources. The evidence presented in this book will suggest that social capital needs to be factored into a nation's resource endowment. The implications of differing endowments of social capital are potentially enormous for the global division of labor. The nature of Chinese Confucianism, for example, may mean that China may never be able to duplicate Japan's development path and will continue to participate in very different economic sectors.

How much the inability to create large organizations will matter for economic growth in the future will depend on unknowable factors, like future directions in technology and markets. But under certain circumstances, this constraint may prove to be a significant one that will harm the long-term-growth potential of countries like China and Italy.

There are, moreover, other benefits to a strong propensity for spontaneous sociability, some of them not economic. A high-trust society can organize its workplace on a more flexible and group-oriented basis, with more responsibility delegated to lower levels of the organization. Low-trust societies, by contrast, must fence in and isolate their workers with a series of bureaucratic rules. Workers usually find their workplaces more satisfying if they are treated like adults who can be trusted to contribute to their community rather than like small cogs in a large industrial machine designed by someone else. The Toyota lean manufacturing system, which is a systematization of a communally organized workplace, has led to enormous productivity improvements as well, indicating that community and efficiency can go together. The lesson is that modern capitalism, shaped by technology, does not dictate a single form of industrial organization that everyone must follow. Managers have considerable latitude in organizing their businesses to take account of the sociable side of the human personality. There is no necessary trade-off, in other words, between community and efficiency; those who pay attention to community may indeed become the most efficient of all.

CHAPTER 4

Languages of Good and Evil

Social capital, the crucible of trust and critical to the health of an economy, rests on cultural roots. At first glance, it seems quite paradoxical that culture should be related to economic efficiency, since culture is totally arational in its substance and in the way it is transmitted. As the subject of scholarly study, it can seem elusive. Economists, believing themselves to be the most hardheaded of social scientists, generally dislike dealing with the concept of culture: it is not susceptible to simple definition and hence cannot serve as the basis for a clear model of human behavior, as in the case of humans as "rational utility maximizers." In one commonly used anthropology textbook, the author provides no fewer than 11 definitions of culture.[1] Another author surveyed 160 definitions of culture that were in use by anthropologists, sociologists, psychologists, and others.[2] Cultural anthropologists insist that there are virtually no aspects of culture that are common to all human societies.[3] Cultural factors are therefore incapable of being systematized into universal laws; they can be interpreted only through what Clifford Geertz calls "thick description," an ethnographic technique that takes account of the variety and complexity of each individual culture. In the view of many economists, culture becomes a grab bag or residual category used to explain whatever cannot be accounted for by general theories of human behavior. Culture, however, can have its own deep adaptive rationality, even if this is not evident at first glance. But first I must define how I will use the concept of culture.

Cultural anthropologists and sociologists distinguish between culture and what they term social structure. Culture in this sense is restricted to meanings, symbols, values, and ideas and encompasses phenomena like religion and ideology. Geertz's own definition of culture is "an historically transmitted pattern of meanings embodied in symbols, a system of inherited conceptions expressed in symbolic forms by means of which men communicate, perpetuate, and develop their knowledge about and attitudes toward life."[4] Social structure, by contrast, concerns concrete social organizations such as the family, clan, legal system, or nation. In this sense, Confucian doctrines about the relationship between fathers and sons belong to culture; the actual patrilineal Chinese family is social structure.

In this book, I will not make use of this distinction between culture and social structure because it is often difficult to distinguish between the two; values and ideas shape concrete social relationships, and vice versa. The Chinese family has a patrilineal structure in large measure *because* Confucian ideology gives preference to males and teaches children to honor their fathers. Conversely, Confucian ideology seems reasonable to those who have grown up in Chinese families.

The definition I will use draws on both culture and social structure, strictly defined, and comes closer to the popularly understood meaning of culture: culture is *inherited ethical habit*. An ethical habit can consist of an idea or a value, such as the view that pork is unclean or that cows are sacred, or it can consist of an actual social relationship, such as the tendency of the eldest son in traditional Japanese society to inherit the whole of his father's estate.

Culture in this sense can perhaps be most easily understood in terms of what it is not. It is not rational choice as used by economists in their basic model of human beings as rational utility maximizers. By "rational choice," I am speaking here in the first instance of rational means rather than rational ends—that is, the consideration of alternative ways of achieving a particular end and the selection of the optimal one based on available information. Choices influenced by culture arise out of habit. A Chinese person eats with chopsticks not because he or she has compared chopsticks to Western knives and forks, and finds the former better suited to manipulating Chinese food, but simply because those are the implements that all Chinese typically use. There is little rational choice involved in the Hindu worship of cows, which protects an economically unproductive bovine population half as large as India's human population. Hindus nonetheless continue to worship cows.[5]

The most important habits that make up cultures have little to do with how one eats one's food or combs one's hair but with the ethical codes by which societies regulate behavior—what the philosopher Nietzsche called a people's "language of good and evil." Despite their variety, all cultures seek to constrain the raw selfishness of human nature in some fashion through the establishment of unwritten moral rules. Although it is possible to affirm an ethical code as a matter of carefully considered rational choice, comparing one's own ethical code against available alternatives, the vast majority of the world's people do not do so. Rather, they are educated to follow their society's moral rules by simple habituation—in family life, from their friends and neighbors, or in school.

A car commercial shown on American television portrays a young girl sitting in an oppressive classroom, being told by a stern teacher in a monotonous voice over and over to "draw between the lines." The scene suddenly cuts to the same girl as a young woman—shown now in color rather than black and white—driving her own car with the top down and the wind ruffling her hair. She not only fails to stay within the lines on the highway but is shown having the time of her life driving off-road across an open field. Though the makers of the commercial did not include this detail, her car might well have sported a bumper sticker reading "Question Authority." The same commercial, were it produced in Asia, would likely portray a sympathetic teacher showing the girl how to draw carefully between the lines. The girl, after patient practice, would do so with the utmost precision. Only then would she be rewarded with a new car, whose bumper sticker would read "Respect Authority." In both cases the moral lessons are conveyed not rationally but through images, habits, and social opinions.

The close relationship between moral virtue and habit is evident in the concept of character. One can easily know the right thing to do intellectually, but only people with "character" are able to do them under difficult or challenging circumstances. Aristotle explains that in contrast to intellectual virtue, "ethical virtue [ēthikē] is for the most part the product of habit [ethos], and has indeed derived its name, with a slight variation of form, from that word." He goes on to explain that "our moral dispositions are formed as a result of the corresponding activities. . . . It is therefore not of small moment whether we are trained from childhood in one set of habits or another; on the contrary it is of very great, or rather of supreme importance."[6]

Traditional religions or ethical systems (e.g., Confucianism) constitute the major institutionalized sources of culturally determined behavior. Ethical systems create moral communities because their shared languages of good and evil give their members a common moral life. To some extent any moral community, regardless of the specific ethical rules involved, will create a degree of trust among its members. Certain ethical codes tend to promote a wider radius of trust than others by emphasizing the imperatives of honesty, charity, and benevolence toward the community at large. This, Weber argued, was one of the key outcomes of the Puritan doctrine of grace, which encouraged higher standards of trustworthy behavior in realms well beyond the family. Trust, which in his view was critical to economic life, arose historically out of religious habit rather than rational calculation.

To identify culture with habit rather than rational choice is not to say that cultures are irrational; they are simply arational with regard to means by which decisions are made. It can be the case that cultures actually embed a high degree of rationality. For example, use of politeness and honorifics in speech serves to convey useful information about the social status of one's interlocutor. Indeed, we could not possibly live day to day without culture in the sense of arational, habitual action. No one has the time or the inclination to come to a rational choice concerning the vast majority of decisions one faces in life—for example, whether to try to sneak out of a restaurant rather than paying the bill, whether to be polite to a stranger, or whether to open a neighbor's letter mistakenly delivered to your mailbox in hopes of finding money in it. Most people are simply habituated to a certain minimal degree of honesty. Gathering the necessary information and considering possible alternatives is itself a costly and time-consuming process, one that can be short-circuited by custom and habit.[7] As the late Aaron Wildavsky has pointed out, this is true even for the seemingly sophisticated political choices made by educated people living in advanced societies. People form attitudes toward risk—for example, which is more dangerous: nuclear power or contact with people with AIDS?—not from any rational analysis of the real risks involved in either case but based on whether they are broadly liberal or broadly conservative.[8]

Modern economists tend to identify rational ends with the maximization of utility, which is usually understood as the greatest possible consumer welfare. In this respect, many traditional cultures (including the traditional culture of the West) are arational or simply irrational with respect to ends because economic well-being ranks lower than other objectives. A devout Buddhist, for example, believes that the end of life is not the accumulation of material possessions but precisely the opposite: the annihilation of the desire for possession and the dissolution of individual personality into a universal nothingness. It is an act of considerable intellectual hubris to believe that only economic goals in the narrow sense can be considered rational. Much of the Western tradition itself, with its rich religious, ethical, and philosophical currents, would have to be discarded as irrational.

Many Westerners tend to dismiss non-Western cultures as irrational. This was frequently said, for example, of Iran after the revolution of 1978, when the country broke its ties with the West and embarked on a program of religiously motivated expansion. If one examines the record closely, however, Iran exhibited behavior that was both rational and maximizing throughout this period in terms of the way it calculated the means used to achieve its goals. What appeared as irrational to Westerners was the fact that many of its ends were not economic but religious.

Conversely, it is entirely possible that arational cultural traditions, practiced as a matter of habit and for the sake of otherworldly ends, can nonetheless advance utility maximization understood in a narrowly materialistic sense. This was the central argument of Max Weber's *The Protestant Ethic and the Spirit of Capitalism,* which showed that the early Puritans, seeking to glorify God alone and renouncing the acquisition of material goods as an end in itself, developed certain virtues like honesty and thrift that were extremely helpful to the accumulation of capital.[9] An argument central to this book is similar to Weber's: there are ethical habits, such as the ability to associate spontaneously, that are crucial to organizational innovation and therefore to the creation of wealth. Different types of ethical habits are conducive to alternative forms of economic organization and lead to large variation in economic structure. In other words, the greatest utility maximizers may not always be the rational ones; people practicing certain kinds of traditional moral and social virtues in an arational way, and who frequently aim at completely noneconomic goals, may not be as disadvantaged or as confused as modern economists would have us believe.

Defining culture as ethical or moral habit can make it difficult to measure cultural variables. Among sociologists' most common tools are opinion surveys, in which a representative sample of a particular population is asked to respond to a series of questions meant to elicit information about underlying values. The problem with this approach, apart from the usual methodological ones (such as the adequacy of sampling or the tendency of respondents to tell interviewers what they think the latter want to hear), is that it confuses opinions with habits. For example, numerous surveys indicate that poor Americans on welfare have similar attitudes toward work, thrift, and dependence that middle-class people do.[10] But having the opinion that it is important to work hard is different from having a work ethic, that is, being habituated to getting up early in the morning to go to a dull or unpleasant job and deferring consumption for the sake of long-term well-being. People on welfare doubtless would like to be off it, but whether they have the habits to enable them to do so is much less clear from the empirical data. Much of the debate over poverty in the United States in the past generation has turned on the question of whether the American urban underclass is poor because it lacks economic opportunities or whether there is something that could be called a "culture of poverty"—dysfunctional social habits like teen pregnancy and drug addiction—that would persist even if the economic opportunities existed.[11]

If we define culture as habit, and particularly as ethical habit, the dividing line between rational choice and culture is still not always clear. What may start out as rational choices can become cultural artifacts over time. For example, it is usually more sensible to speak of the American preference for democracy and free markets as a matter of ideology rather than culture. Many Americans could give a reasonable account of why democracy is preferable to tyranny, or why the private sector can do things better than "big government," based on either their own experience or the persuasiveness of broader political and economic ideologies they absorb as part of their general upbringing.

On the other hand, it is certainly the case that many Americans adopt such attitudes without thinking much about them and pass them on to their children, so to speak, with their toilet training. While the American founding was highly self-conscious and rational, subsequent generations of Americans accepted the principles of the founding not because they gave them the same conscious consideration as the Founding Fathers but because they were traditional. Hence, when people sometimes describe the United States as having a "democratic" or a "free market" culture, they mean that Americans are inclined to distrust big government and authority in general, prize individualism, and have an easygoingness bred of equality—all the traits of national character that Tocqueville described so perceptively in *Democracy in America*. They behave this way without thinking about why they do so or whether there might be better alternative ways of seeing and doing things. Hence Americans have a democratic *ideology* and act out of ideological motivations, but they also have an egalitarian *culture,* which has developed out of the ideology (in combination with other factors) over time.

It is often the case that what starts out as a political act ends up embodying itself in a cultural attribute. For example, in the sixteenth and seventeenth centuries, England and France experienced a series of wars between the monarchy and the various nobles, independent cities, and ecclesiastical authorities among which sovereignty was divided at the time. In England, the monarchy lost the struggle and was ultimately forced to accept a series of constitutional constraints on its power that in time became the foundations for modern parliamentary democracy. In France, the monarchy won and began a long-term process of centralizing authority around the absolute power of the state. There is no deep historical reason I know of why the monarchy should have lost in England and won in France; one could easily have imagined the opposite outcome.[12] But the fact that it happened as it did had profound consequences for the political culture of both countries subsequently. The centralization of political authority in France undermined the autonomy of voluntary associations and made the French more dependent on centralized authority in later generations, whether that authority was monarchical or republican. In England, by contrast, society became far more self-organizing because people were not dependent on centralized authority to adjudicate their differences, a habit that was carried over by the English settlers to the New World.[13]

To complicate matters further, there are times when apparently political choices have cultural roots. The French proclivity for political centralization, which started out as a political act but later became a cultural attribute, influenced subsequent political decisions. Thus, the adoption of the centralized, hyperpresidential constitution of de Gaulle's Fifth Republic in 1958 was a political act in response to the crisis in Algeria, but also very much in keeping with French politicocultural traditions. It was a characteristically French solution to the problem of the political disorder of the Fourth Republic, a solution that had many precedents in French history.

Because culture is a matter of ethical habit, it changes very slowly—much more slowly than ideas. When the Berlin Wall was dismantled and communism crumbled in 1989–1990, the governing ideology in Eastern Europe and the Soviet Union changed overnight from Marxism-Leninism to markets and democracy. Similarly, in some Latin American countries, statist or nationalist economic ideologies like import substitution were wiped away in less than a decade by the accession to power of a new president or finance minister. What cannot change nearly as quickly is culture. The experience of many former communist societies is that communism created many habits—excessive dependence on the state, leading to an absence of entrepreneurial energy, an inability to compromise, and a disinclination to cooperate voluntarily in groups like companies or political parties—that have greatly slowed the consolidation of either democracy or a market economy. People in these societies may have given their intellectual assent to the replacement of communism with democracy and capitalism by voting for "democratic" reformers, but they do not have the social habits necessary to make either work.

On the other hand, people sometimes incorrectly make the opposite assumption: that culture is incapable of changing and cannot be influenced by political acts. In fact, we see evidence of cultural change all around us. Catholicism, for example, has often been held to be hostile to both capitalism and democracy. Weber's *Protestant Ethic* argued that the Reformation was in some sense a precondition for the industrial revolution. Even after it occurred, the Catholic church was frequently a critic of the economic world built by capitalism, and Catholic countries as a group industrialized later than Protestant ones.[14] In the battles between dictatorship and democracy of the first half of the twentieth century such as the Spanish Civil War, throne and altar were closely aligned.

And yet by the end of the second half of the twentieth century, a great transformation of Catholic culture had occurred. The church in its official pronouncements reconciled itself to democracy and, with some qualifications, to modern capitalism.[15] The vast majority of the new democracies that emerged between 1974 and 1989 were Catholic societies, and in a number of them the Catholic church had played a key role in the struggle against authoritarianism.[16] Furthermore, for various stretches during the 1960s, 1970s, and 1980s, Catholic countries like Spain, Portugal, Italy, Chile, and Argentina grew faster than their Protestant counterparts like Britain or the United States. The reconciliation between Catholic culture and either democracy or capitalism is hardly complete, yet there has been a "Protestantization" of Catholic culture that makes the differences between Protestant and Catholic societies much less pronounced today than in times past.[17]

There is no doubt that human beings are, as the economists say, fundamentally selfish and that they pursue their selfish interests in a rational way. But they also have a moral side in which they feel obligations to others, a side that is frequently at cross-purposes with their selfish instincts.[18] As the word *culture* itself suggests, the more highly developed ethical rules by which people live are nurtured through repetition, tradition, and example. These rules may reflect a deeper adaptive rationality; they may serve economically rational ends; and in the case of a few individuals they may be the product of rational consent. But they are transmitted from one generation to another as arational social habits. These habits in turn guarantee that human beings never behave as purely selfish utility maximizers postulated by economists.

CHAPTER 5

The Social Virtues

I t is fashionable to shy away from value judgments when comparing different cultures, but from an economic standpoint, some ethical habits clearly constitute virtues while others are vices. Among the cultural habits that constitute virtues, not all contribute to the formation of social capital. Some can be exercised by individuals acting alone, while others—in particular, reciprocal trust—emerge only in a social context. The social virtues, including honesty, reliability, cooperativeness, and a sense of duty to others, are critical for incubating the individual ones, however, and have received considerably less attention in discussions of this subject. This is one important reason that I will focus on them here.

The literature on the impact of culture on economic life is voluminous, and the bulk of it by far revolves around a single work, Max Weber's *The Protestant Ethic and the Spirit of Capitalism,* published in 1905. Weber stood Karl Marx on his head by arguing that it was not underlying economic forces that created cultural products like religion and

ideology but rather culture that produced certain forms of economic behavior. Capitalism did not simply emerge in Europe when technological
conditions were propitious; a "spirit," or a certain condition of the soul,
enabled technological change to take place. That spirit was the product
of Puritan or fundamentalist Protestantism, with its sanctification of
worldly activity and its emphasis on the possibility of individual salvation
unmediated by traditional hierarchies like the Catholic church.[1]

To this day, Weber's work continues to engender controversy, with
some taking for granted the underlying truth of his hypothesis and others
contesting virtually every assertion in his book.[2] There are many empirical anomalies in the correlation between Protestantism and capitalism—
for example, the vigorous commercial development of the Catholic
northern Italian city-states in the fourteenth and fifteenth centuries, or
the failure of the Calvinist Afrikaners to develop a thriving capitalist culture until the last quarter of the twentieth century.[3]

On the other hand, the correlation between Protestantism and capitalism is strong enough that few are willing to assert there was no causal
connection whatsoever.[4] It is clear, moreover, that on a doctrinal level,
Catholicism retained a greater hostility to modern capitalism than did the
leading Protestant churches, until the last decades of the twentieth century.[5] Many scholars consequently take an intermediate position. They
agree that Weber may have been mistaken on the specific ways that capitalism and Protestantism were causally related and had various empirical
facts wrong. But, according to one contemporary theory, although there
was nothing inherent in Catholicism that constrained economic modernization as Weber asserted, the Counter-Reformation provoked by Protestantism had the effect of stifling the possibility of innovation in the
countries where it triumphed.[6]

Much of the empirical work on cases that have occurred since Weber
wrote have tended to confirm the broad outlines of his hypothesis. Perhaps
the most intriguing findings come from Latin America, where North American Protestants have been evangelizing for the past two or three generations. Many traditionally Catholic Latin American countries now have
substantial Protestant populations, which provides a kind of laboratory for
measuring the consequences of cultural change. The kind of Protestantism
being exported to Latin America from the United States is predominantly
Pentecostal, which the sociologist David Martin argues constitutes the
third great wave of fundamentalist renewal (the other two having been the
original Puritanism of the Reformation and the Methodist revival of the

eighteenth and nineteenth centuries). Twenty percent of Brazil's population is estimated now to be Protestant, of whom over 12 million are evangelicals. Chile's Protestant population is believed to be fifteen to twenty percent of the total; Guatemala's is thirty percent, and one-fifth of Nicaragua's population has been converted.[7] Most empirical sociological work that has been done on this subject, including Martin's own comprehensive study, tends to confirm the Weber hypothesis. That is, Protestant conversions in Latin America have been associated with significant increases in hygiene, savings, educational achievement, and ultimately per capita income.[8]

The term *work ethic*, Protestant or otherwise, is actually something of a misnomer for the collection of related personality traits that are usually placed under its rubric in the post-Weberian literature. If by "work ethic" we mean a general propensity of the working population to get up early in the morning and labor long hours at physically or mentally taxing pursuits, then the work ethic by itself was hardly sufficient to create the modern capitalist world.[9] The typical peasant in fifteenth-century China probably worked significantly harder and for longer hours than does a modern assembly line worker in Detroit or Nagoya.[10] But the peasant's productivity is an infinitesimal fraction of that of the modern worker, because modern wealth is based on human capital (knowledge and education), technology, innovation, organization, and a host of other factors related to the quality rather than the simple quantity of labor used to create it.[11]

Weber's spirit of capitalism refers, then, not just to the work ethic narrowly defined but to other related virtues like frugality (the propensity to save), a rational approach to problem solving, and a preoccupation with the here-and-now that inclines individuals to master their environment through innovation and labor. These are characteristics that apply primarily to entrepreneurs and owners of capital rather than to the workers they hire.

As a set of qualities pertaining to entrepreneurs, however, the "spirit of capitalism" has a real meaning, particularly for societies at an early stage of economic development. This meaning is well understood by development economists who have spent time in the field in preindustrial societies. In the absence of "modern" habits of mind, the most theoretically correct International Monetary Fund stabilization plan will have little effect.[12] In many preindustrial societies, one cannot take for granted that businessmen will show up for meetings on time, that earnings will not immediately be siphoned off and spent by family and friends rather than reinvested, or that state funds for infrastructure development will not be pocketed by the officials distributing it.

The capacity for hard work, frugality, rationality, innovativeness, and openness to risk are all entrepreneurial virtues that apply to individuals and could be exercised by Robinson Crusoe on his proverbial desert island. But there is as well a series of social virtues, like honesty, reliability, cooperativeness, and a sense of duty to others, that are essentially social in nature. While *The Protestant Ethic* focuses on the former, Weber discussed the social virtues in a separate and much less well-known essay, "The Protestant Sects and the Spirit of Capitalism."[13] In that work he argued that another important effect of Protestantism—or more accurately, the sectarian Protestantism that exists in parts of England and Germany and throughout the United States—was to heighten the capacity of its adherents to cohere in new communities.

Sectarian religious communities like the Baptists, Methodists, and Quakers created small, tightly knit groups whose members were bound to each other through common commitments to values like honesty and service. This cohesion served them well in the business world, since business transactions depend to a great degree on trust. In traveling through the United States, Weber observed that many businessmen would introduce themselves as some kind of Christian believer, in order to establish credentials for honesty and trustworthiness. In one case,

> On a long railroad journey through what was then Indian territory, the author, sitting next to a traveling salesman of "undertaker's hardware" (iron letters for tombstones), casually mentioned the still impressively strong church-mindedness. Thereupon the salesman remarked, "Sir, for my part everybody may believe or not believe as he pleases; but if I saw a farmer or a businessman not belonging to any church at all, I wouldn't trust him with fifty cents. Why pay me, if he doesn't believe in anything?"[14]

Weber noted as well that the small sectarian communities created natural networks through which businessmen could hire employees, find customers, open lines of credit, and the like. Precisely because they were members of voluntary rather than established churches, adherents of Protestant sects had a deeper degree of commitment to their religious values and stronger ties with one another. Rather than being compelled to be observant, they had internalized their sect's moral values.

The importance of the sectarian form of Protestantism, and its impact on both spontaneous sociability and economic life, is suggested by differences between Canada and the United States. Most Americans would not be able to identify significant social differences between themselves and their northern neighbors (the reverse, however, being much less true). But the difference in the social spirit of the two countries can sometimes be quite striking. Canada has had two centralized churches (one Catholic and one Protestant), that have received substantial support from the state, and despite many similarities with the United States, Canadian society has always resembled a European country with an established church more than its neighbor to the south. Many observers over the years have noted that Canadian businesses were less vigorous than their American counterparts. Even Friedrich Engels, the supposed economic determinist, asserted after visiting Canada that "one imagines that one is in Europe again. . . . Here one sees how necessary the feverish speculative spirit of the Americans is for the rapid development of a new country."[15] Seymour Martin Lipset notes that statistically, there are characteristic differences in the English-speaking Canadian and American approaches to economic life that mirror those between Protestants and Catholics within Canada. Canadians are more risk averse; they invest less of their assets in stocks; they prefer general humanistic to practical business education; and they are less prone to debt financing than are Americans.[16] While there are structural differences between the U.S. and Canadian economies that help explain these differences, Lipset tends to correlate these economic trends with the sectarian nature of Protestantism in the United States.

Spontaneous sociability is critical to economic life because virtually all economic activity is carried out by groups rather than individuals. Before wealth can be created, human beings have to learn to work together, and if there is to be subsequent progress, new forms of organization have to be developed. While we typically associate economic growth with technological development, organizational innovation has played an equal if not more important role since the beginning of the industrial revolution. The economic historians Douglass North and Robert Thomas put it bluntly: "Efficient economic organization is the key to growth; the development of an efficient economic organization in Western Europe accounts for the rise of the West."[17]

The development of transoceanic commerce in the fifteenth century depended on invention of the carrack, which could sail beyond coastal waters. But it also depended on the creation of the joint-stock company, by which individuals could pool their resources and share the risks entailed in funding great voyages. The extension of railroads across the continental United States in the mid-nineteenth century required large, hierarchically organized companies with geographically dispersed managers. The kinds of businesses that had existed previously were owned and operated by families. Not only could family businesses not keep the trains running on time; they could not keep them from running into one another on the same track, as occurred in an infamous accident that took place in 1841 on a line between Massachusetts and New York.[18] Henry Ford made possible the mass-produced automobile at the beginning of the twentieth century by putting the chassis on a moving conveyor belt and then subdividing the work into easy, repeatable steps. Complicated machines like automobiles no longer needed the services of specialized craftsmen but could be assembled by workers with virtually no education or experience. In the past generation, Toyota rose to international prominence in the global auto industry by partly undoing Henry Ford's factory system and giving workers on the factory floor a greater share of the responsibility of running the assembly line. In the 1990s, massive changes are occurring in the American economy under the rubrics of "downsizing" and "restructuring." Corporations are finding they can produce the same goods with fewer workers, changing not so much their technology but the way their employees work together.

In contrast to the work ethic and its associated individual virtues, which has been discussed extensively in the literature, the social virtues that encourage spontaneous sociability and organizational innovation have been studied much less systematically for their impact on economic life.[19] A strong argument can be made that social virtues are prerequisites for the development of individual virtues like the work ethic, since the latter can best be cultivated in the context of strong groups—families, schools, workplaces—that are fostered in societies with a high degree of social solidarity.

Most economists have assumed that group formation does not depend on ethical habit but arises naturally following the establishment of legal institutions like property rights and contract law. To see whether this is the case, we need to compare propensities for spontaneous sociability across cultural groups, holding constant to the extent possible economic institutions and environmental conditions.

CHAPTER 6

The Art of Association Around the World

Industrial structure tells an intriguing story about a country's culture. Societies that have very strong families but relatively weak bonds of trust among people unrelated to one another will tend to be dominated by small, family-owned and-managed businesses. On the other hand, countries that have vigorous private nonprofit organizations like schools, hospitals, churches, and charities, are also likely to develop strong private economic institutions that go beyond the family.

Conventional wisdom has it that Japan is the model of a group- and state-oriented "communitarian" society, while the United States is the epitome of an individualistic one. It is an omnipresent theme of the extensive competitiveness literature that the United States lives according to the principles of Anglo-Saxon liberalism in which people pursue their own aims and resist cooperation in larger communities. As such, it constitutes Japan's polar opposite in terms of sociability.

But if we look at the industrial structures of Japan and the United

49

States, we find a number of interesting similarities. Both economies are dominated by large corporations, relatively few of which are owned or subsidized by the state. In both countries, family businesses have evolved into professionally managed, rationally organized corporations relatively early in their developmental histories—beginning in the 1830s in the United States and in the last decades of the nineteenth century in Japan. Although Japan and America retain important small-business sectors run largely by families, the bulk of employment today is provided by large, publicly traded companies with highly dispersed ownership. These industrial structures are much more similar to one another than either is to those of Chinese societies like Taiwan and Hong Kong, on the one hand, or of France, Italy, or Spain on the other.

If Japan and the United States represent polar opposites in terms of their propensity for community, why then do their industrial structures resemble each other so closely and differ from other industrialized countries at a comparable level of development? The reason is that the characterization of American and Japanese societies as polar opposites is wrong. The United States is not nearly as individualistic, nor is Japan as state centered, as conventional wisdom holds. The competitiveness literature, by focusing on the question of industrial policy versus free markets, has missed a key factor critical to a robust economy and society.

Consider the United States. Although Americans commonly characterize themselves as individualistic, most serious social observers have noted in the past that the United States historically has possessed many strong and important communal structures that give its civil society dynamism and resilience. To a greater degree than many other Western societies, the United States has a dense and complex network of voluntary organizations: churches, professional societies, charitable institutions, private schools, universities, and hospitals, and, of course, a very strong private business sector. This complex associational life was noted first by the French traveler, Alexis de Tocqueville, during his visit to America in the 1830s.[1] This aspect of American society was also observed by the sociologist Max Weber after visiting the United States around the end of the nineteenth century: "In the past and up to the very present, it has been a characteristic precisely of the specifically American democracy that it did *not* constitute a formless sand heap of individuals, but rather a buzzing complex of strictly exclusive, yet voluntary associations."[2]

It is true that Americans have a strong antistatist tradition, evident in the relatively small size of the American public sector when compared to virtually all European nations,[3] and in opinion polls that show Americans expressing decidedly lower levels of confidence in and respect for government than do citizens of other industrialized nations.[4] But antistatism is not the same as hostility to community. The same Americans who are against state regulation, taxation, oversight, and ownership of productive resources can be extraordinarily cooperative and sociable in their companies, voluntary associations, churches, newspapers, universities, and the like. Americans say they feel a strong distrust of "big government," but they are very good at creating and maintaining very large, cohesive *private* organizations; they pioneered the development of the modern hierarchical (and later multinational) corporation, as well as the huge labor unions spawned by them.[5]

The American proclivity for associating in voluntary organizations continues up to the present, but it has been weakened in key respects over the past couple of generations. Family life, which constitutes the smallest and most basic form of association, has deteriorated markedly since the 1960s with a sharp increase in rates of divorce and single-parent families. Beyond the family, too, there has been a steady breakdown of older communities like neighborhoods, churches, and workplaces. At the same time, there has been a vast increase in the general level of distrust, as measured by the wariness that Americans have for their fellow citizens due to the rise of crime, or in the massive increases in litigation as a means of settling disputes. In recent years the state, often in the guise of the court system, has supported a rapidly expanding set of individual rights that have undermined the ability of larger communities to set standards for the behavior of their members. Thus, the United States today presents a contradictory picture of a society living off a great fund of previously accumulated social capital that gives it a rich and dynamic associational life, while at the same time manifesting extremes of distrust and asocial individualism that tend to isolate and atomize its members. This type of individualism always existed in a potential form, yet through most of America's existence it had been kept in check by strong communal currents.[6]

Not only is American society incorrectly portrayed as exclusively individualistic in conventional analyses, but Japan is also misunderstood as representing the opposite extreme of a statist communitarian society. Among the prominent scholars who over the years have emphasized the role of the state in Japanese development are the economic historian Alexander Gerschenkron and the Japanologist Chalmers Johnson.[7]

Like the view that Americans are individualistic, the assertion that Japan is a statist society is based on a certain core of truth, but it also misses a critical aspect of Japanese society. There is no question that the Japanese state plays a much larger role in Japanese society than does its American counterpart, and that this has been true throughout the two countries' national histories. In Japan, the best and brightest young people aspire to become bureaucrats, not businessmen, and there is intense competition for bureaucratic jobs. The state regulates the economy and society to a far greater extent than in the United States, and Japanese corporations and individuals defer to the state's authority much more readily than in the United States. From the Meiji Restoration in 1868 on, the Japanese state has played a key role in Japanese economic development, directing credits, protecting industries from foreign competition, financing R&D, and the like. The Ministry of International Trade and Industry (MITI) has become famous around the world as the guiding intelligence behind postwar Japanese economic development. The United States, on the other hand, has never had an explicit industrial policy.[8] There is a strong tradition of hostility to bureaucrats and a widespread feeling that anything the government can do, the private sector can do better.

But compared to highly statist societies like France, Mexico, or Brazil (not to speak of socialist societies like the former Soviet Union or China), the Japanese state's direct role in the economy has always been limited. Indeed, the Japanese state has been much less activist than in other fast-developing Asian countries like Taiwan (where state-owned industries have accounted for as much as a third of gross domestic product) or Korea (where state intervention to create Japanese-style conglomerates has been much more overt).[9] To this day, the Japanese government's direct role in the economy remains small; the Japanese public sector as a percentage of gross national product was for many years the lowest in the Organization of Economic Cooperation and Development, lower even than in the United States.[10]

Those who have argued for a statist interpretation of Japanese economic development point, of course, not to direct government intervention but to the subtle interaction between government and big business in Japan—a relationship characterized by the familiar term *Japan, Incorporated*. The degree of collusion between public agencies and private businesses is much higher than in the United States, to the point that it is often difficult to know what is public and what is private. It is frequently asserted that Japanese economic life has a nationalistic element missing in Western countries. When a Japanese executive goes to work, he toils not just for himself, his family, and his company but for the greater glory of the Japanese nation as well.[11]

Because government-business collusion and a nationalistic mind-set make it hard to draw a precise line between public and private in Japan, many have leaped to the conclusion that there is no difference between the two. The obscurity of Japanese society to most outsiders reinforces such conspiracy theories. But the great engines of Japanese economic growth—the prewar *zaibatsu,* or giant industrial conglomerates, the postwar multinational corporations with their *keiretsu* networks, as well as the often underestimated myriad of small businesses in the Japanese economy's surprisingly vigorous second tier—have (with the brief exception of the first two Meiji decades) all been private enterprises.[12] While Japan's entrepreneurs have seen their interests paralleling that of the state, it is they who provided the capital accumulation, technological innovation, and organizational skill to create a modern economy. William Lockwood, a historian of the Japanese economy, surveying the early history of Japanese industrialization, states, "The foregoing remarks . . . all cast doubt on the thesis even in the case of Japan that the State was 'the chief element in economic development' or the statesmen 'the chief actors.' . . . The energies, the skills, and the ambitions which provided the real motor force of Japanese industrialization were much too pervasive and too diverse to be compressed into any such formula."[13] In the postwar period, there is accumulating evidence that the Japanese government and private sector have often clashed and that growth has occurred despite, rather than because of, MITI's efforts. In any event, seeing the Japanese private sector as a mere extension of the state obscures the remarkable self-organizing characteristic of Japanese society.

Like the United States, Japanese society supports a dense network of voluntary organizations. Many of these are what the Japanese call *iemoto* groups, centered around a traditional art or craft like Kabuki theater, flower arranging, or classical tea ceremony. These groups are hierarchical like families, with strong vertical ties between masters and disciples, but they are not based on kinship and are entered into on a voluntary basis. *Iemoto*-type organizations, which have no counterpart in China, pervade

Japanese society, extending far beyond the traditional arts to encompass religious, political, and professional organizations. Unlike the Chinese but similar to Americans, the Japanese tend to exhibit a high degree of religiosity.[14] They belong to individual Shinto, Buddhist, and even Christian temples and churches, supporting a dense network of religious organizations with their contributions. The sectarian character of Japanese religious life would also be more familiar to Americans than to Chinese. Throughout Japanese history there has been a constant succession of monks and preachers who have established cult followings, frequently clashing with the political authorities and with each other. Finally, Japan is the only country in Asia with a strong system of private universities—institutions like Waseda, Keio, Sophia, and Doshisha—started, like their American counterparts at Harvard, Yale, or Stanford, by wealthy businessmen or by religious organizations.

It is more accurate to say that the Japanese have a group-oriented rather than a state-oriented culture.[15] While most postwar Japanese respect the state, their primary emotional attachments—the loyalties that make them stay in the office until ten at night or miss weekends with their families—are to the *private* corporations, businesses, or universities that employ them. There was a period before World War II when the state did serve as a primary object of loyalty and private citizens were much more self-conscious about the national purposes they hoped to serve, but defeat in war all but discredited this kind of nationalism except on the extreme right.

The groups to which Japanese owe loyalties may be stronger and more cohesive than in the United States, and there is no doubt that the Japanese state is more intrusive than its American counterpart. But Japan shares with the United States an ability to spontaneously generate strong social groups in the middle part of the spectrum—that is, in the region between the family on the one hand and the state on the other. The significance of this ability becomes much more evident if we contrast both the United States and Japan to socialist societies, Latin Catholic countries, or Chinese society.

Perhaps one of the most devastating consequences of socialism as it was actually practiced in the Soviet Union and Eastern Europe was the thorough destruction of civil society that took place there, a destruction that has hampered the emergence of both working market economies and stable democracies. The Leninist state set about deliberately to destroy all possible competitors to its power, from the "commanding heights" of the economy down through the innumerable farms, small businesses, unions, churches, newspapers, voluntary associations, and the like, to the family itself.

The extent to which the totalitarian project succeeded varied from one socialist society to another. The destruction of civil society was perhaps the most thorough in the Soviet Union. Russian civil society before the Bolshevik Revolution, weakened by centuries of absolutist rule, was not strong. What existed, such as the small private sector and social structures like the peasant commune, or *mir,* were ruthlessly eradicated. By the time of Stalin's consolidation of power in the late 1930s, the Soviet Union exhibited a "missing middle": the complete dearth of strong, cohesive, or durable intermediate associations. That is, the Soviet state was very powerful, and there were many atomized individuals and families, but in between there were virtually no social groups whatsoever. The ironic consequence of a doctrine designed to eliminate human selfishness was that people were made *more* selfish. It was a common observation, for example, that Soviet Jewish émigrés to Israel were much more materialistic and less public spirited than Jews who had come from bourgeois countries. Virtually everyone in the Soviet Union had become cynical about public spiritedness as a result of a state that constantly hectored and coerced them into "voluntarily" giving up their weekend for the sake of Cuban or Vietnamese people or some other such cause.

But socialist societies were not the only ones to have weak intermediate associations. Many Latin Catholic countries like France, Spain, Italy, and a number of nations in Latin America exhibit a saddle-shaped distribution of organizations, with strong families, a strong state, and relatively little in between. These societies are utterly different from socialist ones in any number of important ways, particularly with regard to their greater respect for the family. But like socialist societies, there has been in certain Latin Catholic countries a relative deficit of intermediate social groups in the area between the family and large, centralized organizations like the church or the state.

The literature on France, for example, has long stressed the absence of communal organizations between the family and the state. In Tocqueville's memorable phrase from *The Old Regime and the French Revolution,* "When the Revolution started, it would have been impossible to find, in most parts of France, even ten men used to acting in concert and defending their interests without appealing to the central power for aid," a characteristic of French society that he compared very unfavorably with the Americans' proclivity for associating with one another.[16] Similarly, Edward Banfield's *The Moral Basis of a Backward Society* introduced the concept of "amoral familism" to describe social life in a southern Italian peasant community after World War II. Banfield found that social ties and moral obligation were limited to the nuclear family alone; outside of this, individuals did not trust each other and therefore did not feel a sense of responsibility to larger groups, whether they were the neighborhood, village, church, or nation.[17] These findings have been largely confirmed, at least for southern Italy, in Robert Putnam's study of civic traditions in that country. And in Spain, according to Lawrence Harrison, excessive individualism, "a narrow radius of trust and the centrality of the family to the exclusion of broader society," has long been characteristic.[18]

The "missing middle" between the family and the state is not unique to these Latin Catholic cultures. In fact, it finds a purer expression in Chinese societies—in Taiwan, Hong Kong, Singapore, and the People's Republic of China itself.[19] As we will see in the following chapters, the essence of Chinese Confucianism is familism. Confucianism promotes a tremendous strengthening of family bonds through moral education and the elevation of the importance of the family above other sorts of social ties. In this respect, the Chinese family is much stronger and more cohesive than the Japanese family. As in Latin Catholic societies, the strength of the family bond implies a certain weakness in ties between individuals not related to one another: there is a relatively low degree of trust in Chinese society the moment one steps outside the family circle. Hence the distribution of associations in Chinese societies like Taiwan or Hong Kong resembles that of France. The industrial structures of Chinese societies are startlingly similar to Latin Catholics: businesses tend to be family owned and managed and tend therefore to be of rather small scale. There is a reluctance to bring in professional managers because this requires reaching outside the bounds of the family, where trust is low. Hence the impersonal corporate structures needed to support large-scale institutions are adopted only slowly. These family businesses are often dynamic and profitable, but they have a hard time institutionalizing themselves into more permanent enterprises not dependent on the health and competence of the founding entrepreneurial family.

In both the Latin Catholic and Chinese cases, the existence of large economic units not based on the family depends in large measure on the role of the state or on foreign investment. The public sectors of France and Italy have traditionally been among the largest in Europe. In the People's Republic of China, virtually all the large enterprises remain state owned, holdovers from the days of orthodox communism, and in Taiwan many of the large manufacturing enterprises—several related to armaments or defense—are owned by the state. Hong Kong, on the other hand, with its highly noninterventionist British government, has had little state involvement in the economy and hence relatively few very large corporations.

With respect to the distribution of social groups, there are significant differences between Japanese and Chinese cultures. Japan and China are both Confucian societies and share many cultural traits; Chinese and Japanese usually feel much more at home in each other's societies than either would feel in Europe or the United States. On the other hand, they are different from one another in striking ways that become evident in all aspects of social life. When compared to Chinese or Latin Catholic cultures with their weak intermediate associations, the similarities between Japan and the United States become more understandable. It is no accident that the United States, Japan, and Germany were the first countries to develop large, modern, rationally organized, professionally managed corporations. Each of these cultures had certain characteristics that allowed business organizations to move beyond the family rather rapidly and to create a variety of new, voluntary social groups that were not based on kinship. They were able to do so, as we will see, because in each of these societies there was a high degree of trust between individuals who were not related to one another, and hence a solid basis for social capital.

II

LOW-TRUST SOCIETIES AND THE PARADOX OF FAMILY VALUES

CHAPTER 7

Paths and Detours to Sociability

During the 1992 American presidential campaign, Vice President Dan Quayle attacked the Democrats on the issue of family values by arguing that the cultural left was glorifying single parenthood through TV characters like Murphy Brown. The question of family life was suddenly politicized, with the left accusing Republicans of narrow-minded gay bashing and hostility to single mothers, and the right countering that feminism, gay rights, and the welfare system had contributed to the precipitous decline in the strength and stability of American families.

After the smoke of the election campaign cleared, it was clear that serious problems beset the American family, problems that have been repeatedly acknowledged by Democratic president Bill Clinton. Nuclear families started to break down throughout the industrialized world in the late 1960s, with some of the most dramatic changes occurring in the United States.[1] By the mid-1990s, the rate of single-parent families in

61

the white community was reaching a rate of close to 30 percent, the level that Daniel Patrick Moynihan found so troubling in the African-American community of the 1960s, and black single parenthood in many inner-city neighborhoods was upwards of seventy percent. As the U.S. Census Bureau has documented in considerable detail, with the growth in numbers of single-parent families in the 1970s and 1980s came a significant increase in poverty and in the social pathologies that are fed by poverty.[2] Swimming against this tide were a number of immigrant groups that seemed to do well in the United States because they retained a strong family structure from the cultures out of which they came, structures that had not yet been undermined by the broader atomizing currents of mainstream American life.[3] Today there is a generally positive evaluation in the United States of the role of the family as an effective institution for socializing individuals, one that cannot easily be replaced by broader community groups and least of all by government programs.

When we step back from contemporary American debates over family values, we find that the family paradoxically does not always play a positive role in promoting economic growth. The earlier social theorists who saw the strong family as an obstacle to economic development were not entirely wrong. In some cultures, such as in those of China and certain regions of Italy, the family looms much larger than other forms of association. This fact has a striking impact on industrial life. As the extraordinarily rapid development of many Chinese economies and of Italy in recent years indicates, familism in itself is a barrier to neither industrialization nor rapid growth if other cultural values are right. But familism does affect the character of that growth—the types of economic organizations that are possible, as well as the sectors of the global economy in which that society will operate. Familistic societies have greater difficulties creating large economic institutions, and this constraint on size limits the sectors of the global economy in which such businesses can operate.

There are three broad paths to sociability: the first is based on family and kinship, the second on voluntary associations outside kinship such as schools, clubs, and professional organizations, and the third is the state. There are three forms of economic organization corresponding to each path: the family business, the professionally managed corporation, and the state-owned or -sponsored enterprise. The first and third paths, it turns out, are closely related to one another: cultures in which the primary avenue toward sociability is family and kinship have a great deal of trouble creating large, durable economic organizations and therefore look to the state to initiate and support them. Cultures inclined toward voluntary associations, on the other hand, can create large economic organizations spontaneously and do not need the state's support.

In part II, we will examine four societies—those of China, Italy, France, and Korea—in which families play a central role and voluntary associations are relatively weak. Part III will then investigate two societies, Japan and Germany, where associations beyond the family are strong and plentiful.

Virtually all economic endeavors start out as family businesses: that is, businesses that are both owned and managed by families. The basic unit of social cohesion serves also as the basic unit of economic enterprise: labor is divided among spouses, children, in-laws, and so on outward to (depending on culture) an ever-widening circle of kin.[4] Family businesses in the form of peasant households were omnipresent in preindustrial agricultural societies, as well as more modern ones, where they formed the backbone of the first industrial revolution in England and the United States.

New businesses in mature economies also usually start out as small family enterprises and only later take on a more impersonal corporate structure. Because their cohesion is based on the moral and emotional bonds of a preexisting social group, the family enterprise can thrive even in the absence of commercial law or stable structure of property rights.

But family businesses are only the starting point for the development of economic organizations. Some societies early on built bridges to other forms of sociability beyond the family. Beginning in the sixteenth century, for example, England and Holland created legal arrangements permitting the vesting ownership in larger groups, such as joint proprietorships, joint-stock companies, or limited liability partnerships. Besides allowing owners to capture the social returns from their investments, legal structures such as these allowed unrelated people to cooperate in the creation of a business. The contract and its associated system of obligations and penalties, enforced through a legal system, could fill in the gap where the trust naturally found in families did not exist. Joint-stock companies, in particular, allowed enterprises to grow in scale beyond the means of a single family by pooling the resources of a large number of investors.

Historians of economic development like Douglass North and Robert Thomas assert that the creation of a stable system of property rights was the crucial development that permitted the process of industrialization to begin.[5] In some countries like the United States, a system of property rights was established early on, such that family businesses were usually also incorporated as legal entities. But in other places, such as China, where there was little security of property rights, family businesses grew quite large without legal protection.

Although legal arrangements like joint-stock companies and limited liability partnerships permitted unrelated people to cooperate with one another in business, they did not automatically lead to that result or to the extinction of family businesses. In many cases, family businesses incorporated under these laws and enjoyed the protection of their property rights but in other respects operated much as before. Virtually all American businesses were family businesses until the 1830s, despite the existence of a rather well-developed system of commercial law and a fledgling stock market. Family-owned businesses can grow to be extremely large, employing tens of thousands of workers and the most modern technology. Indeed, many large contemporary corporations such as the Campbell Soup Company, familiar to American consumers, are still family owned.[6]

But as a business grows, its increasing scale usually outstrips the capabilities of a single family to operate it. First to fall away is family management: a single family, no matter how large, capable, or well educated, can only have so many competent sons, daughters, spouses, and siblings to oversee the different parts of a rapidly ramifying enterprise. Family ownership often persists longer, but here too, growth often requires raising more capital than one family can provide. Family control is diluted first through bank borrowing, which gives the creditor some voice in the running of the business, and then through public equity offerings. In many cases the family gets out or is pushed out of the business it founded, as the latter is bought out by nonfamily investors. Sometimes the families themselves disintegrate as a result of jealousy, squabbling, or incompetence—something that has happened in innumerable Irish bars, Italian restaurants, and Chinese laundries.

At this point family businesses face a critical choice: try to retain control of their enterprises within the family, which is often tantamount to opting for continuing small size, or give up control and become, in effect, passive shareholders. If they opt for the latter, family business gives way to the modern corporate form of organization. In place of the family proprietors who founded the company come professional managers, chosen not for their bloodline but for their competence in some aspect of management. The enterprise becomes institutionalized, taking on a life of its own beyond the control of any single individual. The often ad hoc decision-making structure of family-owned businesses gives way to a formal organization chart with structured lines of authority. Instead of everyone reporting directly to the firm's founder, a hierarchy of middle managers is created to insulate the top decision makers from the overload of information coming up from below. Ultimately the sheer complexity of running very large-scale businesses requires the evolution of a decentralized form of decision making centered around separate divisions, which top management treats as independent profit centers.[7]

The corporate form of organization did not appear until the middle of the nineteenth century, first in the United States and then somewhat later in Germany. But by the first decades of the twentieth century, it had become the dominant form of economic organization in the United States. The classic description of the rise of managerialism in American business was given by Adoph Berle and Gardner Means in their 1932 book, *The Modern Corporation and Private Property.* They noted that with the new corporate form of organization, the link between ownership and management increasingly was broken, opening up the possibility of a conflict of interest between owners and professional managers.[8] The business historian Alfred Chandler has chronicled the rise of the modern, multidivision, hierarchical corporation, in both the United States and abroad, in great detail.[9] Many of the brand names of modern corporate America, such as du Pont, Eastman Kodak, Sears, Roebuck, Pitney-Bowes, and Kellogg started out as small family businesses in the nineteenth century.

For decades, social scientists believed that there was a natural development path that led from family businesses based on traditional moral reciprocity to the modern, impersonal, professionally managed corporation based on contract and property rights. As a consequence, many sociologists argued that too strong an insistence by society on maintaining family ties at the expense of other kinds of social relationships—what is called *familism*—was detrimental to economic development. Max Weber, in his book *The Religion of China,* argued that the strong Chinese family created what he called "sib fetters" (overly restrictive family bonds), constraining the development of universal values and the impersonal social ties necessary for modern business organization.

In the West, many observers believed that family ties had to weaken if economic progress was to occur. The following passage, from one of the standard works on industrial development typical of the early postwar modernization school, illustrates this view of the breakdown of the extended family:

> [The extended family] provides shelter and food for all its members, regardless of their individual contributions, so that the indigent and the indolent alike are cared for in a sort of "social security" system. Working members are expected to pool their earnings for the benefit of everyone; individual saving is discouraged. The behavior and careers (including marriage) of its members are the close concern of the elders. Family loyalty and obligations take precedence over other loyalties and obligations. Thus, the extended family tends to dilute individual incentives to work, save, and invest.[10]

It was not only Western social scientists and management experts who held a negative view of the role of the family in economic life. Chinese communists also believed this, hoping to break the hold of the traditional Chinese family by encouraging other sorts of loyalties—to the commune, the party, and the state itself.[11]

Though familism was considered an obstacle to economic development, social scientists also tended to believe that it would be eroded as an inevitable result of socioeconomic change. There was a widespread belief that in premodern agricultural societies, some type of extended family was the norm and that these extended families were replaced by nuclear families as a result of industrialization. Although there was great variety in family structure among cultures before the industrial revolution, a consensus developed that these differences would erode over time and that cultures would come to share the nuclear family structure typical of industrialized North America and Europe.

More recently, it has become much less widely accepted that there is a single path of economic development that all societies must follow as they modernize. The economic historian Alexander Gerschenkron, for example, noted that late modernizers like Germany and Japan did things rather differently from early modernizers like England and the United States, with the government playing a much more active role in promoting development.[12] In terms of the evolution of corporate organization, the large, vertically integrated firm described by Chandler is not the only way to deal with problems of scale. The Japanese *keiretsu* system constitutes an alternative form of corporate organization based on networks rather than hierarchy and in effect achieves the scale economies of vertical integration with a much more flexible form of organization. An advanced industrialized country's economy can, moreover, remain dominated by modern family businesses, as we will see in the cases of Taiwan and Italy. Craft traditions and small-scale production have survived alongside large-scale, mass production facilities.[13]

Recent research on the history of the family has indicated that the evolutionary account of the "modern" family's progressing steadily from extended to nuclear was not quite accurate. Historical studies have shown that the nuclear family was much more prevalent in preindustrial societies than was previously thought, and in some cases extended kinship groups first disintegrated but later reconstituted themselves as industrialization progressed.[14] Most important from the standpoint of culture, causation was not a one-way street: just as economic change affected the nature of the family, family structure had an impact on the nature of industrialization. As we will see, the economies of China and Japan are structured very differently, and those differences can be traced back ultimately to family structure.

In the United States over the past generation, the harsh view of the family as an obstacle to development has softened considerably and has been replaced—as the Dan Quayle family values debate indicated—with a more positive assessment of the impact of family life on economic well-being. In retrospect, it seems clear that modernization theorists writing in the 1950s or 1960s were wrong to assume that the breakdown of family structure would end with the nuclear family, whose stability and cohesion they took for granted. As it turned out, nuclear families began to break down into single-parent families at an alarming rate, with much less benign consequences than the breakdown of the extended family in earlier generations.

Hence, the impact of family values on economic life poses a complex and contradictory picture: it is possible for families in some societies to be too strong to permit the formation of modern economic organizations, while in others they can be too weak to perform their basic task of socialization. How this can be so simultaneously is elucidated in the following chapters.

CHAPTER 8

A Loose Tray of Sand

W ang Laboratories of Lowell, Massachusetts, began as a small family business. A maker of computer equipment, Wang had revenues of $2.28 billion by 1984 and at one time employed 24,800 people, eventually making it one of the Boston area's largest employers.[1] An Wang, who founded Wang Laboratories in 1951, was born in Shanghai and emigrated to the United States when he was twenty-five. Wang Laboratories went public in the late 1950s and was one of the great American high-tech entrepreneurial success stories of the next generation. But when An Wang got ready to step down in the mid-1980s, he insisted on having his American-born son, Fred Wang, take over the business. Fred Wang was promoted over the heads of several more senior managers with proven track records, including John Cunningham, whom most people inside the company believed to be the logical successor to An Wang. The blatant nepotism evident in his promotion alienated a string of American managers, who quickly left the company.[2]

Wang Laboratories' subsequent fall was stunning, even for a company in the volatile computer industry. The company posted its first loss the year after Fred Wang took over the company. Ninety percent of its market capitalization had disappeared in four years, and in 1992 it filed for bankruptcy. The elder Wang eventually admitted that his son was in over his head as a manager and was forced to fire him. Whether the one Chinese brand name familiar to many Americans will survive to the end of the 1990s is an open question.

The story of Wang Laboratories, though far removed from China itself, reveals a fundamental truth about Chinese business: despite the explosion of Chinese industry around the world in the past twenty years and the high-tech, modern facade of many Chinese companies, Chinese businesses continue to be based on family ties. The Chinese family provides the social capital with which to start up new businesses, but it also constitutes a major structural constraint on these enterprises that in many cases prevents them from evolving into durable, large-scale institutions.

Wang Laboratories' debacle demonstrates other aspects of Chinese culture. Some observers note that many of the problems that emerged after Fred Wang took over the company were actually the result of his father's management style. An Wang remained a highly autocratic CEO, unwilling to delegate authority. In 1972, when the company already had 2,000 employees, 136 people reported to him directly.[3] An Wang was energetic and capable enough to make this typically Chinese hub-and-spoke management system work, and in some respects it increased esprit de corps throughout the company. But this management system is exceedingly difficult to institutionalize and hastened the company's decline when the elder Wang retired. We will see these management practices repeated throughout the Chinese business world. Their origins in the Chinese family are as strong as they are deep.

The Chinese constitute the world's largest racial, linguistic, and cultural group. They are spread across a vast geographic area and live in a wide variety of states, from the still-communist People's Republic of China, to overseas Chinese settlements in Southeast Asia, to industrial democracies like the United States, Canada, and Great Britain.

Despite this variation in political environment, it is nonetheless possible to speak of a relatively homogeneous Chinese economic culture. Its purest manifestations are in Taiwan, Hong Kong, and Singapore, where the Chinese are an ethnic majority and the state has not forced economic development along an ideologically determined path, as in the PRC. But this culture can also be seen within the minority Chinese ethnic enclaves in Malaysia, Thailand, Indonesia, and the Philippines, and it has appeared in the open, private economy that has flourished in the PRC since Deng Xiaoping's economic reforms of the late 1970s. And, as the story of Wang Laboratories suggests, it is even evident among Chinese in the United States, despite the relatively higher degree of assimilation into the dominant culture there than in Southeast Asia. The fact that a similar pattern of economic behavior emerges whenever governments allow Chinese communities to organize their own affairs suggests that it is in some sense a natural outgrowth of Sinitic culture.

The first thing we notice in the industrial structure of Chinese societies like Taiwan, Hong Kong, and Singapore is the small scale of enterprises.[4] In the West, Japan, and Korea, economic development has been accomplished more through rapid increases in the scale of economic enterprises than through growth in the number of enterprises. The opposite is true in Chinese cultures. In Taiwan, for example, of the 44,054 manufacturing enterprises that existed in 1971, 68 percent were small-scale enterprises, and another 23 percent were classified as medium scale, employing up to 50 workers.[5] The number of such firms increased between 1966 and 1976 by 150 percent, while the average size of an individual enterprise measured by number of workers increased by 29 percent. In Korea, which followed a development path more like that of Japan or the United States, the opposite was the case: the number of manufacturing firms increased in the same period by only 10 percent, while the employees per enterprise increased by 176 percent.[6] Although there are some large private Taiwanese companies, their scale is dwarfed by large private corporations in Korea. This difference clearly cannot be explained by the level of development, since Korea is usually held to be slightly behind Taiwan. Taiwan's largest private company in 1983, Formosa Plastics, had sales of $1.6 billion and 31,211 employees, compared to the Korean conglomerates Hyundai and Samsung, which in that same period had sales of $8.0 and $5.9 billion and 137,000 and 97,384 employees, respectively. In 1976 the average Taiwanese firm was only half the size of the average Korean firm.[7]

Small firm size is, if anything, even more the rule in Hong Kong, which has long been famous as an exemplar of a highly competitive market composed of atomistic firms. Indeed, the average size of Hong Kong firms has actually declined: in 1947, there were 961 firms in Hong Kong employing 47,356 people, for a mean of 49.3 employees per firm, while in 1984, there were 48,992 firms employing 904,709 people, or 18.4 employees per firm.[8] Even in the industrial suburb of Kwun Tung, which was deliberately zoned to encourage larger firms, some 72 percent of the firms there employed fewer than 50 workers each, while only 7 percent had more than 200.[9] This decline in firm size was partly due to the opening up of the PRC's Guangdong Province to Hong Kong business in the 1980s; many larger manufacturing firms moved to the mainland to take advantage of lower labor costs there. On the other hand, capital from the PRC poured into Hong Kong in a reverse flow and was used to establish a number of large corporations there. Data from other overseas Chinese communities suggest a similar pattern. In the Philippines, for example, the assets of Chinese firms are only one-third the size of non-Chinese firms.[10] Of the 150 companies in a 1990 *Fortune* survey of the largest Pacific Rim corporations, only one—a Taiwanese state-owned oil company—was Chinese.[11]

The small scale of Taiwanese industry is associated with another unique feature of Taiwanese development: much manufacturing is carried on outside large urban areas. As late as the mid-1960s, more than half of Taiwan's manufacturing labor force was employed outside the seven largest cities and nine largest towns.[12] A good deal of manufacturing consisted of cottage industries run by part-time farmers, as was the case also in the PRC after decollectivization. These firms were financed almost entirely from household savings, using family labor to produce low-tech plastic components, paper products, and the like.[13]

There have always been a number of large, state-owned companies in Taiwan, particularly in petrochemicals, shipbuilding, steel, aluminum, and most recently semiconductors and aerospace. Some of these companies were started during the Japanese colonial period and were taken over by the Nationalist government after it assumed power on the island in 1949. Alice Amsden has argued that the Taiwanese state sector has been ignored in many accounts of Taiwanese development, and these firms did indeed play an important role in the early years of the island's industrialization.[14] But these large state enterprises were always the least dynamic part of the island's economy, and have accounted for a steadily decreasing share of gross domestic product over time. Many of them have run in the red and are kept going by the state for national security reasons, or because state ownership may be the only way for such a society to develop large-scale enterprises.[15] It is the private business sector, dominated by small enterprises, that has piled up such impressive growth statistics since the 1950s.

As in all other Asian societies, there exists among the Chinese another level of economic organization above that of individual enterprises, which might be collectively titled "network organizations."[16] The largest and most famous of these are the Japanese *keiretsu* (known before World War II as *zaibatsu*) like the Sumitomo and Mitsubishi groups: alliances of companies, often centering around a bank, that hold each other's shares and deal with each other on a preferential basis. The Korean version of the network organization is known as the *chaebol,* among which are such well-known names as Samsung and Hyundai. These network organizations achieve economies of scale and scope on the level of leading Western firms but within a looser organizational form that permits a greater degree of flexibility than the equivalent vertically integrated American firm.

Taiwan also has network organizations, but of a very different nature. In the first place, they are much smaller than their Japanese or Korean counterparts: the six largest Japanese *keiretsu* average thirty-one firms per group,[17] the Korean *chaebol* have eleven, and the Taiwanese network organizations average only seven firms each. The average firm size within each Taiwanese business group is smaller, and their role in the economy is much smaller. While the Japanese and Korean network organizations include the largest and most important enterprises in their respective economies, the Taiwanese groups are much more marginal: of the largest 500 manufacturing firms in Taiwan, only forty percent belong to business groups.[18] These network organizations do not, like the Japanese *keiretsu,* center on a bank or some other financial institution. Most Taiwanese firms deal with a number of different banks, and the latter were, in any case, largely state owned.[19] Finally, the nature of the ties linking members of the Taiwanese network organizations is different: they are largely based on family. In this respect they are much more similar to the Korean *chaebol,* whose linkages are also kinship based, than to the Japanese *keiretsu,* which are publicly owned corporations tied to one another through cross-shareholdings.[20]

The reason for the small scale of enterprises in Chinese societies is that virtually all private-sector businesses are family owned and family managed.[21] Although it is difficult to find accurate ownership statistics, evidence indicates that a vast majority of the small businesses dominating the economic life of Hong Kong, Taiwan, and Singapore are owned by single families.[22] The large, hierarchical, publicly owned, professionally managed corporation, which has been the dominant organizational form in Japan and the United States for many years, does not exist in culturally Chinese societies for all practical purposes.

This is not to say that there are not large enterprises or professional managers in the PRC, Taiwan, Hong Kong, or Singapore. The World Wide Shipping Company of Hong Kong, owned by the late Sir Yue-kong Pao, was at one time the largest in Asia, with offices around the world.[23] The gigantic Li Ka-shing empire, also based in Hong Kong, has successfully incorporated a large number of professional managers. There are a dozen billionaire families controlling large businesses in Taiwan and a comparable number in Hong Kong. Fifty-four percent of the Hong Kong stock market's capitalization is controlled by ten family groups (seven Chinese, one Jewish/British, and two British).[24]

From the outside, these look like modern corporations, with far-flung offices in San Francisco, London, New York, and elsewhere. But these large companies remain family managed, with the regional offices often headed by a brother, cousin, or son-in-law of the founder back in Hong Kong or Taipei.[25] At the top levels of the company, the divorce of family ownership and family management has been much slower to occur than in Japan or the United States. The Li Ka-shing empire is being taken over by the elder Li's two Stanford-educated sons. The Pao empire, for its part, was run largely by four sons-in-law. The empire was split four ways among these branches of the family just before the elder Pao's death.[26]

The fact that many of these large businesses are publicly listed on their local stock exchanges does not necessarily make them any less family controlled than their private counterparts. Families are usually reluctant to let their shares in their companies fall below thirty-five to forty percent—enough to guarantee them a major voice in management.[27] Moreover, many of the publicly listed shares are owned by a bank or financial company that is also controlled by the same family.[28] These layers of ownership often obscure the fact that a single family remains in control.

Family businesses are not unique to Chinese societies; almost all Western firms initially started out as family enterprises and only later acquired a corporate structure. What is striking about Chinese industrialization, however, and demonstrated dramatically in the case of Wang Laboratories, is the *very great difficulty Chinese family businesses seem to have in making the transition from family to professional management,* a step that is necessary for the enterprise to institutionalize itself and carry on beyond the lifetime of the founding family.

The Chinese difficulty in moving to professional management is related to the nature of Chinese familism.[29] There is a very strong inclination on the part of the Chinese to trust only people related to them, and conversely to distrust people outside their family and kinship group.[30] According to Gordon Redding's study of Hong Kong businesses,

> The key feature would appear to be that you trust your family absolutely, your friends and acquaintances to the degree that mutual dependence has been established and face invested in them. With everybody else you make no assumptions about their goodwill. You have the right to expect their politeness and their following of the social proprieties, but beyond that you must anticipate that, just as you are, they are looking primarily to their own, i.e., their family's, best interests. To know your own motives well is, for the Chinese more than most, a warning about everybody else's.[31]

The lack of trust outside the family makes it hard for unrelated people to form groups or organizations, including economic enterprises. In sharp contrast to Japan, Chinese society is *not* group oriented. This difference is captured in the saying of Lin Yu-tang, who spoke of Japanese society as being like a piece of granite, while traditional Chinese society was like a loose tray of sand, each grain being an individual family.[32] This is what makes Chinese society at times appear highly individualistic to Western observers.

In traditional Chinese economic life, there is no figure comparable in social importance to the Japanese *banto,* the professional manager brought in from the outside to run the affairs of the family business.[33] Even small family businesses in Chinese societies frequently need the labor of nonfamily employees, but the relationship of these employees to the family-owners/managers is quite distant. The Japanese sense of the enterprise or company as a surrogate family does not exist. Nonfamily employees generally do not like working for other people and aspire not to lifetime employment with the same company but to break free and start a company of their own.[34] Comparative management studies have found that Chinese managers keep a much greater social distance between themselves and their employees.[35] The kind of spontaneous, egalitarian camaraderie that emerges when a Japanese manager goes out drinking in the evening with the people he supervises is much rarer in a

Chinese cultural context. Japanese-style company-sponsored events, in which an entire office—supervisors together with those supervised—will leave Tokyo or Nagoya on a retreat to a resort in the countryside for several days, are as foreign in a Chinese cultural setting as they are in the West. In Hong Kong or Taipei, the retreats and common vacations would be reserved for family members only, or perhaps occasionally for larger kinship groups.[36] Nonfamily managers in Chinese companies are not given large equity stakes in their businesses and often complain of a lack of openness when dealing with the boss. Furthermore, they usually hit a glass ceiling in promotion, since a family member will always be preferred for important positions.

In other words, the problem of nepotism, which Weber and others saw as a severe constraint on modernization, has not disappeared from Chinese economic life despite the remarkable recent economic growth of Chinese societies. It has been more tenacious in part because the family is more central to Chinese than to other sorts of cultures, and also because the Chinese have found ways of working around it. The founding entrepreneurs of many large, modern Chinese businesses try to deal with the problem of incompetent offspring by educating their children very well, sending them to business or engineering school at Stanford, Yale, or MIT. An alternative is to marry one's daughters in such a way as to bring new managerial talent into the family. The obligations of family run both ways: there are many instances of sons trained as doctors or scientists in America who have been summoned home to take over control of the family business. But there are limits to such strategies, particularly as the scale of the firm grows and the family is stretched thin.

The strong influence of family values leads to some unusual dilemmas for Chinese consumers that do not occur in other cultures. Consider the following description of shopping in Hong Kong:

> Retailers are expected to give close kinsmen a lower price, but the kinsman is also expected to buy without a lot of quibbling. . . . One old lady carefully avoided shopping at the mixed goods shop run by her sister's son because she would feel obligated to buy once she went in. If she wanted a blue thing and all they had were red ones, she would have to take a red one. So she went to the shop of a non-kinsman where she could carefully look for something that exactly suited her taste, walk out if she didn't find it, and bargain fiercely if she did.[37]

The strong distrust of outsiders and preference for family management in Chinese societies leads to a distinctive three-stage evolutionary cycle for Chinese businesses.[38] In the first stage, the business is founded by an entrepreneur, usually a strong patriarch who then places his relatives in key management positions and rules the company in an authoritarian manner. The solidarity of the Chinese family does not mean that there are not significant tensions within it, but toward the outside world the family shows a united front, and disputes ultimately are settled by the authority of the founding entrepreneur. Since many Chinese entrepreneurs started out poor, the entire family is willing to work extraordinarily hard to make the business succeed. Although the business may hire nonfamily employees, there is little separation between the firm's finances and those of the family.

Under first-generation entrepreneur-managers, even if the business prospers and grows to a large scale, there is often no effort to move to a modern management system with a formal division of labor, a managerial hierarchy, and a decentralized, multidivisional form of organization. The company remains organized according to a highly centralized hub-and-spoke system, with the organization's various branches all reporting directly to the founding entrepreneur.[39] Chinese management style is frequently described as personalistic—that is, rather than relying on objective performance criteria, personnel decisions are made on the basis of the boss's personal relations with his subordinates, even if they are not relatives.[40]

The second stage in the evolution of the family firm—assuming the business has been successful—occurs on the death of the founding patriarch. The principle of equal inheritance among male heirs is deeply ingrained in Chinese culture, and as a consequence all of the founder's sons find themselves with an equal stake in the family business.[41] Although considerable pressure exists for all the sons to take an interest in the family business, not everyone is always so inclined. As in other cultures, pressures for conformity lead to rebellion, and many stories are told of sons who, having been sent off to business school in the United States or Canada, decide to major in the arts or some other field removed from their father's money-making world. The partnership of those sons interested in managing the business is fraught with inherent tensions. Although they start with equal equity stakes, not all are equally competent or equally interested. The business has the best chance of surviving if one of the sons takes over leadership and recentralizes authority in himself. If this does not happen, authority is fragmented among the brothers. The frequent result is disputes, which sometimes have to be resolved through formal, contractual delineations of authority. If the division of responsibility is not settled amicably, the heirs can descend into a power struggle for ultimate control of the company, which in some cases can lead to its breakup.

The third phase occurs when control passes to the founding entrepreneur's grandchildren. Those businesses that have survived this long tend to disintegrate thereafter. Since the sons often have unequal numbers of children, the grandchildren's shares vary in size. In the case of very successful families, the grandchildren have grown up in very well-to-do surroundings. Unlike the founding entrepreneur, they more readily take their prosperity for granted and are typically less motivated to make the sacrifices needed to keep the business competitive, or else they have developed interests in other types of activities.

The gradual decline in entrepreneurial talent from the first generation to the third is not, of course, something that occurs only in Chinese culture. It characterizes family businesses in all societies and has been labeled the "Buddenbrooks" phenomenon. There is, indeed, a traditional Irish saying reflecting the rise and fall of family fortunes: "Shirtsleeves to shirtsleeves in three generations." In the United States, the Small Business Administration estimates that eighty percent of all businesses are family owned, and only a third of them survive at all into the second generation.[42] Many of the great American entrepreneurial families—the du Ponts, the Rockefellers, and the Carnegies—have seen similar declines. The children and grandchildren may go on to distinguished careers in other fields like the arts or politics (as Nelson and Jay Rockefeller did), but they seldom excel at running their forefather's organization.

The big difference between Chinese and American entrepreneurial families, however, is that by the time of the third generation, very few Chinese businesses have succeeded in institutionalizing themselves. American family businesses are quick to bring in professional management, particularly after the passing of the company's founder, and by the third generation, the company has usually passed entirely into the hands of professional managers. The grandchildren's generation might still retain ownership of the enterprise as majority stockholders, but few of them actively manage the company.

In Chinese culture, by contrast, the strong distrust of outsiders usually prevents the institutionalization of the company. Rather than let professional managers take over management of the firm, family owners of

Chinese businesses tend to acquiesce in its fragmentation into new concerns, or in its total disintegration. In this respect, the experience of one of imperial China's early successful entrepreneurs, Sheng Hsuan-huai, is typical. Rather than reinvest profits in his family businesses, sixty percent of his fortune went into a foundation to aid his sons and grandsons and was dissipated within a generation after his death.[43] We must, of course, allow for the unpropitious political conditions in Sheng's time, but his would seem to be a case in which the capital behind a potential Chinese Sumitomo empire was dissipated because of Chinese attitudes toward the family.

The difficulty that Chinese businesses have in institutionalizing themselves, as well as the Chinese principle of equal inheritance, explains why firm size in Chinese societies has remained relatively small. It also gives a very different character to the industrial organization of overall economy: companies are constantly being formed, rising, and then going out of business. In the United States, Western Europe, and Japan, many sectors (particularly the more capital-intensive ones) are oligopolistically organized, with a small number of giant firms sharing the market. The opposite is true in Taiwan, Hong Kong, and Singapore, where markets resemble the neoclassical ideal of perfect competition, with hundreds or thousands of tiny firms all fiercely competing to stay in business. If the cartel-like structure of the Japanese economy seems anticompetitive, the kaleidoscopically changing world of Chinese family firms appears, if anything, overly competitive.

A further consequence of the relatively small scale of Chinese firms is the dearth of Chinese brand names.[44] In the United States and Europe, the rise of branded and packaged goods in the late nineteenth century in sectors like tobacco, food, clothing, and other consumer goods was the product of the forward integration of manufacturers that wanted to control the new mass markets opening up for their products. Brand names can only be established by companies able to exploit economies of scale and scope in marketing. The companies owning them must be relatively large and must stick around long enough for consumers to develop an awareness of the quality and distinctiveness of their products. Names like Kodak, Pitney-Bowes, Courtney's, and Sears all date back to the nineteenth century. Japanese brand names like Sanyo, Panasonic, or Shiseido have been around a shorter time but were created by very large, well-institutionalized corporations.

In the Chinese business world, by contrast, there are very few brand names. The only one familiar to most Americans is Wang, which is the exception that proves the rule. Chinese companies in Hong Kong and Taiwan produce textiles that go into American brand names like Spaulding, Lacoste, Adidas, Nike, and Arnold Palmer, but only rarely does a Chinese company establish the brand name itself. The reasons that this is so should be clear from the account of the evolution of Chinese family firms. Because of their reluctance to develop to professional management, they are constrained from integrating forward, particularly into unfamiliar overseas markets, which require the marketing skills of native inhabitants. It is difficult for small Chinese family firms to grow to a scale where they can produce a distinctive mass-market product, and few survive long enough to establish a reputation with consumers. As a result, Chinese firms usually seek Western business partners to do their marketing rather than creating their own marketing organizations like large Japanese companies. This turns out to be a comfortable relationship for the Western company, since there is less likelihood that the Chinese partner will seek to dominate marketing in that particular sector in the manner of a Japanese corporation.[45] In other cases, like the Bugle Boy line of clothing, the marketing organization has been done by a Chinese-American familiar with American culture.

The tendency of Chinese firms to remain small and family managed is not necessarily a disadvantage and in some markets may even constitute an advantage. They have done best in relatively labor-intensive sectors and in sectors with fast-changing, highly segmented, and therefore small markets such as textiles and apparel, trading, timber and other commodities, PC components and assembly, leather goods, small-scale metalworking, furniture, plastics, toys, paper products, and banking. A small, family-managed firm is highly flexible and can make decisions rapidly. Compared to a large, hierarchical Japanese firm with its cumbersome system of consensual decision making, a small Chinese business is much better equipped to respond to overnight changes in market demand. Where Chinese firms do less well is in sectors that are highly capital intensive, or in which returns to scale are very large due to complex manufacturing processes—sectors like semiconductors, aerospace, autos, petrochemicals, and the like. Private Taiwanese companies cannot even hope to compete with Intel and Motorola in producing the latest generation microprocessor, as the Japanese firms Hitachi and NEC conceivably could.[46] But they are highly competitive at the commodity end of the personal computer business, where countless no-name PCs roll off small assembly lines.

There are three routes open to a Chinese society to overcome the inability to create large corporations. The first is through network organizations. That is, Chinese firms can develop the equivalent of scale economies through family or personal ties with other small Chinese firms. There is today throughout the Pacific Rim an enormous series of overlapping and constantly ramifying networks of Chinese firms. Much of the hothouse development going on in the PRC's Fujian and Guangdong provinces is the work of Hong Kong–based family networks spreading through the adjoining regions of China. Families are important to network organizations as well as to individual firms, though perhaps to a somewhat lesser degree. Many networks take advantage of kin ties outside the family, such as the very large lineage (or clan) organizations that exist in southern China. (On the other hand, some network relationships are not based on kinship at all but simply on personal trust and contact.)

The second method of developing large-scale industries is to invite in foreign direct investment. Chinese societies have typically been wary in permitting foreigners to play such an influential role in their economy. In Taiwan and the PRC, the practice has been tightly regulated.

The third way that Chinese societies can achieve economies of scale is through state promotion or ownership of enterprises. An atomistic, highly competitive market of small private businesses is not a new phenomenon; this system in fact characterized Chinese economic life for many centuries, in both the countryside and the cities. Traditional China had, in addition, very sophisticated manufacturing capabilities and a high level of technological sophistication in the early modern period (that is, when compared to Europe at the time), but these all lay within the state sector. For example, the porcelain metropolis of Jingdezhen had hundreds of thousands of inhabitants, and it is said that individual pieces passed through seventy or more pairs of hands in the manufacturing process. Yet porcelain manufacturing there was always a state-owned and-operated business, and there are no records of comparably sized private firms.[47] Similarly, the government of late Qing China—the last dynastic state—established a number of so-called *kuan-tu shang-pan* enterprises ("officially supervised, privately owned"), including a monopoly of salt production and a number of armaments industries believed necessary for national security purposes. In these cases, the state appointed official supervisors, while the right to manufacture was sold to private merchants from whom the government extracted taxes.[48] When the Chinese communists won the civil war in 1949, they immediately set about nationalizing Chinese industry in accordance with their Marxist principles. In good socialist fashion, the PRC today has any number of gigantic (and hugely inefficient) state-run enterprises. But the Nationalists as well inherited several large state-owned businesses from the Japanese and until recently have not been in any hurry to privatize them. If Taiwan hopes to be a major player in sectors like aerospace and semiconductors, state sponsorship (whether in the form of outright ownership or subsidy) would appear to be the only way.

The familism evident in Chinese business life has deep roots in Chinese culture, and it is there that we have to go to understand its unique characteristics.

CHAPTER 9

The "Buddenbrooks" Phenomenon

The Chinese communists came to power in 1949 determined to break the hold of Chinese familism on Chinese society. They believed, incorrectly, that the traditional patrilineal Chinese family was a threat to economic modernization. But they also saw, with greater clarity, that the family was a political competitor, one that weakened the hold that ideology and nation would have over this vast country. As a consequence they undertook a series of measures designed to destroy the traditional family: "modern" family law, outlawing polygamy and guaranteeing the rights of women, was introduced; the peasant household was split asunder through collectivization of agriculture; family businesses were nationalized or otherwise expropriated; and children were indoctrinated to believe that the party, not the family, was the ultimate source of authority. The family planning measures designed to constrain China's explosive population growth by limiting families to a single child was perhaps the most frontal assault on traditional Confucianism, with the latter's millennia-old imperative to have many sons.[1]

But the communists vastly underestimated the staying power of Confucian culture and the Chinese family, the latter of which emerged from the past half-century of political upheaval stronger than ever. A proper understanding of the role of the family in Chinese culture is key to understanding the nature of Chinese economic society, as well as that of other familistic societies around the world today.

Confucianism, to a much greater degree than Buddhism or Taoism, has defined the character of social relations within Chinese society over the last two and a half millennia. It consists of a series of ethical principles that are said to undergird a properly functioning society.[2] Such a society is regulated not by a constitution and system of laws flowing from it but by the internalization of Confucian ethical principles on the part of each individual as the result of a process of socialization. These ethical principles define the proper nature of a wide variety of social relationships, the central five of which are held to be those of ruler-minister, father-son, husband-wife, elder–younger brother, and friend-friend.

A great deal has been written about what Tu Wei-ming characterizes as "political Confucianism," that is, Confucianism's support for a hierarchical system of social relations, with an emperor at the top and a class of gentlemen-scholars manning an elaborate centralized bureaucracy below him. This political structure was considered to be a "super family" of the Chinese people, and the relationship of the emperor to his people like that of a father toward his children. In this system, meritocratic advancement was possible through a series of imperial examinations for entry into the bureaucracy, but the social ideal to which the examinees aspired was that of a scholar versed in the traditional Confucian texts. The superior man (*chun tzu*) possessed *li,* the ability to behave in accordance with the elaborately articulated rules of propriety,[3] and as such was very far from the modern entrepreneur. He sought leisure rather than hard work, derived his income from rents, and saw himself as a guardian of Confucian tradition, not as an innovator. In a traditional, stratified Confucian society, the merchant was not held in high esteem. If a merchant's family grew rich, his sons would hope not to carry on his business but to take the imperial examination and enter the ranks of the bureaucracy. Instead of reinvesting, many merchants diverted the profits from their businesses to landownership, which conferred much higher social prestige.[4]

Many of the negative assessments of the economic impact of Confucianism in the first half of the twentieth century arose in part because the political aspects of the doctrine were taken to be the core of the cultural system as a whole. Political Confucianism, however, has virtually disappeared from the scene. The last Chinese dynasty was overthrown in 1911 and the imperial bureaucracy abolished. Although various generalissimos and commissars have been compared to emperors in later years, the imperial system has been long dead and in little danger of being revived. The social stratification supported by political Confucianism has also largely been dismantled. The old class structure was dissolved by force in the PRC after the revolution and eaten away as the result of successful economic development on Taiwan. In the other overseas Chinese communities, the traditional Chinese political system could not be exported to what were from the start relatively homogeneous ethnic communities of merchants and small businessmen.[5] Some Chinese societies like Singapore have tried to revive a form of political Confucianism as a means of legitimizing their particular version of "soft authoritarianism," but these efforts have a rather artificial character to them.

In any event, the true essence of Chinese Confucianism was never political Confucianism at all but rather what Tu Wei-ming calls the "Confucian personal ethic." The central core of this ethical teaching was the apotheosis of the family—in Chinese, the *jia*—as the social relationship to which all others were subordinate. Duty to the family trumped all other duties, including obligations to emperor, Heaven, or any other source of temporal or divine authority.

Of the five cardinal Confucian relationships, that between father and son was key, for it established the moral obligation of *xiao,* or filial piety, which is Confucianism's central moral imperative.[6] Children are encouraged to defer to parental authority in all cultures, but in traditional China this is taken to an extraordinary degree. Sons have the duty to defer, even as adults, to their parents' wishes, to support them economically when they are old, to worship their spirits once they are dead, and to keep alive a family line that can be traced backward through generations of ancestors. In the West, the father's authority has had to compete against a number of rivals, including teachers, employers, the state, and ultimately God.[7] Rebellion against parental authority has become virtually institutionalized in a country like the United States as a coming-of-age ritual. In traditional China, this would be unthinkable. There is no counterpart to the Judeo-Christian concept of a divine source of authority or higher law that can sanction an individual's revolt against the dictates of his family. In Chinese society, obedience to paternal authority is akin to a divine act, and there is no concept of individual conscience that can lead an individual to contradict it.

The centrality of the family in traditional Chinese culture becomes evident when there is a conflict between loyalties to one's family and loyalties to higher political authorities such as the emperor or, in the PRC, the commissar. Of course, by the tenets of orthodox Confucianism, such conflicts should never even arise; in a well-ordered society, all social relationships are harmonious. But arise they do, most acutely when one's father has committed a crime and the police come looking for him. Many classical Chinese dramas portray the moral agony of a son forced to choose between loyalty to the state and loyalty to the family but in the end the family wins: you do not turn your father in to the police. In a classical story involving Confucius and the head of a neighboring kingdom, "The king boasted to Confucius that virtue in his land was such that if a father stole, his son would report the crime and the criminal to the state. Confucius replied that in his state virtue was far greater for a son would never think of treating his father so."[8] The communists rightly saw that the authority of the family was a threat to their own and engaged in an extended struggle to subordinate the family to the state: for them, the virtuous son reported his criminal father to the police. There is good evidence, however, that they failed completely in their attempts to subvert the family. The priority of the family over the state, indeed over any other relationship outside the family, makes orthodox Chinese Confucianism very different from its Japanese offshoot, with important consequences for business organization.

Competition between families makes Chinese societies seem individualistic, but there is no competition between the individual and his or her family in the Western sense. An individual's sense of self is defined by the family to a much greater extent. According to the anthropologist Margery Wolf's study of a Taiwanese village,

> A man not thoroughly imbedded in a network of kinship cannot be completely trusted because he cannot be dealt with in the normal way. If he behaves improperly, one cannot discuss his behavior with his brother or seek redress from his parents. If one wants to approach him about a delicate matter, one cannot use his uncle as a go-between to prepare the way.

Wealth cannot make up for this deficiency any more than it can make up for the loss of arms and legs. Money has no past, no future, and no obligations. Relatives do.[9]

The weakness of a sense of duties and obligations to anyone outside the family in traditional China is manifested by the self-sufficiency of the peasant household.[10] Peasants usually tried not to rely on their neighbors for anything, though there might be some collective labor at peak harvest times. In contrast to the European manorial system of the Middle Ages in which peasants were closely tied to the households of their seigneurs and dependent on them for land, credit, seed, and other kinds of services, the Chinese peasant usually owned his own plot and had minimal contact with social superiors except when he was taxed. The household was an independent unit for both production and consumption. There was little division of labor in the countryside; the peasant household produced itself as many of the nonagricultural goods it needed from day to day rather than obtaining them through markets. The cottage industries in the countryside that were encouraged in the PRC and sprang up spontaneously in Taiwan thus have deep roots in Chinese culture.[11]

The degree of self-sufficiency among gentry families was lower, though it remained as a social ideal. In a well-born family, there was sufficient surplus to support larger households and more women. Members of the family did not work but managed and were dependent on the labor of nonfamily employees. The imperial examination system existed as a route of upward social mobility out of the family. Gentry families often lived in cities, where there were more distractions and opportunities for social relations outside the family. Nevertheless, Chinese aristocratic families remained more self-sufficient than their European counterparts.[12]

If one looks at Chinese familism in historical perspective, it is clear that there was a good deal of economic rationality behind it. In traditional China, there were no established property rights. Through much of Chinese history, taxation was highly arbitrary; the state subcontracted tax collection to local officials or tax farmers, who were free to set the level of taxation at whatever the local population could endure.[13] Peasants could also be drafted arbitrarily for military duty or to work on public works projects. The state provided few social services in return for its taxes. The sense of paternalistic obligation between lord and peasant that existed in the European manorial system, however inconsistent and hypocritical it often was, did not have a counterpart in China. Traditional

China faced chronic situations of overpopulation and resource (i.e., land) scarcity, and the competition among families was always intense. There was no formal system of social security, an absence that has persisted in most Confucian societies up to the present day.

In this sort of environment, a strong family system can be seen as an essentially defensive mechanism against a hostile and capricious environment. A peasant could trust only members of his own family, because those on the outside—officials, bureaucrats, local authorities, and gentry alike—felt no reciprocal sense of obligation to him and felt no constraints about treating him rapaciously. With most peasant families living perpetually at the edge of starvation, there was little surplus with which one could be generous to friends or neighbors. Sons—as many as one could afford while one's wife was of childbearing age—were an absolute necessity, for without them there was no way one could hope to support oneself in old age.[14] Under such harsh conditions, the self-sufficient family was the only rational source of shelter and cooperation available.

Traditional China failed to develop concentrated wealth that could have capitalized early industries, because of the principle of equal male inheritance, which was deeply ingrained in the culture.[15] The Chinese family system is strictly patrilineal; inheritance flows through males only and is shared equally by all of a father's sons. With increases in population, land was constantly subdivided from one generation to the next, resulting in individual peasant plots that were too small to feed a family adequately. This phenomenon occurred into the twentieth century.[16]

Even among rich families, equal division of inheritances meant that fortunes were dissipated in a generation or two. One consequence was that there are very few large noble houses or estates as in Europe—that is, large family dwellings that were built to be occupied by the same aristocratic family over generations. The houses of wealthy families were small, single-story affairs clustered around a common courtyard, which could accommodate the families of the patriarch's sons. In contrast to societies with a system of primogeniture like England and Japan, there was no stream of younger sons who, left out of the family inheritance, would be forced to seek their fortunes in commerce, the arts, or the military. The labor supply was therefore kept in the countryside to a greater extent than in countries with a system of primogeniture.

Sons were important both for inheritance and as a form of social security. But it was extremely difficult to adopt outsiders into the family in the event one had no sons or one's sons died early or were incompetent.[17] Although it was in theory possible in traditional Chinese culture to adopt a son not biologically related into the family (usually by marrying him to one's daughter), this was not a preferred way of proceeding. An adopted son would not feel the same obligations to his new family that a biological son would, and from the father's perspective there was always the danger that the adopted son would take his children and leave the family altogether if, for example, he felt he had not received an adequate share of the inheritance. Because of the danger of disloyalty, infant adoptions were preferred, and the adopter went to elaborate pains to keep the identity of the adoptee's birth family secret. Adoptions were carried out within the kinship group if at all possible.[18] Going to a complete outsider was usually an extraordinary event, one that was commemorated by public humiliation of the sonless adopter.[19] The borderline between family and nonfamily is thus sharply drawn in Chinese culture. Again, as we will see, Japanese practice with regard to adoption could not be more different.

The combination of intense familism, equal male inheritance, lack of a mechanism for adopting outsiders, and distrust of nonkin has led to a pattern of economic behavior in traditional China that anticipated the business culture of contemporary Taiwan and Hong Kong in many respects. In the countryside, there were no large estates but microscopic land holdings that tended to shrink with each generation. There was a constant rising and falling of families: those that were industrious, thrifty, and able would accumulate money and move up the social scale.[20] But the family fortune—not only land but the family residence(s) and household items—would be dissipated in the second generation by its equal division among sons. The ability and moral virtue of succeeding generations was never ensured, and so the family would eventually sink back into obscurity and poverty. The anthropologist Hugh Baker noted of Chinese village life: "No family in our village has been able to hold the same amount of land for as long as three or four generations."[21] Peasant communities experienced the constant rise and fall of different families over time: "What this process of rise and fall in family fortunes meant was a society like a seething cauldron, with families bubbling to the top only to burst and sink back to the bottom. When they burst they shattered their land-holdings too, and the patch-work quilt effect posed by the constant fragmentation and re-agglomeration of land-holdings was a distinctive feature of the Chinese landscape."[22] Families could not grow too rich, at least given the technological opportunities of traditional Chinese agriculture; nor could they grow too poor, since below a certain level of poverty men could not afford to marry and produce offspring.[23] The only opportunity for breaking out of this cycle came if a particularly able son was permitted to take the imperial examination, but that happened rarely and in any event affected only individuals.

Up to this point, I have been using the term *family* as if the Chinese family were identical to its Western counterpart. This is not the case.[24] Chinese families have generally been larger than their Western counterparts, both before and after industrialization, so that they could support somewhat larger economic units. The ideal Confucian family is in fact a five-generation household with great-great-grandfathers living near their great-great-grandchildren. Obviously, this kind of extended family was seldom practicable; more common was the so-called joint family in which a father and mother (and possibly the father's brothers' families) lived together with the families of their grown sons.[25] Historical research on the Chinese family has shown that even this type of joint family was more of an ideal than a reality. Nuclear families have been much more common in China than many Chinese themselves believe, even among traditional peasants in the countryside.[26] The large joint family was in many ways a privilege of the well-to-do: only the wealthy could afford many sons and their wives and could support so many family members in a single household. Among wealthy families, there was a cyclical evolution of families from nuclear to stem to joint and back to nuclear, as children grew up, parents died, and new households established.

It is a mistake to think of the traditional Chinese family as the harmonious and unified whole as it is sometimes perceived to be from the outside. The *jia* was in fact fraught with a number of inherent tensions. It was both patrilineal and patriarchal: the woman marrying into the family was expected to shed her ties to her own family and was strictly subordinate to her mother-in-law (not to mention the males in the family) until she herself became the mother-in-law.[27] In traditional China, wealthy men would often take multiple wives and/or concubines to the extent of their ability to support them.[28] Women contributed a greater share of work in poor peasant families than in rich ones and therefore had more leverage over the men. The result was the more frequent fission of such families. The strength and stability of the traditional Chinese family came about, therefore, through its ability to control and subordinate women; when that control weakened, families tended to split.

In addition, the equal status of the brothers led to considerable rivalry, and stories about the conflicts and jealousies that arose between the brothers' wives are legion. Indeed, the traditional living arrangement for well-to-do joint families—with the families of the different brothers either living under the same roof or in separate houses around a common courtyard—was often an explosive recipe, and many such families dissolved into nuclear ones because they could not contain the tension. Hence, while the large five-generation family remained an ideal, there were considerable pressures for disintegration into smaller units.[29]

Beyond the *jia,* in either its nuclear or joint forms, there were further concentric circles of kinship with great economic significance. The most important of these was the lineage, defined as "a *corporate group* which celebrates *ritual unity* and is based on *demonstrated descent* from a common ancestor."[30] Alternatively, it can be understood as a family of families, all tracing common descent.[31] Lineages are common primarily in southern Chinese coastal provinces like Guangdong and Fujian, while being much rarer in the north. Chinese lineages, sometimes described as clans, can encompass entire villages, with each family sharing the same surname. Beyond the lineage, there are what are termed "higher-order lineages," in which distinct lineages are bound into a giant clan by ancient ancestry. For example, in Hong Kong's New Territories there are several villages containing lineages with the surname Deng, who all trace their ancestry to a single individual who settled in the area nearly a thousand years earlier.[32] Lineages usually possess some common property, such as an ancestral hall that is used for ritual purposes, and some of them maintain highly developed sets of rules and genealogical records dating back over many centuries.[33]

Economically, lineages have performed the function of widening the circle of kinship, and therefore the number of people who can be trusted in an economic enterprise. Obligations to members of one's lineage are of a much lower order than toward one's family. The same lineages can encompass very rich families and very poor ones, and the richer members have no particular obligation to help the poorer ones.[34] Lineages can often be fictitious: people with the same surname like Chang or Li and coming from the same area will assume that they belong to the same lineage, while their actual degree of kinship may be nonexistent.[35] Nonetheless, kinship ties, however attenuated, provide the basis for a degree of trust and obligation not present in the case of complete strangers, and vastly increase the pool of people one can safely bring into a family business.[36]

Lineage ties are extremely important in understanding the nature of contemporary Chinese economic development. Many of the overseas, or *nanyang*, Chinese in the thriving communities of the Pacific Rim—Singapore, Malaysia, Indonesia, Hong Kong, Taiwan—originated from the two southern Chinese provinces of Fujian and Guangdong. Although the emigration occurred in many instances three or four generations ago, the overseas Chinese have retained ties to kin in China. Much of the economic development that has taken place in Fujian and Guangdong in the past decade consists of expatriate Chinese capital ramifying backward into its hinterland along family- and lineage-based networks. This is particularly true of Hong Kong and its New Territories, which is physically contiguous with Guangdong and whose lineage organizations overlap to some extent. In many instances, overseas Chinese entrepreneurs have been welcomed back to their home villages or regions by local authorities who have given them particularly favorable treatment because of their kinship ties—actual or sometimes merely presumed. The existence of these kinship ties has given the overseas Chinese the confidence to invest in the PRC, even in the absence of property rights or a stable political environment. It also explains why the overseas Chinese have a leg up on other foreign investors—Japanese, American, or European.

The priority of family and, to a lesser extent, lineage ties in Chinese culture give an entirely different meaning to nationalism and citizenship. Many observers over the years have remarked that, in contrast to neighbors of China like Vietnam or Japan, the Chinese sense of national identity is weaker, as are citizenship and public spiritedness. The Chinese do, of course, have a highly developed sense of national identity supported by their old and rich common culture. As we have seen, national identity was undergirded by political Confucianism in traditional China, which laid down a series of obligations to a hierarchy of political authorities, culminating in the emperor. A negative, antiforeigner sense of national identity was forged in the late nineteenth and early twentieth centuries by China's occupation, first by European colonial powers and then by Japan. In the twentieth century, the Chinese Communist party tried to put itself in place of the emperor and acquired an aura of nationalist legitimacy by virtue of its role in the struggle against the Japanese.

But from dynastic times up through the communist victory in 1949, the primary loyalties of individual Chinese have been not to whatever political authorities were in power but to their families. The concept of "China" never had the same sort of emotional significance as a community of shared value, interest, and experience that "Japan" did for the Japanese. In Chinese Confucianism, there is no such thing as a universal moral obligation to all human beings as there is in the Christian religion.[37] Obligations are graded and fall off in intensity the further one moves from the inner family circle.[38] In Barrington Moore's words, "The Chinese village, the basic cell of rural society in China as elsewhere, evidently lacked cohesiveness in comparison with those of India, Japan, and even many parts of Europe. There were far fewer occasions on which numerous members of the village cooperated in a common task in a way that creates the habits and sentiments of solidarity. It was closer to a residential agglomeration of a number of peasant households than to a live and functioning community."[39] Chinese societies have been able to enforce citizenship through authoritarian power in places like the PRC, Singapore, and Taiwan, just as these same governments have been able to subsidize the growth of large companies. But as many Chinese have noted about themselves, they suffer from a low degree of "spontaneous" citizenship, measured by such things as the proclivity of people to abuse common areas, their willingness to contribute to charity, keep public spaces clean, volunteer for public interest–oriented groups, or die for their country.[40]

And yet the usual forces of socioeconomic change have altered traditional Chinese families and lineages in both the PRC and among the overseas Chinese.[41] Urbanization and geographic mobility weaken lineage organizations, because the latter's members can no longer live in the same village as their ancestors. Large joint or even extended families are harder to maintain in an urban environment and are gradually being replaced by conjugal ones.[42] Women are increasingly educated and, as a consequence, less willing to accept subservient positions in traditional households.[43] Both peasant household agriculture and rural industrialization may be reaching the limits of possible productivity gains. Further economic progress will require the peasant population of China either to urbanize further or create some new form of economic organization in the countryside, thereby disrupting the self-sufficiency of the peasant household. Many of these changes have already taken place in noncommunist Chinese societies like Taiwan and Hong Kong.

Nonetheless, it is very premature to talk about the death, or even the eroding, of the *jia*. Growing evidence indicates that changes in family patterns have been less dramatic in China than was once thought.[44] In modern, urban environments family relationships have actually reconstituted themselves. In its contest with the traditional family, communism has clearly lost. The Australian Sinologist W. J. F. Jenner has remarked that out of the wreckage of twentieth-century Chinese history, the one institution that has emerged stronger than all the others is the patrilineal Chinese family.[45] The latter has always been a refuge against the capriciousness of political life, and Chinese peasants have understood that in the end, the only people they could really trust were members of their immediate family. The political history of this century has reinforced that feeling: two revolutions, warlordism, foreign occupation, collectivization, the insanity of the Cultural Revolution, and then decollectivization after the death of Mao have all taught the Chinese peasant that nothing is certain in the political environment. Those in power today may be the underdogs of tomorrow. By contrast, the family provides at least a modicum of certainty: in providing for one's old age, it is far better to put one's faith in one's sons than in the law or changeable political authorities.

Monumental changes have taken place in China since Deng Xiaoping's reforms of the late 1970s and the marketization of a large part of the Chinese economy since then. But the reform was, in another sense, simply the restoration of older Chinese social relationships. It turned out that the self-sufficient peasant household had not been destroyed by communism, and it came roaring back when given a chance by the rural responsibility system. The anthropologist Victor Nee admitted, somewhat poignantly, that he had wanted to find that social bonds created by the communist commune system had survived and were even strengthened by two decades of collective farming. What he (and many others) found instead was only the individualism of the peasant household.[46] Jenner points out that many Chinese Communist party officials, despite their Marxist ideology, have spent the past decade establishing foreign bank accounts and educating their children in the West, in preparation for the day that they may be out of power. For them no less than for the most humble peasant, the family will remain the only safe refuge.[47]

In the previous chapter I noted the small scale of Chinese businesses and the fact that they tend to be owned and operated by families. The reasons for the persistence of small scale cannot be traced to either the level of development of contemporary Chinese societies or their lack of modern legal or financial institutions. Other societies at lower levels of development and with weaker institutions have nonetheless been able to move beyond the family as the dominant form of business organization.

On the other hand, it seems quite likely that the modern Chinese business structure has its roots in the singular position of the family in Chinese culture. The pattern of economic life was the same in traditional as in modern China. The constant rise and fall of atomistic, family-operated enterprises; the failure of these enterprises to institutionalize themselves or survive beyond two or three generations; the pervasive distrust of strangers and reluctance to bring nonkin into the family; and the social obstacles to the accumulation of large fortunes due to inheritance customs all existed in Chinese society well before the postwar industrialization of Taiwan, Hong Kong, Singapore, and the PRC.

CHAPTER 10

Italian Confucianism

Over the past decade and a half, one of the most interesting new economic phenomena to be studied by business schools and management experts has been small-scale industry in central Italy. Italy, which industrialized late and has usually been regarded as one of Western Europe's economic backwaters, saw certain regions explode in the 1970s and 1980s with the emergence of networks of small businesses making everything from textiles and designer clothes to machine tools and industrial robots. Some enthusiasts of small-scale industrialization have argued that the Italian model represents an entirely new paradigm of industrial production, one that can be exported to other countries. Social capital and culture give us considerable insight into the reasons for this miniature economic renaissance.

Though it may seem a stretch to compare Italy with the Confucian culture of Hong Kong and Taiwan, the nature of social capital is similar in certain respects. In parts of Italy and in the Chinese cases, family bonds

97

tend to be stronger than other kinds of social bonds not based on kinship, while the strength and number of intermediate associations between state and individual has been relatively low, reflecting a pervasive distrust of people outside the family. The consequences for industrial structure are similar: private sector firms tend to be relatively small and family controlled, while large-scale enterprises need the support of the state to be viable. And for both Chinese and Latin Catholic societies broadly, the causes of this lack of spontaneous sociability are similar: the dominance of a centralized and arbitrary state during an earlier phase of historical development, which deliberately eviscerated intermediate groups and sought to control associational life. These generalizations, like all other large abstractions, need to be qualified in many ways to fit conditions of time and place, but they are striking nonetheless.

We noted that individuals in Chinese society are tightly subordinated to families and indeed have little identity outside their families. Because a high degree of competition exists among families, reflecting the absence of a generalized sense of trust within the society, cooperation in group activities outside family or lineage ties is strictly limited. Compare this situation to the description of social life in the small southern Italian town of "Montegrano" in Edward Banfield's classic study, *The Moral Basis of a Backward Society:*

> The individual's attachment to the family must be the starting place for an account of the Montegrano ethos. In fact, an adult hardly may be said to have an individuality apart from the family: he exists not as "ego" but as "parent". . . .
>
> In the Montegrano mind, any advantage that may be given to another is necessarily at the expense of one's own family. Therefore, one cannot afford the luxury of charity, which is giving others more than their due, or even of justice, which is giving them their due. The world being what it is, all those who stand outside of the small circle of the family are at least potential competitors and therefore also potential enemies. Toward those who are not of the family the reasonable attitude is suspicion. The parent knows that other families will envy and fear the success of his family and that they are likely to seek to do it injury. He must therefore fear them and be ready to do them injury in order that they may have less power to injure him and his.[1]

Banfield lived in the impoverished village of Montegrano for an extended period in the 1950s and noted that the most remarkable feature of this village was its almost complete lack of associations. Banfield had just completed a study of St. George, Utah, a town that was crisscrossed by a dense network of associations, and he was struck by the utter contrast presented by the Italian village. The only moral obligations that the residents of Montegrano felt were to members of their own nuclear families. The family was a person's only source of social security; people were consequently fearful that they would fall through the cracks should a father die young. The Montegranesi were totally unable to come together to organize schools, hospitals, businesses, charities, or any other form of activity. As a result, whatever organized social life there was in the town depended on the initiative of two external, centralized sources of authority: the church and the Italian state. Banfield summarized Montegrano's moral code: "Maximize the material, short-run advantage of the nuclear family; assume that all others will do likewise." He titled this type of family-based isolation "amoral familism," a term that subsequently entered the broader social science lexicon.[2] With some modification, it could be applied to Chinese society as well.

Banfield was primarily interested in the political rather than the economic consequences of amoral familism. He noted, for example, that in such a society people will fear and distrust the government while simultaneously believing in the need for a strong state to control their fellow citizens. As in noncommunist Chinese societies, the degree of citizenship and identification with larger institutions is weak. But the economic effects of amoral familism were evident as well: "Lack of such association [beyond the family] is a very important limiting factor in the way of economic development in most of the world. Except as people can create and maintain corporate organization, they cannot have a modern economy."[3] Most of the residents of Montegrano were peasants very close to subsistence; the industrial employment that existed in such communities would have to come from the outside, probably in the form of a state-run company. Noting that the large landowners of the region could have built a profitable factory, they nonetheless chose not to do so because they believed that the state had an obligation to shoulder the risk.[4]

Banfield's argument needs to be qualified and updated in several respects. The most important caveat is that the atomistic individualism of Montegrano is not characteristic of the whole of Italy but rather of the southern regions. Banfield himself noted the stark contrasts between northern and southern Italy; the North, with a much denser web of intermediate social organizations and a tradition of civic community, resembles Central Europe more than the *Mezzogiorno* (literally, "mid-day," the area south of Rome). In the past fifteen years, observers of Italy have come to speak not just of two but of three Italies: the impoverished South, including the islands of Sicily and Sardinia; the industrial triangle formed by Milan, Genoa, and Turin in the North; and what is labeled the *Terza Italia,* or "Third Italy," in between, constituting the central regions of Emilia-Romagna, Tuscany, Umbria, and the Marche, and, to the northeast, Veneto, Friuli, and Trentino. The Third Italy has some unique characteristics that differentiate it from the two traditional Italies.

Robert Putnam has extended Banfield's findings by measuring throughout Italy what he calls "civic community": the propensity of people to form organizations not based on kinship, that is, spontaneous sociability. Putnam found a stark dearth of civic community in southern Italy, reflected in such measures as the smaller number of associations like literary guilds, sports and hunting clubs, local press, music groups, labor unions, and the like.[5] Italians in the South were much less likely than others to read newspapers, belong to unions, vote, and otherwise take part in the political life of their communities.[6] Moreover, people in the South expressed a much lower degree of social trust and confidence in the law-abiding behavior of their fellow citizens.[7] Putnam argues that Italian Catholicism correlates negatively with civic-mindedness: when measured by indexes like attendance at mass, religious marriages, rejection of divorce, and so on, it grows stronger the farther south one moves, and civic-mindedness grows weaker.[8]

Putnam found that Banfield's amoral familism continues to thrive in the South, though the competitive pressures of a society at the margins of subsistence have eased somewhat with Italy's postwar economic growth. Nevertheless, he argues that the isolation and distrust that exist among families in the South go back for generations and have persisted up through the present. One report from 1863 noted that in Calabria, there were "no associations, no mutual aid; everything is isolation. Society is held up by the natural civil and religious bonds alone; but of economic bonds there is nothing, no solidarity between families or between individuals or between them and the government."[9] Another Italian historian noted at the turn of the century that "the peasant classes were more at war amongst themselves than with the other sectors of rural society. . . . That such attitudes triumphed can only be understood in the context of a society which was dominated by distrust."[10] These characterizations are quite similar to those encountered in Chinese peasant life.

In southern Italy, we notice another phenomenon that has its counterpart in other atomized societies with relatively weak intermediate social organizations: the most powerful communal groups are "delinquent communities," not sanctioned by prevailing ethical laws.[11] In the Italian case, they are famous criminal organizations like the Mafia, 'Ndrangheta, or Camorra. Like the Chinese *tongs,* an Italian criminal gang is family-like but not literally a family. In a society where bonds of trust outside the family are weak, the blood oaths taken by members of La Cosa Nostra serve as surrogate kinship bonds that allow criminals to trust one another in situations in which betrayal is very tempting.[12] Highly organized criminal gangs are characteristic of other low-trust societies with weak intermediate institutions, such as postcommunist Russia and American inner cities. Naturally, corruption of political and business elites is more prevalent in the South than in the North.

By contrast, the regions of Italy where social capital is the highest are in the North (Piedmonte, Lombardy, and Trentino), and particularly in regions of *La Terza Italia* like Tuscany and Emilia-Romanga.[13]

The broader theme of this book, that social capital has a significant impact on the vitality and scale of economic organizations, suggests that there should be important differences in the character of economic organizations in the different regions of Italy. And indeed, this overall pattern is confirmed by the data emerging from a comparison of the North and the South. Italy has a much smaller number of large corporations than European countries that are comparable to it in terms of absolute gross domestic product such as England or Germany; indeed, countries like Sweden, Holland, and Switzerland, with gross domestic products one-fifth to one-quarter of Italy's, have comparably sized corporations.[14] If one subtracts state-owned businesses, the gap widens even further. Italy, like Taiwan and Hong Kong, has very few large, publicly owned, professionally managed, multinational corporations. Those that exist, like the Agnelli family's FIAT group or Olivetti, are clustered in the northern industrial triangle. Southern Italy, by contrast, is a relatively good illustration of the saddle-shaped distribution characteristic of Taiwan. Private firms are small, weak, and family based, forcing the state to intervene to maintain employment by subsidizing a number of large, inefficient public sector companies.

Many people think of the Italian state as weak or even nonexistent, but this is to confuse weakness with ineffectiveness. In terms of its formal powers, the Italian state is as strong as its French counterpart, having been deliberately designed after unification along French lines. Until the early 1970s, when various decentralizing reforms were introduced, policy in the regions was centrally dictated from Rome. To an even greater degree than in France, the state directly manages numerous large enterprises, including Finmeccania, Enel, the Banca Nazionale Del Lavoro, the Banca Commerciale Italiana, and Enichem. There has been talk of privatizing a significant part of the Italian state sector since the election of the short-lived rightist government of Silvio Berlusconi in April 1994, just as there has been in France since the coming to power of Edouard Balladur's conservative government. Whether either country will be able to carry out these privatizations remains to be seen.

The part of Italy that has been the most economically dynamic over the past generation, and presents the greatest puzzle in terms of social capital, is also that part that most resembles Taiwan and Hong Kong: the *Terza Italia,* in the center. Those Italian sociologists who first began writing about the Third Italy noted that its industrial structure is largely composed of small, family-owned, family-managed businesses.[15] While peasant familism remains characteristic of the impoverished South, the family businesses of the *Terza Italia* were, by contrast, innovative, export oriented, and in many cases high-tech. For example, this region is the home of the Italian machine tool industry, with a large number of very small producers of numerically controlled (NC) machine tools (i.e., machine tools controlled by computers) whose output, by the end of the 1970s, had propelled Italy to the position of the second largest machine tool producer (behind Germany) in Europe.[16] Indeed, many of those machine tools find markets in the powerful German auto industry. Despite the large aggregate output, the production runs of the Emilian machine tool industry tend to be very low, often amounting to a single, custom- designed machine.[17]

Other highly competitive products from the *Terza Italia* include textiles and apparel, furniture, farm machinery, other sorts of advanced capital goods such as shoemaking equipment and industrial robots, high-quality ceramics, and ceramic tile. This confirms that there is no necessary connection between small-scale industry and technological backwardness. Italy is the world's third-largest producer of industrial robots, and yet a third of that industry's output is produced by enterprises with fewer than fifty employees.[18] Italy has in many ways become the center of the European fashion industry, with many labels shifting there from France in the 1960s and 1970s. In 1993, Italian textiles and apparel racked up a trade surplus of $18 billion, as much as the trade deficit in food and energy. In this industry, there are only two large-scale, publicly traded manufacturers, Benetton and Simint; sixty-eight percent of the workers are employed in companies of fewer than ten employees.[19]

Many observers of small family businesses in the *Terza Italia* have noted their tendency to cluster together into industrial districts of the sort first identified in the nineteenth century by Alfred Marshall, where they can take advantage of local pools of skills and knowledge. These districts were regarded as Italy's version of California's Silicon Valley or Boston's Route 128. In certain cases, these industrial districts have been deliberately fostered by local governments, which have provided training, financing, and other services. In other cases, small family businesses have formed spontaneous networks with other like-minded companies, and they subcontract with other small firms for supplies or marketing services. These networks resemble the network organizations that exist in Asia, though they are more similar in scale to the family-based networks of Taiwan and other Chinese countries than the giant *keiretsu* organizations of Japan. The Italian networks appear to perform an economic function similar to their Asian counterparts, providing what amount to economies of scale and vertical integration while retaining much of the flexibility inherent in small, owner-managed businesses.

The dynamism and success of the small-business sector in the *Terza Italia* have made it the subject of intense scrutiny. This kind of industrial district, populated by small, craft-oriented, high-tech firms, was one of the chief illustrations of the "flexible specialization" paradigm articulated by Michael Piore and Charles Sabel.[20] Piore and Sabel argued that mass production involving large-scale enterprises was not a necessary consequence of the industrial revolution. Not only have smaller-scale enterprises based on craft skills survived alongside giant ones, but with the evolution of highly segmented, sophisticated, and rapidly changing consumer markets, there may be a premium on the flexibility and adaptiveness that only small organizations can provide. For Piore and Sabel, the congeries of small, family-based producers is not just an interesting quirk of Italian development but represents a possible growth for other countries in the future—one that avoids the worst alienating features of the mass production paradigm. Whether they are right depends, as we will see, on the degree to which small-scale industrialization has a cultural basis.

Many outside observers looking at the phenomenon of small-scale industrialization in Italy have hoped that it could become a generalizable model of industrial development, either in Europe or around the world more broadly. The European Commission, for example, latched onto the Italian industrial districts in recent years as a positive example of job-creating, small-scale business development. While large corporations in Europe have been shedding jobs steadily through the postwar period as they learned to be more productive, the share of employment provided by the small- to medium-enterprise sector has grown.[21] But the growth in small-business employment has not been distributed evenly within Europe and has been much less vigorous for Europe as a whole than for the United States.[22] Many promoters of the idea of industrial districts are inclined to believe that the path of small-scale industrialization is a good thing in itself, and they tend to emphasize those aspects of this phenomenon that can be affected by public policy, such as the creation of educational and skill infrastructures by local and regional governments.

It is clear that the high degree of social capital in northern and central Italy has been critical in explaining their greater economic prosperity. Robert Putnam is certainly correct in saying that economics does not predict the degree of spontaneous sociability (or, in his terminology, civic community) that exists in a society; rather, spontaneous sociability predicts economic performance, better even than economic factors by themselves.[23] At the time of unification in 1870, neither northern nor southern Italy was industrialized; indeed, a slightly higher percentage of the population worked the land in the North. But industrial development took off rapidly in the North, while the South actually became slightly less urban and industrial between 1871 and 1911. Per capita incomes in the North moved steadily ahead, and the gap between regions remains high today. These regional variations cannot be explained adequately by differences in government policy, since that has (for the most part) been set nationally since the emergence of a unified Italian state. They do, however, correlate very strongly with the degree of civic community or of spontaneous sociability that prevails in the respective regions.[24] There are family firms in all parts of Italy, but those in the high-social capital center have been far more dynamic, innovative, and prosperous than those in the South, characterized by pervasive social distrust.

The small family firms of central Italy nevertheless constitute something of an anomaly in the argument concerning scale. It is understandable that northern Italy should have larger firms than the South, given its higher degree of social capital, but why do small family firms predominate in central Italy, which by Putnam's account have the highest degree of social capital of any of Italy's regions? The high degree of social trust in this region should have allowed producers to go well beyond the family in business organizations, just as political life there is not based on family and personal patronage to the degree it is in the South.

Possibly there are external factors having nothing to do with social capital—political, legal, or economic—that have promoted large-scale organizations in the North and discouraged them in the center. In the absence of such an explanation, however, two sets of answers suggest themselves. The first is that in assessing the industrial structure of *La Terza Italia,* we should pay more attention to the networks than to the individual firms themselves. Like comparable organizations in Asia, these Italian networks allow small companies to achieve scale economies without having to create large, integrated corporations. Unlike Chinese networks, however, the Italian version is not based on family but involves the cooperation of nonkin on a professional and functional basis. By this account, the networked small firm is a matter of deliberate organizational choice on the part of entrepreneurs with a relatively high degree of spontaneous sociability who could, if they wanted, opt for scale.

On the other hand, there is also evidence that the small size of these firms and their networked structure is sometimes the result of weakness and inability to institutionalize rather than being a matter of deliberate choice. Hence a second explanation is that strong family bonds remain important in central Italy and put a distinctive stamp on business life there, without simultaneously undermining the sense of broader civic community in the political realm. That is, there is no necessary trade-off between strong families and strong voluntary associations in this part of Italy; both can be cohesive simultaneously, just as both can be weak in other societies.

There is indeed some evidence for the latter thesis. Familism remains a more powerful force throughout Italy—North, South, and center— than in other European countries, though it varies considerably within Italy's different regions. A number of observers have pointed to revealing differences in family structure between the different parts of the country. As in the case of China, recent research has shown that the nuclear family was much more common throughout Europe than was previously thought, since at least the fourteenth century.[25] One exception, however, was in central Italy, where the complex Italian family persisted in a relatively strong and cohesive form since the Middle Ages.[26] "Complex family" means something not entirely dissimilar to the Chinese joint family: a father and mother living together or in close proximity with their married sons and their families. The pattern of extended families continues to be true to the present. In the *Terza Italia,* 50 percent of the population lives in complex families, compared to 27 percent in the northern triangle (Lombardy, Piedmonte, and Liguria) and only 20 percent in the South. Correspondingly, the incidence of nuclear families is much higher in the northern triangle (64.6 percent of the population) and, interestingly, even higher in the impoverished South (74.3 percent).[27] The last figure supports Banfield's claim that the nuclear family is the primary kinship unit to which people feel moral obligation in the South.

One might be tempted to say that the part of Italy that resembles China the most closely is the South, where the radius of trust does not extend beyond the nuclear family and unrelated people have great difficulties cooperating with one another. In fact, it is the *Terza Italia* whose family structure resembles that of the Chinese most closely.[28] The peasant families in Montegrano whom Banfield described are far more atomized and isolated than a typical Chinese peasant family or than the larger families of central Italy. Consider Banfield's description of tensions within the family:

> At the time a new family is established, attachments to the old ones weaken. The wedding arrangements provide opportunities for the bride and groom to get on bad terms with their in-laws. . . . Ill will serves the useful function of protecting the new family against demands that might be made upon it by the old. But it also prevents cooperation among members of the family. The division of land into tiny, widely scattered parcels occurs partly because of family squabbles. For example, Prato's half-sister owns a patch of land next to his. She cannot work it herself, but she will not sell or rent it to him, and consequently it lies idle. If peasants were generally on good terms with their siblings, it might be possible in some cases to rationalize the distribution of land by a series of exchanges. . . . Even when there is no falling out between them, the son's attachment to his parents all but dissolves when he marries. Once he has a wife and children of his own, it is not expected that he will concern himself with the welfare of his parents, unless, perhaps, they are nearly starving.[29]

The society Banfield described is not that of China, with its powerful sense of family obligation. These southern Italian families are so small, atomized, and weak that they serve poorly as building blocks for economic enterprises. The Chinese family, and consequently the Chinese family business, can call upon sons, daughters, uncles, grandparents, and even more distant kin within the lineage organization to provide staffing for business enterprises. And this is precisely the kind of family structure that exists in the *Terza Italia*: a family structure that serves as a source of support for the modern Italian family business.

Another factor that some sociologists have pointed to as a possible explanation for the prevalence of family firms in central Italy was the institution of sharecropping there.[30] Sharecropping was based on a long-term contract between the landowner and the head of a family, who contracted on behalf of the other family members. The landowner had an incentive to keep tenant families large enough to farm his estate efficiently, and the sharecropping contract gave him a great deal of control over whether family members could move away or even marry. In many cases the plots were too large for nuclear families to farm by themselves. Hence there was an economic incentive for extended families, who tended to live as groups on the land that they farmed. In southern Italy, by contrast, the predominant form of agricultural labor was the *bracciante,* or day laborer, who sold his labor on the market and had no long-term relationship to the land that he worked. The *bracciante* was hired as an individual and usually lived in town, not on the land that he worked. The sharecropping family in central Italy worked as a unit and owned property—tools and animals—in common. Incentives were structured in ways that encouraged thrift and entrepreneurship, incentives that were nonexistent among the agricultural wage laborers of the South.[31] It would appear, then, that the extended sharecropping family in central Italy constituted a cohesive economic unit very much like the Chinese peasant household. This occurred before industrialization and served as a natural basis for family firms in later years.

Why does the degree of spontaneous sociability vary so dramatically across Italy, being so much lower in the South than in the North and center? Much of the explanation appears to have to do with the degree of political centralization that existed historically in each region, long before industrialization ever began. The amoral familism of the South had its origins in the Norman kingdoms in Sicily and Naples, particularly under Frederick II. The southern kingdoms established an early form of monarchical absolutism, snuffing out the independence of towns that displayed a desire for autonomy. A steep social hierarchy was established in the countryside, with a landed aristocracy wielding vast powers over a peasantry close to subsistence. Although in some societies religion may serve to strengthen intermediate institutions and the propensity to organize spontaneously, in southern Italy the Catholic church served only to reinforce monarchical absolutism. The church was regarded as an external obligation and burden, not as a community voluntarily entered into and controlled by its members.

This centralized authority contrasted sharply with the decentralization of the North and center, where a number of city-states like Venice, Genoa, and Florence were independent republics at the end of the Middle Ages. Not only were they politically autonomous, but these commercial city-states practiced, on and off, a republican form of government that demanded a high degree of political participation from its members. Under such shelter, a rich associational life could flourish, including guilds, neighborhood associations, parish organizations, confraternities, and the like. In the North and center, the church was simply one social organization among many. In Robert Putnam's words, "By the beginning of the fourteenth century, Italy had produced, not one, but two innovative patterns of governance with their associated social and cultural features—the celebrated Norman feudal aristocracy of the South and the fertile communal republicanism of the North."[32] In subsequent years, the North was "refeudalized" and brought under the control of a succession of centralized sources of authority (many of them foreign), but the republican traditions forged during the Renaissance survived well enough as part of the northern culture to become, in modern times, the source of a higher degree of spontaneous sociability than in the South.

As its name implies, the *Terza Italia* occupies a kind of alternative position between the poles represented by the North and the South. On the one hand, it is imbued with a familism in some ways more developed and intense than that of the South. That familism makes the family business a natural economic building block, even as it tends to constrain the growth of family businesses into larger organizations. On the other hand, much of central and northeastern Italy is imbued with the North's spirit of republican communalism, which sharply tempers the highly atomistic familism of the South. The networked family businesses of Emilia-Romagna or the Marche are therefore of an intermediate scale between the tiny peasant proprietors of the South and the much larger, professionally managed corporations of the North—neither completely atomized nor completely integrated into large organizations.

The proponents of flexible specialization tend to portray Italian small-scale industrialization as the ideal form of industrial organization. In this view, the Italian family firm combines unalienating small size, craft skills, and respect for family traditions with efficiency, technological sophistication, and other benefits usually associated with large scale. Robert Putnam portrays economic activity in these regions as the epitome of civic-minded cooperativeness, where business networks dovetail with local government to provide job satisfaction and prosperity for everyone.[33] But is this network organization of small-scale firms the wave of the future, a New Age form of industrial organization that combines economies of scale with the intimacy of small workplaces and the reunion of ownership and management?[34]

It is certainly not the case that Italy has had to pay an economic price for the relatively small scale of its businesses. Up until the recession of 1992–1994, the Italian economy was one of the fastest-growing in the European Community, in large measure because of the dynamism of its small-firm sector. Smallness of scale is thus no more of a constraint on aggregate gross domestic product growth in Italy any more than it is in Taiwan or Hong Kong. In an industry like apparel, which, in the words of a leading Italian designer, "every six months or so . . . reinvents itself with extraordinary speed," small scale is undoubtedly an advantage.[35]

But there are some negative aspects to this form of industrialization as well. Italian family firms tend to have short life histories and often fail to adopt efficient management practices, just like their Chinese counterparts. Silicon Valley and Route 128 hosted many small, entrepreneurial start-up firms, but a number of them like Intel and Hewlett-Packard grew up to be enormous, bureaucratically organized corporations; indeed, they could not have risen to industrial dominance in their sectors without adopting the corporate form of organization. While there are exceptions like Benetton and Versace, many fewer of central Italy's small family firms have made the same transition. In the words of Michael Blim, who has studied small-scale industrialization in the Marche intensively,

Almost all of the San Lorenzo entrepreneurs have resisted the institutionalization of their firms through installation of a management structure; and thus, they tend to live by their wits and to persevere, at times, by sheer gall. Eventually, however, fatigue affects even the most protean among them, and they then retire—or go out of business before they, in fact, fail. Fortunately—given the small start-up costs—there are still young ones imbued with that irreplaceable virginal spirit, to take their place. Too often, though, the second generation of entrepreneurs leave out the hard-fisted habit of savings that has fostered firm accumulation. Profits are soon diverted, instead, to conspicuous consumption and social status advancement.[36]

Like their Taiwanese counterparts, these small family firms are intensely competitive and, despite their networking, much more atomized and distrustful of one another than some of their foreign proponents suggest. The degree of civic-mindedness manifest in the relationships between family businesses and their employees and suppliers is thrown into question by the widespread practice of *lavoro nero* ("black labor"), a variety of generally illicit practices including the refusal to pay fringe benefits or report income, taking deliveries "off the books," and the like.[37] In many cases, small businesses are successful in central Italy because their employees are not unionized, as in the northern industrial triangle, and therefore can be paid less.[38]

Although bigger is not necessarily better, for some lines of business it undoubtedly is, and the familistic nature of these businesses prevents them from moving into new markets or taking advantage of scale. Despite trends in some consumer markets toward increased segmentation and product differentiation, mass production has not gone away, nor have the economies of scale in many industries. Just as in Taiwan and Hong Kong, the family orientation of businesses may be a constraint as well as an advantage, one that limits Italy's ability to move into certain sectors of the global economy that require larger scale. In this respect, the networks that have sprung up among small Italian family firms may not be so much the wave of the future as much as a reflection of the inability of these small firms to grow to a more efficient scale or integrate vertically in ways that would be necessary if they were to exploit new markets and technological opportunities. It is no accident that these firms—just like small firms in Taiwan—have specialized in machine tools, ceramics, apparel, design, and other activities that do not reward large scale. On the other hand, it is doubtful whether any amount of networking among small family firms will be sufficient to produce, for example, an Italian semiconductor industry.

Many observers have compared Italy to continental Europe, but none that I know of has tried to compare Italy to China. Although these regions vary enormously in terms of history, religion, and other aspects of culture, they are in fact quite similar in several critical respects. In both cases, the family plays a central role among social structures, with a corresponding weakness of nonkinship-based organizations, and in both industrial structure consists of relatively small family businesses networked together in complex webs of interdependence. The similarities go further; because of small scale and simple decision-making structures, firms in both the *Terza Italia* and Taiwan and Hong Kong are admirably suited to serve rapidly-changing, highly segmented consumer markets, or markets for producer goods like machine tools that do not require large scale. In both societies, small family businesses rely on networks to achieve what amount to economies of scale. On the other hand, neither the Italian nor the Chinese family firm has been able to break out of those sectors to which they are limited by their scale and therefore occupy similar niches within the global economy. In terms of industrial structure, therefore, these parts of Italy are essentially Confucian in nature, and their challenge in adapting to changing economic conditions will be similar.

CHAPTER 11

Face-to-Face in France

I n recent decades the French state has placed a high priority on making France a leader in a number of high-technology fields, such as aerospace, electronics, and computers. Its approach was consistent with those taken by French governments for at least the past five hundred years: a group of bureaucrats in Paris drew up plans for the promotion of technology, which it carried out through protection of domestic industries, subsidies, government procurements, and (after the Socialist victory in 1981) outright nationalization of a number of high-tech firms, including the entire electronics sector. This type of unapologetic industrial policy or *dirigisme* yielded some results: a viable aerospace industry, including the Concorde supersonic transport; a series of exportable military aircraft; an active space launch program; and, with the help of its European consortium partners, a commercial airliner, the Airbus.[1]

But the overall record of French high-tech industrial policy has been dismal. The government's Plan calcul of the late 1960s predicted that computing power would be concentrated in just a few mammoth time-sharing mainframe computers, and on the eve of the microcomputer revolution it subsidized development in this direction.[2] The French computer industry, nationalized and heavily subsidized in the early 1980s, began to hemorrhage money almost immediately, increasing the government's budget deficit and depressing the franc. In the end, French firms never succeeded in becoming a leading-edge supplier of hardware or software, except to the captive French telecommunications market. Nor has government policy succeeded in fostering world-class semiconductor, biotech, or, indeed, auto industries.

The poor record of French industrial policy is often held by free market economists to be an indictment of industrial policy per se, and it does indeed provide a sobering lesson about the limits of a government's ability to pick industrial winners. But what many of these critics fail to take into account is that French governments have been constantly tempted to intervene in the economy because the French private sector has never been dynamic, innovative, or entrepreneurial. In the words of Pierre Dreyfus, one-time minister of industry and former head of the Renault automobile company, "private enterprise in France does not take risks; it is chilly, timid, shy."[3] Private firms in France over the past 150 years have never been leaders in new organizational forms, nor have they been noted for their large scale or ability to master complicated industrial processes. The most successful, apart from those owned or subsidized by the state, have tended to be family concerns serving relatively small, high-quality consumer or specialty markets.

If this pattern sounds familiar, it is. While it might seem quite presumptuous to compare as complex and highly developed a society as that of modern France to small, upstart Chinese societies in the Far East, there are in fact a number of close parallels with respect to their endowments of social capital. France shares with the typical Chinese society a weakness in intermediate associations between the family and the state that has constrained the French private sector's ability to produce large, strong, and dynamic enterprises. As a result, French economic life has clustered around either family-oriented businesses or giant state-owned companies that were founded when the French government stepped in to rescue faltering large private corporations. This missing layer of intermediate organizations has had an impact not only on French industrial structure writ large but also on the way that French workers and managers deal with each other.

We should note at the outset the various significant ways in which France differs from a Confucian society. It would be wrong to say that France is familistic in anything like a Chinese sense, or even that it has anything resembling central Italy's familism. Beyond the general sanctioning of the family given by the Catholic church and the Latin tradition of the *familia,* France has never had an elaborate ideology that gave the family special privileges. Even in premodern times, kinship never played the same sort of role that it did in China; France in the Middle Ages was richly endowed with a variety of intermediate organizations—guilds, religious orders, municipalities, and clubs—almost none of which were based on kinship. In later years, France was to become the country that invented the concept of *la carrière overte aux talents* ("careers open to talent"), based on objective criteria of merit rather than birth or inherited social status. The French family, regardless of social class, never aspired to be a self-sufficient economic unit and never possessed the strict patrilineality of the Chinese *jia.* The large number of hyphenated names in the French aristocracy and *haute bourgeoisie* is itself testimony to the importance of matrilineal inheritance.

The French state, moreover, has had, since at least the early modern period, a legitimacy and a *gloire* that was quite different from China. The Chinese emperor, his court, and the imperial bureaucracy all stood, in theory, at the pinnacle of Chinese society and were legitimated by Confucian ideology. But there was a parallel tradition among the Chinese of distrust for the state and a jealous guarding of the prerogatives of their families against its depredations. In France, by contrast, service to the state continues to be an aspiration of the best and the brightest, who can hope to attend the École nationale d'administration (ENA) or another of the *grandes écoles* and land a job in the bureaucracy or running one of France's large state-owned companies. Though wariness about bureaucratic careers may be in the process of changing, relatively few ambitious Chinese have yet chosen public service over seeking a fortune for themselves and their families in private business, whether in the PRC, Taiwan, Hong Kong, or Singapore.

The real significance of the French family lies not so much in the fact that it is particularly strong or cohesive but rather that it has been thrust forward as one of the major poles of social cohesion because of a lack of other intermediate groups between the family and the state that can claim individual loyalties. This was true, above all, in economic life.

In a seminal article written in the late 1940s, the economic historian

David Landes argued that France's relative economic retardation when compared to England, Germany or the United States was due to the predominance of the traditional family firm.[4] Landes asserted that the typical French family businessman was fundamentally conservative, with a distaste for the new and unknown. He was primarily interested in the survival and independence of his family enterprise, and he was therefore reluctant to go public or seek sources of capital that would dilute his control over the business. Strongly protectionist and much less export oriented than the Germans, the French manufacturer regarded himself more as a functionary than an entrepreneur, and "came to look on the government as a sort of father in whose arms he could always find shelter and consolation."[5]

The Landes thesis was extended by Jesse Pitts, who argued that the successful French bourgeoisie was co-opted by the mores and values of the aristocracy. The latter held capitalism in low esteem and prized the noble, individualistic act of *prouesse,* or prowess, over the process of steady, unremitting rational accumulation.[6] The French bourgeois family did not seek to overturn the status quo through growth and innovation but rather aspired to the settled, landed, *rentier* status of the aristocracy. Large accumulations of wealth were hard to achieve, in part because entrepreneurial families were not willing to take significant risks and also because of the nature of the family itself. Primogeniture had been abolished as undemocratic during the Revolution, and the matrilineality of the French family often led to internal fractiousness and the splitting of fortunes. Pitts might have added that the conservative anticapitalism of the aristocracy was replaced, in the twentieth century, by the equally anticapitalist *snobbisme* of a largely Marxist intelligentsia. This had a telling effect on the French businessman's view of the legitimacy of his own calling.

The Landes thesis about the familistic roots of French economic backwardness was attacked repeatedly in subsequent years from a number of perspectives. Most important, the French economy began to grow quite rapidly in the 1950s, producing its own miniature "miracle" not much less impressive than that of the Germans. Hence the very premise of French backwardness or retardation was thrown into question.[7] Today, the French have one of the highest per capita incomes in the industrialized world when measured in terms of parity purchasing power rather than dollars. There has been a substantial amount of revisionism by scholars who have argued, first, that French growth rates were never significantly lower than those experienced by supposedly more advanced countries like England and Germany,[8] and second, that family firms are no less capable than their professionally managed counterparts at producing innovation and generating new wealth.[9] Both the automaker Renault and the retailer Bon Marché, the latter virtually having invented the department store, were examples of dynamic family businesses that grew to large size.[10]

Despite these criticisms, however, few would deny that the French economy was organized familistically until well into the second half of the twentieth century; that the French were very late when compared to Germany and the United States in making a transition from family business to the professionally managed corporation; and that the French state played a very large role in promoting that transition. While German businesses had started to acquire a corporate form of organization in the 1870s, the legitimacy in France of family leadership of businesses was unquestioned and family firms retained their hold through the interwar period.[11] Family control was weakened by a number of laws passed in the mid-1930s that, among other things, equalized voting rights among shareholders, but the broad transition to corporate management did not take place until well after World War II.[12] While the French growth rate may have kept up with Britain's on a per capita basis, few economic historians would dispute that the French were slower to adopt new technologies, particularly those of the "second" industrial revolution (in chemicals, electrical equipment, coal, steel, etc.) than were the Germans or Americans. Trade associations have always been rather weak when compared to their German counterparts, which play an extremely important role in promoting standards, training, markets, and the like. Although they have modernized since then, French trade associations were more typically designed to protect established sectors from competition through tariffs and subsidies.[13] There is also general consensus that French production remained geared toward traditional manufacture of high-quality consumer goods during much of the nineteenth century, which was particularly well served by small-scale family firms.[14]

Indeed, many of the distinctive characteristics of the French economy can be traced to French familism. Some observers have argued that French industry suffered from a Malthusian market organization that exposed a large number of small firms to "excessive" competition, driving down their profitability or leading them to cartelize to protect market shares.[15] But market structure is an effect, not a cause, of firms trying to reap scale economies. If French firms were unable to do so effectively, the problem was much more likely not the market itself but the proclivities of family businesses that were unwilling to expand and dilute their control. Similarly, others hold that the French emphasis on small-lot production of traditional high-quality goods stemmed from the small and segmented nature of such markets. It is true that the survival of class distinctions and certain aristocratic traditions has had an important impact on French consumer tastes. But it is also the case that large, modern, marketing organizations tend to create their own demand. The French market for mass consumer goods eventually came into existence after World War II, just as it had earlier in the United States and Germany, but the relative lateness with which this happened may also be traceable to the slow withering away of the family business.[16]

The solidarity of the traditional French bourgeois family, with its tendency to look inward and its concern for its status and traditions, has been a staple of French literature and social commentary. As in other familistic societies, there has been a long-standing cultural discomfort with adoption, which was reflected in the debates in the Conseil d'état when the basic law on adoption was introduced under Napoleon.[17] French familism, however, is not nearly as strong as Chinese familism or even the familism of central Italy. Why, then, were French family businesses so slow in making the transition to professional management and a modern corporate structure?

The answer has to do with the low level of trust among the French and their traditional difficulties associating with each other spontaneously in groups. The relative paucity of intermediate groups between the family and the state in France has been noted over the years by a wide variety of observers, the first and most important of whom was Alexis de Tocqueville. Tocqueville explained in *The Old Regime and the French Revolution* that on the eve of its Revolution, France was pervaded with large class divisions and minuscule status hierarchies within classes that prevented people from working with one another, even when they had important interests in common.

The French sociologist Michel Crozier noted that this was also characteristic of the post–World War II clerical agency and industrial monopoly that he studied. Within each bureaucracy, there were no groups or teams of any sort, no associations related either to work or leisure; indeed, employees seldom had friendships inside the organization and preferred to relate to one another through the formal, hierarchical rules that defined the organization.[18] Crozier pointed to a wide variety of other studies indicating the absence of informal groups in French society: children in one village do not form groups or cliques and fail to develop lasting ties that continue through adulthood;[19] the adults in another have a hard time cooperating on tasks of common interest because this would disrupt the theoretical equality of the villagers.[20]

There is, in other words, a very pronounced French cultural distaste for informal, face-to-face relationships of the type required in new informal associations and a strong preference for authority that is centralized, hierarchical, and legally defined. Frenchmen of equal status, in other words, find it difficult to solve problems between themselves without reference to a higher, more centralized form of authority.[21] In Crozier's words,

> Face-to-face dependence relationships are, indeed, perceived as difficult to bear in the French cultural setting. Yet the prevailing view of authority is still that of universalism and absolutism; it continues to retain something of the seventeenth century's political theory, with its mixture of rationality and *bon plaisir.* The two attitudes are contradictory. However, they can be reconciled within a bureaucratic system, since impersonal rules and centralization make it possible to reconcile an absolutist conception of authority and the elimination of most direct dependence relationships. In other words, the French bureaucratic system of organization is the perfect solution to the basic dilemma of Frenchmen about authority.[22]

The dislike of direct, face-to-face relationships is apparent in many aspects of French economic life. French workers on the shop floor are reluctant to form teams spontaneously; their preference is to cooperate on the basis of formal rules established centrally by management or by centralized bargaining between management and labor. Labor relations as a whole tend to suffer from the same formalism; labor unions tend not to settle disputes with management locally but refer problems up the ladder of authority—ultimately to the government in Paris.

The historical origins of this French propensity for centralization and the corresponding weakness of associational life can be found in the victory of the French monarchy over its aristocratic rivals in the sixteenth and seventeenth centuries and its systematic suppression and subordination of alternative centers of power. In this respect, it was similar to both the Chinese imperial system and the Norman kingdom in southern Italy.[23] The rise of a centralized French state was motivated originally not by economic but by political pressures—in particular, by the need to field a sufficiently large army to protect and extend the French monarchy's dynastic possessions.[24] Local administration was abolished in favor of a system of *intendants* appointed from Paris and supervised by a Royal Council with ever-expanding duties. According to Tocqueville, the result of this political centralization was that "there was in France no township, borough, village, or hamlet, however small, no hospital, factory, convent, or college which had a right to manage its own affairs as it thought fit or to administer its possessions without interference."[25]

In economic affairs, absolute royal control over fiscal matters in France developed during the reign of Charles VII (1427–1461), and was extended—as manifested by a more or less continually rising tax rate—through the subsequent reigns of Louis XI, Louis XII, and Francis I in the late fifteenth and early sixteenth centuries. Tocqueville notes that the most pernicious aspect of the tax system was its inequality, since it made people conscious of their differences and jealous of each other's privileges.[26] In addition to taxes, the Crown developed a new means of raising revenue through the sale of offices in an expanding royal bureaucracy. Holders of these offices did not usually perform official functions, or at least, any that were socially useful, but they were thereby exempted from a variety of taxes and received a title that conferred considerable social prestige.[27] Like the Chinese bureaucracy, the French bureaucracy constituted a huge black hole that would consume the energies of anyone with ambition or talent: "There can be few, if any, parallels for this intense desire of the middle-class Frenchman to cut an official figure; no sooner did he find himself in possession of a small capital sum than he expended it on buying an official post instead of investing it in a business."[28]

The sale of offices had a more pernicious long-term effect, dividing French society into classes and subdividing those classes into smaller and smaller strata that saw themselves in a bitter competition with one another for offices and royal favor. This process is described admirably by Tocqueville: "Each group was differentiated from the rest by its right to petty privileges of one kind or another, even the least of which was regarded as a token of its exalted status. Thus they were constantly wrangling over questions of precedence, so much so that the *Intendant* and the courts were often at a loss for a solution of their differences."[29]

The status distinctions fostered by the tax and privileges policies of the Old Regime survived in modern France and have affected economic life in countless ways. France has remained in many respects a class-ridden society. The relatively late growth of a mass consumer market in France and the persistence of small markets for expensive, high-quality goods is testimony to the lingering effects of aristocratic sensibilities among middle-class French consumers. The gulf between labor and management was traditionally very wide. Like other southern European countries, the French labor movement flirted with anarchosyndicalism at the close of the nineteenth century and in the twentieth was heavily ideologized and dominated by the French Communist party. Labor disputes that in the United States would have been settled pragmatically often took on political overtones and usually required the intervention of the central government to settle. Stanley Hoffmann has noted how aristocratic values survived even among the French working class, in its emphasis on the demonstration of prowess in its struggles with the bourgeoisie.[30] In such an atmosphere of shop floor militancy, the Japanese idea of teams that blur distinctions in bureaucratic hierarchies or the concept of the company's constituting a "family" that cuts across class lines would have been particularly foreign.

These class divisions in French society, combined with traditional attitudes toward authority, have created a system of legalistic and inflexible shop floor relations. Observers of the French political system have noted that the dislike of face-to-face participation reduces opportunities for pragmatic adjustment and creates blockages and a lack of feedback. Routine politics entails a dull acceptance of strong, centralized bureaucratic authority and is very fragile; when pressures for change build to a breaking point, participants in the system lurch to the opposite extreme, revolting and questioning all authority.[31] This pattern is replicated in French labor-management relations, which are seldom capable of small, incremental adjustments but tend to explode periodically in crisis periods of highly politicized labor actions designed to achieve goals at a national level.

Among the class of managers—the *patronat*—there have been historic tensions between the grand and petty bourgeoisie, or between France's "two capitalisms," the first Catholic and family and producer oriented, the other dominated by Jews and Protestants who were heavily involved in finance, banking, and speculation.[32] Just as in England, where speculators of the City in London looked down upon the provincial manufacturers in northern cities like Manchester or Leeds, so too in France was there a mutual distrust between finance capital in Paris and manufacturing in the provinces. The bank-centered industrial group, found in Germany and Japan, which depends on a high degree of trust between the group's financial and manufacturing arms, was much less plausible in such circumstances. An early French effort to establish such a group, the Crédit mobilier, ended in spectacular failure in 1867.

To the extent that the bureaucracy under the Old Regime performed an economic function, it was to regulate all aspects of French economic life. The guilds were one form of medieval social organization that could in theory have retained a degree of independence and thereby acted as a bulwark against the centralizing tendencies of the French state. But they were in effect taken over by the state and became an instrument by which the latter could control economic life. In each traditional industry, state regulations covered virtually every aspect of the production process. According to the historians Douglass North and Robert Thomas, the regulations governing the dyeing of cloth ran to 317 articles. The guilds were used to establish standards that limited markets and posed formidable barriers to entry; in their words, "The system of control and inspection by guild officials could be so comprehensive that, during the time of Colbert, even ordinary cloth required at least six inspections."[33] Thus, the guilds did not see their purpose as the defense of craft traditions against the encroachments of outsiders, including the state. Rather, they depended on the state to protect them from competition, to legitimate their powers and to enforce their control over economic life.

The consequence of this high degree of centralization was, naturally, a high degree of dependence of French private businesses on the protection and subsidy of the state. While English law had been changed by the seventeenth century to allow state-chartered companies to keep a large part of the income they earned through innovation, the French state kept such benefits to itself. Colbert, Louis XIV's legendary minister of finance, had great difficulties setting up a French equivalent of the British and Dutch East India companies, complaining, like the Renault executive quoted above, that "our merchants . . . have not the capacity to take up any matter with which they are not acquainted."[34] A habit of dependence on government favor took hold throughout the French private sector well before the Revolution, which is described in the following terms by Tocqueville:

> The government having stepped into the place of Divine Providence in France, it was but natural that everyone, when in difficulties, invoked its aid. We find a vast number of petitions which, though the writers professed to be speaking on behalf of the public, were in reality intended to further their own small private interests. . . . They make depressing read-

ing. We find peasants applying for compensation for the loss of their cattle or their homes; wealthy landowners asking for financial aid for the improvement of their estates; manufacturers petitioning the *Intendant* for monopolies protecting them from competition.[35]

The tradition of heavy French government intervention in the economy, especially on behalf of large-scale firms, has continued up to the present. Many private, family-owned businesses were nationalized after they had grown to a certain size and had, for one reason or another, gotten into trouble under their private owners and/or managers. These have included, over time, the automaker Renault, the steel company Usinor-Sacilor, the chemical company Pechiney, the energy company ELF, the bank Crédit Lyonnais, and the high-tech aerospace and electronics firms Thomson-CSF, Snecma, Aérospatiale, and Companies des Machines Bull.

French *dirigisme,* or the active involvement of the state in economic life, was thus both the cause and the effect of the weakness of the French private sector and of its inability to create competitive large-scale enterprises on its own. That is, in the distant historical past, the centralized French state deliberately undermined the independence of the private sector through taxes and privileges in order to bring it under political control, which had the effect of weakening the entrepreneurial and organizational habits of businesses. But in later years, that very weakness of entrepreneurial spirit became a motive for the renewed intervention of the state, which sought to reenergize a cautious and unimaginative private sector. The willingness of the state to step in then perpetuated the dependence of the private sector. The issue became complicated in the twentieth century by socialist governments, which wanted to nationalize private businesses for ideological reasons, even when they would have been viable on their own, and later by conservative governments, which wanted to privatize out of similarly ideological convictions. (It should be noted, however, that truly market-oriented conservative French governments are a relatively new phenomenon; many conservatives have been quite happy to preside over an enormous state sector.)

Most neoclassical economists would argue that state-owned firms will inevitably be less efficient than private ones because the state lacks the proper incentives to run enterprises efficiently. The state does not have to fear bankruptcy, since it can keep businesses going out of tax dollars or, at worst, by printing money. It also has strong incentives to use the firm for political ends like job creation and patronage. These deficiencies of public ownership have been the underlying justification for the global move toward privatization over the past decade. But state-owned enterprises can be run more or less efficiently, and any final judgment as to the efficiency price paid for nationalization has to be measured against the entrepreneurial capabilities of that society's private sector. In France, nationalized companies have often been allowed considerable managerial discretion and operate not much differently from their private sector counterparts.[36]

The opposite side of the coin of French private sector weakness is the talent and strength of its public sector bureaucrats. The French state since its modern emergence has always had a prestige, *élan,* and respect lacking in other centralized bureaucracies. Tocqueville at one point remarks that "in France the central government never followed the example of those governments in Southern Europe which seem to have laid hands on everything and sterilized all they touched. The French Government always displayed much intelligence and quite amazing energy in handling the tasks it set itself."[37] One of those southern European governments Tocqueville was thinking of was undoubtedly the Norman kingdom in southern Italy. By contrast, the centralized French state succeeded in modernizing France and making it into a major modern technological power. In contrast to nationalized industries in formerly socialist countries or in Latin America, French nationalized industries have been run relatively efficiently. When they came to power in 1981, for example, the Socialists undertook a major reorganization of the French steel and chemical industries that involved, among other things, the laying off of substantial numbers of workers as a result of restructuring. The French steel industry became more competitive as a result of state management, though at a huge cost to French taxpayers in the form of investment in industrial infrastructure.[38] There have, of course, been major debacles as well, such as the mismanagement of the state-owned Crédit Lyonnais, which in the early 1990s ran up an expensive portfolio of bad debts that had to be made good by the French treasury.[39]

An issue further complicating this picture is the question of cultural change. The difficulty the French have in spontaneous association, and the consequent weakness of intermediate groups, has been one of the more remarkable continuities over the centuries of French history, one in which the Old Regime and modern France "join hands across the abyss made by the Revolution."[40] But just as the culture of centralization in French social life was the product of a specific period of French history, so too this culture has itself been exposed to other influences that have modified it. As the post–World War II recovery got under way, observers like Charles Kindleberger pointed to important changes going on in the culture of the French family business, which had become more open to innovation and professional management.[41] France in the past couple of generations has been undergoing a process of cultural homogenization as it has integrated into the broader European community and participated in the globalization of the world economy. The imperatives of industrial modernization have eaten away at important aspects of French economic culture as French corporations strove to be competitive on a global stage. Many prominent French economists have studied neoclassical economics at American universities. More French young people now attend American-style business schools than previously, and a greater number of them speak the international language of business: English. In what is far from an unmixed blessing, the communications revolution has made it more difficult to preserve French cultural traditions intact. The traditional French weakness in associations has been changing: there is today an impressive array of voluntary private French groups like the humanitarian association *Médecins sans frontières,* which has been active in Third World trouble spots.

Cultural change by its very nature occurs slowly, however. A gulf of distrust continues to characterize relations among French workers, and between them and their managers. In terms of social capital, France continues to resemble Italy and Taiwan, despite enormous differences in other respects, more than it does Germany, Japan, or the United States, with important implications for France's economic future. If France wishes to remain a player in sectors where size matters, the state will have to remain heavily involved. Despite the economically liberal professions of recent conservative French governments, privatization will work less well in a French cultural setting than in certain others, and the state may well have to intervene at a later date to rescue key privatized industries deemed strategic.

CHAPTER 12

Korea: The Chinese Company Within

The low-trust, family-oriented societies with weak intermediate organizations we have observed have all been characterized by a similar saddle-shaped distribution of enterprises. Taiwan, Hong Kong, Italy, and France have a host of smaller private firms that constitute the entrepreneurial core of their economies and a small number of very large, state-owned firms at the other end of the scale. In such societies, the state plays an important role in promoting large-scale enterprises that might not be spontaneously created by the private sector, albeit at some cost in efficiency. We might postulate then that as a general rule, any society with weak intermediate institutions and low trust outside the family will tend to have a similar distribution of firms in its economy.

The Republic of Korea, however, presents an apparent anomaly that needs to be explained in order to preserve the validity of the larger argument. Korea is similar to Japan, Germany, and the United States insofar as it has very large corporations and a highly concentrated industrial structure. On the other hand, Korea is much closer to China than to Japan in terms of family structure. Families occupy a similarly important place in Korea as in China, and there are no Japanese-style mechanisms in Korean culture for bringing outsiders into family groups. Following the Chinese pattern, this should lead to small family businesses and difficulties in institutionalizing the corporate form of organization.

The answer to this apparent paradox is the role of the Korean state, which deliberately promoted gigantic conglomerates as a development strategy in the 1960s and 1970s and overcame what would otherwise have been a cultural proclivity for the small- and medium-size enterprises typical of Taiwan. While the Koreans succeeded in creating large companies and *zaibatsu* in the manner of Japan, they have nonetheless encountered many Chinese-style difficulties in the nature of corporate governance, from management succession to relations on the shop floor. The Korean case shows, however, how a resolute and competent state can shape industrial structure and overcome long-standing cultural propensities.

The first thing to note about Korean industrial structure is the sheer concentration of Korean industry. Like other Asian economies, there are two levels of organization: individual firms and larger network organizations that unite disparate corporate entities. The Korean network organization is known as the *chaebol,* represented by the same two Chinese characters as the Japanese *zaibatsu* and patterned deliberately on the Japanese model. The size of individual Korean companies is not large by international standards. As of the mid-1980s, the Hyundai Motor Company, Korea's largest automobile manufacturer, was only a thirtieth the size of General Motors, and the Samsung Electric Company was only a tenth the size of Japan's Hitachi.[1] However, these statistics understate their true economic clout because these businesses are linked to one another in very large network organizations. Virtually the whole of the large-business sector in Korea is part of a *chaebol* network: in 1988, forty-three *chaebol* (defined as conglomerates with assets in excess of 400 billion won, or US$500 million) brought together some 672 companies.[2] If we measure industrial concentration by *chaebol* rather than individual firm, the figures are staggering: in 1984, the three largest *chaebol* alone (Samsung, Hyundai, and Lucky-Goldstar) produced 36 percent of Korea's gross domestic product.[3] Korean industry is more concentrated than that of Japan, particularly in the manufacturing sector; the three-firm concentration ratio for Korea in 1980 was 62.0 percent of all manufactured goods, compared to 56.3 percent for Japan.[4] The degree of concentration of Korean industry grew throughout the postwar period, moreover, as the rate of *chaebol* growth substantially exceeded the rate of growth for the economy as a whole. For example, the twenty largest *chaebol* produced 21.8 percent of Korean gross domestic product in 1973, 28.9 percent in 1975, and 33.2 percent in 1978.[5]

The Japanese influence on Korean business organization has been enormous. Korea was an almost wholly agricultural society at the beginning of Japan's colonial occupation in 1910, and the latter was responsible for creating much of the country's early industrial infrastructure.[6] Nearly 700,000 Japanese lived in Korea in 1940, and a similarly large number of Koreans lived in Japan as forced laborers. Some of the early Korean businesses got their start as colonial enterprises in the period of Japanese occupation.[7] A good part of the two countries' émigré populations were repatriated after the war, leading to a considerable exchange of knowledge and experience of business practices. The highly state-centered development strategies of President Park Chung Hee and others like him were formed as a result of his observation of Japanese industrial policy in Korea in the prewar period.

As with Japanese *keiretsu,* the member firms in a Korean *chaebol* own shares in each other and tend to collaborate with each other on what is often a nonprice basis. The Korean *chaebol* differs from the Japanese prewar *zaibatsu* or postwar *keiretsu,* however, in a number of significant ways. First and perhaps most important, Korean network organizations were not centered around a private bank or other financial institution in the way the Japanese *keiretsu* are.[8] This is because Korean commercial banks were all state owned until their privatization in the early 1970s, while Korean industrial firms were prohibited by law from acquiring more than an eight percent equity stake in any bank. The large Japanese city banks that were at the core of the postwar *keiretsu* worked closely with the Finance Ministry, of course, through the process of overloaning (i.e., providing subsidized credit), but the Korean *chaebol* were controlled by the government in a much more direct way through the latter's ownership of the banking system. Thus, the networks that emerged more or less spontaneously in Japan were created much more deliberately as the result of government policy in Korea.

A second difference is that the Korean *chaebol* resemble the Japanese intermarket *keiretsu* more than the vertical ones (see p.197). That is, each of the large *chaebol* groups has holdings in very different sectors, from heavy manufacturing and electronics to textiles, insurance, and retail. As

Korean manufacturers grew and branched out into related businesses, they started to pull suppliers and subcontractors into their networks. But these relationships resembled simple vertical integration more than the relational contracting that links Japanese suppliers with assemblers. The elaborate multitiered supplier networks of a Japanese parent firm like Toyota do not have ready counterparts in Korea.[9]

Finally, the Korean *chaebol* tend to be considerably more centralized than the Japanese *keiretsu*. Since the *chaebol* are kinship based, there is a natural unity among the heads of the member firms that differs from relations among *keiretsu* members in Japan. The Korean *chaebol* typically have centralized staffs for the organization as a whole—usually not as large as the central staffs of former American conglomerates like ITT and Gulf +Western but more institutionalized than the Presidents' Councils that link Japanese network organizations. These central staffs are responsible for planning the allocation of resources across the organization. The central planning staffs can also play a role in personnel decisions for the organization as a whole. In addition, certain *chaebol* are centered on a single holding company, like the Daewoo Foundation, that holds shares in the network's members. The result of these differences is that the boundaries between *chaebol* are more distinct than between *keiretsu* in Japan. In the latter country, there are a few cases where the same company can be in the Presidents' Council of two or more different *keiretsu*.[10] I am not aware of parallel cases in Korea. The Korean *chaebol* therefore look somewhat more like hierarchical organizations and less like networks than their Japanese counterparts.

If we turn now to the structure of the Korean family, we find that it is much more similar to that of China than Japan. The traditional Korean family was, like its Chinese counterpart, strictly patrilineal; inheritance did not pass, as it often did in Japan, through daughters. In the Japanese *ie,* or household, the actual roles of father, eldest son, and the like did not have to be played by blood relatives. In Korea, by contrast, there was no equivalent of the Japanese *mukoyoshi,* or nonbiologically related adopted son. Adopted sons had to come from a kin group, most typically from among the sons of the adopting father's brothers.[11]

The practice of primogeniture in Japan helped greatly in concentrating wealth in preindustrial times and in creating a surplus of younger sons who had to make their fortunes outside the family's farm and household. Korean inheritance practices differ from those of both Japan and China but had an economic impact closer to the latter. Inheritance was partible but not equally divided among male heirs as it was in China. Generally the eldest son received twice as much as the other sons, and in any event not less than half of the estate.[12] In practice, the actual amounts could be adjusted to suit the circumstances; if the pieces into which the family property was to be divided were too small to be economical, the younger sons would receive only a token inheritance. As in China, however, there were many potential claimants on the property of a rich father, and consequently a tendency to dissipate wealth after two or three generations.

Families tended to be smaller, however, in Korea than in China. There were fewer large joint families where the adult sons and their families could continue to live together in the same household or compound. Instead, younger sons were expected to move out of the family house, as in Japan, taking their part of the inheritance with them to start their own household.[13] Unlike Japan, however, legal succession to the position of head of the household did not occur on the father's retirement but on his death.[14]

Korea has for long been a more strictly Confucian society than Japan, consistent with the fact that it is closer and more accessible to China. Some, indeed, have said that Korea is more Confucian than China itself.[15] While Confucian influences in Japan date back to the Taika period in the seventh century A.D., the importance of this doctrine has waxed and waned. In Korea, Confucianism was made the state ideology during the Yi dynasty (1392–1910), while Buddhism was officially suppressed and Buddhist monks driven into the mountains. Apart from the very strong Protestant Christian influence in the twentieth century, there was a less active and diverse religious life in Korea than in Japan, as reflected in the much smaller number of Buddhist temples and monasteries throughout the country. The Confucian virtue of filial piety is strongly stressed in Korea relative to loyalty, as it is in China. This means that in traditional Korean society, primary loyalties go not to the political authorities but to one's family.[16] As in the case of China, Korean familism makes the society appear to be more individualistic than Japan, though what is perceived as individualism is actually the competition of families or lineages.[17]

Korea's social structure was similar to that of China: a king and mandarinate at the top, and families and lineages below, but relatively few intermediate organizations not based on kinship (like the *iemoto* groups in Japan). Although Korea was beset by outside invaders from Mongolia, Japan, and China, it remained a unitary kingdom from its unification under the Silla kingdom. There was no genuinely feudal period, as during the Tokugawa period in Japan, or like Europe in the Middle Ages, when political power was widely diffused among a class of nobles or warlords. Like China, Korea was ruled by gentlemen-scholars—the *yangban* class—rather than by soldiers. In preindustrial times, all three societies were rigidly stratified into official classes, but the porousness of class boundaries was perhaps a bit less in Korea than in either Japan or China. The lowest social class, that of *chonmin,* were in effect slaves who could be bought or sold by their masters, and the civil service examination, which was the route to government service and the highest status positions, was open only to members of the *yangban* class.[18] By all accounts, premodern society in Korea was extremely stagnant and inert, internally rigid and closed off to foreign influences.

As in southern China, the primary social structure standing between the family and the state is kinship based: the lineage. Korean lineages are even larger than in China; people claim descent from a common ancestor going back thirty generations or more. Lineages can come to include hundreds of thousands of people.[19] The influence of large lineages in Korea may be seen in the fact that there are even fewer surnames in Korea than in China; some forty percent of all Koreans are named Kim and another eighteen percent Park.[20] Korean lineages were also more homogeneous, failing to segment like those in southern China along class or status lines.[21]

Given this kind of family and social structure, one would expect modern Korea's business structure to resemble that of capitalist Chinese societies like Taiwan and Hong Kong. That is, most businesses would be family businesses of a relatively small scale; to the extent that they broadened beyond the family, recruitment would be based on lineages or regional origin. Korea, like China, lacks an easy method of adoption of nonkin and hence should tend to resist the introduction of nonfamily members into the family business (i.e., the professionalization of management). Without the precedent of a broad range of premodern, intermediate social organizations not based on kinship, trust should be limited to kinship groups. One would therefore expect modern corporations based on a nonkinship principle to be introduced into modern Korea only very slowly. Partible inheritance should contribute to the instability of Korean businesses and their likelihood of fragmenting after a generation or two. Given a conflict of interest between family and company, one would expect Koreans to choose family. If culture is important, in other words, Korean industrial structure should look very much like that of Taiwan or Hong Kong.

The truth of the matter is that Korean businesses, despite their large scale, *do* look and behave more like Chinese businesses than like Japanese corporations. Beneath the imposing exteriors of corporate behemoths like Hyundai and Samsung lie familistic interiors that are slowly and grudgingly accommodating themselves to professional management, public ownership, the divorce of management and ownership, and an impersonal, hierarchical corporate form of management.

Korean *chaebol* started as family businesses; most remain family owned and, at the upper reaches, family managed. Like large Hong Kong companies, giant enterprises like Daewoo and Ssangyong obviously have long since outstripped the ability of any one family to manage in their entirety, and so they are populated by legions of professional middle managers. But family control remains relatively tight at the top. One study conducted in 1978 found that of 2,797 executives of large Korean enterprises, some twelve percent were directly related to the founders by blood or marriage (this figure excludes the 76 founders themselves).[22] Another study found that of the top twenty *chaebol,* thirty-one percent of the executive officers were family members, forty percent were recruited from outside, and twenty-nine percent were promoted from within the organization.[23] A third study showed that as of the early 1980s, twenty-six percent of all large company presidents were founders, nineteen percent the sons of founders, twenty-one percent promoted from within, and thirty-five percent recruited from outside. Chung Ju Yung, founder of the Hyundai *chaebol,* had seven sons, known as the "seven princes," who were moved into leadership positions at various Hyundai companies at early ages.[24] This pattern contrasts sharply with that of Japan, where a far smaller number would be founders or relatives of founders, and a much higher proportion recruited from inside (but still unrelated to the founding family).[25] There is also a relatively high rate of intermarriage among descendants of *chaebol* founders. According to one study, half of the offspring of the top one hundred *chaebol* groups married spouses with a similar social background, while the remainder married within an elite circle of government officials, military officers, and the like.[26]

The Korean *chaebol* have been around a much shorter time than the Japanese *zaibatsu/keiretsu,* so it is not surprising that the founding entrepreneurs would in many cases still be in the driver's seat up through the 1980s. As one would expect from a culture heavily influenced by China, succession has proven to be a very difficult problem in Korea—much more so than it has been in Japan. Most of the founding entrepreneurs have wanted to turn their businesses over to their eldest sons, and in one survey of Korean business successions, sixty-five percent had done so.[27] (One notable exception is the Daewoo *chaebol,* which has made it a policy not to turn to family members for leadership.)[28] The proper education of a founding entrepreneur's children becomes extremely important, a need that dovetails nicely with Korean Confucianism's strong emphasis on education. As in China, however, the familistic principle of succession leads to substantial problems if the eldest son is incompetent or uninterested in taking over the corporation's leadership.

Something like this happened in the case of Korea's largest *chaebol,* Samsung, when its founder, Lee Byung Chul, decided he wanted to step down. The elder Lee had three sons, the first of whom was an invalid and apparently incapable of running the company. Rather than give him control of the company or divide it into three parts, the father decided to bypass the first two sons in favor of the youngest, Kun Hee. This kind of decision would have been relatively easy under the Japanese *ie* system, but it went against the grain of Korean familism. To mask the nature of his decision, the elder Lee had to go through an elaborate charade of passing the vast majority of his shares to two family foundations to prevent the older sons from seeking controlling interests in parts of the company. Once the youngest son was safely in control, the shares passed back from these foundations to him.[29] Lee Byung Chul got around the problem of an incompetent eldest son and kept the Samsung family fortune undivided, but the method was haphazard and messy.

In other less prominent cases, *chaebol* have split apart like Chinese family businesses because of the practice of partible inheritance and familistic succession. Taehan Textile and Taehan Electric Wire were once part of the same *chaebol* founded by Ke Dong Sol but split between his sons after his death. Similarly, the Kukjae and Chinyang companies were formerly part of the same *chaebol* and are now owned by two sons of the founder.[30] Despite the size of Korean enterprises, maintaining scale over an extended period of time is more difficult to do than for large, publicly owned Japanese corporations.

A second way in which Korean familism affects Korean business practices lies in management style. Virtually all comparative studies of Korean management indicate that Korean businesses tend to be run in a hierarchical, authoritarian, and centralized manner.[31] This type of authority structure makes them similar to Chinese family enterprises but different from both the consensual style of Japanese corporate management and the classic American decentralization of authority in multidivisional corporations. This was particularly true of the *chaebol* still run by founding entrepreneurs, who insisted on making virtually all major management decisions personally. Chung Ju Yung, founder of Hyundai, was said to talk to all of his overseas branch managers daily from 6:00 to 6:30 in the morning and to meet with the forty or so presidents of the *chaebol* member companies twice a week. The meetings were marked by a great deal of formality; in the words of one Korean newspaper, "The meeting of group presidents often serves to impress on the presidents that the distance between them and the group chairman is as great as the distance between them and new recruits. . . . And they all, even those who are formerly ranking government officials or comrades of the founding group chairman, must stand at attention when the group chairman enters the meeting room, even though he may be only in his thirties."[32] The more authoritarian nature of decision making in Korea makes it easier for Korean companies to move quickly and decisively; they are not bogged down by the Japanese-style need to develop extensive consensus throughout the hierarchy before making a move. This more decisive style, however, can also mean that decisions are not adequately vetted by staff and are made on the basis of insufficient knowledge.[33]

The Korean *chaebol* resembles, in other words, a Chinese family business writ large rather than a Japanese corporation, or *kaisha*. The forms of communal solidarity that permeate the Japanese corporation are largely missing from Korean ones. There is, for example, no permanent lifetime employment system based on unwritten reciprocal obligation, and layoffs in large companies are more common than in Japan.[34] Employment of managers in Korean corporations has tended to be relatively stable only because the country's steady rate of economic expansion has not made layoffs a serious issue. The group of core employees, to whom the company feels a strong commitment, is smaller than in a Japanese corporation, and there is a ring of expendable marginal employees who have no ready counterpart in Japan.[35] Korean corporations have never had the sense of managerial paternalism that exists in Japan or Germany, with extensive privately developed welfare systems for employees. The Koreans have no equivalent of the Japanese concept of *amae,* the unwillingness of members of a group to take advantage of each other's weakness that breeds such strong mutual dependence in Japan. The effect is, in the words of one observer, that "while Koreans also are relatively group-oriented, they also have a strong individualistic streak like most Westerners. Koreans frequently joke that an individual Korean can beat an individual Japanese, but that a group of Koreans are certain to be beaten by a group of Japanese."[36] The rate of employee turnover, raiding of other companies' skilled labor, and the like are all higher in Korea than in Japan.[37] Anecdotally, there would seem to be a lower level of informal work-oriented socializing in Korea than in Japan, with employees heading home to their families at the end of the day rather than staying on to drink in the evenings with their workmates.[38]

Although it is very homogeneous racially and linguistically, Korea is a class-ridden society when compared to a similarly homogeneous Japan. A large number of Korean entrepreneurs come out of the gentleman-scholar *yangban* class, which was relatively less open to outsiders than the Japanese *samurai* class. These traditional class differences have been sharpened in certain ways through the growth of a fabulously wealthy business elite, whose children tend to intermarry with one another. These sorts of class cleavages are mitigated, on the other hand, by the development of a system of universal education, standardized examinations, and certain status-leveling institutions like the army.

Given this general background, it should not surprise us to find that labor-management relations in Korea are far more adversarial and similar to those of North America and Western Europe than to Japan. According to one observer, "Koreans also seem to have a much weaker sense of indebtedness (*un* in Korean, *on* in Japanese) to an organization and one's fellow members. Once the organizational bonds are strained or broken by internal frictions, Koreans are less likely than the Japanese to feel guilty and more likely to feel anger and a sense of betrayal."[39] The authoritarian governments that ruled Korea until the late 1980s effectively outlawed strikes and made it illegal for unions to intervene in labor-management disputes. The state provided very little in the way of social welfare services and did not compel employers to do so either.[40] While this helped keep Korean wages and other costs down for the first few postwar decades, it also bred labor militancy and encouraged the unions to take a strong antigovernment position.[41]

In addition to a national culture there are also individual corporate cultures, which to some extent override the broader tendencies. Thus, among the large *chaebol,* Samsung's founder, Lee Byung Chul, made greater efforts to create a collegial atmosphere within the company than did Hyundai's more authoritarian Chung Ju Young. As a result, Samsung experienced a significantly lower level of strike activity than did Hyundai.[42]

The impact of Korean familism on Korean industrial structure should not be overstated. The traditional Korean family and its bonds have been weakening to some extent with the urbanization of the country.[43] Growing scale has simply outstripped the capabilities of most founding families to produce competent managers, and many of them have been forced to adopt institutionalized recruitment systems by which competent professional managers can be selected out of the university system on an impartial basis. Moreover, the large *chaebol* have become brand names and broadly recognized national champions; letting such a large enterprise split apart over a succession squabble would be a blow to national pride and might have harmful economic consequences in some cases as well.[44] Korean firms therefore have stronger incentives to keep their enterprises intact than do Chinese companies.

The need to sustain the Samsung or Hyundai names once they became major institutions is understandable, but the question remains: How did they grow into such formidable competitors in the first place? The rise of very large-scale enterprises in the context of such a highly Sinified culture as that of Korea is due to one primary factor: the behavior of the Korean state and its desire to imitate the industrial model of Japan. Indeed, this phenomenon was very much the result of the predilections of one man, President Park Chung Hee, the former military officer who more than anyone else oversaw Korea's rise as a developmental state from the time he took over the presidency in 1961 until his assassination in 1979.

Of all of the fast-developing countries in East Asia, South Korea has had perhaps the most hyperactive state (with the exception of communist countries). State-owned companies, including the entire banking sector, produced nine percent of Korean gross domestic product in 1972, or thirteen percent of all nonagricultural output.[45] The rest of the economy was highly regulated through the state's control over credit and its ability to reward or punish private companies through the granting of subsidies, licenses, and protection from foreign competition. The Korean state established a formal planning process in 1962 that has resulted in a series of Five-Year Plans that have governed the overall strategic direction of investment in the country.[46] Given the high debt-equity ratios of Korean corporations, access to credit was the key to control over the economy as a whole, and in the words of one observer, "All Korean businessmen, including the most powerful, have been aware of the need to stay on good terms with the Government to assure continuing access to credit and to avoid harassment from the tax officials."[47]

Up to this point, the behavior of the Korean state does not look much different from that of Taiwan. Taiwan had an even larger state sector and the government owned all of the commercial banks and yet its economy was dominated by small- and medium-sized producers. The key difference between Korea and Taiwan was not in the degree of state involvement, but in its direction: whereas the Guomindang government of Chiang Kai-shek did not want to foster large companies that would someday become competitors to the party, the Korean government under Park Chung Hee sought to create large national champions that it hoped would rival the Japanese *keiretsu* in world markets.[48] Park explicitly looked to other political revolutionaries as models, including Sun Yat-sen, Ataturk, Nasser, and the Meiji rulers of Japan. He evidently shared a bit of the Leninist infatuation with scale and believed that large size was a necessary component of modernization. As he explained in his autobiographical manifesto, he initially wanted to create "millionaires who promoted the reform [of the economy]" and thereby hoped to encourage "national capitalism."[49] While Taiwanese planners were content to create the proper infrastructural and macroeconomic conditions for rapid growth, the Park regime intervened in a microeconomic fashion to encourage particular companies and particular investment projects.[50]

The Korean government used a number of mechanisms to encourage large scale. First and most important was its control over credit: in contrast to Taiwan, which used a high-interest-rate policy to encourage savings, the Korean government shoveled money out the door to large *chaebol* in an effort to strengthen their global competitive position. This credit often came at negative real interest rates, a fact that goes far to explain the willy-nilly expansion of these conglomerates into businesses where they had scant management expertise.[51] The share of so-called policy loans, that is, loans explicitly directed by the government, increased from forty-seven percent of all loans in 1970 to sixty percent in 1978.[52] The government also could manipulate the credit markets, as in the Emergency Decree of 1972 controlling curb market loans, in such a way as to benefit large over small- and medium-sized companies.[53]

A second method at the government's disposal was to accredit only a limited number of firms to participate in lucrative export markets.[54]

Thus, for example, the government set standards by which a company would be considered a general trading company (on the model of the Japanese GTCs) based on a certain minimum level of paid-in capital, exports, overseas branches, and so on. Once qualified, a company would have preferential access to credit, markets, and licenses.[55] Finally, by doing a high degree of indicative planning, the Korean government created a reasonably predictable domestic economic environment in which large companies could operate, knowing that they would be protected from foreign competition in their (albeit small) domestic markets and supported in their export drives abroad.[56]

The Korean state could control corporate behavior through more direct authoritarian methods as well, by putting out-of-favor executives on trial and letting their businesses fail. Park Chung Hee believed not only in the need for Korean "millionaires" but also in the need for a strong state to control their behavior. One month after coming to power in 1961, Park's regime passed the Law for Dealing with Illicit Wealth Accumulation and under a glare of publicity arrested a number of wealthy businessmen from the Syngman Rhee era. They were exempted from prosecution and from having their property confiscated if they established firms in industrial sectors dictated by the government and if they sold shares directly to the state.[57] To a greater extent than in Japan, the close ties between government and the business community were based on fear and the implicit threat that the state would use its coercive power if entrepreneurs did not take its direction.[58]

The willingness of the Korean state to intervene in the economy with these instruments meant that the broad course of that country's post-1961 economic development was very much dictated by the vision of economic bureaucrats rather than by the market. Thus, in the 1970s Korean planners decided to move out of labor-intensive industries like textiles and into heavy industry: construction, shipbuilding, steel, petrochemicals, and the like. In 1976, seventy-four percent of all manufacturing investment (of which government-directed loans were a major part) went to heavy industries; by 1979 this figure was over eighty percent.[59] Within a decade, the entire sectoral makeup of the Korean economy had shifted. This industrial forced march led to predictable consequences. For example, President Park urged Chung Ju Yung of Hyundai to get into shipbuilding in the early 1970s. The Korean shipbuilding industry, which had never constructed a vessel of more than 10,000 tons previously, jumped into the production of 260,000-ton very large crude carriers. The first ship had just come off the ways when the oil crisis of 1973 hit and global tanker overcapacity sent the market for large tankers into a tailspin.[60] A similar problem arose in the petrochemical industry, where the massive new capacity added during the 1970s far outstripped domestic Korean demand, and Korean producers were forced to dump their products in international markets.

Although the state played an important role in fostering large-scale industry, it would be a mistake to argue that there is no spontaneous social basis for large-scale organizations in Korea. Several other bridges to sociability have allowed Koreans to transcend the bounds of narrow familism. The first, as in southern China, is the lineage. Korea's extremely large kinship groups have meant that kinship-based recruiting can draw on extensive pools of individuals, thus mitigating the negative consequences of nepotistic employment.

A second bridge is regionalism, a phenomenon that has a counterpart in China but not in Japan. Korea's different regions have distinct identities that date back to before the unification of the country under the Silla kingdom in the seventh century. The country's political and business elites come disproportionately from the Kyongsang provinces (those surrounding the southern cities of Pusan and Taegu) and from the area around Seoul; by contrast, Chungchon, Cholla, and Kangwon provinces are relatively underrepresented.[61] Samsung's founder, Lee Byung Chul, came from the Yong-nam region. Although Samsung has implemented an ostensibly objective personnel system to recruit competent professional managers, a large number of Samsung employees also happened to come from Yong-nam.[62]

The further bridge to sociability beyond the family is university class. As in Japan, large corporations recruit heavily from Korea's most prestigious universities.[63] Samsung, in addition to favoring staff from Yong-nam, has also been known to give preference to graduates of Seoul National University. A considerable degree of solidarity develops among members of the same graduating class, a solidarity that remains with them as they move upward in the industrial workplace and constitutes the basis for later networking.

A fourth source of sociability outside the family, and one that does not have a counterpart in contemporary Japan, is the army. Since the Korean War, there has been universal male conscription in Korea. Virtually all young men go through the socialization provided by military or police service and are required to remain on reserve duty for a number of years thereafter. The army is, of course, the prototypical example of a large, rational, hierarchical organization, and the discipline of serving within its ranks is said by many to carry over into business life.[64] One would surmise that the army was particularly important as a socializing force in the early phases of industrialization, when peasants were first coming off the farm into an urban industrial workplace.

Finally, in Korea's contemporary urban culture, a number of new study or hobby groups have sprung up that are usually focused, like their American counterparts, on shared interests or activities of their members. These groups provide a space for sociability separate from the family and the workplace.

It is important to point out that nationalism and national identity are much more highly developed in Korea than they are in China, for all of the similarities between the two cultures. Korea has always been an isolated and hermetic state caught between two powerful neighbors, and the experiences of the past century—Japanese colonization, revolution, war, and the struggle with the North—have if anything reinforced the Koreans' sense of themselves as a distinct ethnic and national group. It is clear that nationalism played an important role in the thinking of leaders like Park Chung Hee. As in the case of the Japanese, economic success was pursued for reasons of national pride; nationalism was one motive, independent of economic rationale, for wanting large-scale industries in leading economic sectors.

Other interesting cultural differences within Korea may have an impact on economic life. For example, entrepreneurship is not distributed evenly among Korea's different regions but is concentrated in particular areas. Many entrepreneurs have come from what is now North Korea and from particular regions within the North. They have also come from the Seoul area and from Kyongsang in the South; Chungchong, Cholla, and Kangwon provinces, by contrast, are underrepresented. The reasons for these variations are unclear, since the parental backgrounds of successful entrepreneurs coming from the North and the South are quite different from one another. A common thread, however, may be that in both cases, the parental backgrounds are different from the rest of Korean society, thereby giving them something of an outsider status.[65]

There is, further, the question of the impact of Christianity on Korean economic development. Korea is the only country besides the Philippines in East Asia that has a significant Christian population. Christian conversion got underway during the Japanese occupation, when it constituted a somewhat less dangerous form of protest against Japanese power. After the Korean War, Korea's vital strategic tie with the United States proved a gateway for American cultural, and hence religious, influence. The Protestant population of Korea mushroomed after the war, and now it alone constitutes upwards of twenty percent of the total. Most of the new converts belong to fundamentalist denominations like the Assemblies of God. The largest Pentecostal church in the world, the Full Gospel Central Church, is located in Seoul and has a membership of 500,000.[66] Christians have been active out of proportion to their numbers in the political and social life of the country. The South's first president, Syngman Rhee, was a Christian; Christians were very active in the democratic protest movements that led ultimately to the fall of the military government in 1987; and three of the best universities in Korea today are Christian sponsored.[67]

Korean Protestants have certainly participated enthusiastically in economic life. Nearly half of the recent Korean immigrants in the United States, who have developed such a formidable reputation for hard work and entrepreneurship, are Christians. It is very difficult, however, to find evidence that Protestants played a role out of proportion to their numbers in promoting Korea's rapid economic development.[68] It may be that both Protestant and Confucian cultures promote similar kinds of economic and entrepreneurial values, so that the role of the former is much more difficult to discern in Korea than in, say, Latin America.[69]

The Korean case demonstrates that a competent and determined state can act decisively to overcome a cultural tendency toward small organizations and create large-scale industries in what it deems to be strategic sectors. In spite of the existence of other sources of sociability in Korea, it is clear that Korean industry would not be nearly as concentrated as it is in the absence of such prolonged activism on the part of the post-1961 Korean state.

Indeed, one could argue that the Koreans managed to shape their economy in the desired direction, while avoiding many of the pitfalls of French- or Italian-style industrial policy, by channeling governmental subsidies through private rather than state-owned companies. That the *chaebol* have remained more competitive than many state-owned or -subsidized firms in Europe or Latin America is due to the single-minded emphasis of their state overseers that they concentrate on and succeed in highly competitive overseas markets. The need to sell abroad under market conditions has imposed a discipline on them similar to that experienced by the German chemical industry in the 1920s when it was merged into a single cartel.

In opting for large scale, Korean state planners got much of what they bargained for. Korean companies today compete globally with the Americans and Japanese in highly capital-intensive sectors like semiconductors, aerospace, consumer electronics, and automobiles, where they are far ahead of most Taiwanese or Hong Kong companies. Unlike Southeast Asia, the Koreans have moved into these sectors not primarily through joint ventures where the foreign partner has provided a turnkey assembly plant but through their own indigenous organizations. So successful have the Koreans been that many Japanese companies feel relentlessly dogged by Korean competitors in areas like semiconductors and steel. The chief advantage that large-scale *chaebol* organizations would appear to provide is the ability of the group to enter new industries and to ramp up to efficient production quickly through the exploitation of economies of scope.[70]

Does this mean, then, that cultural factors like social capital and spontaneous sociability are not, in the end, all that important, since a state can intervene to fill the gap left by culture? The answer is no, for several reasons.

In the first place, not every state is culturally competent to run as effective an industrial policy as Korea is. The massive subsidies and benefits handed out to Korean corporations over the years could instead have led to enormous abuse, corruption, and misallocation of investment funds. Had President Park and his economic bureaucrats been subject to political pressures to do what was expedient rather than what they believed was economically beneficial, if they had not been as export oriented, or if they had simply been more consumption oriented and corrupt, Korea today would probably look much more like the Philippines. The Korean economic and political scene was in fact closer to that of the Philippines under Syngman Rhee in the 1950s. Park Chung Hee, for all his faults, led a disciplined and spartan personal lifestyle and had a clear vision of where he wanted the country to go economically. He played favorites and tolerated a considerable degree of corruption, but all within reasonable bounds by the standards of other developing countries. He did not waste money personally and kept the business elite from putting their resources into Swiss villas and long vacations on the Riviera.[71] Park was a dictator who established a nasty authoritarian political system, but as an economic leader he did much better. The same power over the economy in different hands could have led to disaster.

There are other economic drawbacks to state promotion of large-scale industry. The most common critique made by market-oriented economists is that because the investment was government rather than market driven, South Korea has acquired a series of white elephant industries such as shipbuilding, petrochemicals, and heavy manufacturing. In an age that rewards downsizing and nimbleness, the Koreans have created a series of centralized and inflexible corporations that will gradually lose their low-wage competitive edge. Some cite Taiwan's somewhat higher overall rate of economic growth in the postwar period as evidence of the superior efficiency of a smaller, more competitive industrial structure.

There are other problems more closely related to the question of culture. The poor fit between large scale and Korea's familistic tendencies has probably been a net drag on efficiency. The culture has slowed the introduction of professional managers in situations where, in contrast to small-scale Chinese businesses, they are desperately needed. Further, the relatively low-trust character of Korean culture does not allow Korean *chaebol* to exploit the same economies of scale and scope in their network organization as do the Japanese *keiretsu*. That is, the *chaebol* resembles a traditional American conglomerate more than a *keiretsu* network: it is burdened with a headquarters staff and a centralized decision-making apparatus for the *chaebol* as a whole. In the early days of Korean industrialization, there may have been some economic rationale to horizontal expansion of the *chaebol* into unfamiliar lines of business, since this was a means of bringing modern management techniques to a traditional economy. But as the economy matured, the logic behind linking companies in unrelated businesses with no obvious synergies became increasingly questionable. The *chaebol*'s scale may have given them certain advantages in raising capital and in cross-subsidizing businesses, but one would have to ask whether this represented a net advantage to the Korean economy once the agency and other costs of a centralized organization were deducted from the balance. (In any event, the bulk of *chaebol* financing has come from the government at administered interest rates.) *Chaebol* linkages may actually serve to hold back the more competitive member companies by embroiling them in the affairs of slow-growing partners. For example, of all the varied members of the Samsung conglomerate, only Samsung Electronics is a truly powerful global player. Yet that company has been caught up for several years in the group-wide management reorganization that began with the passing of the conglomerate's leadership from Samsung's founder to his son in the late 1980s.[72]

A different class of problems lies in the political and social realms. Wealth is considerably more concentrated in Korea than in Taiwan, and the tensions caused by disparities in wealth are evident in the uneasy history of Korean labor relations. While aggregate growth in the two countries has been similar over the past four decades, the average Taiwanese worker has a higher standard of living than his Korean counterpart. Government officials were not oblivious to the Taiwanese example, and beginning in about 1981 they began to reverse somewhat their previous emphasis on large-scale companies by reducing their subsidies and redirecting them to small- and medium-sized businesses. By this time, however, large corporations had become so entrenched in their market sectors that they became very difficult to dislodge. The culture itself, which might have preferred small family businesses if left to its own devices, had begun to change in subtle ways; as in Japan, a glamour now attached to working in the large business sector, guaranteed it a continuing inflow of Korea's best and brightest young people.[73]

The great concentration of wealth in the hands of the owners of *chaebol* has also had the consequence feared by the KMT in Taiwan: the entry into politics of a wealthy industrialist. This happened for the first time with the candidacy of Chung Ju Yung, founder of Hyundai, for president in the 1993 election. There is, of course, nothing wrong with a Ross Perot–style billionaire's entering politics in a democracy, but the degree of concentrated wealth in the Korean business community has made other political actors on both the right and the left nervous. The result for Korea thus far has not been propitious; while losing the election to Kim Young Sam, the seventy-seven-year-old Chung was jailed in late 1993 on rather specious corruption charges—a warning to all would-be politicians among the business class that their participation in politics would not be welcome.[74]

Despite the apparent anomaly between its Chinese-style familistic culture and its large corporations, Korea continues to fit my overall hypothesis. That is, Korea, like China, is a familistic culture with a relatively low degree of trust outside kinship. In default of this cultural propensity, the Korean state has had to step in to create large organizations that would otherwise not be created by the private sector on its own. The large Korean *chaebol* may have been run more efficiently than the state-owned companies of France, Italy, and a number of countries in Latin America, but they were no less the product of subsidy, protection, regulation, and other acts of government intervention. While most countries would be quite happy to have had Korea's growth record, it is not clear that they could achieve it using Korean methods.

III

HIGH-TRUST SOCIETIES AND THE CHALLENGE OF SUSTAINING SOCIABILITY

CHAPTER 13

Friction-Free Economies

Why is it necessary to turn to a cultural characteristic like spontaneous sociability to explain the existence of large-scale corporations in an economy, or prosperity more generally? Wasn't the modern system of contract and commercial law invented precisely to get around the need for business associates to trust one another as family members do? Advanced industrialized societies have created comprehensive legal frameworks for economic organization and a wide variety of juridical forms, from individual proprietorships to large, publicly traded multinational enterprises. Most economists would add rational individual self-interest to this stew to explain how modern organizations arise. Don't businesses based on strong family ties and unstated moral obligations degenerate into nepotism, cronyism, and generally bad business decision making? Indeed, isn't the very essence of modern economic life the replacement of informal moral obligations with formal, transparent legal ones?[1]

The answer to these questions is that although property rights and other modern economic institutions were necessary for the creation of modern businesses, we are often unaware that the latter rest on a bedrock of social and cultural habits that are too often taken for granted. Modern institutions are a necessary but not a sufficient condition for modern prosperity and the social well-being that it undergirds; they have to be combined with certain traditional social and ethical habits if they are to work properly. Contracts allow strangers with no basis for trust to work with one another, but the process works far more efficiently when the trust exists. Legal forms like joint-stock companies may allow unrelated people to collaborate, but how easily they do so depends on their cooperativeness when dealing with nonkin.

The question of spontaneous sociability is particularly important because we cannot take these older ethical habits for granted. A rich and complex civil society does not arise inevitably out of the logic of advanced industrialization. On the contrary, as we will see in the upcoming chapters, Japan, Germany, and the United States became the world's leading industrial powers in large part *because* they had healthy endowments of social capital and spontaneous sociability, and not vice versa. Liberal societies like the United States have a tendency toward individualism and a potentially debilitating social atomization. As noted earlier, there is evidence that in the United States, trust and the social habits that underlay its rise to greatness as an industrial power have eroded significantly in the past half-century. Some of the examples from part II should serve as a warning: it is possible for societies to lose social capital over time. France's once-flourishing and complex civil society, for example, was later undermined by an overly centralizing government.

The countries we will examine in this part and in part IV are all high-trust societies, inclined toward spontaneous sociability and possessing dense layers of intermediate associations. In Japan, Germany, and the United States, powerful, cohesive, large-scale organizations have developed spontaneously primarily out of the private sector. Although the state on occasion has stepped in to bolster sagging industries, sponsored technological development, or operated large economic organizations like telephone companies and postal services, the degree of intervention has been relatively minor compared to the cases in part II. In contrast to the saddle-shaped distribution of organizations at the poles of family and state in China, France, and Italy, these societies have strong organizations in the middle. These nations have also tended to be, from the moment they first industrialized, leaders in the global economy and today are the wealthiest societies in the world.

In terms of industrial structure and their civil societies more generally, the countries analyzed here have more in common with each other than any does with more familistic societies like Taiwan, Italy, or France. The source of spontaneous sociability in each of these cases has very different historical roots. Japan's stem from family structure and the nature of Japanese feudalism; Germany's is related to the survival of traditional communal organizations like the guilds into the twentieth century; and that in the United States is the product of its sectarian Protestant religious heritage. As we will see in the chapters at the end of this part, the more communal nature of these societies is manifest at a micro- as well as a macrolevel, in the relationships that develop on the shop floor among workers, foremen, and managers.

Before considering these cases in detail, however, we need to step back and consider the economic function of trust and spontaneous sociability. There is no question that institutions like contract and commercial law are necessary preconditions for the emergence of a modern industrial economy. No one would argue that trust or moral obligation alone can take their place. But if we presume that such legal institutions exist, the presence of a high degree of trust as an additional condition of economic relations can increase economic efficiency by reducing what economists call transaction costs, incurred by activities like finding the appropriate buyer or seller, negotiating a contract, complying with government regulations, and enforcing that contract in the event of dispute or fraud.[2] Each of these transactions is made easier if the parties believe in each other's basic honesty: there is less need to spell things out in lengthy contracts; less need to hedge against unexpected contingencies; fewer disputes, and less need to litigate if disputes arise. Indeed, in some high-trust relationships, parties do not even have to worry about maximizing profits in the short run, because they know that a deficit in one period will be made good by the other party later.

In fact, it is very difficult to conceive of modern economic life in the absence of a minimum level of informal trust. In the words of the economist and Nobel laureate Kenneth Arrow,

Now trust has a very important pragmatic value, if nothing else. Trust is an important lubricant of a social system. It is extremely efficient; it saves a lot of trouble to have a fair degree of reliance on other people's word. Unfortunately this is not a commodity which can be bought very easily. If you have to buy it, you already have some doubts about what you've bought. Trust and similar values, loyalty or truth-telling, are examples of what the economist would call "externalities." They are goods, they are commodities; they have real, practical, economic value; they increase the efficiency of the system, enable you to produce more goods or more of whatever values you hold in high esteem. But they are not commodities for which trade on the open market is technically possible or even meaningful.[3]

We often take a minimal level of trust and honesty for granted and forget that they pervade everyday economic life and are crucial to its smooth functioning. Why, for example, do people not walk out of restaurants or taxicabs without paying their bills more often, or fail to add the customary fifteen percent tip to restaurant meals in the United States? Not paying your bills is, of course, illegal, and in some cases people might be deterred by the thought of getting caught. But if they were intent, as economists assert, simply on maximizing their incomes unconstrained by noneconomic factors like convention or moral considerations, then they ought to calculate every time they go into a restaurant or cab whether they could get away without paying. If the cost of cheating (in terms of embarrassment or, at worst, a minor legal run-in) were higher than the expected gain (a free meal), then a person would stay honest; if not, he or she would walk out. Were this kind of cheating to become more prevalent, businesses would have to bear higher costs, perhaps by stationing someone at the door to make sure customers did not leave before they paid or by demanding a cash deposit in advance. The fact that they typically do not do so indicates that a certain basic level of honesty, practiced as a matter of habit rather than rational calculation, is fairly widespread throughout the society.

It is perhaps easier to appreciate the economic value of trust if we consider what a world devoid of trust would look like. If we had to approach every contract with the assumption that our partners would try to cheat us if they could, then we would have to spend a considerable amount of time bulletproofing the document to make sure that there were no legal loopholes by which we could be taken advantage of. Contracts would be endlessly long and detailed, spelling out every possible contingency and defining every conceivable obligation. We would never offer to do more than we were legally obligated to in a joint venture, for fear of being exploited, and we would regard new and possibly innovative proposals from our partners as tricks designed to get the better of us. Moreover, we would expect that, despite our best efforts in the negotiations, a certain number of people would succeed in cheating us or defaulting on their obligations. We would not be able to resort to arbitration, because we would not trust third-party arbitrators sufficiently. Everything would have to be referred to the legal system for resolution, with all of its cumbersome rules and methods, or potentially even to the criminal courts.

That this description sounds increasingly familiar to American ears as a characterization of the general business environment is one indication of a rising level of distrust in U.S. society. There are, moreover, specific areas of American economic life that resemble this no-trust world more completely. The reason Americans found the Pentagon paying $300 for hammers and $800 for toilet seats in the 1980s can ultimately be traced back to the absence of trust in the defense contracting system. Defense contracting is a unique area of economic activity insofar as many weapons systems are one-of-a-kind products. Since they have few commercial counterparts, their prices have to be set through negotiation on a cost-plus basis rather than through markets. This system naturally invites manipulation and occasional fraud on the part of either the contractors or the government officials writing the contracts. One way of handling this problem is to cut red tape by trusting key Pentagon officials to use their best judgment in their procurement decisions, which would require tolerating occasional scandals and errors in judgment as a cost of doing business. Certain high-priority weapons have in fact been successfully developed in this fashion.[4] But routine procurement is done under the assumption that trust does not exist in the system: contractors will try to cheat taxpayers if at all possible, and government officials given any degree of discretion in dealing with contractors will abuse their freedom.[5] Costs have to be justified through extensive documentation, which requires both contractors and the bureaucracy to hire layers of auditors to keep track of them. All of this regulation saddles government procurement with enormous extra transaction costs, which is the single most important reason that military procurement is so expensive.[6]

As a general rule, trust arises when a community shares a set of moral values in such a way as to create expectations of regular and honest behavior. To some extent, the particular character of those values is less important than the fact that they are shared; both Presbyterians and Buddhists, for example, would likely find they had a great deal in common with their coreligionists and therefore form a moral basis for mutual trust. This is not always the case, however, since certain ethical systems encourage some forms of trust over others: societies of witches and cannibals are presumably fraught with certain internal tensions. In general, the more demanding the values of the community's ethical system are and the higher are the qualifications for entry into the community, the greater is the degree of solidarity and mutual trust among those on the inside. Thus Mormons and Jehovah's Witnesses, who have relatively high standards for community membership like temperance and tithing, would feel stronger mutual bonds than, for example, contemporary Methodists or Episcopalians, who allow virtually anyone into their communities. Conversely, communities with the strongest internal ties will have the weakest bonds with those outside. Hence the gulf between a Mormon and non-Mormon will be greater than between a Methodist and a non-Methodist.

It is in this context that the economic significance of the Protestant Reformation can be seen. The economic historians Nathan Rosenberg and L. E. Birdzell note that in the early capitalist period (from the late fifteenth century on) people had to outgrow firms based on kinship and separate their personal finances from their firm's finances. In this respect, a technical innovation like double-entry bookkeeping was indispensable. But technical advances were not, in themselves, enough:

> The need for a form of enterprise which could command trust and loyalty on some basis other than kinship was only one facet of a broader need: the rising world of trade needed a moral system. It needed a morality to support reliance on its complex apparatus of representation and promise: credit, representations as to quality, promises to deliver goods, or to buy goods in the future, and agreements to share in the proceeds of voyages. A moral system was also needed . . . to supply the personal loyalties necessary to the development of firms outside the family, as well as to justify reliance on the discretion of agents, ranging from ships' captains to the managers of remote trading posts and including merchants' own partners. The ethical system of feudal society had been built around the same military hierarchy as the rest of feudalism, and it did not meet the needs of the merchants. It was out of the turbulence of the Protestant Reformation that there developed a morality and patterns of religious belief compatible with the needs and values of capitalism.[7]

Religion can be an obstacle to economic growth, as when clerics rather than markets establish a "just" price for goods or declare a certain interest rate to be "usurious." But certain forms of religious life can also be extremely helpful in a market setting, because the religion provides a means of internalizing the rules of proper market behavior.

There is another reason that societies manifesting a high degree of communal solidarity and shared moral values should be more economically efficient than their more individualistic counterparts, which has to do with the so-called "free rider" problem. Many organizations produce what economists call public goods, that is, goods that benefit the members of the organization regardless of the amount of effort they contribute to their production. National defense and public safety are classic examples of public goods that are provided by the state and accrue to its citizens simply by virtue of citizenship. Smaller organizations also produce goods that are public with respect to its members. A labor union, for example, negotiates a higher wage that benefits all of its members, regardless of how militant they as individuals were, or even whether they paid their union dues.

As the economist Mancur Olson has pointed out, all organizations producing public goods of this sort suffer from the same inner logic: the larger they become, the greater the tendency is for individual members to become free riders. A free rider benefits from the public goods produced by the organization but fails to contribute his or her individual share to the common effort.[8] In a very small group, like a partnership of half a dozen lawyers or accountants, the free rider problem is not severe. A single partner slacking off will be noticed immediately by colleagues, and the failure to perform will have relatively large and noticeable consequences for the profitability of the group as a whole. But as the size of organizations increases, the output of the group affected by the actions of any one of its members decreases at the margin. At the same time, the probability that the free-riding individual will be caught and stigmatized falls. It is much easier for an assembly line worker in a factory employing thousands to fake sickness or to take extra-long breaks than in the small partnership, where the group members are highly dependent on one another.

The free rider problem is a classic dilemma of group behavior.[9] The usual solution is for the group to impose some form of coercion on its members to limit the free riding they can do. That is why, for example, unions demand closed shops and mandatory dues; otherwise, it would be in the self-interest of any individual member to leave the union and break the strike, or alternatively to skip the dues but benefit from the higher wage settlement. Needless to say, this also explains why governments resort to criminal sanctions to get people to serve in the military or to pay their taxes.

The problem of free riding could be mitigated in another way, however, if the group possessed a higher degree of social solidarity. People become free riders because they put their individual economic interests ahead of that of the group. But if they strongly identified their own well-being with that of the group, or even put the group's interests ahead, then they would be much less likely to shirk work or responsibilities. This is why family businesses are a natural form of economic organization. Much as many American parents feel that their teenage children have become free riders, family members usually contribute to the success of a family enterprise more energetically than if they were collaborating with strangers and do not worry nearly so much about questions of relative contributions and benefits. Victor Nee points out that free riding crippled the efficiency of the peasant communes established in the People's Republic of China under Mao. Dissolution of the communes in the late 1970s and their replacement with peasant households as the basic unit of agricultural production permitted a dramatic increase in productivity because it solved the free rider problem.[10]

It is particularly easy for an individual to identify with the aims of an organization over his or her narrow self-interest if the purpose of the organization is not primarily economic. Commando units and religious sects are examples of organizations in which individuals will be self-motivated to advance the group's interests ahead of their own. This is perhaps one reason that Weber's early Puritan entrepreneurs, or recent converts to Protestantism in Latin America, do so well: it is much harder to be a free rider when God (rather than, say, an accountant) is watching. But even in more ordinary kinds of organizations that serve economic ends, good managers learn to instill a certain sense of pride in their employees, a belief that they are part of something much larger than themselves. People feel better motivated to do their share if they believe that their company's purpose is, for instance, to push back the frontiers of information technology rather than, as former IBM chairman John Akers once said, to maximize their stockholder's return on equity (which was, of course, the truth).

While groups exhibiting a high degree of trust and solidarity can be more economically efficient than those lacking either, not all forms of trust and solidarity are necessarily advantageous. If loyalty overrides economic rationality, then communal solidarity simply leads to nepotism or cronyism. A boss's favoritism to his children or a particular subordinate is not good for organizations.

There are many groups exhibiting a high degree of solidarity that are highly inefficient from the standpoint of the economic welfare of the society as a whole. While groups and organizations are necessary for any sort of economic activity to take place, not all groups serve economic ends. Many groups are engaged in the redistribution rather than the production of wealth, from the Mafia and the Blackstone Rangers to the United Jewish Appeal and the Catholic church. Their purposes range from sinister to divine, but from an economist's point of view, all of them lead to "allocative inefficiencies," that is, a mismatching of resources to their most productive uses. Many important economic actors are cartels that seek to promote their own well-being by controlling the entry of other players into the market. Contemporary cartels include not just oil producers and suppliers of gold and diamonds but professional associations like the American Medical Association or the National Educational Association, which set standards for entry into the medical and teaching professions, respectively, or labor unions that regulate the entry of new workers into the labor market.[11] In a developed democracy like the United States, virtually all significant sectors of society are represented in the political process through well-organized interest groups. The latter seek to advance or protect their positions not merely through economic activity but through rent seeking or by exercising influence over the political process.

The countries of medieval and early modern Europe were in many respects highly communitarian societies, with a large number of overlapping sources of communal authority—princely, ecclesiastical, seigneurial, and local—constraining the behavior of individuals. Economic life in the towns was strictly regulated by traditional craft guilds that established qualifications for membership and limited both the number of new entrants into the craft and the types of work they could engage in. In the early phases of the industrial revolution, new enterprises had to be located outside the towns so as to escape the restrictions imposed by the guilds—an ironic upending of the aphorism *Stadtluft macht frei* ("city air liberates"). Many of the milestones of advancing industrialization in Britain and France were marked by the destruction of the guilds and the liberation of economic activity from their authority.

Cartels, guilds, professional associations, unions, political parties, lobbying organizations, and the like all serve an important political function by systematizing and articulating interests in a pluralistic democracy. But although they usually serve the economic ends of their members by seeking to redistribute wealth to them, they seldom serve the broader economic interests of society as a whole. For this reason many economists regard the proliferation of such groups as a drag on overall economic efficiency. In fact, Mancur Olson has formulated a theory that maintains that economic stagnation can be traced to the growing proliferation of interest groups that occurs in stable democratic societies.[12] In the absence of shocks from the outside—wars, revolutions, or market-opening trade agreements—a society's organizational ability tends to go increasingly into the creation of new distributional cartels that inject stifling rigidities into the economy. Olson suggests that one of the reasons for British economic decline over the past century is the fact that, unlike its continental neighbors, Britain experienced continuous social peace in a way that permitted the steady accretion of efficiency-destroying groups.[13]

Societies that are good at producing wealth-creating economic organizations most likely are also good at creating wealth-redistributing interest groups that harm efficiency. The positive economic effects of spontaneous sociability have to be calculated net of the costs incurred as a result of interest group activity. There can be societies that are good at producing only interest groups without being able to create effective businesses, in which case sociability would have to be considered an overall liability. Medieval Europe resembled such a society in many ways, as do certain contemporary Third World societies that have an excess of parasitic employers' groups, labor unions, and community organizers and a dearth of productive corporations. While the argument has been made that the United States suffers increasingly from paralysis due to the proliferation of interest groups, it would be difficult to argue that the American propensity for association has historically been a liability for either its economic or political life.[14]

Since social groups in any society overlap and crosscut each other, what looks like a strong sense of social solidarity from one perspective can seem to be atomization, divisiveness, and stratification from another. Strongly familistic societies like China and Italy look highly communitarian when viewed from within the family but rather individualistic when one observes the rather low level of trust and mutual obligation between families. This is also true from the perspective of class consciousness. The British working class has always shown a greater degree of solidarity and militancy than its American counterpart. There has been a consistently higher level of trade union membership in Britain than America, a fact that has led some to argue that Britain is a less individualistic, more communally oriented society than the United States.[15] But that very class solidarity deepens the divisions between management and labor in Britain. Under such conditions, workers scoff at the idea that they and management together constitute one large family or team with common interests. Class solidarity can impede communitarian innovations in worker-management relations like work teams or quality circles.

By contrast, horizontal working-class solidarity exists to a much lesser degree in Japan than in Britain, and in this respect the Japanese would be said to be *less* group oriented than the British.[16] Japanese workers tend to identify with their companies rather than with their fellow workers; because they are company unions, Japanese trade unions are despised by their more militant brethren abroad. But the reverse side of the coin is a much higher degree of vertical enterprise solidarity in Japan, which is why we correctly think of Japan as more group oriented than Britain. This kind of vertical group solidarity would appear to be more conducive to economic growth than its horizontal alternative.

Clearly social solidarity is not always beneficial from the standpoint of economic well-being. In Schumpeter's phrase, capitalism is a process of "creative destruction," in which older, economically harmful or inefficient organizations have to be modified or eliminated and new ones created in their place. Economic progress demands the constant substitution of one kind of group for the other.

Traditional sociability can be said to be loyalty to older, long-established social groups. Medieval producers following the economic doctrines of the Catholic church fall into this category. Spontaneous sociability, by contrast, is the ability to come together and cohere in new groups, and to thrive in innovative organizational settings. Spontaneous sociability is likely to be helpful from an economic standpoint only if it is used to build wealth-creating economic organizations. Traditional sociability, on the other hand, can frequently be an obstacle to growth.

With these general considerations in mind, we will proceed to an analysis of the society that displays perhaps the greatest degree of spontaneous sociability among contemporary nations: Japan.

CHAPTER 14

A Block of Granite

After a generation of competition with Japanese firms, Americans have come to a much better understanding of the nature of the Japanese economy and the ways in which it differs from that of the United States. But the differences between the Japanese economy and that of a Chinese society, or indeed of any other familistic society, are much less clear, and they are critical to understanding how culture influences an economy. Many Americans and Europeans assume that most Asian economies are similar, a view that is encouraged by promoters of the idea of an "East Asian Miracle" on both sides of the Pacific, who sometimes speak as if Asia were a single, undifferentiated cultural area. In fact, however, Japan is more like the United States than it is like China with respect to spontaneous sociability and the capacity of the society to create and manage large-scale organizations. The differences between Japanese and Chinese culture, particularly with regard to family structure, reveal the profound impact of Japanese culture on economic life and clarify the basis for its similarity to the high-trust societies of the West.

The first thing that is notable about Japan's modern industrial structure is that it has always been dominated by very large organizations. Its rapid rise from a predominantly agricultural society to a modern industrial power following the Meiji Restoration of 1868 is closely associated with the growth of the *zaibatsu,* the huge family-owned conglomerates like Mitsubishi and Sumitomo that dominated Japanese industry before World War II. (*Zai* in Japanese means "fortune" or "money," while *batsu* is a clique.) Before World War II, the ten largest *zaibatsu* accounted for fifty-three percent of total paid-in capital in the financial sector, forty-nine percent in the heavy industrial sector, and thirty-five percent for the economy as a whole.[1] By the end of the war, the "big four"—Mitsui, Mitsubishi, Sumitomo and Yasuda—controlled fully one-quarter of the paid-in capital of all businesses in Japan.[2]

The *zaibatsu* were dissolved under the American occupation but gradually reconstituted themselves as the present-day *keiretsu.* Japanese industry continued to grow in scale, and today the Japanese private sector is far more highly concentrated than is that of any Chinese society. The ten, twenty, and forty largest Japanese companies are second in size, in terms of revenues, only to those of the United States; the top ten are twenty times larger than those of Hong Kong, and fifty times larger than those of Taiwan.

One might object that while Japanese companies are much larger, on average, than Chinese ones, they are not large in a broader global comparison. Table 1, for example, measures the size of the largest firms in ten industrialized nations in terms of employment rather than revenues. The largest Japanese firms are, on average, smaller than those of the United States, Germany, Britain, and France. As a percentage of total industrial employment, Japanese firms are the least concentrated of the entire group, and particularly so when compared to the smaller European countries like Holland, Switzerland, and Sweden.

This comparison is misleading, however, because of the nature of Japanese network organizations. Many of the Japanese companies considered in the table as separate organizations, such as Mitsubishi Heavy Industries (MHI) and Mitsubishi Electric Co. (MELCO), are linked to each other in *keiretsu* relationships. Not quite independent and yet far from integrated, the *keiretsu* allows nominally separate organizations to share capital, technology, and personnel in ways not open to firms outside the network.

TABLE I

Aggregate Industrial Concentration:

Japan versus Other Industrialized Nations, 1985

	AVERAGE SIZE OF LEADING FIRMS (NUMBER OF EMPLOYEES)		LEADING FIRM EMPLOYMENT AS PERCENTAGE OF TOTAL EMPLOYMENT	
NATION	*Top 10*	*Top 20*	*Top 10*	*Top 20*
Japan	107,106	72,240	7.3	9.9
United States	310,554	219,748	13.1	18.6
West Germany	177,173	114,542	20.1	26.0
United Kingdom	141,156	108,010	23.1	35.3
France	116,049	81,381	23.2	35.3
South Korea	54,416	N.A.	14.9	N.A.
Canada	36,990	26,414	15.3	21.9
Switzerland	60,039	36,602	49.4	60.2
Holland	84,884	47,783	84.5	95.1
Sweden	48,538	32,893	49.4	66.9

Source: F. M. Scherer and David Ross, Industrial Market Structure and Economic Performance, 3d ed. (Boston: Houghton Mifflin, 1990), p. 63.

To illustrate the impact of networks on firm size, in the late 1980s Toyota, Japan's largest industrial corporation by sales, produced 4.5 million cars per year with 65,000 workers. General Motors, by contrast, produced 8 million cars with 750,000 workers—that is, less than twice as many cars with more than ten times as many workers.[3] Part of this difference is due to Toyota's greater productivity: Toyota's Takaoka facility required sixteen man-hours to produce a car in 1987 compared to thirty-one hours at GM's Framingham, Massachusetts, plant.[4] But even more important is the fact that Toyota subcontracts out the lion's share of the assembly for each car, while GM is a vertically integrated company that owns many of the parts suppliers for its vehicles. Toyota is the lead company in a so-called vertical *keiretsu,* itself performing only design and final assembly functions. It is, however, linked with hundreds of independent subcontractors and parts suppliers in an informal but durable network. Through its *keiretsu* partners, Toyota is able in effect to reap the scale economies in design, manufacturing, and marketing of an organization half GM's size but with less than one-tenth the number of workers. It is, by any account, a very large organization.

While Japan has many large corporations, it may surprise some to know that it also has a sizable and important small-business sector. Indeed, the existence of the small-company sector in Japan has been one of the more durable aspects of industrial structure there and one that has been extensively studied. According to the census figures of 1930, nearly a third of the Japanese working population could be classified as small, independent entrepreneurs, and thirty percent of all manufacturing output came from factories with fewer than five workers.[5] These businesses tended to be family owned and managed, just like their Chinese counterparts, and included retail stores, restaurants, noodle shops, cottage industry (including many small machinist's shops in the metalworking sector), and traditional crafts like weaving and pottery. Many people believed that these small, traditional firms would disappear with progressing industrialization, as they did in India. But by and large, they did not. Traditional independent weavers, for example, expanded market share more rapidly than large textile firms in the 1930s.[6] Between 1954 and 1971, the number of manufacturing firms in Japan doubled, while increasing by only twenty-two percent over the same period in the United States.[7] In 1967, sixteen percent of manufacturing employment in Japan was in firms with fewer than ten workers, whereas the corresponding figure for the United States was only three percent.[8] David Friedman has gone so far as to argue that dynamic small businesses, and not the well-known giant corporations, are the essence of the Japanese "miracle."[9] In this respect, Japanese industrial structure would appear to bear many similarities to those of Chinese societies, with their myriad small family businesses.

The latter position, however, overstates and misrepresents the significance of small businesses in Japan. Although the number of small Japanese manufacturing firms is impressive, many of them are not truly independent companies but are linked with larger firms in *keiretsu* relationships. The *keiretsu* involves a much more permanent and intimate relationship than the networks of small firms in an American industrial district like Silicon Valley. The suppliers and subcontractors to the large firms are very heavily dependent on them not only for orders but often for personnel, technology, and management advice as well. Because the *keiretsu* relationship imposes reciprocal moral obligations to deal with one another, they are not free to sell their products where they wish or to get the most competitive price. They behave, in fact, much more like captive suppliers in a vertically integrated American firm than like truly independent small companies.

Moreover, it is a mistake to argue that small companies are the leading edge of the Japanese economy, as they are in Taiwan or Hong Kong. The vast bulk of small Japanese businesses are situated in relatively unglamorous, inefficient sectors like retail, restaurants, and other services. In manufacturing, they tend to be clustered in the machine tool industry, which has always lent itself to small scale in Japan and elsewhere. Most of the important technological innovations and productivity gains, however, have been achieved by Japan's large, highly competitive, export-oriented companies.

Consider, for example, the computer industry. This is preeminently a sector in which large scale is not an advantage, and indeed often constitutes a liability. In the United States, IBM's domination of the computer business, which reached over eighty percent of the total U.S. market in the 1970s, was steadily eroded by a series of much smaller start-up companies. One such firm was Digital Equipment (DEC), which began to undercut IBM's mainframe business in the 1970s with a new generation of technology, the minicomputer. Then in the late 1980s, DEC's minicomputer market was in turn undercut by still newer and smaller producers of workstations, such as Sun Microsystems and Silicon Graphics. In each case, the large company's product line and innovative capacity had ossified, and the leading-edge technological development was carried out by smaller and nimbler competitors.

The Japanese computer industry, by contrast, is dominated by four large producers—the Nippon Electric Company (NEC), Hitachi, Fujitsu, and Toshiba—which have been responsible for virtually all the indigenous technological innovation in the past generation. There is no dynamic second tier of small, aggressive Japanese start-up companies that are constantly challenging the dominance of the big four. Because Japanese industry lacks this tier, large companies have had to purchase small American ones to establish footholds in new markets (as when Fujitsu purchased the small Silicon Valley firm HAL Computer Systems in 1990)[10] or form alliances with larger ones (as in the case of the Hitachi-IBM and Fujitsu-Sun alliances announced in 1994).[11] While a small company will occasionally come out of nowhere in Japan and rise to be an industry leader, as the Honda Motor Company did in the 1950s and 60s, such instances are rare. Small companies frequently participate in innovative projects but often under the direction of a larger partner that is the true source of leadership and dynamism. The ability of small businesses in Japan to cooperate with large ones in *keiretsu* networks is in itself an important organizational innovation, but it does not contradict the argument that the Japanese economy is dominated, quantitatively and in terms of innovation and dynamism, by very large-scale organizations.

A second notable feature of Japanese industrial structure closely related to the first is that family management was replaced by professional management relatively early in Japan's economic development. Japan was quick to adopt the corporate form of organization; today, there are many professionally managed, multidivisional, hierarchical, publicly owned Japanese companies. The adoption of the corporate form of organization, in turn, permitted Japanese companies to grow to very large size and was a permissive condition of their rise in sectors characterized by large scale, capital intensity, and complicated manufacturing processes.

As in other parts of the world, virtually all Japanese corporations started out as family businesses. This was especially true of the great *zaibatsu*, which remained family owned until their dissolution after the war. The eleven branches of the Mitsui family, for example, held ninety percent of their wealth collectively and had a formal arrangement for acting as a collective entity. The Mitsubishi *zaibatsu* was controlled by the two branches of the Iwasaki family, with control alternating between the branches, and Sumitomo interests were directed by the single head of the family.[12]

But while the *zaibatsu* remained family owned until the end, they had moved to professional management much earlier. The *banto* was a hired executive, often unrelated to the controlling family, who was brought in to oversee the family business. In sharp contrast to China, the role of the *banto* was solidly established in Japan well before the Meiji Restoration and the beginning of industrialization.[13] By the eighteenth century, the traditional merchants of Osaka, for example, had established a pact among themselves not to turn their businesses over to their children, and they made extensive use of the *banto* instead. The *banto* went through an apprenticeship much as in a traditional craft occupation, and though their status was like that of a vassal to a feudal lord, they were given a large degree of autonomy in managerial decision making. Indeed, awareness of the dangers of excessive familism is evident in an old Japanese proverb: "The fortune made through the hard work of the first generation is all lost by the easygoing third generation."[14] Nepotism certainly exists in Japan, but it appears to be much less prevalent than in China. Many large Japanese firms prohibit employees from marrying, and entry into firms is usually based on objective criteria like university credentials or entrance exams.[15] The unfamilial orientation of Japanese businessmen is reflected in the determination of Soichiro Honda (founder of the Honda Motor Company) not to let his sons into the business, lest it become a dynasty.[16]

The professionalization of management occurred in several ways. In traditional family firms before the Meiji Restoration, salaried managers were delegated top authority for long periods of time; in the twentieth century, the level of education and sophistication of such executives rose steadily. In newer firms established after 1868, the original founder-entrepreneur would rule the company in cooperation with professional middle managers. This pattern was common to China also, but the second generation would tend to recede into the background as passive shareholders, while effective control passed to salaried managers. Finally, in joint-stock companies not controlled by a single family, the professional managers would frequently come to own equity stakes in the business and sometimes rise to become exclusive owners as well.[17] While the different *zaibatsu* moved to professional management at different points—it happened much earlier in the Mitsubishi combine than for the more traditionally oriented Mitsui, for example—virtually all of them had ceased relying on family members for top managerial positions by the 1930s.[18]

The shift from family to public ownership in Japan took somewhat longer to accomplish. Although the family owners of the *zaibatsu* and other businesses had gotten out of management early on, they were reluctant to give up ownership and formal control of their companies. Despite the introduction of legal provisions for joint-stock companies early on in the Meiji period, many family owners continued to hold their shares very closely. Occasionally branch families and unrelated employees were allowed to buy equity stakes, but these were usually small and encumbered with legal restrictions, left over from the preceding Edo period, as to their voting rights and disposition. Such inequalities in shareholder voting rights were abolished as a result of the Commercial Law of 1893 and the Civil Law of 1898.[19] Thereafter, to avoid dilution of family control, many families made arrangements so that the shares would be held collectively, precluding a descendant from selling off his or her stake to outsiders. Within *zaibatsu* families, there were usually arrangements by which proceeds from investments could be reinvested only with companies affiliated with the *zaibatsu*.[20]

Family ownership of large companies in Japan ended abruptly with the American occupation in 1945. The New Deal administrators advising General Douglas MacArthur believed that the large concentrations of wealth represented by the *zaibatsu* holdings were undemocratic and a source of support for Japanese militarism (this was one of the weaker ideological assumptions they brought with them). The owners of the large family trusts were ordered to deposit their equity stakes with the Commission for Dissolution of Zaibatsu, which then sold them to the public.[21] At the same time, the shareholders and top management of the *zaibatsu* who had overseen their operations before and during the war were purged. The huge management vacuum left at the top of many large Japanese corporations was filled for the most part by younger middle managers without particularly large equity stakes in their companies. The *zaibatsu* networks quickly reconstituted themselves as *keiretsu* under these new managers, but ownership had already become highly deconcentrated. Land reform, which broke up large agricultural estates, a steep tax on personal assets, and the deflation of equity values as a result of the war left few large fortunes available to flow into the void.[22]

The result of these developments was the emergence of Japanese firms in the postwar period that more closely fit the description of the modern corporation set forth by Berle and Means than they did in the prewar period. Japanese businesses were, for the most part, professionally managed, with publicly dispersed ownership and, consequently, a disjuncture between ownership and management. Japan came to have one of the lowest percentages of family ownership (in terms of total market capitalization) among the industrialized countries, with only fourteen percent of all equity being owned by families or individuals in 1970.[23] While Japanese industry is highly concentrated, ownership is much less so. Most Japanese corporations are owned by other institutions: pension funds, banks, insurance companies, and other corporations (particularly within the company's own *keiretsu,* where cross-shareholding is commonly practiced). As they grew in scale, Japanese companies also abandoned the hub-and-spoke system of organization prevalent in many family-managed businesses for a hierarchical, multidivisional table of organization.

The widespread use of professional managers even in preindustrial times has allowed the Japanese to create extremely durable economic organizations. The roots of the Daimaru department store chain go back a couple of centuries to the Shimomura family, and the Mitsui and Sumitomo *keiretsu* are even older. Sumitomo was founded in 1590 by Soga Riemon as a copper-crafting shop in Kyoto, which quickly developed mining, banking, and trading interests. While many Japanese small enterprises are constantly being created and going out of business, large Japanese firms have a great deal of staying power—a staying power enhanced by the mutual support they receive from their *keiretsu* partners. Large firms and institutional continuity have meant that the Japanese can create brand names quite easily. In sharp contrast to the Chinese, they have established extensive marketing organizations in the United States, Europe, and other target markets.

Was the large scale of Japanese industry the result of deliberate government policy, or did it arise out of cultural factors? As in Korea, the answer is that the state did play a certain role in promoting large-scale industry, but the scale of Japanese firms would have grown very large even in the absence of state intervention. In the early Meiji period, the government played an important role in promoting some of the large *zaibatsu* family fortunes. The *han* industries, owned prior to 1868 by the local provincial governments, were abolished in 1869, and their assets in effect were privatized. Other businesses owned by the central government in Tokyo were sold off a few years later after the failure of Japan's initial effort at state capitalism. Together, these former state industries formed the core of a number of large-scale private firms. In addition, the Japanese government worked closely with the *zaibatsu,* directing credit and business toward them. This pattern was repeated again after World War II, when the Bank of Japan guaranteed credit for a number of large city banks, which passed on their lower borrowing costs to their large corporate clients. The Japanese government is known for working hand in glove with large Japanese firms and has never developed the kind of adversarial posture toward big business that has characterized many American administrations.

The government's support for large-scale industry encouraged a trend that already existed in the Japanese private sector and in all likelihood would have continued to develop without the state's help. The Japanese state never played as direct or important a role in subsidizing large-scale industry as, for example, the Korean or French governments have. State support was more episodic and does not correlate particularly well with periods of growth in large-scale industry. Because Japanese firms could institutionalize themselves with professional managers and administrative hierarchies, they never faced the problems of breakdown or loss of entrepreneurial energy after the founder's passing that Chinese enterprises did. Many of the unique organizational characteristics of large Japanese companies—the practices of network organization, relational contracting, lifetime employment, cross-shareholding, and the like—were all innovations of the Japanese private sector.

Large firms and administrative hierarchies are not always an advantage. We have already noted how Japan lacks a tier of aggressive small companies in computers and other high-tech sectors. The four large Japanese computer companies were deliberately created on the model of IBM, and all suffer from IBM's inertia and lack of nimbleness in identifying new technologies and markets. Within a large Japanese corporate bureaucracy, decision making is notoriously slow; the need for consensus in Japanese culture has led to a process by which even routine, low-level decisions have to be approved by half a dozen or more higher administrative levels before being sent down again.[24] Small family firms with less structured administrations can often respond more quickly.

On the other hand, large scale has allowed Japan to play in key sectors from which it otherwise would have been excluded. It is hard to imagine that the assaults on the American auto and semiconductor industries that were mounted in the 1970s and 1980s by Japanese companies could have been carried out by any but the very largest corporations, ones with extensive technological resources and deep pockets. In order to build market share, Japanese semiconductor companies like NEC and Hitachi had to cut prices and, consequently, profit margins sharply, to the point where they were frequently accused by their American competitors of dumping.[25] They were able to get through this period of low profitability because their semiconductor operations could be cross-subsidized by other more profitable divisions like consumer electronics. In addition, they had not only corporate treasuries but financial backing from their *keiretsu* partners. Korean semiconductor companies can aspire to duplicate this feat because they are large, concentrated companies to an even greater extent than their Japanese counterparts. But it is very hard to imagine even large Hong Kong or Taiwanese firms pulling this off without substantial state support.

The Japanese firm was able to grow beyond a family business early on because the Japanese family is very different from its Chinese counterpart. It is to this issue that we turn now.

CHAPTER 15

Sons and Strangers

The Japanese early on developed the habit of associating in ways that were not based on kinship. Although the Japanese had clans in feudal times, which are often compared to Chinese lineages, these groups did not claim ancestry from a common progenitor but were united instead around loyalty to a particular feudal lord, or *daimyo*. The Japanese thus developed a range of nonkinship-based associations centuries before the industrial revolution, at approximately the same time that similar groups existed in Europe.

The fundamental basis for the greater Japanese proclivity for spontaneous sociability is the structure of the Japanese family. The bonds uniting the Japanese family are much weaker than those of the Chinese family. It is smaller and weaker, in terms of traditional obligations, than extended families in central Italy. Indeed, in emotional terms, the Japanese family probably exerts less of a pull than the American family, though it is clearly more stable. The distinct lack of familism in Japan permitted the growth of other sorts of associations, particularly at the beginning of the Edo period (1600–1867), that is the basis for Japan's extraordinary degree of spontaneous sociability in the twentieth century.

Japan is, of course, a Confucian society, and shares many values with China, from which much of Japanese culture was adopted.[1] For both the Japanese and Chinese, filial piety is a central virtue; children owe extensive obligations to their parents that do not exist in Western cultures. A son is traditionally supposed to feel greater affection for his parents than for his wife. In both cultures there is a strong tendency to defer to age, as reflected in the Japanese seniority-based compensation system. Both cultures practice ancestor worship and, under their traditional legal systems, recognize joint family responsibility before the law. In both systems, women were held strictly subordinate to men.

But there are very important differences in family ideology between the two cultures that have had a direct impact on modern economic organization. Central to this distinction is the Japanese *ie,* usually translated as "household," and which differs significantly from the Chinese *jia,* or family.

The Japanese *ie* usually, but not necessarily, corresponds to a biological family. It is more like a trust for the assets of the household, which are used in common by family members, with the head of the household acting as chief trustee.[2] What is important is the continuity of the *ie* through the generations; it is a structure whose positions could be occupied temporarily by the actual family acting as its custodian. But these roles do not have to be played by biological relatives.

For example, the position of household head is usually passed from father to eldest son, but the *role* of eldest son could be played by any outsider to the family, provided he had undergone the appropriate legal procedures for adoption.[3] In Japan, in sharp contrast to China, the practice of adoption of nonbiological outsiders is both widespread and relatively easy. The most common way that this occurred was for a family without a male heir, or with an incompetent one, to marry a daughter to a son-in-law, who would subsequently take his wife's family's surname. He would then inherit the *ie*'s wealth and would be treated no differently than if he had been born into the family. This would continue to be true even if a son were born to the family subsequently.[4] In ancient times Japanese families did not exhibit the strict patrilineality of their Chinese counterparts, with some court families practicing matrilineal-uxorilocal marriage (inheritance and residence passed through females).[5] Occasionally even a servant would be adopted into the household. For many *ie,* the nonrelated servants living under the same roof would have a more intimate relationship with the family than blood relatives living in separate households and could become ritual kin by worshipping the family ancestors and being buried in the family grave.[6]

Not only was it possible to adopt a son, but there was a certain wariness in the culture about nepotism, reflected in a number of sayings warning against the dangers of lazy or incompetent sons. Evidently it was fairly common to pass over a biological son who for one reason or another was deemed unfit to succeed to leadership of the *ie,* in favor of a total stranger. This practice was more common in premodern times than since the Meiji Restoration, particularly in merchant and *samurai* households (which had more assets to pass on). The rate at which natural sons were passed over in favor of adoptive heirs for such groups ranges from twenty-five to thirty-four percent.[7] These sorts of practices were far less common in China.

In Japan, no stigma attaches to adoption outside the kinship group.[8] The adopting family is not publicly humiliated, as in China; indeed, the Chinese occasionally criticized Japan's "promiscuous" adoption practices as "barbarous" and "lawless" because of their openness to strangers.[9] It is quite common for younger sons in socially prominent families to themselves become *mukoyoshi,* or adopted sons, in other families. For example, Eisaku Sato, prime minister of Japan from 1964 to 1972 was an adopted son, coming himself from a prominent family (his brother, Nobusuke Kishi, had been prime minister some years before).[10] If we go back further into Japanese history, there are many other examples of adopted sons' rising to great prominence. Toyotomi Hideyoshi, the great shogun who reunified Japan at the beginning of the Tokugawa period, was the son of a peasant who was adopted into an aristocratic family. Uesugi Yozan, the *daimyo* of Yonezawa, was similarly adopted from another *daimyo* family.[11] These examples, which have no counterpart in Chinese history, can be multiplied indefinitely. According to one study, the percentage of adoptions within *samurai* families in the four feudal domains studied rose from 26.1 percent in the seventeenth century, to 36.6 percent in the eighteenth, to 39.3 percent in the nineteenth.[12]

The second great difference between Japanese and Chinese family structure concerns primogeniture. The Chinese, as we have seen, have practiced equal division of estates among male heirs for thousands of years. Japan, however, developed a system of primogeniture during the

Muromachi period (1338–1573) comparable to that of England and other European countries.[13] Under it, the bulk of the estate, including the family house and (if there was one) the family business, was inherited by the oldest son, or by the heir designated by the family as the oldest son.[14] This son had various obligations to his younger siblings; he might, for example, employ a younger brother in the family business or help him get established in another career. But he was not obliged to share the family wealth. The younger sons were not expected to remain in the household; indeed, they were required to establish separate households of their own. Hence families quickly divided in the second generation into *honke* and *bunke*—senior and junior branches, respectively. Moreover, the Chinese custom of having multiple wives was not as widespread in Japan. This did not mean that Japanese men were any more faithful to their wives—the practice of concubinage was common—but it did mean that the rich had fewer sons with a legal claim on the family inheritance.

The institution of primogeniture had several consequences for family and business life. In the first place, large family fortunes that had been acquired through trade or other forms of commercial activity were not dissipated within two or three generations, as they tended to be in China. Second, Japanese households were smaller. In China, the social ideal was a joint family in which the married sons lived in the same residence as their parents. Separate residence was something to be avoided and would occur only if the brothers' wives did not get along. In Japan, by contrast, it was normal for the younger brothers to move out of the family house once the eldest son had taken effective control of the *ie,* and to establish households of their own. The smaller household meant that the *ie* could not aspire to the same degree of self-sufficiency as the traditional Chinese "big family" but would be forced to go outside itself in regular economic dealings. It also implied a somewhat greater degree of mobility in general, as families would constantly ramify into new households.[15] As Chie Nakane points out, there is a relationship between family size and the practice of adoption: the Chinese do not need to adopt strangers as frequently because their large families and kinship networks provide them with a much larger pool of heirs if a father's biological sons do not work out.[16] Finally, the fact that younger sons did not inherit substantial parts of the family fortune meant that there was a constant supply of them for other sorts of activities, in the bureaucracy, in the military, or in commerce. These alternatives undoubtedly had an effect on the rate at which Japan urbanized, once opportunities for expanded urban employ-ment opened up.

The differences between Chinese and Japanese families are evident in naming conventions. There are many more surnames in Japan than in China, just as there are more Chinese than Korean surnames. The rela-tively small number of surnames in China is testimony to the inclusive-ness of family and lineage organizations. Chinese family names are very old, and many have been in use for over two thousand years. It is not un-common, after the passage of a long period of time, for all residents in a village to have the same last name. Families will seek out long-lost distaff branches and try to reincorporate them into the main line, and offshoots with only distant connections to a prominent lineage will try to prove close affinity. In addition, males of the same generation and surname usually have one common element in their given names. In Japan, by contrast, many families did not make use of surnames before the Toku-gawa period, so even fathers and sons were not linked by a common last name. Households tended to fissure into smaller ones more readily, and there was no great pressure on the *bunke* households to retain their ties with the dominant *honke* household. Because of the relatively easy divisi-bility of households and the fact that families could adopt outsiders read-ily, one or two prominent lineage names did not come to dominate a single geographic area.[17]

The differences between the Japanese *ie* and Chinese *jia* are replicated in larger social groups. As we have seen, beyond the family in China is the lineage, and occasionally a higher-order lineage that is like a family of clans. While Chinese lineages are one path to sociability beyond the immediate family, they are still based on kinship. In Japan there were larger organiza-tions called *dozoku,* usually translated as "clans" as well, but they were never based on kinship like their Chinese counterparts.[18] Nor were they territorially based or linked directly to landownership.[19] They were based, rather, on mutual obligations undertaken voluntarily during Japan's period of feudal warfare and internal chaos. Thus, for example, a samurai would become linked to a group of peasants in a village, providing them protec-tion from roving bands of robbers in return for a share of their agricultural output. Similar obligations would be undertaken by a lord or *daimyo* and the *samurai* who fought for him.[20] These obligations in time would take on a ritualized character, but they were not inheritable, and the organizations therefore did not survive without voluntary renewal from generation to generation, as did Chinese lineage associations. But neither were they American-style voluntary associations like the United Methodist church or the American Medical Association. Although entry into the relationship was voluntary, exit was not; the moral commitment of mutual obligation lasted an entire lifetime and took on the character of a religious vow.

From the beginning of Japan's feudal period, then, the character of Japanese society was very different from that of China. The former had relatively small and fragile families, while developing a significant number of nonkinship-based social organizations.[21] On the other hand, the strength of groups outside the family meant that ties within the family were weaker, particularly when viewed from a Chinese perspective. Chie Nakane reports that "even in pre-war times the behaviour of Japanese children toward their parents often surprised Chinese who visited Japan, because of the lack of respect toward parents as measured by Chinese standards."[22] Like the Chinese family, the Japanese family has been changing in response to urbanization and economic growth.[23] Unlike the situation in China, however, these changes make less difference to Japanese social and business organizations, since the latter were much less family based to begin with.

Iemoto refers to the heads of *ie*-like groups that are omnipresent in Japanese society. They are particularly important in traditional arts and crafts, like archery, swordsmanship, tea ceremony, Noh theater, Kabuki drama, flower arrangement, and the like. *Iemoto* groups are associations of unrelated people who behave as if they were related. A master plays the role of father, and disciples play the role of children; authority within the *iemoto* group is hierarchical and paternalistic, as in a traditional family. The most important social bonds are not horizontal ones between equals (such as, between the disciples of a given master) but the vertical ones between senior and junior.[24] This relationship is comparable to the situation in the Japanese family, where that between parents and children is much stronger than those between siblings. *Iemoto* groups are like modern Western voluntary associations insofar as they are not based on kinship; anyone can join them initially. But they are like families because relations within the group are not democratic but hierarchical and because the moral obligations taken on by joining are not so easily given up. Membership in the group is not hereditary, however, and cannot be passed on from father to son.[25]

The anthropologist Francis Hsu argues that *iemoto*-like groups are characteristic not only of the traditional arts and crafts, with which they are commonly associated, but constitute the structure of virtually all organizations in Japan, including business organizations.[26] Japanese political parties, for example, are divided up into quasi-permanent factions led by a senior member of the party. These factions do not represent different ideological or policy positions, as do, for example, the Black Caucus or the Democratic Leadership Council in the American Democratic party. Rather, they are *iemoto*-like groups based on the mutual obligations undertaken between the faction leader and his followers, based on arbitrary personal association. Japanese religious organizations also manifest this *iemoto*-like structure of disciples and followers. In contrast to China, where people visit whatever temples or shrines they please, most Japanese "belong" to a temple the way that Americans "belong" to a particular church, supporting it with charitable donations and developing a personal relationship with the monk or abbot in charge.[27] Hence religious life in Japan is more organized and sectarian than it is in China.

This form of social organization creates habits that are carried into the business world: while Japanese firms are frequently said to be "family-like," Chinese companies are literally families.[28] The Japanese corporation has an authority structure and sense of moral obligation among its members that is similar to what prevails in a family, but it also has elements of voluntarism, unconstrained by kinship considerations, that make it much more like a Western voluntary association than like a Chinese family or lineage.

The very different position of the family in Japanese society when compared to China was reinforced by Japanese Confucianism as well. Japan has been a Confucian country since at least the seventh century, when Prince Taishi Shotoku wrote a seventeen-article constitution for Japan based on Confucian principles.[29] Some authors speak of Japanese Confucianism as if it imposed the same imperatives as its Chinese counterpart, but in migrating to Japan, it assumed a rather different character in key respects.[30] Confucian doctrine supports a number of different virtues, and the relative emphasis that these virtues receive can have important implications for real-world social relationships. For example, of the five principal virtues in orthodox Chinese Confucianism, benevolence (*jen*), or the goodwill that people naturally feel within the family, and *xiao*, or filial piety, were of central importance.[31] Loyalty is also a virtue in Chinese Confucianism, but it is considered more of an individual than a social virtue: one is loyal to oneself and one's beliefs, not to a particular political source of authority. Moreover, for the Chinese, the virtue of loyalty had to be tempered by the virtue of justice, or righteousness (*i*).³² Presumably if an external source of authority demanding loyalty acted unjustly, the requirements of *jen* would not necessitate blind obedience.

When Confucianism was imported and adapted to Japanese conditions, however, the relative weight of these virtues changed considerably. In a document typical of the Japanese interpretation of Confucianism, the imperial injunction to the armed forces issued in 1882, the virtue of loyalty was elevated to the first rank, and the virtue of benevolence was dropped from the list altogether.³³ In addition, the meaning of loyalty changed subtly from its Chinese version. In China, there was an ethical sense that one had duties to oneself, that is, personal standards of behavior to which one had to conform that served as the functional equivalent of a Western individual conscience. Loyalty to a lord had to be reconciled to this sense of duty to one's own principles. Duty to a lord in Japan, by contrast, had a much more unconditional character.³⁴

The impact of the elevation of the virtue of loyalty to a cardinal position in Japanese Confucianism and the downgrading of filial piety can be seen in the case of conflicting social obligations. We have seen how in traditional China, when a father breaks the law, the son is usually not obligated to inform the police or other authorities. Ties to family trump ties to political authorities, even the authority of the emperor. In Japan, by contrast, a son in a similar dilemma would have a duty to report his father to the police: loyalty to the *daimyo* trumps loyalty to the family.³⁵ The central role of obligations to the family gave Chinese Confucianism its special character. For while orthodox Confucian doctrine stressed loyalty to the emperor and his supporting bureaucratic elite of gentlemen-scholars, the family loomed large as a bulwark protecting a significant degree of private autonomy from the control of the state. In Japan, just the opposite is the case: the political authorities have control over the family, and in theory no autonomous sphere is safe from their intrusion.³⁶

The contemporary manifestation of the loyalty of the *samurai* to his *daimyo* is the loyalty of the contemporary Japanese executive, or "salaryman," to his company. The salaryman's family gets sacrificed in the process: he is seldom home and sees his children only rarely while they are growing up; weekends and even vacations are devoted to the company rather than his wife and children.

The Japanese altered the Confucian teachings they imported from China to suit their own political circumstances. In China, even the emperor's authority was not absolute; it could be undermined altogether if he lost the "mandate of heaven" by behaving immorally. The succession of Chinese dynasties, none lasting more than a few hundred years, is testimony to the impermanence of Chinese political authority. In Japan, by contrast, there has been a single, unbroken dynastic tradition since the mythical founding of the country, and no political equivalent of the loss of the "mandate of heaven" by which a Japanese emperor could lose his throne. In importing neo-Confucianism, the Japanese were careful not to have its political dictates impinge on the prerogatives of the emperor and the political ruling class.

Moreover, those at the apex of the Japanese political system have tended to be soldiers, while China has traditionally been run by a bureaucracy of gentlemen-scholars. The militaristic class running Japan developed its own ethical code—*bushido,* or the so-called *samurai* ethic—that stressed the military virtues of loyalty, honor, and courage. Family ties were strictly subordinate to feudal ones.[37] When Chinese Confucianism of the Sung dynasty, particularly the Chu Hsi school, was brought to Japan at the beginning of the Tokugawa period, it was made consistent with *bushido* by giving greater emphasis to loyalty. Although there was debate over the relative priority of loyalty and filial piety at this time, the former in the end emerged on top.[38]

The elevation of the virtue of loyalty in Japanese Confucianism occurred many centuries ago, but after the Meiji Restoration, further efforts were made to promulgate Confucianism as an ideology that would support the government's goals of modernization and national unity.[39] This nineteenth-century Japanese effort to use Confucianism to shape culture is not dissimilar to the efforts of former prime minister Lee Kwan Yew of Singapore to do the same thing in the 1990s. The Imperial Injunction to Soldier and Sailors of 1882 and the Imperial Rescript on Education of 1890 both used Confucian language to emphasize the virtue of loyalty to the state.[40] At the turn of the century, Japanese officials and businessmen, facing the problem of labor shortages and the mobility of skilled workers, began to extend what had previously been a doctrine taught primarily to the upper classes to the society as a whole. The principle of loyalty was broadened to include not just the state but the company as well, and it was inculcated through the educational system and in the workplace.[41] Chalmers Johnson is correct in arguing that this was done as a political act to meet the needs of the Japanese state and society at a particular juncture in its history.[42] It was carried out successfully, however, only because the concept of loyalty was so deeply embedded in

Japanese culture. Whether similar doctrines could have been promulgated nearly as easily in China is unclear.

One of the consequences of these modifications of Chinese Confucianism in Japan is that citizenship and nationalism are much more important in Japanese than in Chinese society. I have noted that the Chinese family in some sense constituted a defensive bulwark against an arbitrary and rapacious state, and consequently Chinese family businesses instinctively thought of ways of hiding income from the tax collector. The situation is quite different in Japan, where the family is weaker and individuals are pulled in different directions by the various vertical authority structures standing above them. The entire Japanese nation, with the emperor at the top, is, in a sense, the *ie* of all *ie*s, and calls forth a degree of moral obligation and emotional attachment that the Chinese emperor never enjoyed. Unlike the Japanese, the Chinese have had less of a we-against-them attitude toward outsiders and are much more likely to identify with family, lineage, or region as with nation.

The dark side to the Japanese sense of nationalism and proclivity to trust one another is their lack of trust for people who are not Japanese. The problems faced by non-Japanese living in Japan, such as the sizable Korean community, have been widely noted. Distrust of non-Japanese is also evident in the practices of many Japanese multinationals operating in other countries. While aspects of the Japanese lean manufacturing system have been imported with great success into the United States, Japanese transplants have been much less successful integrating into local American supplier networks. Japanese auto companies building assembly plants in the United States, for example, have tended to bring over with them the suppliers in their network organizations from Japan. According to one study, some ninety percent of the parts for Japanese cars assembled in America come from Japan or from subsidiaries of Japanese companies in America.[43] This is perhaps predictable given the cultural differences between the Japanese assembler and the American subcontractor but has understandably led to hard feelings between the two. To take another example, while Japanese multinationals have hired a great number of native executives to run their overseas businesses, these people are seldom treated like executives at the same level in Japan. An American working for a subdivision of a Japanese company in the United States might aspire to rise within that organization but is very unlikely to be asked to move to Tokyo or even to a higher post outside the United States.[44] There are exceptions. Sony America, for example, with its largely American staff, is highly autonomous and often influences its parent in Japan. But by and large, the Japanese radius of trust can be fully extended only to other Japanese.

A further element of Japanese culture that permitted an added element of flexibility in business relationships was the long-standing Japanese tradition that actual power holders do not have to correspond to the nominal power holders. This again constitutes a major point of difference between Japanese and Chinese culture. In Japan, frequently the real holder of power is an anonymous person behind the scenes, who is content to exercise rule indirectly. The Meiji Restoration itself, which nominally restored the emperor Meiji to the throne at the expense of the shogunate, was engineered by a group of nobles from Satsuma and Choshu who acted in the emperor's name. The emperor himself wielded very little power, either before or after the restoration. In fact, the only reason that Japan has an unbroken dynastic tradition is that Japanese emperors have been powerless. In sharp contrast to China, where emperors often ruled, the real struggles for leadership in Japan occurred among the emperor's advisers, who maintained the facade of unbroken rule and legitimacy while contesting for real power so vigorously that the country was frequently plunged into civil war.

Like the widespread practice of adoption, the fact that real and nominal power holders do not have to correspond in Japan has been of great advantage in both political and business successions. In the late 1980s and early 1990s, many of the leaders exercising real power in the People's Republic of China were men in their eighties who had fought together with Mao as companions on the Long March or started their careers at the time of the 1949 revolution. There was no way that they could be gently kicked upstairs in favor of younger leaders, and the process of political reform in that country was delayed as the country waited for them to die.[45] (A similar situation exists in Korea, whose cultural practices are closer to those of China than Japan; North Korean politics was very much hostage to the longevity of its leader, Kim Il Sung.) The situation is much different in Japan, where leaders who grow too old or incompetent can be gently nudged aside into honorific positions, while real authority is assumed by younger people. The origins of this practice may perhaps be seen in the traditional peasant household. There, it was not uncommon for the family's head to move out of the main house to a smaller one in favor of his eldest son, when the latter was of an age at which he could assume leadership responsibilities. Although the Japanese respect old age, they also respect an old man who, like Soichiro Honda, understands when his time is up and relinquishes power to someone younger and more vigorous.[46]

Tracing the historical origins of Japanese institutions like the *ie* and *iemoto,* primogeniture, adoption rules, and so on are beyond the scope of this book. One critical factor, however, that many authors have pointed to in explaining why these institutions arose in Japan and not elsewhere in East Asia, has to do with the decentralized nature of political power in Japan.[47] Like Germany and northern Italy, but unlike southern Italy, France, and China, Japan was never ruled in its premodern period by a powerful, centralized government with a large, intrusive bureaucracy. Although Japan boasts an unbroken dynastic tradition, Japanese emperors have always been weak and were never in a position to subdue, as in France, the country's feudal aristocracy. Power was broadly distributed among a series of warring clans whose fortunes were constantly waxing and waning. The failure of central authority to consolidate control left a certain free space in which small associations could spawn. During the period of the seventh-century Taika reforms, for example, peasants could be attracted away from imperial estates by local lords in exchange for military protection from the imperial authorities.[48] As in Europe, prolonged periods of civil war gave rise to autonomous fiefdoms based on the exchange of protection for rice between samurai and peasant, in which kinship played no role. The idea of reciprocal obligation based on exchange of services is therefore deeply entrenched in Japanese feudal traditions.[49] Decentralized political power permitted considerable scope for private economic activity. Just prior to the Meiji Restoration, for example, many of the local *han* governments into which Japan had been divided in Tokugawa times sponsored their own industries, and a number of these *han* industries became the basis for the major industrial enterprises after 1868. Again as in Europe, fractured power permitted the growth of cities like Osaka and Edo (Tokyo), which sheltered a large and increasingly powerful merchant class.[50] Such a class could not arise in China without soon clashing with imperial authority and facing takeover or regulation by it.

Doubtless other aspects of Japanese culture have played a significant role in Japan's economic success. An important one concerns the special character of Japanese Buddhism. As Robert Bellah and others have shown, the doctrines of the Buddhist monks Baigan Ishida and Shosan Suzuki in the early Tokugawa period sanctified mundane economic activity and promulgated a commercial ethic in a manner comparable to early Puritanism in England, Holland, and America.[51] There was, in other words, the Japanese counterpart to the Protestant work ethic, formulated at around the same time as its European version. This phenomenon is closely related to the Zen tradition of perfectionism in everyday, secular activities—swordsmanship, archery, carpentry, silk weaving, and the like—that comes about through inner meditation rather than explicit technique.[52] Those who have seen the early Akira Kurosawa film *The Seven Samurai* will remember the figure of the Zen master swordsman who, after meditation, was able to disembowel his opponent with a single, graceful blow, before the latter was even aware of what had happened to him. This obsessive perfectionism, critical to the success of Japanese export industries, has religious rather than economic roots. Although other areas in Asia share the Japanese work ethic, few share Japan's tradition of perfectionism. I have not dwelt on these aspects of culture, however, since they are not specifically related to the proclivity for spontaneous sociability.[53]

We now need to understand the way in which these cultural practices play themselves out in the contemporary Japanese business world.

CHAPTER 16

Job of a Lifetime

Over the past two decades, the American economy has undergone a wrenching series of transformations as old, large companies began to downsize, restructure, and in some cases go out of business. "Reengineering the corporation" is the latest of a series of euphemisms used by management consultants to describe the firing of workers in the name of greater productivity. President Clinton and a host of other experts have warned Americans that they cannot expect to hold the same job over their lifetime and that they have no choice but to accept a higher level of economic change and insecurity in their working lives than their parents did.

It is interesting to speculate on what would happen, given current global economic conditions, if some occupying Martians suddenly declared that large American corporations were not allowed to lay off workers. Economists, once they regained their composure, would doubtless argue that this would spell the death of the U.S. economy, for without what they call "factor mobility," labor markets would not be able to adjust to rapid changes in demand or adopt more efficient technologies. But if the Martian overlords insisted, while being flexible on all other issues, one could imagine certain changes taking place. First, employers would start demanding greater flexibility in work rules and conditions, for if a worker was not needed in one job, the company would have great incentive to move him or her to a position where this person's labor could be of greater use. Second, there would be a strong incentive for companies to train their workers in-house to learn new skills and jobs, so that those whose jobs were no longer needed would not be a dead loss to the company. The structure of the companies themselves would change: they would have an incentive to move into a number of different activities such that workers no longer needed to make steel or textiles, could be moved to jobs in electronics or marketing. And finally, there would have to be some small-firm sector of the economy exempt from the lifetime employment rule, into which unneeded workers could be pushed as a last resort. It is doubtful whether these adjustments could compensate for the lost efficiency of companies unable to fire workers, but the change might buy one intangible commodity that could have a large bottom-line payoff: worker loyalty and a greater disinclination to free ride on the company's time.

The previous paragraph describes, in essence, the nature of the Japanese lifetime employment system that is practiced in large firms. Lifetime employment and the high degree of communal solidarity that exists within Japanese companies is one of the two distinctive and perhaps sui generis features of the Japanese economy. The other, discussed in the following chapter, has to do with the long-term stability of relations among different companies belonging to the same network organization. Both practices have a common source in the high degree of reciprocal moral obligation that the Japanese develop toward each other within the groups that they form spontaneously.[1] This sense of obligation is not based on kinship, as it is in China, nor does it arise out of legal contractual relationships. It is more like the moral obligation felt by members of a religious sect toward one another, where entry into the relationship is voluntary but exit much less so.

The first manifestation of reciprocal obligation exists in the Japanese labor market, and in the relations that Japanese workers and managers maintain with one another. In China, as we have seen, nonfamily employees are usually not eager to remain with family businesses for extended periods of time if they have other options. They know that they will probably not be accepted into top management as fully trusted and equal partners, nor do they feel comfortable in a relationship of day-to-day dependence with their employers. Employees in Chinese firms therefore tend to switch employers readily and ultimately hope to accumulate the capital to start their own businesses.

Large Japanese companies, by contrast, have institutionalized the practice of lifetime employment (in Japanese, *nenko*) since at least the early postwar period.[2] When an employee starts out his (or much less frequently, her) career with a given company, there is an agreement that management will continue to provide employment, while the employee for his part agrees not to jump ship to seek a better job or higher wage elsewhere. Although there may be a written contract, the force of the agreement does not lie in the contract itself. Indeed, insisting on putting the arrangement into legal language is usually considered very bad form and could result in the employee's being banned from the lifetime employment system altogether.[3] The penalties for violating the informal contract can be severe: an employee who leaves a lifetime employment firm for another because it pays better may subsequently be ostracized, as will a company that tries to raid employees of another firm. Enforcement of these sanctions rests not on law but on moral pressure alone.

The lifetime employment system has the effect of locking workers into a single track for most of their careers. Japanese society can be highly egalitarian and meritocratic, but the opportunity for social mobility usually comes only once in a lifetime, when a young person takes the grueling exam for entrance into a Japanese university. The exams are open to all and graded objectively, and it is on the basis of them that universities admit students. The quality of jobs available after college depends heavily on which school one went to (more so than one's actual performance at school), and once in the company, there is very little opportunity to leapfrog one's peers on the seniority ladder. The company may move workers around at will, but these individual workers usually have relatively little to say in the matter. A student who fails to reach the cutoff at the entrance exam stage is virtually barred thereafter from working in the large-company sector with its good jobs and salaries, though there may be opportunities for employment in the small-company sector.[4] (Japanese schoolchildren feel themselves under intense pressure to succeed, sometimes from the moment they enter kindergarten.) All of this stands in sharp contrast to the United States, where it has always been possible, even at an advanced age, to start over again after failure.

Workers are compensated in what would appear to be a totally irrational way from the standpoint of neoclassical economics.[5] There is no such thing as a principle of equal pay for equal work; rather, compensation is broadly based on seniority or other factors unrelated to the worker's performance, such as whether he has a large family to support.[6] Japanese companies pay a relatively larger share of total compensation to their workers in the form of bonuses. Some bonuses are granted as a reward for individual effort, but more often they are paid to larger groups—say, a section within a company or the company as a whole—in return for its collective efforts. A worker, in other words, knows that he will not be fired except in cases of extreme misbehavior, and he also knows that his compensation will rise only as a result of getting older, and not in return for increased individual effort on his part. If the worker proves incompetent or unfit in some other way, the company, rather than firing him, will often find some part of the enterprise where he can be safely tucked away. From the standpoint of management, labor becomes a large fixed cost that can be reduced only with great difficulty in times of economic downturn.[7]

This kind of compensation system would seem to invite free riding: any increased benefits arising from superior performance are in effect a public good with respect to the company as a whole, giving an individual an incentive to shirk his part of the burden. In only one other type of society was compensation delinked from performance in such a thoroughgoing way: the former communist world. And there, as we know well, it had the effect of undermining productivity and the work ethic completely.

That lifetime employment does not undermine the productivity or the work ethic in Japan, that it is in fact compatible with an extraordinarily vigorous work ethic, is testimony to the power of reciprocal obligation in Japanese society. For part of the tacit lifetime employment contract is the agreement that in return for stable employment and steady advancement, the worker will provide the company with his or her best effort. The employee, in other words, wants to do his best for the company because it looks after his long-term welfare. The sense of obligation is not formal or legal; it is entirely internalized, the result of a subtle process of socialization. Public education in Japan does not shy away from teaching children proper "moral" behavior, and moral education continues in the worker training programs sponsored by Japanese corporations.[8]

Communist states tried to inculcate a similar sense of moral obligation to the larger social group through constant propaganda, indoctrination, and intimidation. This kind of ideological hectoring not only proved ineffective in motivating people to work but promoted a widespread cynicism, which, since the fall of communism, has resulted in a pronounced lack of work values, public-spiritedness, and citizenship in Eastern Europe and the former Soviet Union.

Employees in the lifetime employment system resist free riding in part because moral obligation is a two-way street. Their loyalty and work are repaid in a variety of ways that go well beyond the commitment to job security. Japanese employers are famous for taking a paternalistic attitude toward the personal lives of their workers. A supervisor will attend weddings and funerals of the people he supervises and may even act as a go-between in arranging marriages. He is more likely than his Chinese counterpart to play a major role in seeing a worker through financial problems or an injury or death in the family.[9] And he is much more likely to socialize after hours with the people under his supervision. Japanese companies typically organize sporting and social events, retreats, and vacations for their workers.

The Japanese corporation is frequently described as family-like.[10] The assertion that "a good foreman looks at his workers as a father does his children" usually elicits strong assent in Japanese opinion surveys.[11] The Japanese are more likely than Americans to say their work supervisor "looks after you personally in matters not connected with work," by eighty-seven to fifty percent.[12] In fact, the moral bonds that arise among employees at a company frequently take precedence over their actual families. Quite typically workers voluntarily attend company-sponsored weekend retreats rather than spend the time with their family, or they go out in the evenings drinking with work associates rather than stay at home with their wife and children. Their willingness to sacrifice the interests of the family for the sake of the firm is taken as a sign of loyalty; reluctance to do so would be seen as a moral failing. And as in a real family, it is very hard to opt out of the relationship: if one's corporate "father" is seen as too overbearing, one usually does not have the option of disowning him by quitting and working somewhere else.

The bonds of reciprocal obligation felt between workers and managers are reflected on a larger scale in Japanese union organization. Postwar Japanese unions are not organized along craft or industrial lines, as in the United States and many European countries, but as company unions; for example, the Hitachi union represents Hitachi workers, regardless of specialty. The attitudes that labor and management hold toward each other reflect a higher degree of trust than in the United States, and much more so than in European countries like Britain, France, and Italy, with histories of militant, ideologized trade unionism. Though Japanese unions stage their spring demonstrations as a kind of nostalgic throwback to their days of militancy earlier in the century, they hold interests in common with management in the overall growth and well-being of the company. Japanese unions thus often act as tools of management, seeking to smooth over complaints about working conditions or disciplining unruly workers. The situation in Britain is utterly different, of course. As the sociologist Ronald Dore explains in his comparative study of a British and a Japanese factory, "In Britain many among both unionists and managers, while accepting the inevitability of the other's existence, refuse fully to accept its legitimacy or at least to accept the legitimacy of the power which the other enjoys. Both sides are apt to consider an ideal society as one in which the other does not exist."[13]

Western managers, observing the apparent docility of Japanese trade unions, often long for similar relations with their workers. They try to appeal to their unions using the Japanese language of common interests between workers and management to convince the latter to loosen work rules or take wage concessions. But if Japanese-style reciprocal obligation is to work, the obligation and trust must flow in both directions. A Western trade unionist would argue, with considerable justification, that it would be naive to trust management to seek the good of workers as well as management; the company would exploit any concessions made by the union while giving back as little as possible in terms of job security or other benefits. In contract negotiations, managers frequently open their books to the union negotiators in order to convince them that they cannot afford to give in to a particular wage demand. This tactic will not work, however, unless the union trusts the management to be honest in its presentation.[14] Knowledge is power, and many Western unions have had the unhappy experience of being outmaneuvered by employers willing to cook the books, overstating costs and understating profits, for bargaining purposes. Japanese unions, then, can come into existence only as the counterpart of Japanese management.

Observers, including many Japanese themselves, have suggested that Japan's lifetime employment system and the labor-management relations it engenders constitute an ancient practice that springs directly out of deep cultural traditions, particularly the Confucian tradition of loyalty.[15] There is in fact a cultural basis for lifetime employment, but the relationship between cultural tradition and contemporary business practice is considerably more complicated than that.[16] Lifetime employment in its current form does not date back further than the end of World War II and in any case does not apply to many small companies in the second tier of Japanese industry. This system represents the culmination of efforts on the part of Japanese employers and government to stabilize the workforce, a struggle that opened as Japan began to industrialize in the late nineteenth century. Particularly at the turn of the century, skilled labor was frequently in short supply, and employers often found themselves unable to retain the workers they needed. There was in fact a tradition dating back to Tokugawa times of highly mobile artisans, who moved from workplace to workplace as the mood struck them. These workers took pride in their intolerance of routine, in their rebelliousness, in their ability to sell their labor where they chose, and in their high living and frequently unconventional lifestyles, all characteristics we tend not to associate with contemporary Japanese.[17] Skilled labor in this period was organized by the *oyakata,* the traditional guilds whose members' first loyalties were to their crafts rather than to their employers.[18]

Stability of employment was particularly important because private companies took on the responsibility for training their employees in basic industrial skills. The cost of separation thus was high to firms that invested in worker training. Mitsubishi was one of the first large concerns that, in 1897, offered a generous package of sickness and retirement benefits in an effort to retain its workers. Despite practices like this, separation rates remained extremely high in subsequent years, seldom falling to less than fifty percent a year, for example, in the engineering industry.[19] Nor were labor relations in Japan always peaceful. Growth of a working class led to considerable union activity and militancy until the military regime dissolved the unions in 1938. When Japanese industry reconstituted itself after the Pacific War, its leaders hoped to create a more harmonious and stable set of labor relations than those that had prevailed earlier. With the support of conservative governments after the late 1940s and a sympathetic American ally that did not want to see leftist labor union militancy, the result was the now-familiar *nenko* system.

The recent origins of the institution of lifetime employment have led some observers to argue that *nenko* is not a culturally determined phenomenon at all but simply an institution created by the political authorities to meet Japan's needs at a particular juncture in its history.[20] This interpretation, however, misunderstands the role that culture played in shaping the institution.[21] Although it is true that lifetime employment is not an ancient practice in Japan, it builds on certain ethical habits with a very long standing in Japanese history. A system based on reciprocal moral obligation to work needs to have a high degree of trust within the society in the first place. A firm could easily exploit workers and unions under such a system, just as workers could become free riders. That neither happens to a noticeable extent in Japan is testimony to the fact that each side has a high degree of confidence that the other will live up to its end of the bargain. It is very difficult to imagine lifetime employment's being implemented successfully in relatively low-trust societies like Taiwan, Hong Kong, southern Italy, or France or a society riddled with class animosities like Britain. Both labor and management would distrust the motives of those setting up the system; the former would think it a plot to undermine union solidarity, and the latter would label it back-door corporate welfare. Governments in such societies could establish lifetime employment as a matter of legal fiat, as many socialist states did, but the likelihood would then be that neither labor nor management would live up to its end of the bargain: workers would pretend to work, and employers would pretend to deliver prosperity. The Japanese system works so efficiently because both labor and management internalize the rules: workers work and managers look out for their interests without coercion or the transaction costs of a formal legal system of rights and duties to regulate their relations.

The bursting of the bubble economy of the late 1980s and the recession of 1992–1993, with continuing problems over the rise of the yen, has put tremendous pressures on the lifetime employment system. In trying to cut costs while honoring their employment commitment, Japanese companies have responded in a number of ways. They have shifted employees around to other lines of business; moved them down to the second, small-company tier; slashed bonuses; forced early retirements; and sidelined other workers entirely, keeping them on the payroll while in effect underemploying them. Perhaps the most serious social consequence has been a sharply lower level of hiring of new university graduates.[22] Company hiring of new graduates fell twenty-six percent in 1992, and another ten percent in 1993, leaving 150,000 graduates still seeking work.[23] Some large corporations have in fact resorted to layoffs, and others have begun to engage in American-style "headhunting," using the weak demand for labor as an opportunity to raid competitors' staff. The lifetime employment system constrains them, however, from downsizing and "reengineering" to take advantage of productivity gains by engaging in wholesale layoffs or buyouts, as many American corporations did in the early 1990s. Lifetime employment is a commitment that was much easier to honor when Japan was experiencing double-digit growth, with few reversals or slowdowns. Whether it will exert a significant drag on the productivity of Japanese companies now that the Japanese economy has matured and fallen into a pattern of slower long-term growth remains to be seen. But even if *nenko* is not the optimal system for the future, it has clearly worked well for Japan in the past, reconciling job security with economic efficiency in a manner that has eluded many Western economies.[24] The fact that it has worked so well until now—indeed, that it has worked at all—is testimony to the power of reciprocal obligation in Japanese social life.

CHAPTER 17

The Money Clique

A recent incident on the Internet—the computer network originally established by the Department of Defense to allow computers to communicate with one another around the globe—demonstrates the importance of reciprocal obligation to the functioning of a network. Many information superhighway enthusiasts believe that networks of small firms or individuals constitute a new organizational form that will prove its superiority to both large, hierarchical corporations, on the one hand, and anarchical market relationships, on the other. If networks are to be more efficient, however, this will come about only on the basis of a high level of trust and the existence of shared norms of ethical behavior between network members. The importance of social obligation may come as a surprise to many of the hackers who built the Internet, who tend to be free spirits hostile to any form of authority, but networks are in fact particularly vulnerable to certain forms of normlessness and asocial behavior.

The Internet is both a physical network, and in a certain limited but critical sense a community of shared values.[1] The Internet community in its early years in the 1970s and '80s was initially composed mostly of government and academic researchers, who were homogeneous enough in their backgrounds and interests to abide by a set of unwritten rules regarding net etiquette. Lacking any formal administrative hierarchy or legal rules, Internet users exchanged data and information freely on the assumption that the cost of putting data on the net eventually would be repaid by free access to other people's data. One of the net's cardinal yet informal rules was a prohibition on the use of electronic mail for commercial advertising, which could clog the network if it got out of hand. The costs of running the system could be kept low because the users had internalized the rules and could be trusted not to abuse it. The Internet culture, limited as it was, produced real economic efficiencies.

But as news of this free (or at least low-cost) service spread in the early 1990s, so did the number of users, including some who did not feel bound by the ethical constraints of the original Internet community. The prohibition against advertising was broken flagrantly in 1994 by a pair of lawyers who bombarded the Internet news groups with advertisements for their services. Despite howls of protest from longtime Internet users, the lawyers argued that they had not broken any laws or official rules, and they could not be shamed into desisting.[2] It was clear that their action threatened the viability of the network as a whole, because over time others would start exploiting what amounted to a public good for private purposes.

The problem could, and may well someday, be solved by turning the network into a hierarchy and writing a set of formal rules with enforcement provisions. Net etiquette then would be maintained through fiat backed by a threat of coercion rather than through an internalized sense of reciprocal obligation. Rules may preserve the viability of the Internet, but they will also raise the transaction costs of maintaining it considerably, since there would then have to be network administrators and police, restrictions on access, and the like. The introduction of computer viruses into the network by inadequately socialized hackers has already imposed substantial extra economic costs on the running of the network, in the form of firewall computers and data compartmentalization. What once was a matter of inward obligation now becomes a matter of external law, with all the cumbersomeness of law; what once was decentralized and self-managing now must acquire a central administration and an accompanying bureaucracy.

The network as a community based on reciprocal moral obligation is perhaps the most fully developed in Japan. Besides lifetime employment, the *keiretsu,* or business network, is the second unique feature of the Japanese economy whose working depends on the pervasive ability to enter into high-trust relationships.[3]

There are two broad categories of *keiretsu.* The vertical *keiretsu,* like that of the Toyota Motor Corporation, consists of a manufacturing firm, its upstream subcontractors and suppliers, and its downstream marketing organizations. The second and more common type is the so-called horizontal or intermarket *keiretsu,* which unites widely differing types of businesses similar to American conglomerates like Gulf+Western and ITT, which had their heyday in the 1960s and 1970s. A typical intermarket *keiretsu* is centered around a large bank or other financial institution and usually also includes a general trading company, an insurance company, a heavy manufacturing firm, an electronics firm, a chemical company, an oil company, various commodity producers, a shipping firm, and others. When the *zaibatsu* began to reconstitute themselves after the end of the American occupation, they started out as so-called President's Councils, where the CEOs of companies with a historical relationship with one another came together on a regular basis. The *keiretsu* members have no formal legal ties, though they have come to be linked to one another through a complicated system of cross-shareholding of each other's equity.

Keiretsu-like business groups exist in many cultures.[4] Chinese societies like Taiwan and Hong Kong have family-based network organizations; the small companies of central Italy are united in complex webs of interdependence; and America had its Morgan and Rockefeller trusts in the late nineteenth century, and even after their breakup it was not uncommon for companies to form long-term alliances with interlocking boards of directors. As Boeing today gears up to produce the 777 airliner, it is in effect acting as a systems integrator whose main business is to organize the activities of a host of independent subcontractors that do much of the actual manufacturing of the airplane. The German economy contains many bank-centered industrial groups that resemble Japanese network organizations in a number of ways.

The Japanese *keiretsu* system, however, is distinguished by a number of features that do not have obvious counterparts in other societies. The first is that they are very large and play an extremely important role in the Japanese economy as a whole. Compared to the average Taiwanese business network with six companies, the six largest Japanese intermarket *keiretsu* unite an average of thirty-one companies.[5] Of Japan's two hundred largest industrial firms, ninety-nine maintain some clear long-term affiliation with a network organization. Firms that do not belong to *keiretsu* tend to be in newer industries, where alliances have not yet had time to form.[6]

A second characteristic is that despite their enormous overall size, the individual member companies of an intermarket *keiretsu* seldom occupy a monopoly position with regard to any single sector of the Japanese economy. Instead, each *keiretsu* is represented by a single oligopolistic competitor in each market sector, in sector after sector. Hence Mitsubishi Heavy Industries, Sumitomo Heavy Industries, and Kawasaki Heavy Industries (a member of the Dai-Ichi Kangyo group) compete with each other in heavy manufacturing and defense, while Mitsubishi Bank, Sumitomo Bank, and Dai-Ichi Kangyo Bank compete with each other in finance.[7]

A third unique characteristic is that network members tend to trade with each other on a preferential basis, even when that does not make strict economic sense. *Keiretsu* members do not trade exclusively with one another, but they do tend to trade more heavily with other group members than with outside companies, frequently paying higher prices or receiving goods of lower quantity than would be the case were these pure market transactions.[8] Another form of preferential trading relationship takes the form of below-market-rate loans from the network's central financial institution to a member company, in effect constituting a subsidy. The tendency of *keiretsu* members to trade with each other on a preferential basis is a major irritant in U.S.-Japanese trade relations and may be the single most important source of misunderstanding between the two countries. An American firm trying to export to Japan will frequently find it incomprehensible that the Japanese customer will pay a higher price to a *keiretsu* partner rather than buy the American import. The Japanese company, for its part, is not necessarily trying to exclude American goods per se; it would prefer dealing with its *keiretsu* partner to another Japanese firm outside the network as well. To outsiders, however, this system looks suspiciously like an informal barrier to trade.

Finally, the degree of intimacy that exists among *keiretsu* partners is frequently very great and reflects a high degree of trust. Companies like GM and Boeing have long-term relationships with suppliers, but these tend to remain somewhat at arms length. The supplier always has to worry that if the prime contractor knows too much about its proprietary processes or finances, it might use that knowledge in a detrimental way, perhaps leaking information to a competitor or entering the same business itself. This uneasiness slows the rate at which more efficient processes spread to business partners. Japanese prime contractors, by contrast, frequently demand that they be able to scrutinize all aspects of a subcontractor's operations for the sake of efficiency, a demand that is accepted because the latter trusts the former not to misuse the information gained in this manner.[9]

The sense of reciprocal obligation felt between *keiretsu* members is illustrated by the well-known case of Toyo Kogyo, the automaker (otherwise known as Mazda Motors) that faced bankruptcy in 1974 when sales of its rotary-engined cars plummeted as a result of the oil crisis. Toyo Kogyo was a member of the Sumitomo *keiretsu,* and the group's chief bank, Sumitomo Trust, was a major lender and shareholder in the car company. Sumitomo Trust took the lead in reorganizing Toyo Kogyo, dispatching seven directors and forcing it to adopt new production techniques. The other members of the *keiretsu* switched their automobile purchases to Mazda, the parts suppliers reduced prices, and lenders provided the necessary credit. As a result, Mazda survived without requiring any layoffs, though management and workers saw their bonuses reduced.[10] Chrysler, which ran into serious trouble a few years later, could not rely on its lenders and suppliers to bail it out and instead had to turn to the U.S. government. Taken alone, none of the decisions to save Toyo Kogyo by the members of the Sumitomo *keiretsu* made economic sense; whether they made economic sense taken together might be questioned by some economists. But this case does serve to illustrate the sacrifices that members of a *keiretsu* are at times willing to make on each other's behalf.

To understand the economics of Japanese network organizations, we need to step back and look more generally at existing economic theories of the firm. While capitalism is supposed to be based on free markets and competition, life inside a Western corporation is at once hierarchical and cooperative. As anyone who has worked in one knows, corporations are the last bastion of authoritarianism: the single CEO at the top has, with the leave of his board of directors, more or less total freedom to order his organization around like an army. At the same time, the people working within this hierarchy are supposed to cooperate, and not compete, against each other.

This apparent contradiction between the competitive free market and the cooperative yet authoritarian firm was the starting point of a seminal article written in the 1930s by the economist Ronald Coase.[11] Coase noted that the essence of the market was the price mechanism, which brought supply and demand into equilibrium, but that within the firm, the price mechanism was suppressed and goods were allocated by command. If the price mechanism was deemed so efficient, the question arose: Why did firms exist at all? It is conceivable, for example, that cars could be manufactured entirely without car companies in a decentralized market. One firm would sell a car design to a final assembler, which would purchase the major components from subcontractors, which would in turn purchase the parts for subassemblies from other independent parts suppliers; the assembled car could then be sold to an independent marketing organization, which would sell it to a dealer and thence to the final consumer. But modern car companies did just the opposite: they integrated backward and forward, purchasing their suppliers and marketing organizations, moving goods along the manufacturing process by fiat rather than through market transactions. Why did the boundaries between the firm and the market end up where they did?

Coase's answer to this puzzle, and the answer of most subsequent economists, was that although markets allocate goods efficiently, they often also entail substantial transaction costs. That is, market transactions entail costs of matching buyers and sellers, negotiating prices, and finalizing deals in the form of contracts. These costs made it more economical for a car company to acquire its suppliers outright rather than haggle with them repeatedly over price, quality, and delivery schedules for every part.

Coase's original thesis has been vastly elaborated, particularly by Oliver Williamson, into a broad theory of the modern corporation.[12] In Williamson's words, "The modern corporation is mainly to be understood as the product of a series of organizational innovations that have had the purpose and effect of economizing on transaction costs."[13] Transaction costs can be substantial, in turn, because human beings are not completely trustworthy. That is, if people pursued their economic self-interest and were at the same time completely honest, it might be possible to build cars by subcontracting. Suppliers could be relied on to provide their best price, not to renege on deals or give competitors proprietary information, to meet delivery schedules and maintain quality to the best of their ability, and so on. But human beings are, in Williamson's words, "opportunistic" and characterized by "bounded rationality" (meaning that they do not always make optimally rational decisions); integrated corporations are necessary because outside suppliers cannot be relied on to do what they contract to do.[14]

Firms integrate vertically, then, in order to reduce transaction costs. They continue to expand until the costs of large size begin to exceed the savings from these transaction costs. That is, large organizations suffer from diseconomies of scale: the free rider problem becomes more severe the larger the organization becomes;[15] they are prone to agency costs, where the firm's bureaucracy develops a stake in its own survival rather than profit maximization; and they suffer from information costs when managers lose track of what is happening in their own organizations. In Williamson's view, the multidivisional corporation, which was pioneered by American corporations at the beginning of the twentieth century, was an innovative response to this problem that combined the transaction cost economies of integration with decentralized, independent profit centers.[16]

It should be clear, however, that the Japanese *keiretsu* is another innovative solution to the problem of scale. The long-term relationships between *keiretsu* partners are a substitute for vertical integration, one that achieves similar efficiencies in terms of transaction cost savings. Toyota could have purchased outright one of its large subcontractors, Nippondenso, just as General Motors acquired Fisher Body in the 1920s. It has not done so, however, because purchase would not necessarily lower transaction costs. Toyota's intimate relationship with Nippondenso allows it to participate in product and quality decisions, just as it would if the latter were a wholly owned subsidiary. Furthermore, the bonds of reciprocal obligation felt between the two companies give Toyota confidence that Nippondenso will continue to meet its needs reliably into the indefinite future. It is the long-term stability of the obligational relationship that is important: both contractors can invest and plan for the future knowing that the other will not jump ship if a third party offering a somewhat better price were to come along.[17] They will, moreover, waste less time haggling over prices for any deal: if one party feels it got a less than optimal price or even suffered a loss in the short run, it knows that its partner will be willing to make this up at a later point.

It is understandable that the *keiretsu* relationship emerged in a Japanese cultural setting: because of the relative ease with which two parties can enter into a durable relationship of mutual obligation, transaction costs are lower across the board in Japan.[18] Transactions that would be expensive to conduct across firm boundaries in a low-trust society like Hong Kong or southern Italy (in effect, between firms without kinship ties) cost much less in Japan, because the contracting parties have a higher level of confidence that the contract will be fulfilled. At the same time, members of a Japanese *keiretsu* do not incur the extra costs of centralized administration that exist within vertically integrated firms.

The transaction cost approach is useful for understanding the economic efficiencies of vertical *keiretsu* like that of Toyota, which are the functional equivalents of vertically integrated Western companies. But what about the horizontal or intermarket *keiretsu,* whose different members have no necessary economic connection with one another? What economic motives, for example, made it important that each of the major intermarket *keiretsu* include a brewery in its group, such that members of the Sumitomo group drink Asahi beer, while those of Mitsubishi prefer Kirin?[19]

To the extent that *keiretsu* members have economic dealings with each other, the intermarket *keiretsu* can share many of the transaction cost efficiencies of its vertical counterpart. That is, group members know each other well and trust one another; to buy from a member of the group will not entail the same information and negotiation costs as buying from a stranger.[20] Losses incurred in one period may be made up in a later period.

A further economic rationale concerns the role of the bank, which is at the center of each intermarket *keiretsu*. The Japanese stock market, though old, has never played an important role in capitalizing Japanese industry. This function instead has been performed by banks and secondarily by debt, the latter more frequently in the case of government agencies. The big city banks have played a key role in financing large-scale manufacturing industry from the beginning of Japan's industrialization. In the early phase of industrialization, it probably made sense for the *zaibatsu* to branch out into unrelated businesses, despite a lack of any natural synergy with existing interests. They could bring modern management techniques to sectors that previously were totally unmodernized and could take advantage of subsidized credit in doing so. During the recovery period of the 1950s, the city banks were the mechanism by which the state-owned Bank of Japan channeled savings into the manufacturing sector, through the process of "overloading." By manipulating reserve requirements and, in effect, guaranteeing a high and stable level of lending activity, the central bank could make available capital that the market alone would not have provided at a similar interest rate.[21]

Large banks independent of *keiretsu* ties could have performed a similar role in capitalizing industry. There are several possible reasons that they developed long-term relations with certain industrial clients even after the practice of overloaning ended. First, the very stability of the relationship gave the bank access to superior information about its clients.[22] This knowledge presumably allowed it to allocate capital more efficiently; it also allowed the bank to intervene directly in the restructuring of a troubled client, as in the Mazda case. Second, the *keiretsu* permitted smaller and riskier ventures, or long-term investments whose returns would accrue very far in the future, to raise capital at lower interest rates than would otherwise be possible. Large corporations are generally able to borrow money at lower real rates of return than small ones;[23] the *keiretsu* in effect socializes the costs of capital among its members and uses the stable income from the older and better-established firms to subsidize the newer and riskier ventures. Finally, the *keiretsu* bank, through preferential lending, can serve as a price-clearing agent, helping to equalize rates of return for member companies whose profits have been adversely affected by noncompetitive pricing, much like a corporate treasury that compensates divisions for losses on distorted intracompany transfer pricing.

There may be other rationales for intermarket *keiretsu*. The *keiretsu*'s brand names, for instance, can be used in new product markets to establish credibility. One very important function that the *keiretsu* played in the 1960s and 1970s was to block or otherwise control the degree of direct foreign investment in Japan. When the Japanese government agreed to liberalize capital markets in the late 1960s, many Japanese companies feared an influx of foreign, mostly U.S., competition as outside multinationals bought stakes in Japanese businesses. The importance of foreign direct investment to exports has typically been insufficiently appreciated; it is often very difficult for a multinational corporation to market in a foreign country unless it also manufactures its products there.[24] As Mark Mason has shown, the level of intra-*keiretsu* cross-shareholding increased dramatically in anticipation of capital market liberalization, so as to make it more difficult for foreigners to acquire majority ownership of Japanese corporations.[25] This tactic proved quite successful: few American multinationals were able to purchase more than minority interests in Japanese companies, even after they were legally permitted to do so. The well-publicized inability of American corporate raider T. Boone Pickens to secure a seat on the board of the Japanese auto parts supplier he had bought a major interest in is testimony to the effectiveness with which *keiretsu* relationships can be used to limit foreign access to Japanese markets. As the last example indicates, some of the functions of the inter-market *keiretsu* may not be economic at all but political.

The unique and intriguing features of Japanese network organizations have led some people to speculate more broadly that network organizations may be an economically efficient way of structuring modern business life, not just in Japan but in other countries as well. Using the categories developed by Coase and Williamson, Western economies have generally encompassed two types of industrial relationships: market ones, in which goods are exchanged on the basis of agreement between completely independent actors, and hierarchical ones, in which goods are exchanged between related actors within the same firm on the basis of administrative fiat. But a network, according to Shumpei Kumon, is "one in which . . . the major type of mutual acts is consensus/inducement-oriented" and in which the actors have some kind of continuing yet informal relationship with one another.[26] Networks thus achieve the savings in transaction costs of large organizations, while retaining the savings in overhead and administrative costs of large organizations. This is a model that, it is argued, can be applied not only to economic relations but to political relations as well, where the large, rigid, centralized government structures of earlier years have proven too inflexible and slow moving to accommodate the needs of complex, modern societies.

There is a degree of truth to the view that network organizations are not necessarily unique to Japanese culture. Germany and the United States, both high-trust societies, have had their own versions of network organizations. They are especially evident in Germany, where cartels and trade associations have played a major role in the economy. Although similar organizations ran up against the barrier of the Sherman and Clayton Anti-Trust acts in the United States by the early twentieth century, informal networks continued to exist nonetheless in the form of related companies with cross-shareholding and interlocking boards of directors (the chemical giant E. I. du Pont de Nemours, for example, was a major shareholder in General Motors, with which it shared directors). American purchasing managers do not always ruthlessly scour the horizon for the lowest cost–highest quality suppliers, shifting from one to the other based on price signals, as neoclassical economics might sometimes suggest. In practice, buyers frequently develop long-term relationships with certain suppliers they trust, feeling that reliability may in the long run be more important than marginally lower prices. They too are often loathe to drop a supplier based on short-term profit considerations, because they calculate that a relationship of trust takes time to build and may lead the other party to give them a break in the future.

But it is hard to imagine that the specifically Japanese form of network organization could ever become a generalizable model, particularly in low-trust societies with a low degree of spontaneous sociability. In a network organization, there is no overall source of authority: if two members cannot agree on a transaction price, there is no central office to resolve the dispute for them. If some action on the part of the network as a whole is required—for example, a decision on the part of the Sumitomo group to rescue Mazda Motors—any individual member has a potential veto because of the need for consensus. Consensus comes about relatively easily in Japan. In a low-trust society, the network form of organization would be a formula for paralysis and inaction. Each member of the network, when faced with the need for collective action, would try to figure out how to exploit the network for its own advantage and would suspect the others of scheming to do the same.

Networks based on reciprocal moral obligation have ramified throughout the Japanese economy because the degree of generalized trust possible among unrelated people is extraordinarily high. This is not to say that all Japanese trust each other or that the radius of trust is coterminous with the country as a whole. There are criminals in Japan who murder, defraud and cheat each other, though many fewer than in the United States. The degree of trust outside the *keiretsu* network is much lower than within. But something in Japanese culture makes it very easy for one person to incur a reciprocal obligation to another and to maintain this sense of obligation over extended periods of time. This suggests that the network structure of the Japanese economy will be only partially replicable, even in other high-trust societies, and will not be the pattern at all for societies with a low degree of trust, where networks will be based on kinship or will be slight modifications of pure market relationships, in which the ties binding networked firms are fragile and subject to frequent change.

Like the practice of lifetime employment, *keiretsu* relationships came under considerable pressure during the recession that began in Japan in

1992. It is one thing to pay an unnecessarily high price to a *keiretsu* partner when times are good but another to do so when losses are mounting and outsiders can offer substantial discounts. The impact of the recession and rising yen fell particularly hard on small companies, which occasionally found themselves unprotected by their *keiretsu* relationships as large manufacturers desperately tried to cut their own costs by pushing them onto subcontractors.[27] The recession also reduced the degree of cross-shareholding, with industrial companies particularly eager to dump the shares of the banks they worked with.[28] Pressure to break apart *keiretsu* relationships has come from external sources as well, including American exporters eager to break into closed Japanese markets. *Keiretsu* relationships can easily entail inefficiencies that might act as serious constraints on the ability of Japanese corporations to control costs in an increasingly competitive international economy. Like the lifetime employment system, however, the recession of the early 1990s seems only to have bent, not broken, the *keiretsu* system.

Japan was the first country in East Asia to move beyond family businesses to the modern corporate form of organization, making use of hierarchical management structures and professional managers. This was done very early in its development, well before industrialization began. It and Korea are the only Asian countries whose economies are dominated by private, large-scale businesses. As a consequence, Japan has been able to participate in a wide range of capital-intensive sectors involving complicated manufacturing processes.

The reason that Japan has achieved this goal is that Japanese society has a much stronger proclivity for spontaneous sociability than societies like China or France with relatively weak middles. The radius of trust in Japan extends well beyond the family or lineage to a wide variety of intermediate social groups.[29] Particularly important were the rules on adoption: the Japanese family could incorporate nonbiologically related strangers into the household much more readily than in China, a characteristic that was extremely important in paving the way for professional management of family businesses. Trust springs up in Japan spontaneously among many different groups of unrelated people on a voluntary basis. Once an *iemoto*-type organization is established, it loses some of its voluntary character; people are not free to drop relationships of reciprocal obligation. But the degree to which nonkin entering into voluntary organizations are willing to trust each other without the benefit of contract or other legal instruments spelling out reciprocal rights and duties is extraordinarily high in Japan—perhaps higher than in any other contemporary society. The intensity of this feeling of reciprocal moral obligation permits the emergence of economic practices like lifetime employment or business networks like the *keiretsu* system that have no ready counterparts around the world, even in other societies characterized by a high degree of spontaneous sociability.

After Japan, the country displaying the highest degree of spontaneous sociability is perhaps Germany. Although the specific cultural origins of communitarianism are quite different in Germany than they are in Japan, the effects are remarkably similar: Germany developed large organizations and professional management early on, has an economy organized into informal networks, and possesses a high degree of enterprise solidarity. It is this case to which we will turn next.

CHAPTER 18

German Giants

The German economy is of particular interest to us for two reasons. First, it has been extraordinarily successful for a very long period of time. When political conditions in the nineteenth century became right for a take-off with the creation of a unified economic space (the *Zollverein*) and then a unified country, Germany raced past its more developed neighbors Britain and France and became the leading economic power in Europe in the space of two generations. This leadership position has not changed up to the present, despite the losses incurred in two horrendous wars. Second, this leadership position has been maintained despite the fact that the German economy has never been organized along the purely liberal lines that neoclassical economists would have recommended. From Bismarck's day, the Germans have always had a sizable welfare state, which today consumes more than half of German gross domestic product. There are numerous rigidities in the German economy, particularly in the labor market; although there is no lifetime employment system, firing a German worker remains far more difficult than firing an American worker.

Germany can be distinguished from its neighbors France and Italy by the same sorts of systematic differences that exist between Japan and China. The German economy has always been pervaded by communal institutions that have no obvious counterparts outside Central Europe.[1] As in Japan, many of these institutions are the result of positive law or administrative policy, but they also draw on strongly communitarian traditions in German culture.

The number of similarities between German and Japanese culture, many of which can be traced to the highly developed sense of communal solidarity shared by both, are intriguing, and they have been remarked upon by numerous observers. Both countries have reputations for orderliness and discipline, reflected in clean public spaces and tidy private homes. These are societies whose members enjoy playing by the rules, thereby reinforcing a sense of belonging to a distinct cultural group. Both peoples have a reputation for going about their work with great intensity and seriousness; neither is known either for lightness of touch or a sense of humor. The obsession for order often shades into fanaticism of both positive and negative sorts. In the former category is the long tradition of perfectionism among both Germans and Japanese, whose contemporary industrial manifestation lies in their great gift for precision manufacturing. Both countries are known for their machine tools and machinists, for their auto and optics industries, their Leicas and Nikons. On the other hand, their communal solidarity within the national community weakens their regard for people who stand outside it; neither country has been known for its friendliness to foreigners, and both became notorious for their brutality to the peoples they conquered and ruled. And both countries have, in the past, let their passion for order lead them to dictatorship and unthinking submission to authority.

At the same time, it is important not to overemphasize the similarities between Japan and Germany, particularly since the end of World War II. Germany has undergone a much more profound cultural change since the war and as a result has become a much more open and individualistic society than Japan. Nonetheless, the two countries' cultural traditions have resulted in similar economic structures.

It should be noted that the continuity of German culture in eastern Germany has been seriously disrupted as a result of communist rule under the German Democratic Republic. Many Germans, both East and

West, have been very surprised since unification at the enormous cultural differences separating them. Managers in the West have said that their Turkish workers possess more classically German virtues like a strong work ethic and self-discipline than the ethnic Germans who grew up under communism. Easterners, for their part, have often felt more akin to Poles, Russians, and Bulgarians in their aspirations, anxieties, and reactions to the postcommunist world. Hence culture is not an unbending, primordial force but something shaped continuously by the flow of politics and history.

Since the individual German states began to industrialize in earnest in the 1840s, the German economy has been characterized by large-scale firms. As table 1 at the beginning of chapter 14 showed, German firms today are the largest in Europe in terms of absolute size. Because of the large overall size of the German economy, the share of the largest ten or twenty German companies of total employment is smaller than for a number of other European countries, but these shares are still larger than the comparable figures for two other big economies with giant corporations, the United States and Japan.

Historically, these differences in scale have been even more pronounced. Because the German courts upheld the legality of large mergers and cartels at around the same time that American courts and administrations were engaged in trust-busting, gigantic German combines in key sectors like chemicals and steel were significantly larger than their next largest international competitors. For example, in 1925 Germany's largest chemical companies, including the giants Bayer, Hoechst, and BASF (the Badische Analin und SodaFabrik), merged into a single concern named IG Farbenindustrie. The German chemical industry at the time was the world's largest and most advanced, and the new IG Farben dwarfed other large international competitors like the American du Pont or the Swiss predecessor of today's Ciba-Geigy. The following year, much of the strong German steel industry was organized into a single trust, the Vereinigte Stahlwerke. These huge concerns were broken up by the Allied Control Council administering occupied Germany after World War II, at the same time and for the same reasons that the Allied occupation forces dismantled the Japanese *zaibatsu.* Vereinigte Stahlwerke was split into thirteen independent companies, while IG Farben's constituent companies reemerged. While the large German IGs (*Interessengemeinschaften,* or "communities of interest") never reunited themselves as did the Japanese *zaibatsu,* Bayer, Hoechst, and BASF remain large and important players in the global chemical and pharmaceutical industries. As in Japan, American-style antitrust laws were passed in the early prewar period, a development that did not unduly hamper the development of large, oligopolistic firms.[2]

The reason there were so many large companies in Germany is the same as in Japan and, as we will see, the United States: the Germans were very quick to move from family businesses to professional management, building rationally organized administrative hierarchies that turned into durable institutions. The corporate form of organization was created in Germany during the second half of the nineteenth century, at roughly the same time that it was being pioneered by American enterprises.

The transition from large family business to corporation did not occur in other European countries until much later. In England, for example, large family-owned and -managed businesses survived through the end of World War II, as they did in France and Italy. (Holland, Switzerland, and Sweden made the transition not long after Germany and today are hosts, despite their relatively small size, to some enormous companies like Royal Dutch/Shell, Phillips Electronics, Nestlé, and ABB Asea Brown Boveri—a story that is beyond the scope of this book.)

There are numerous examples of German enterprises that organized themselves into mammoth multinational concerns in the space of just a few decades. Emil Rathenau, for example, founded the Deutsche Edison-Gesellschaft in 1883 to exploit the Edison patents he had recently acquired. Changing its name to the Allgemeine Elektricitäts-Gesellschaft (AEG), the concern had forty-two offices in Germany, thirty-seven elsewhere in Europe, and thirty-eight overseas by 1900.[3] The other great German electrical equipment giant, Siemens, created an industrial facility in Berlin that Alfred Chandler describes in the following terms:

> By 1913 Berlin's Siemensstadt had become the world's most intricate and extensive industrial complex under a single management. There was nothing approaching it in either the United States or Britain. Indeed, the locational contrast between Siemens and GE is striking. A similar complex would have appeared in the United States only if the GE plants at Schenectady, New York, Lynn and Pittsfield, Massachusetts; Harrison, New Jersey; and Erie, Pennsylvania had been placed along with Western Electric's large Chicago plant, which produced nearly all of the nation's telephone equipment, at one site in the neighborhood of 125th Street in New York City, or at one near Rock Creek Park in Washington, D.C.[4]

A British industrialist, Sir William Mather, acquired the Edison patents at the same time as Rathenau but failed to create a similar organization. Britain was certainly at no disadvantage with respect to technical expertise or the availability of capital or skilled manpower to create a great electrical industry. And yet no British equivalent of AEG, Siemens, General Electric, or Westinghouse appeared, leaving the British electrical equipment industry to play catch-up to the German and American leaders throughout the twentieth century.[5] The German Stollwercks company, originally a family-run chocolate maker, hired a large professional management team and in the 1870s and 1880s created a large marketing organization throughout Europe and North America. The British Cadbury company (now Cadbury-Schweppes), by contrast, competing in similar markets, remained family managed, and therefore smaller, for two or three more generations.[6] The key difference between the German and British concerns lay in the quality of their entrepreneurs, and in particular in tremendous organizational ability of the leading German industrialists.

There are a number of German communal economic institutions whose closest parallels are in Japan rather than elsewhere in Europe. The first is the bank-centered industrial group. Like Japan and other late-modernizing countries in Asia, German industrial growth in the second half of the nineteenth century was financed primarily by banks rather than through equity offerings. Once private limited-liability banks were made legally possible, a number of them grew to extremely large size in close relationship with a particular industry they knew intimately and to which they supplied the capital. Thus the Diskontogesellschaft became known as the "railway bank"; the Berliner Handelsgesellschaft was closely associated with the electrical equipment industry; and the Darmstadter bank financed the development of railroads in Hesse and Thuringia.[7]

The investments that these banks made in particular companies and industries were neither short-term nor arms-length. As in the case of the Japanese *zaibatsu*, bank representatives became involved in the affairs of their client companies over prolonged periods of time. It became common practice for bank representatives to sit on the *Aufsichtsrat*, the higher of the two boards of directors that oversaw the activities of German companies. German investment banks were the first to create large staffs of specialists in particular industries, which would be responsible for the bank's relations with them.[8] Today these bank-centered groups (like their Japanese counterparts) provide a degree of stability in financing that permits German companies to take a longer-term perspective in their investments than American market equity–financed companies.[9] Together with the fact that by law a hostile takeover must acquire seventy-five percent of voting shares to succeed, the large equity positions of banks allows them to block unwanted acquisition attempts. The Deutsche Bank's successful effort to prevent an Arab buyout of Daimler-Benz, mentioned in the first chapter, is one example.

This kind of bank-centered group was not nearly as common in other advanced societies. Some of the late-nineteenth-century trusts in the United States included financial institutions that were used to capitalize the trust's industrial firms. Many were broken up during the antitrust movement at the turn of the century and finally made illegal with the passage of the Glass-Steagall Act in 1933 that separated commercial from investment banking. The French Crédit Mobilier, established as an investment bank in 1852 by Emile and Isaac Pereire, collapsed in 1867 in an infamous scandal. British banks turned away from the long-term financing of industry, particularly after the failure of the City of Glasgow Bank in Britain in 1878. This reflected a deeper social cleavage in that country between the financiers, working out of the City of London, and the manufacturers in northern cities like Liverpool, Leeds, and Manchester. The former were more easily assimilated into Britain's upper-class culture and tended to look down upon the less refined, more pragmatically educated industrialists from the grimy towns of the North. They often opted for safety and stability, in preference to the long-term risks inherent in funding new industries, and as a result the British electrical and automobile industries never received the level of financing they needed to make them globally competitive.[10] As was typical throughout British economic history, development was hobbled by class and status barriers that undercut the sense of community and erected unnecessary obstacles to economic cooperation. Though Germany too was a class-ridden society, no similar status distinction existed between bankers and industrialists; the two groups were neither physically nor culturally isolated as in England.

The second characteristic communitarian economic institution in Germany were industrial cartels, which also existed in Japan. Cartels have never had the same negative associations in Germany as in the United States. There was no German equivalent of the Sherman and Clayton Anti-Trust acts prohibiting combinations in restraint of trade; indeed, at the same moment that the U.S. Supreme Court was upholding the constitutionality of the Sherman Act, the German high court upheld the enforceability of contracts between firms in setting prices, output, and market shares. The number of cartels increased steadily in the late nineteenth century, rising from 4 in 1875 to 106 in 1890, to 205 in 1896, and 385 in 1905.[11] These cartels would share research and development costs, or engage in industry-wide plans for industrial restructuring. Cartel arrangements tended to become more important in times of recession than in times of growth; in such periods firms would agree to share markets rather than turn on each other to drive weaker competitors out of business. During the 1920s the cartels tended to be replaced by more formal intercorporate arrangements like IGs (as in the case of IG Farben noted above) or by *Konzerne,* which were smaller cross-shareholding arrangements controlled by families or groups of individuals.

While the dismantling of trusts in the United States and the creation of cartels, IGs, and *Konzerne* in Germany were thus products of differences in positive law in the two countries, the laws themselves reflected certain underlying cultural biases. In the United States, there has always been a strong popular distrust of concentrated economic power, despite the powerful American proclivity for creating large organizations. The Sherman Anti-Trust Act was passed as a result of public resentment against enterprises like the Standard Oil Trust that had managed to corner a large portion of the American oil market, and enforcement of the act was one of the populist hallmarks of Theodore Roosevelt's presidency. Political populism was supplemented by a liberal economic ideology that believed that social welfare was maximized by vigorous competition, not by cooperation among large companies.

In Germany, by contrast, there has never been a comparable distrust of size per se. German industries from the beginning were export oriented; their size was more often compared to the global markets they served rather than to narrow domestic ones. Unlike American firms, whose competitive world often began and ended completely inside the United States, German companies had a much stronger sense of national identity in a world of strong international competitors. Because they were export oriented, the potential inefficiencies of domestic monopoly were minimized; large German firms were kept honest by large firms in other countries rather than by each other.

Although the German economy is dominated by large firms, it (like Japan) also has a large and dynamic small-firm sector, the so-called *Mittelstand.* Family businesses are as prevalent and important in Germany as anywhere else; indeed, there are more cases of families' retaining management control of large businesses in Germany than in the United States.[12] But the family has never constrained the creation of large, professionally managed firms to the degree it has in China, Italy, France, or even Britain.

Although large, formal industrial combines like cartels or IGs were broken up during the Allied occupation after the war, their place has been taken in a more informal way by the powerful German trade associations, or *Verbände*. These include the Federal Association of German Employers, the Federal Association of German Industry, and various other groups connected with specific industrial sectors.[13] These trade associations do not have ready counterparts outside Central Europe. Their activities and responsibilities are far broader than those of political lobbying associations like the American Chamber of Commerce or the National Association of Manufacturers. The German *Verbände* act as the counterparts of the trade unions during collective bargaining negotiations, by which wages, benefits, and work conditions are set on an industry-wide basis; they are actively involved in setting standards for training and product quality; and they engage in long-range planning for the strategic future of particular industrial sectors. The trade associations played a key role in initiating negotiations leading to the Investment Aid Act of 1952, for example, by which the relatively well-off sectors of German industry were taxed in order to subsidize certain bottleneck sectors like coal, steel, electricity, and railways.[14]

The third set of communitarian economic institutions consists of the complex of labor-management relations that were codified as part of Ludwig Erhardt's postwar *Sozialmarktwirtschaft,* or social market economy. Germany has had a powerful and well-organized labor movement, which has been represented politically since the late nineteenth century by the influential Social Democratic party (SPD). Despite the Marxist currents that have existed historically within the German workers' movement, labor relations in the postwar period have been remarkably consensual. Germany has not experienced the bitter class antagonisms that have frequently characterized labor relations in Britain, France, and Italy. The number of days lost to strikes in Germany, for example, have been among the lowest in the developed world, comparable to the rates of Austria, Sweden, and Japan.[15] In contrast to other national labor movements, German labor unions have not taken strongly protectionist positions to defend declining industries and generally have behaved in ways that management would consider responsible. There is, in short, a much higher degree of mutual trust between labor and management in Germany than there is in less communally oriented societies.

This degree of harmony stems primarily from the labor-management reciprocity that has been institutionalized in Germany over the years. German managers and the German state have traditionally shown a high degree of paternalistic concern for worker interests. It was Bismarck, after all, who implemented Europe's first social security system in the 1880s (albeit as the counterpart to his antisocialist legislation that included a ban on the SPD).[16] The *Sozialmarktwirtschaft* actually had its origins in the Weimar period in the 1920s, when various forms of labor legislation, including the right of free collective bargaining and workers' councils, were introduced.[17] After the tumultuous 1930s and 1940s, when the Nazis banned independent trade unions and set up their own "yellow" corporatist organizations, postwar German leaders shared a broad consensus that a new, more cooperative system needed to be established. Major elements of the *Sozialmarktwirtschaft* were *Mitbestimmung,* or codetermination, a system under which labor representatives sat on boards of the companies they worked for, with access to corporate information and a real, if limited, participation in governance; a network of workers' councils for managing problems and conflicts on an enterprise level; the system of collective bargaining between the industry associations and the labor unions, by which wages, hours, benefits, and the like are set on a sector- or industry-wide basis;[18] and finally, the extensive social welfare legislation that stipulates health benefits, working conditions, hours, job security, and the like. This entire system is mediated and administered by a series of intermediate organizations, primarily the nationally organized unions and the trade associations, in such a way as to exclude independent employers or union locals.[19]

Institutionalized reciprocity arises out of an intellectual climate in Germany that has always been uneasy with the atomizing, individualistic implications of classical and neoclassical economics.[20] In the nineteenth century, there was a nationalist-mercantilist school of economic thought represented by Friedrich List, which tended to define economic goals in power-prestige terms while advocating strong state guidance of the economy.[21] The post–World War II "ordo-liberal" school associated with intellectuals at the University of Freiburg, which influenced the development of the *Sozialmarktwirtschaft,* opposed any kind of simple return to laissez-faire capitalism. This school argued that the state needed to intervene to set strict rules for the regulation of the market and for the protection of the interests of the groups participating in it.[22] The mainstream conservative parties in Germany—the Christian Democratic Union and its Bavarian wing, the Christian Socialist Union—have never accepted liberal economic ideas unleavened with a heavy dose of social welfare, leaving this position to the much smaller Free Democratic party. The *Sozialmarktwirtschaft* itself was originally conceived as an attempt to find a third way between purely market-oriented capitalism and socialism and was put into place not by a socialist but by a Christian Democratic chancellor, Ludwig Erhard.[23]

German labor-management relations are similar to those in Japan, involving a relatively large degree of worker-management reciprocity and depending on a high level of generalized social trust. There are, however, important differences in the way that the two countries understand their communal institutions. Although they have collaborated effectively with management, German unions remain far more politicized than their Japanese counterparts and are more independent. There are no German company unions as in postwar Japan; this alternative was promoted (and severely discredited) during the Nazi period and is no longer an option.

A further important difference is that German institutions are codified in law to a much greater extent than Japanese ones, though this does not necessarily make them more institutionalized. In Japan, lifetime employment, *keiretsu* relations, and the appropriate level of company-provided private welfare benefits are not as a rule written into law. They are based instead on informal moral obligation and would not be enforceable in a court of law. In Germany, by contrast, virtually all of the elements of the *Sozialmarktwirtschaft* are backed by legislation that spells out, often in great detail, the terms of the relationship. Even communal institutions that are deeply embedded in and dependent on the intermediate organizations of German civil society, such as codetermination and collective bargaining, came into being as the result of a top-down political process led by the state. Japan's communal institutions, on the other hand, just seemed to jell out of civil society without the benefit of an explicit political decision. Although it is hard to argue that the Japanese economy is less heavily regulated than its German counterpart, much of the communal interaction in Japan is done off the books, so to speak. Welfare services, for example, have historically been provided more by private companies than by the state. The result is that although the German public sector is one of the largest in the industrialized world, consuming nearly half of German gross domestic product, Japan has historically had one of the smallest public sectors among the member nations of the Organization for Economic Cooperation and Development. In terms of delivered benefits, however, such as job security and other forms of social welfare, the gap between Japan and Germany is not nearly as great as the difference in size of state sectors would indicate.

The role of the state in organizing the postwar German economy follows a long tradition of state intervention in the economy. As in Japan and other newly industrializing countries in Asia, the German government in the nineteenth century protected and subsidized various industries, most notably through Bismarck's famous "marriage of iron and rye," in which protection of the new steel industry in the Ruhr was linked to Prussian agricultural tariffs. The German state or its predecessors owned many industries, particularly railroads and communications, outright. Perhaps the most important achievement of the German government was to establish first-class universal and higher education systems. That system's technical schools served as the underpinning of German economic prowess during the so-called second industrial revolution in the second half of the nineteenth century that saw the birth of the steel, chemical, and electrical industries.[24] Then, during the National Socialist period, the state took over important parts of the economy directly, allocating credit, setting prices and wages, and engaging in manufacturing.[25]

The role of the German state in the economy is familiar and has been commented on quite often. These policies are neither unique to Germany nor necessarily characteristic of high-trust societies with a strong proclivity for spontaneous sociability.[26] Indeed, as we have seen, various forms of economic statism are practiced intensively by low-trust, familist-statist countries from Taiwan to France. What is far more uniquely characteristic of German economic life, and has arisen more spontaneously out of everyday social life, is the group-oriented nature of shop-floor relations in German enterprises. These relations are intimately connected, in turn, with the apprenticeship system. These economic relationships will be the subject of the chapters that follow. It will be necessary, however, first to take a slight detour to discuss the ways in which relationships of trust are reflected on the factory floor.

CHAPTER 19

Weber and Taylor

One revealing fact about German society concerns the role of noncommissioned officers (NCOs) in the German army. From well before the democratizing reforms of the post-1945 period, NCOs in Germany have been trusted with broader authority than their counterparts in France, Britain, or the United States, performing functions usually reserved for commissioned officers elsewhere. NCOs in any army tend to be less educated and come from blue-collar backgrounds; putting them rather than a "white-collar" lieutenant in charge consequently reduces status distinctions within the unit. The resulting small-unit cohesion was one of the reasons for the extraordinary fighting prowess of the Reichswehr and Wehrmacht. The relationship between a German NCO and his men is paralleled on the factory floor by the relationship of the shop foreman, or *Meister,* and the team of workers he supervises, which is similarly face-to-face, egalitarian, and intimate.

It might seem surprising that small-group relations, whether in the army or factory, should be so egalitarian in Germany, given that country's reputation for hierarchy and authority. But a high degree of generalized trust in German society allows individuals to enter into direct relations with one another rather than having them mediated by rules or formal procedures established by third parties. To understand how trust plays itself out in the most basic factory floor relationships, we need to understand on a more general level the somewhat complicated relationship between trust and formal rules.

According to Max Weber and the sociological tradition that he founded, the very essence of modern economic life is the rise and proliferation of rules and law. One of his most famous concepts was the tripartite division of authority into traditional, charismatic, and bureaucratic forms. In the first, authority was inherited from long-standing cultural sources like religion or patriarchal tradition. In the second, authority came from a "gift"; a leader was chosen by God or some other supernatural power.[1] The rise of the modern world, however, was bound up with the rise of rationality, that is, the ordered structuring of ends to means, and for Weber the ultimate embodiment of rationality was modern bureaucracy.[2] Modern bureaucracy was based on "the principle of fixed and official jurisdictional areas, which are generally ordered by rules, that is, by laws and administrative regulations."[3] The stability and rationality of modern bureaucratic authority arose from the fact that it was rule bound; the ability of superiors to have their way was limited in a transparent and clearly articulated manner, and the rights and duties of subordinates were spelled out in advance.[4] Modern bureaucracies are the social embodiment of regular rules and govern virtually every aspect of modern life, from corporations, governments, and armies to labor unions, religious organizations, and educational establishments.[5]

The modern economic world was, for Weber, bound up as well with the rise of contract. Weber noted that contracts, particularly regarding marriage and inheritance, have existed for thousands of years. But he distinguished between "status" contracts and what he called "purposive" ones.[6] In the former, one person agreed in a general and diffuse way to enter into a relationship with another (e.g., as a vassal or apprentice); duties and responsibilities were not clearly spelled out but based on tradition or the general characteristics of the particular status relationship. Purposive contracts, on the other hand, were entered into for the sake of some specific act of economic exchange. They did not affect broad social relationships but were limited to the particular transaction at hand. The proliferation of the latter kind of contract was characteristic of modernity:

> In contrast to the older law, the most essential feature of modern substantive law, especially private law, is the greatly increased significance of legal transactions, particularly contracts, as a source of claims guaranteed by legal coercion. So very characteristic is this feature of private law that one can *a potiori* designate the contemporary type of society, to the extent that private law obtains, as a "contractual" one.[7]

As we saw in the earlier discussion of the stages of economic development (see chapters 7 and 13), development of institutions like property rights, contract, and a stable system of commercial law was critical to the rise of the West. These legal institutions served as a substitute for the trust that existed naturally within families and kinship groups and constituted a framework under which strangers could interact in joint business ventures or in the marketplace.

Granting the general importance of rules and contract to modern business, it is also evident that rules and contract have not done away with the need for trust in the modern workplace. Consider professionals like doctors, lawyers, or university professors. The professional receives both a general college education and several years of technical education in his or her specialty and is expected to display a high degree of judgment and initiative as a matter of course. The nature of this judgment is often complex and context dependent and therefore cannot be spelled out in detail in advance. This is the reason that professionals, once they have received their technical accreditation, can go completely unsupervised if they are in business for themselves, or else are relatively loosely supervised if they work in an administrative hierarchy. In other words, professionals tend to be trusted to a higher degree than nonprofessionals and therefore operate in a less rule-bound environment. Although they are perfectly capable of betraying the trust placed in them, the concept of a professional serves as a prototype of a high-trust, relatively unregulated occupation.[8] It is inevitable that there should be a decrease in trust as education and skill levels decrease: a skilled worker, such as an experienced lathe operator, is given less autonomy than a professional, and an unskilled assembly line worker requires more supervision and rules than the skilled craftsman.

From an economic standpoint, there are certain clear advantages to being able to operate in a relatively rule-free environment. This is evident from the pejorative connotations of the term *bureaucratization*. Workplaces would run more efficiently if all employees, and not only the most skilled ones, behaved and were treated like professionals, with internalized standards of behavior and judgment. Past a certain point, the proliferation of rules to regulate wider and wider sets of social relationships becomes not the hallmark of rational efficiency but a sign of social dysfunction. There is usually an inverse relationship between rules and trust: the more people depend on rules to regulate their interactions, the less they trust each other, and vice versa.[9]

It was for many years a common belief that the process of industrialization, and in particular the rise of mass production, would inevitably lead to the proliferation of rules and the virtual elimination of both skill and trust relationships from the workplace. Prior to the twentieth century, any sort of complicated manufacturing was done primarily by craftsmen. Under the craft paradigm, a skilled worker using general-purpose tools performed a variety of tasks to make a small number of products. The worker, although not "educated" in the sense of a professional, required a long apprenticeship to acquire his skills. He could generally be trusted to supervise himself and consequently was given a substantial degree of autonomy to organize production as he saw fit. Craft production was well suited to relatively small, upper-class consumer markets; this was how automobiles were initially produced at the beginning of the twentieth century, when they were still very much a luxury item.[10]

Mass production was made possible through the growth of large national and international markets as a result of the nineteenth-century communications revolution (railroads and other forms of transportation) and from the spread of consumer wealth to broader parts of the population. As Adam Smith noted, "The division of labour is limited by the extent of the market." With the growth of mass markets, it became economically efficient to produce even complicated products by subdividing the work to a high degree. Longer production runs made it economical to purchase more expensive, specialized machines that could take the place of skilled craftsmen. A door panel that would have to have been shaped by hand by a craftsman could now be stamped out by an unskilled worker pressing the button on a large, automated metal press. In other words, the increasingly commodity-like character of manufactured output led to growth in the sophistication of production machinery and, in turn, a decreasing need for skilled labor to operate that equipment.

The shift to mass production started in the textile industry in the first half of the nineteenth century and spread to other types of manufacturing relatively slowly. The enterprise that symbolized the dawning of the mass production age most clearly was the assembly plant opened in 1913 by the Ford Motor Company in Highland Park, Michigan.[11] Never before had a complicated product like an automobile been produced with mass production methods. The plant itself was the result of engineering studies that sought to break down and routinize the thousands of steps in the automobile production process. By putting the cars on a moving belt passing a series of workstations, the labor of each worker could be limited to a single set of simple operations that could be performed repetitively by people of limited skills.

The increases in productivity brought about by Ford's innovation were startling and revolutionized not just the automobile industry but virtually every industry serving a mass market. Introduction of "Fordist" mass production techniques became something of a fad outside America: German industry went through a period of "rationalization" in the mid-1920s as manufacturers sought to import the most "advanced" American organizational techniques.[12] It was the Soviet Union's misfortune that Lenin and Stalin came of age in this period, because these Bolshevik leaders associated industrial modernity with large-scale mass production *tout court.* Their view that bigger necessarily meant better ultimately left the Soviet Union, at the end of the communist period, with a horrendously overconcentrated and inefficient industrial infrastructure—a Fordism on steroids in a period when the Fordist model had ceased to be relevant.

The new form of mass production associated with Henry Ford also had its own ideologist: Frederick W. Taylor, whose book *The Principles of Scientific Management* came to be regarded as the bible for the new industrial age.[13] Taylor, an industrial engineer, was one of the first proponents of time-and-motion studies that sought to maximize labor efficiency on the factory floor. He tried to codify the "laws" of mass production by recommending a very high degree of specialization that deliberately avoided the need for individual assembly line workers to demonstrate initiative, judgment, or even skill. Maintenance of the assembly line and its fine-tuning was given to a separate maintenance department, and the controlling intelligence behind the design of the line itself was the province of white-collar engineering and planning departments. Worker efficiency was based on a strict carrot-and-stick approach: productive workers were paid a higher piece rate than less productive ones.

In typical American fashion, Taylor hid a number of ideological assumptions under the guise of scientific analysis. For him, the average worker was comparable to the "economic man" of classical economics: a passive, rational, and isolated individual who would respond primarily to the stimulus of narrow self-interest.[14] The goal of scientific management was to structure the workplace in such a way that the only quality required of a worker was obedience. All of the worker's activities, down to the very motions by which he moved his arms and legs on the production line, were dictated by detailed rules prescribed by the production engineers. All other human attributes—creativity, initiative, innovativeness, and the like—were the province of a specialist somewhere else in the enterprise's organization.[15] Taylorism, as scientific management came to be known, epitomized the carrying of the low-trust, rule-based factory system to its logical conclusion.

The consequences of Taylorism for labor-management relations in the industries in which it was implemented were both predictable and, in the long run, quite harmful. A factory organized according to Taylorite principles broadcasts to its workers the message that they are not going to be trusted with significant responsibilities and that their duties will be laid out for them in a highly detailed and legalistic form. It is only natural, then, that trade unions respond with demands that the employers specify their duties and responsibilities in explicit detail as well, since the latter could not be trusted to look out for the welfare of the workers in return.[16]

Just as the general level of trust varies greatly among societies, it can also change over time within a society as a result of specific conditions or events. Alvin Gouldner argues that reciprocity is a norm that is shared to some degree by virtually all cultures: that is, if person X does a service for person Y, that person Y will then feel grateful and seek to reciprocate in some manner. But groups can enter into a downward spiral of distrust when trust is repaid with what is perceived as betrayal or exploitation.[17]

This spiral of distrust occurred in key American manufacturing industries like automobiles and steel in the first half of the twentieth century. The result, by the 1970s, was an adversarial pattern of labor-management relations characterized by a high degree of legal formalism. For example, the 1982 national agreement between the United Auto Workers (UAW) union and Ford consisted of four volumes, each two hundred pages in length, and supplemented at the plant level by another thick collective bargaining agreement specifying work rules, terms and conditions of employment, and the like.[18] These documents had a heavy job-control focus;

that is, they concentrated less on wages than the specific conditions of employment. There was, for example, a detailed job classification system with extensive descriptions of each position. Wages were tied not to the worker but to the job classification, and procedures for bumping rights, seniority privileges, and the like were all set forth in explicit detail. Union locals tended to be ever vigilant in preventing workers from doing work not specified in their job classifications. A pipefitter might run into trouble with his local if he helped out in the repair of a machine, even if he had the time and skills to do so, because this was not part of his job description. The unions also strongly preferred promotion based on seniority rather than skill. To promote workers on the basis of ability required trusting management to make difficult judgment calls about individual abilities, which they were not willing to concede. The agreements called for a four-level grievance procedure that in effect created a miniature court system within the auto industry, mirroring the extensive legalization of the larger American society.[19] Disputes arising in the workplace tended not to be worked out informally through group discussions but were referred to the legal system for resolution.

The unions that negotiated these contracts were saying, in effect, that if management insisted on subdividing labor in Taylorite fashion into small and specified tasks, they would accept the outcome but hold management to that specification very rigidly. If the worker was not to be trusted to exercise judgment or take on new responsibilities, then management would not be trusted to assign workers new duties or to judge their skills and abilities. It would be wrong to argue that the job control focus of labor contracts at midcentury came about simply because of pressure from the unions. Management, under the sway of Taylorism and scientific management, liked it as well because it prevented workers from usurping what they believed were managerial privileges. The job control system reserved all decisions about business and production for the managers and gave them a clearly defined sphere of responsibility.[20]

The question facing many twentieth-century observers of industrial development was whether Taylorism was an inevitable consequence of advancing technology, as Taylor himself would have maintained, or whether there were alternative forms of factory organization that permitted workers a greater degree of personal initiative and autonomy. An important school of American sociologists believed that there would be a gradual convergence on the Taylorite labor-management relations model in all advanced societies.[21] This view was shared by many of the critics of modern industrial society from Karl Marx to Charlie Chaplin, who believed the Taylorite division of labor was the inevitable consequence of the capitalist form of industrialization.[22] Under this system, man was destined to become alienated: the machines he had built to serve himself had in effect become his masters, reducing the human being to a cog in a system of mechanical production. The deskilling of the workforce would be accompanied by a decrease in trust in society as a whole; people would relate to each other through the legal system, not as members of organic communities. The pride in skill and work that accompanied craft production would be gone, as well as the unique and varied products that craftsmen produced. With each new technological innovation, new fears arose that it would have a particularly devastating effect on the nature of work. Thus, when numerically controlled machine tools were introduced in the 1960s, many people assumed that they would eliminate the need for skilled machinists.

The prospect of alienation as industries move from craft to mass production raises another fundamental question about the nature of economic activity. Why do people work? For the sake of the wages they earn, or because they enjoy working and are fulfilled by it? The answer traditionally provided by neoclassical economics is fairly clear on this subject. Work is essentially regarded as disutility: something painful that people would rather not do. They do not work for the sake of work but rather for the sake of the incomes that they receive in return for work, which they spend in their leisure time. All work, therefore, is undertaken ultimately for the sake of leisure. This view of work as essentially painful has deep roots in the Judeo-Christian tradition. Adam and Eve, after all, did not have to work in the garden of Eden; it was only as a result of the original sin that God required as punishment that they work to support themselves. Death, in the Christian tradition, is regarded as a respite from the toil that accompanies life; hence the inscription on tombstones reading *Requiescat in Pacem*.[23] Given this view of work, the shift from craft to mass production should not matter much as long as real incomes were rising, which they did for the most part as a result of the transition.

There is another tradition, however, and it is more closely associated with Marx: people are both productive and consuming creatures and find satisfaction in the mastery and transformation of nature through work. Work in itself therefore has a positive utility apart from the way it is compensated. But the type of work matters very much. The autonomy of craftsmen—the skills they marshaled and the creativity and intelligence they displayed in fabricating a finished product—were essential to satisfaction. For this reason, the shift to mass production and the deskilling of the workforce robbed workers of something very important that could not be compensated by higher wages.

As mass production proliferated, however, it became evident that Taylorism was not the only model of industrial modernity, that skill and craftsmanship did not disappear, and that trust relationships remained critical to the proper functioning of modern workplaces. As Charles Sabel, Michael Piore, and other proponents of flexible specialization have pointed out, craft production techniques have survived "in the penumbra" of giant, mass production facilities. There are various reasons for this, beginning with the fact that the highly specialized machines producing commodity-like mass production goods cannot themselves be mass produced; they have to be virtually hand-built since they usually have unique designs. (This explains why the small family businesses in central Italy have been so successful in the machine tool business.) As consumers have become more affluent and educated, their desire for differentiated products has grown, leading to greater market segmentation, smaller production runs, and the consequent need for craftlike flexibility in manufacturing.

The fact that small-scale, craft-based industries have survived and even shown surprising vitality does not, however, invalidate the case for spreading Taylorism. The overwhelming majority of workers in most industrialized countries continue to work in mass production facilities. The real alternatives to Taylorism lie in the mass production sector itself, where, it turns out, there has been a surprising degree of variance in the way that production is carried out and in the degree of social trust that comes into play. Advances in technology, for example, created demands for new skills even as they destroyed old ones.[24] Adam Smith's pin factory worker doing a numbingly simple, repetitive task proved much easier to replace with a machine than the worker who kept the machines in order or rebuilt the jigs to accommodate production of a new product. NC (numerically controlled) machine tools did not eliminate the need for skilled machinists, since it proved rather difficult to program these tools without having direct hands-on experience of such operations. It led, instead, to what Sabel calls the "intellectualization of skill," by which mechanical skills were replaced with quasi-mechanical ones requiring a much greater intellectual input from the worker.[25] Empirically, there was little evidence to support the view that workers in mass production facilities hated their jobs because the work was dehumanizing.[26]

From the beginning of mass production, then, evidence has been mounting that workers are in fact not the passive, isolated, self-interested individuals assumed by Taylor. The Hawthorne experiments conducted in the 1930s demonstrated that organizing workers into small groups had a large, positive effect on productivity.[27] Workers whose work rules were not rigidly defined but were instead allowed to make their own decisions about the production process turned out to be both more productive and better satisfied with their jobs. Workers under these conditions showed considerable interest in helping one another and created their own system of leaders and mutual support if left to themselves. These experiments gave support to Elton Mayo's so-called "human relations" movement of the 1930s, which sought less rigid, more communally oriented workplaces.[28]

The fact that trust and sociability are not evenly distributed among cultures but exist more in some than others would suggest that the success of Taylorism would be culture bound as well. That is, Taylorism may be the only way in which factory discipline could be achieved in certain low-trust societies, whereas high-trust societies would be inclined to generate alternatives to Taylorism that were based on greater dispersion of responsibility and skills. And indeed, a number of management studies conducted after World War II indicated that the principles of Mayo's human relations school did not apply uniformly across cultures; the experiments could not be duplicated in different parts of the United States.[29]

The most convincing evidence that Taylorism is not a necessary consequence of industrialization comes from the experience of other countries. The German workplace was never organized along pure Taylorite lines but rather has institutionalized a large number of trust relationships that gave it a greater degree of flexibility when compared to the American workplace of the 1960s and 1970s. It is to these relationships that we turn now.

CHAPTER 20

Trust in Teams

American mass production ideology arrived in Germany with the publication of a German edition of Taylor's *The Principles of Scientific Management* in 1918 and of Henry Ford's autobiography in 1923. The former sold 30,000 copies by 1922, and the latter went through thirty successive printings in the following years, leading to minor cults of *Taylorismus* and *Fordismus*.[1] The enormous advance in productivity represented by Ford's Highland Park facility impressed on German manufacturers the need to adopt mass production techniques in their own operations, and lay behind the "rationalization" movement in German industry during the mid-1920s.

But while German industry adopted mass production, *Taylorismus* never sat very well with German managers and industrial engineers, much less German workers. The deskilling of the workforce, its overspecialization, and the unsatisfying nature of blue-collar work in a Taylorite factory threatened the long-standing German belief in the importance of

231

Arbeitsfreude, or "joy in work," whose origins lay in Germany's powerful premodern craft traditions. Industrial engineers who wrote on the subject of factory organization in this period, like Gustav Frenz, Paul Rieppel, Friedrich von Gottl-Ottlilienfeld, and Goetz Briefs, all tended to distinguish between Taylorism and what they regarded as the more human system that Ford actually implemented.[2] That is, while Taylor and Ford are closely linked in historical memory as the codifier and implementer, respectively, of the low-trust mass production factory system, Ford's early plants actually practiced a form of company paternalism that was never part of Taylor's scientific management principles. Until the Great Depression cut sharply into sales and profits, Ford provided housing and welfare benefits for his workers, attracted them with continually rising wages, and tried to cultivate a spirit of community within the plant between labor and management. These German organizational theorists argued that Taylorism as such was ill adapted to German conditions but that the paternalistic side of *Fordismus* would serve as a useful model for rationalization. Many of their critiques of Taylorism anticipated those of Elton Mayo and the human relations school of the following decade.

The idea of a community of interest between workers and management was given institutional form with the works council legislation of 1920. The works councils (*Betriebesräte*) established the principle of elected worker representation on an enterprise level, with representatives participating in decision making that formerly had been the exclusive province of management. The more radical wing of the German labor movement viewed the *Betriebesräte* with suspicion, because they believed in complete worker control (a number of Bolshevik-style workers' soviets having been established during the revolutionary period immediately following the end of World War I), and the works councils failed to achieve their purpose of creating a sense of community during the interwar period.[3] This early Weimar legislation did, however, establish the precedent for an institutionalized worker-management community that would eventually be incorporated into the postwar *Sozialmarktwirtschaft,* and it indicated the seriousness of German interest in the concept from the moment that mass production was introduced.

Regardless of the fate of this particular piece of social legislation, actual relations on the shop floor had evolved in a distinctly communitarian manner in Germany by the second half of the twentieth century. One of the curious features of modern Germany is the coexistence of two very different images of German society. On the one hand, Germany (like any other European society) is riven by significant class differences and obstacles to social mobility. It possesses a powerful and sophisticated labor movement that for many years subscribed to a Marxist analysis of the need for class struggle, and which continues to try to extract its fair share from management and the owners of capital. There are no Japanese-style company unions in Germany; this sort of "yellow" labor organization was promoted by the state in the National Socialist period and thoroughly discredited. At the same time, there is a high degree of pride in labor on the part of the German working class and a sense of professionalism that allows German workers to identify not simply with their social class but with their industry and its managers. This sense of professionalism and calling has moderated the inclination toward class warfare in Germany and has led to a very different set of workplace relationships than might otherwise have been the case.

If we consider in the abstract what a more communally oriented workplace would look like, it does not imply a return to craft production—that would be impossible for most modern, large-scale industries—but rather a series of un-Taylorite rules for the organization of work. Instead of subdividing labor further and further into simple tasks performed repeatedly by specialized workers, a communally oriented factory would maintain a maximum amount of flexibility in the way that it used its workers. Each worker would be trained to do a number of different tasks and could be moved from workstation to workstation depending on the day's particular production needs. Responsibility would be pushed as far down the production hierarchy as possible. Rather than maintaining a rigid hierarchy of job classifications that established firewalls between management and labor, a communally organized factory would deemphasize status distinctions and permit a high degree of career mobility from blue-collar to white-collar occupations. Work would be done by teams, in which (as a result of multiple skills) workers could substitute for one another if the need arose. In contrast to Taylorite organization, which mandated a sharply graded piece rate system with large financial incentives for extra individual effort and equally broad wage differentials between management and labor, a communally oriented system would tend to have relatively flat pay scales and bonuses paid on the basis of group effort. A Taylorite system tends to be highly legalistic, because of the detailed way that work is laid out by the industrial engineers who design the factory and because of the manner in which labor reacts to it. A communally oriented workplace, by contrast, makes greater use of face-to-face interactions and informal channels of communications to settle problems. Finally, a Taylorite factory deskills blue-collar workers and removes the need for trust; an un-Taylorite factory would tend to improve worker skills such that workers could be trusted with a higher degree of responsibility for both the design and implementation of the production process.

A variety of detailed case studies comparing factory organization in Germany and other industrialized nations reveals that the German facilities do in fact exhibit all of these characteristics to a significantly higher degree than those in many other European countries. Consider the related question of flexibility in skills and the organization of the workplace by teams. Even before the use of work teams became a trendy imported practice in American factories, German factory work was organized on a team basis. German labor unions never insisted on the rigid job classifications and work rules that characterized the American workplace in the heyday of mass production unionism. The German foreman (*Meister*) is trusted with greater responsibility than, for example, his French counterpart. The foreman, together with his shift leaders (*Vorarbeiter*), are given authority to move workers around to perform different functions within the group for which they are responsible. The foreman notes the skills of the workers in his group as they develop and can make use of them to the best of his judgment based on the workers' actual performance. There is a tendency to rotate workers to different workstations as part of a process of socialization. Thus, when a machinist gets sick or an emergency arises on the production line, the group leader can shift workers from other jobs to fill in without legal constraint.[4]

In France, by contrast, there is a single, nationally established job classification system that assigns a coefficient to every position in the hierarchy from unskilled worker to top manager. Workers are placed in job categories and then moved up based on seniority; as in classic American job control unionism, there is labor resistance to out-of-step promotion based on skills. The system is as universalistic and Cartesian as it is rigid: the coefficients (and therefore pay) are attached to the job rather than to the worker, and therefore the struggles are not over improving skills and productivity but over moving up in the job hierarchy. In sharp contrast to Germany, a French worker can get ahead only through job turnover, not by upgrading his or her skills. There is consequently a strong temptation to push for an expansion of the number of jobs at higher classifications whether they are needed or not, a result that can be obtained only through high-level bargaining within each branch of industry. This means that labor and management expend a great deal of time negotiating at a sectoral level over the formal table of organization rather than in bargaining at a plant level over how to assign workers to the most appropriate jobs and remunerate them properly.

The job classification system in French industry is highly centralized and legalistic, like that prevailing in the French civil service. Its most important effect is to undermine the possibility of developing a sense of workplace community. Recall what Tocqueville said about the Old Regime's system of privileges: "Each group was differentiated from the rest by its right to petty privileges of one kind or another, even the least of which was regarded as a token of its exalted status." Something similar happens with the industrial job classification system: its hierarchy and formalism tends to isolate workers from each other, forcing them to look to the center rather than to their coworkers for solutions. The system impedes both the development of work teams and the moving around of workers as the need arises.[5]

In Germany, the work group as a whole is sometimes spoken of as the *"Meister's* group," and frequently develops its own esprit de corps. The *Meister* must know his workers well, since he has to evaluate them personally. On this evaluation bonuses and future mobility will depend. The foreman is able to perform this kind of assessment because he has worked his way up from the ranks of skilled workers and therefore is personally familiar with the tasks he supervises. In France, as in the United States under traditional job control unionism, the formation of work groups is hindered by the fact that each workstation is assigned a particular job category and coefficient through the formal industry-wide job classification system. It would not be possible to move a worker off one station to another if they did not belong to the same category.[6] In contrast to the German *Meister,* the French foreman is frequently described as suffering from malaise, because he is caught between labor and management: no longer a working man but rejected by his white-collar superiors as an equal.[7] Consistent with the French dislike for face-to-face authority relationships described by Crozier and others, there is no need for a French foreman to evaluate his workers personally, since their pay rests on seniority and job classification alone. (The same system applies to professors in French public universities, who are not promoted on the basis of an evaluation by their academic peers, as in the United States, but by bureaucrats in the education ministry based on formal criteria.)

Labor-management hierarchies also demonstrate the higher degree of communal organization in Germany. British companies, following a more Taylorite model, tend to segregate a greater number of technical and managerial tasks from production line jobs than German ones do. That is, production line workers in Germany have a higher level of skill and technical knowledge and are therefore able to operate their lines with a lesser degree of managerial supervision than in Britain.[8] For example, a greater proportion of German machinists were able to program their own NC machine tools than in Britain, where programming was a skill reserved for workers with white-collar status who worked in separate offices from the production line workers.[9] In Germany, management tends to be done by people with the same technical skills as the workers they manage rather than by a separate class of people who think of themselves as skilled in management.

The consequence of the greater responsibility and skills of blue-collar workers and low-ranking supervisory personnel is that the cutoff point for white-collar work is higher in Germany. Hence the ratio of white-collar to blue-collar workers is much lower in Germany than in either Britain or France. In France, there are forty-two white-collar workers for every one hundred blue-collar workers, whereas in Germany there are only thirty-six per one hundred. The average French foreman supervises only sixteen blue-collar workers, while the average German foreman supervises twenty-five.[10] In France, there is a correlation between industries with stable workforces and strong worker influence, on the one hand, and the growth of valuable white-collar jobs on the other. Achieving white-collar status means a leap in prestige and income, but also a new social wall erected between oneself and one's former colleagues. Germany, by contrast, has been much more successful in holding the line against the growth of white-collar jobs and in retaining a wide range of skills and functions within the blue-collar workforce.[11] All of this permits a higher degree of solidarity and of flexibility on the production line.

As one would expect from a more communally organized society, the variation in pay for different job categories is smaller in Germany than in France. The ratio of pay between white-collar and blue-collar workers in Germany is 1.33, compared to 1.75 for France. Given the higher proportion of white-collar workers in French industry, this tends to raise French labor costs as a whole. The flatness of pay in Germany is very much related to the system of work groups there. Productivity bonuses in Germany are determined at a relatively low level in the organization, being based ultimately on the *Meister*'s evaluation of worker performance. Obviously, large or capricious variations in compensation would hurt the morale of a small group and undermine the workers' trust in their immediate supervisor. Hence pay differentials in Germany are based more directly on differences in skill and, on the whole, evened out.[12] The formal nature of the French job classification system removes responsibility for pay issues from the shop floor to the company's personnel office, or to the even higher level of industry-wide labor-management negotiations. Without the need for face-to-face interactions, greater variations in compensation become more tolerable.

The willingness of German managers to trust blue-collar workers with greater responsibilities is closely related to the high level of worker skills in Germany, and consequently to the apprenticeship system that has served to develop and maintain them. It is hard to measure absolute industrial skill levels across cultures, but some measure of their relative importance is indicated by the fact that only ten percent of all skilled workers in Germany do not possess some form of certification, whereas in France more than half the skilled workers lack similar credentials.[13] The German apprenticeship system has been credited with providing German industry with the skill base needed to maintain its reputation for quality, as well as with dampening rates of youth unemployment relative to other European countries. For these reasons the industrial training system has been widely admired, most notably by the Clinton administration, which made German-style vocational training a campaign issue in the 1992 presidential election campaign. The apprenticeship system in Germany arises, however, in the context of a broader educational system that would not be easy to break apart into pieces for export and rests ultimately on the survival of certain social and cultural traditions that are unique to Central Europe.

The German apprenticeship system is significantly broader than that of Britain, where it exists only in certain industries like engineering, building, and construction, or in France, where it feeds the traditional artisanal sector.[14] Some seventy percent of all young Germans start their working careers as apprentices; only ten percent of all Germans fail to pass through either an apprenticeship or higher education.[15] Training lasts two to three or more years, during which the apprentice works at substantially reduced rates of pay. There are apprenticeships in virtually all sectors, for both blue- and white-collar work. These include services like retail merchandising, banking, or clerical work, for which little or no professional training is customarily provided in the United States and other European countries. A sales clerk in a German department store will have received three years of training; an American in a comparable position at JC Penney will have received three days of on-the-job training.[16] Part of the purpose of the training is to socialize young people into the rhythms and requirements of work life, but they also receive training specific to a particular trade, and at the end of the program the apprentice receives certification by taking a detailed examination. The certificates represent a standardized qualification to practice a particular trade and are therefore accepted by employers throughout Germany. Like professional credentials in the liberal or free professions (medicine, accountancy, law, etc.), these certificates are the source of a considerable amount of pride. To be a baker, secretary, or car mechanic in Germany requires substantially more effort and knowledge than in the United States, England, or France.

The system is administered in part by private companies of all sizes and in part by state-supported schools that provide generalized work training. Participation in the program on the part of both workers and companies is voluntary, though virtually all companies participate and submit to heavy regulation by the state. The costs of training are split among companies, the government on various levels, and individuals (who must work for below-market wages while doing their training). For the apprenticeship system to work, there has to be a high degree of consensus among both employers and workers as to its value. In-company training is costly for the companies that provide it (though exactly how costly is debated), and unlike Japan, the firms that provide the training make and receive no promises of lifetime employment and loyalty to those workers who go through the program. Separation rates are rather high; in the 1970s, only forty percent of graduating apprentices were still with the company that had trained them eighteen months after receiving their certificates.[17]

Given the likelihood of separation, it would seem that the temptation to free-ride on other companies' training programs would be strong.[18] That this does not happen to any large extent appears to be the product of several factors. First, the program is nearly universal; even if a company loses a trainee in whom it has invested time and effort, it is confident it can hire a comparably trained employee from a different company. At the same time, the training is usually a mixture of general and company specific; although comparable labor can be acquired externally, there is an incentive for both company and trainee to stay together. Most important, all employers feel a strong degree of social pressure to take care of their employees by giving them the skills to make them employable. Companies that fail to do this face ostracism and would not have the same kind of trust relationship with their workers as ones that did. This in the end is deeply cultural. An astonishing variety of institutions in Germany contributes to the training system: federal, state, and local governments, towns, churches, and unions, to name some of them. To opt out of this system, then, is to reject the value placed on work by the culture as a whole.

If moral pressure is not enough, the works councils—those enterprise-level labor-management groups whose precedents lay in the Weimar period—have the legal power to establish rules that sharply limit the ability of employers to hire and fire workers at will. Companies seeking to downsize must submit plans for compensating, retraining, or relocating workers to be laid off. This restricts the ability of free riders to "poach" the skilled labor of other companies.[19] These works councils have effects somewhat similar to the Japanese lifetime employment system insofar as they impede labor mobility. Were institutions with similar powers to exist in different cultural settings—in Britain, say, or Italy—they would likely use their political power to hold on to jobs at any cost, regardless of the effect on productivity. (Recall the bitter struggle waged by Arthur Scargill and the British mine workers to prevent the closing of inefficient mines in the early 1980s.) That this problem is not nearly as severe in Germany has to do with the much greater degree of trust between the works councils and management.[20] The works councils have a better sense of the need to keep their companies competitive and often press for retraining or moving workers so that they can continue to be productive. Just as in the Japanese system, the fact that companies cannot fire workers easily gives them a strong incentive to retrain them and makes an apparently inflexible labor market less so in actuality. While higher than in other European countries, however, German workplace solidarity still falls rather short of Japanese levels.

One of the paradoxes of the German industrial training system is that while it tends to produce a strong sense of workplace solidarity, it is fed by a broader educational system that at first glance appears much more highly inegalitarian than those of France, the United States, or Japan. The most notable feature about German secondary education is tracking. After four years of elementary schooling, students have to decide whether to enter one of three tracks: the *Hauptschule,* the *Realschule,* or the *Gym-*

nasium. The first two tracks lead into the apprenticeship system; only those passing through a *Gymnasium* can expect go on to receive a higher education. Indeed, a student who passes the *Abitur,* or final examination, at the end of secondary education is entitled to enter any German university. Thus by the age of ten, German children face important educational choices that will determine their occupational prospects for the rest of their life. The tracking system reflects existing class differences in German society and does little to encourage mobility; of children of working-class parents, only fifteen percent entered Gymnasia during the 1960s.[21] In contrast, university entrance in France and Japan is determined by the results of a single, nationally administered examination given toward the end of high school education—an exam that is theoretically open to all takers regardless of their previous educational background. The French secondary educational system is much more open in class terms; in the 1960s, forty percent of students in the *lycées* (the French college-preparatory upper track) were from working-class backgrounds.

How is it, then, that it is the French, and not the German, educational system that leads to a workplace that is much more highly stratified into groups of differing status that find it hard to work with one another? Much of the answer has to do with the nature of the training that occurs after students have received their general education. In France, there is a relatively open primary and secondary educational system leading to the *baccalaureate* exam. Based on the results of this test, a poor but talented student can enter first a good university and then go on to one of the *grandes écoles* that is the key to a job at the pinnacle of the French administrative system, in the public or private sector. But talents are distributed as unevenly in France as everywhere else, and the vast majority of students wash out of the system at the *baccalaureate* or later. (In France, forty-five percent of those attending the upper secondary track fail to achieve the *baccalaureate,* whereas the comparable figure for Germany is only ten percent.)[22] As in the United States, vocational education has a certain stigma in France: it is what one does if one has failed in the general educational system and is not good enough to go on to a university. Washouts who end up in blue-collar or low-skill white-collar positions have less reason to take pride in their work; it is what they end up doing in a society with high expectations for higher education. In Germany, by contrast, working-class students know from a relatively early age that they will not be going on to a university, but because the apprenticeship system provides them with training and a professional qualification appropriate to their skill level, they tend to regard themselves not as people who failed in the general educational system but as ones who succeeded in a demanding vocational training track.

Moreover, the dynamism of the German vocational training system is such that training opportunities do not end with the completion of an apprenticeship program. Beyond the basic apprenticeship program has grown up a system of intermediate certifications that allow older workers to increase their skill levels. These intermediate certifications constitute an entirely separate route to upward social mobility of a sort that does not exist in most other countries. For example, in France or the United States, it is not possible to receive professional credentials as an engineer without having gone to college and obtained a higher degree, usually requiring several years of graduate study. This is not the case in Germany, where there are two routes to being an engineer: attending university and obtaining an engineering degree, as in other countries, or working one's way up through an intermediate occupational training program.[23] Indeed, with the passage of time, many new routes to higher educational, and therefore occupational and social status, have been opened up. Thus the decision of a ten-year-old German child to enter the *Hauptschule* track is not nearly as career limiting a decision as it might at first seem. At the same time, the apprenticeship system leaves the bottom two-thirds of the workforce with a high level of skills and, perhaps just as important, a considerable degree of pride in their abilities.

There are a number of questions overhanging the future of the German apprenticeship system and its ability to support the future competitiveness of German industry. In the early 1980s, the system appeared to be in a state of crisis because the large number of young people applying for apprenticeships outstripped the number of openings and opportunities for employment once they had completed their training. This problem disappeared, however, once the baby boom turned to baby bust by the end of the decade.[24] The current question is whether the types of apprenticeships available will endow the German workforce with appropriate skills for the future, particularly in a twenty-first-century information-age economy. The system is extremely dynamic. Both the sectoral trade associations and the unions work together to make sure that the types of apprenticeships and standards for certification match the needs of industry. The system is very well suited to train workers for the kinds of medium-technology industries at which the Germans traditionally have excelled, such as automobiles, chemicals, machine tools, and other producer goods.

It is less clear, however, that apprenticeships can be a source of skills for the much more highly knowledge-intensive industries such as telecommunications, semiconductors and computers, and biotechnology. These skills may require, instead, a vast expansion of the university system.[25]

The issue here, however, is not whether the apprenticeship system will be the appropriate institutional mechanism for training in the next century. The German training system is of interest because it constitutes a critical bridge to sociability in the German workplace.

By raising the skill levels of workers, it allows managers to trust them to work autonomously, with fewer detailed rules and less supervision. As well, it socializes new workers both to the norms of a particular trade and to those of the company in which they are trained. A worker who undergoes a three-year apprenticeship with a particular firm is likely to develop a higher degree of loyalty to the organization than one whose training lasts three days. And by giving professional credentials to even the lowest-ranking employee, workers develop a much greater sense of pride in their work. To the extent that workers regard work not merely as a burden or a commodity to be exchanged for other goods, the workplace becomes a less alienating venue, one that is better integrated into the worker's social life. In Charles Sabel's words,

> German superiors assume the opposite [from their French counterparts], namely, that their subordinates want and are able to acquire the kind of knowledge about their jobs that allows them to work autonomously. The task of the German supervisor is thus not to tell those charged with execution how to do their work, but rather to indicate to them what needs to be done. Conversely, in return for not being hedged in by a thicket of rules, German subordinates must count on their supervisors not to make abusive use of their discretionary powers. German society is "high trust" because it discourages the separation of conception and execution.[26]

The 1992–1993 recession created high and seemingly intractable levels of unemployment in Germany, and in the view of many observers it was precisely the communitarian aspects of the German postwar *Sozialmarktwirtschaft* that were to blame. The German welfare state has grown enormous, consuming half the nation's gross domestic product by the early 1990s. German labor had become very expensive, and employers were burdened with the mandatory costs of health care, unemployment, training, and vacation benefits, as well as sharp constraints on their ability to lay off workers and downsize their companies.

Although there are many similarities between the communal and paternalistic orientation of German and Japanese industry, the Japanese system remains considerably more flexible. The group orientation of Japanese business is, for the most part, not written into law; neither lifetime employment nor the *keiretsu* system is based on anything more than informal moral obligation. Companies have greater room for maneuver in terms of cutting costs in Japan, either by shifting employment elsewhere, forcing down wages (mostly in the form of forgone bonuses), or insisting that workers increase their efforts. The Japanese government pays a lower level of welfare benefits (having kept this function in the private sector to a greater extent). In Germany, by contrast, most welfare benefits are written into law and administered by the state on various levels. They are therefore much harder to adjust during downturns. The competitiveness of the German economy depends on a delicate balancing act: labor, although expensive, is also very highly skilled, and has found high value-added niches in the world economy. The system can go out of balance if the value-added produced by the skills fails to keep up with costs, both direct and social. On the other hand, these communal institutions have produced a remarkable record of economic growth coupled with a high level of social benefits throughout much of the postwar period, something that has eluded many of Germany's neighbors.

Before concluding our discussion of Germany and returning to the question of workplace relations in Japan, we need to examine briefly the historical origins of the apprenticeship system.

CHAPTER 21

Insiders and Outsiders

One of the great ironies of the modern German economy is that the apprenticeship system, which is broadly credited as the basis of Germany's industrial dominance in Europe, is the direct descendant of the medieval guild system. Throughout the industrial revolution, the guilds were the *bête noire* of liberal economic reformers, who believed the latter represented hidebound tradition and a hindrance to modernizing economic change.

The role of the guilds in the development of free institutions in the West is quite complex. The guilds, closed corporations existing in virtually all European (and most Asian) countries, were the distant forerunners of modern organizations like the American Bar Association and the American Medical Association. With some variations, they restricted entry into a particular trade or profession by setting standards or qualifications for membership, thereby also artificially raising the income of their members. The guilds regulated the quality of products and occasionally engaged in training their members. In the late Middle Ages, they played an important part in the breakdown of the manorial system. Particularly in central Europe, the guilds sank deep roots in the imperial free cities, where they won the right to manage their own affairs and became bastions of independence from seigneurial and patrician control.[1] The guilds were therefore key intermediate organizations, constitutive of the rather rich civil society of the late Middle Ages. Their existence limited the power of absolute sovereigns and therefore played an important role in the development of free Western political institutions.

The guilds, with their self-governing practices and often considerable wealth, represented a challenge to ambitious princes, who eyed them with a mixture of envy and resentment. With the rise of large, centralizing monarchies in countries like France and Spain in the sixteenth and seventeenth centuries, the guilds were seen as rivals for power. As we saw in an earlier chapter, the French monarchy succeeded in subordinating them to the goals of the state, where they became a sort of regulatory appendage to the political authorities in Paris. The situation was quite different in Germany, however, where no centralized state was established until 1871. The decentralized nature of political power in the German lands kept alive a host of feudal communal institutions like the guilds for much longer than in other parts of Europe.

While some have argued that the guilds were important in preserving craft traditions and maintaining quality standards,[2] by the early eighteenth century the tide of progressive opinion in England and France had shifted decisively against them.[3] Though differently motivated, early liberals carried on the work of the absolute monarchs in reducing the guilds' power and influence. The first modern factories had to be built in the countryside, outside the cities with their guild restrictions. In England, liberal reformers pushed for abolition of the Statute of Artificers and an end to compulsory guild membership, particularly in the middle decades of the eighteenth century.[4] In France and the parts of Europe occupied by the French, the guilds, whose independence had already been undermined by the Old Regime, were officially abolished during the Revolution.

The liberals' struggle against the guilds in the German-speaking lands was considerably more drawn out and convoluted. As elsewhere, one of the rallying cries of liberal reformers in Prussia was *Gewerbefreiheit,* or "freedom of occupation," a principle that was introduced on a limited basis beginning in 1808.[5] While trade was liberalized under the Stein-

Hardenberg reforms of 1807–1812 and in areas that had been under French control, a period of reaction set in throughout many of the German states in the following decades that reasserted guild privileges. This movement was spearheaded by the traditional artisans, whose livelihoods were being threatened by advancing industrialization. The General Industrial Ordinance of 1845 in Prussia, while abolishing certain corporate privileges, established the need for certification of master craftsman status and means tests for entrepreneurs.[6] Even as the liberal Frankfurt Vorparliament was meeting in 1848, the independent craft sector had organized itself and staged a United German Craftsmen's Congress (*Allgemeiner Deutscher Handwerker-Kongress*) in the same city to lobby for the protection of craft privileges.[7] In the decade after the defeat of the revolutions of 1848, guild ordinances were tightened in several German states. The history of the struggle of liberal economic reformers against the guilds thus paralleled the struggle of political liberalism in Germany. While liberal principles made cautious advances in 1815 and 1848, frequent setbacks occurred both before and after unification, and they never achieved the ascendancy they did in England and France.

By the end of the nineteenth century, the actual power of the guilds had been undermined in practice by the growth of entirely new industries like railroads and steel that emerged outside their purview. Legal control over product quality and craft certification existed only in the traditional handicraft sector. But the guilds had the last word, so to speak. As Germany industrialized, large numbers of craftsmen from the traditional artisanal sector moved over into modern manufacturing to become machinists or other skilled craft workers, and they brought their corporatist traditions with them. Both the German Committee for Technical Schooling (*Deutscher Ausschuss für technisches Schulwesen*) and the German Institute for Training in Technical Work (*Deutsches Institut für technische Arbeitsschulung*) were established early in the twentieth century to provide systematic craft training for industry.[8] In 1922 the *Handwerkskammer Tag* (Chamber of Craft Confederation) was legally recognized as the representative of craft interests.[9] A basic framework for vocational training founded in the Weimar period provided for apprenticeships and technical colleges, involving industry and labor unions as corporate bodies. Then in 1935, under National Socialism, trade associations were assigned legal responsibility for vocational training, similar to what existed in the handicraft guilds.[10] It was in this period also that systematic training for the *Meister*, or foreman, was developed. This particular legacy of

National Socialism was never rejected after the formation of the Federal Republic of Germany in 1949, but in fact continued and strengthened up through the Vocational Education and Training Act of 1969.

In Germany, then, the guilds were never ruthlessly destroyed as they were in France. They survived and were transmuted into a modern form, becoming the basis of the country's postwar apprenticeship system. England, by contrast, had no comprehensive vocational training system in place after the war due, in part at least, to its own liberal principles. Not only had elimination of guild privileges been on the liberal reform agenda, but a somewhat laissez-faire attitude toward education in general contributed to the slowness with which the British established a modern educational system suitable to a twentieth-century industrial power. Free universal education was not instituted in Britain until 1891, considerably later than in Germany, and English higher educational institutions did not orient their curricula toward science and technology until well into the twentieth century.[11]

The incomplete victory of liberalism in Germany had a disastrous effect on a political level.[12] The German state at the beginning of the twentieth century was considerably more authoritarian than that of Britain or France, with significant powers reserved for the kaiser and the Junker aristocracy surrounding him. The Junkers, with their military traditions and authoritarian social relations, set the tone for German politics and foreign policy. Apart from institutions, the communitarian nature of German culture itself bred intolerance and lack of openness. That is, the very strength of the bonds uniting Germans gave them a clear sense of their own distinct cultural identity and provided a powerful boost to German nationalism in the first half of the century. Historians have also argued that Germany's late statehood made German insistence on a distinct national identity all the more insistent and aggressive. When, as a result of defeat in World War I and economic disaster, the Germans could also look upon themselves as victims, that strong sense of cultural identity began to take extreme and ugly forms. It took defeat in World War II and the painful legacy of National Socialism to break down the Germans' closed sense of community and to build the basis for the kind of tolerance and openness in German society that had existed in Britain and France for several generations. Even today, German democracy is more corporatist and less individualistic than England or France because of the legally recognized role that established social groups play in it.

What had grim consequences from the standpoint of political development, however, turned out to be very useful from the standpoint of economic modernization. Accordingly, the Federal Republic did not reject the National Socialist legislation on training out of hand, as it did most other Nazi legal innovations, but rather preserved and extended certain aspects of it. In this, the German case is parallel to the Japanese, who took cultural traditions like the *iemoto* group and the Confucian virtue of loyalty and modernized them as part of a new industrial synthesis.

None of this should be construed as implying that preservation of cultural traditions per se is a precondition for successful economic modernization. Just as many immigrants to the United States do well because they combine their particularistic cultural traditions with freedom of a liberal society, so too the countries that appear to be successful industrial powerhouses are those that manage to combine older institutions and/or cultural characteristics with a broadly liberal economic framework. The Germans hardly preserved the guild system intact any more than the Japanese preserved feudal clan structures, but neither did they remake society entirely anew based on purely liberal principles. Instead, the liberal framework was moderated and given cohesiveness by certain premodern holdover institutions.

Indeed, the German case shows the importance of being either clever or lucky in the kinds of traditional culture that has been preserved. After all, modern British society is also a mixture of liberal institutions and ancient cultural traditions, but in the English case the mixture has not worked out as well from an economic point of view. I said earlier that the British took a more laissez-faire attitude toward education when compared to the Germans. This was as much a matter of liberal ideology as the product of a traditional upper-class aristocratic culture that was hostile to the sort of technical and pragmatic education necessary to create a modern industrial economy. The United States was no less liberal a society than Britain and yet established universal education earlier and developed a much superior system of higher technical education.[13] Higher educational institutions in Britain remained devoted to classical humanism rather than science well into the twentieth century. Engineering was not regarded as a high-status occupation and tended to be the province of the children of skilled workers rather than the country's elite. The upper classes cultivated a belief in the ideal of the educated amateur and the practical tinkerer, both of whom disdained systematic technical education.[14]

Martin Wiener has argued that the very gradualism and tolerance of English politics, which was a boon from the standpoint of the development of decent liberal political institutions, had the perverse effect of leaving intact an upper-class culture that was openly hostile to the values of a modern industrial society.[15] The landed aristocracy in Britain was far more willing to admit upstart middle-class industrialists and financiers into its ranks than the Prussian Junkers ever were. But this acceptance proved to be a poison pill: rather than energizing the aristocracy, the entrepreneurial middle classes were co-opted by the leisured values of the aristocracy. Wiener relates the story of Marcus Samuel, a once ambitious Jew from the East End of London who founded the Shell Oil Company in the late nineteenth century. Samuel's real ambition was not to become a fabulously wealthy industrialist but to have a country house (which he acquired in 1895) and a title (he became Lord Mayor of London in 1902), and to send his children to Eton and Oxford (which also happened). In so doing, he lost control of the company to Henry Deterding, head of Royal Dutch, who retained more of the classic middle-class virtues and was not seduced by the appeal of fox hunting or charitable social events.[16]

From the standpoint of economics, then, the Germans were fortunate that as a result of a half-century of war, revolution, economic instability, foreign occupation, and rapid social change, a number of their traditional social institutions other than the guild system were destroyed. The Prussian aristocracy lost its hold, actual and figurative, on German society in the aftermath of the Great War, a process that was, if anything, accelerated by Hitler and the National Socialist revolution. Virtually all of the traditional social hierarchies were discredited with the defeat in 1945. The engineer and entrepreneur, both of whom had a more valued social status in nineteenth-century Germany, became central players as the whole nation focused its energies on economic recovery.

At the beginning of the nineteenth century, Britain, Germany, and Japan were ruled by aristocratic classes that disdained commerce, technology, and moneymaking. All three societies retained communal institutions left over from feudal times (guilds, churches, or temples) and pockets of local political authority. Japan by the turn of the twentieth century and Germany by its middle had succeeded in neutralizing their aristocracies, either by turning the energies of the ruling classes to business (as in the case of Japan) or by simply marginalizing them (as in the case of Germany). Japan and Germany at the same time modernized many of their traditional communal cultural practices or institutions by transforming them into the building blocks of a modern industrial society, whether in the form of the bank-centered industrial group, *keiretsu,* industry association, or apprenticeship. Both were able to master the problem of organization at both ends of the scale, creating extremely large, hierarchical corporations while giving their immediate workplaces a more human face by encouraging the solidarity of small groups.

The English did something of the opposite: they undercut many traditional communal institutions like the guilds and were slow to create modern organizations to replace their functions of training and quality control. English society demonstrated a high propensity for spontaneous sociability. Never having been subjected to a powerful modernizing state, it retained a large number of very rich intermediate organizations during the entire period it industrialized, including dissenting or free churches (like the Quakers, Congregationalists, and Methodists), charitable institutions, schools, clubs, and literary societies. But it also retained a sharp sense of class stratification that balkanized British society and made it impossible, in the twentieth century, for workers and managers ever to feel that they were part of the same team. Even as the real power of the English aristocracy declined, its anticapitalist attitudes were taken up by a Marxist intellectual class that retained the aristocracy's snobbishness toward industry, technology, and men of affairs. For such people, "making three-dimensional artifacts" was a dubious activity.[17] Class consciousness and a sense of tradition delayed the full emergence of the corporate form in Britain until after World War II. Despite the fact that British society is not nearly as familistic as China or Italy, many large British firms remained family owned and family managed until the middle of the twentieth century.[18] In many ways the Thatcher revolution was aimed as much against the antientrepreneurial aristocratic right as against the trade unionist left. Margaret Thatcher's impact on the former culture, at this point, would seem to have been rather small.

The survival of communitarian structures in the German and Japanese economies points to what seems at first like a strange paradox. In the past, both Germany and Japan have been known for authoritarian government and for having sharply hierarchical societies. A popular stereotype of both groups is that they like to obey authority—a view that, like all other stereotypes, was never quite true and has become less so over time. And yet, as we have seen, the German and Japanese factory floors are much more egalitarian than their English, French, or American counterparts. There are many fewer formal status distinctions between supervisors and workers; wage differentials tend to be lower; and authority is devolved to lower levels of the organization rather than being husbanded by central managers or offices. How can it be that societies that were never "dedicated to the proposition that all men are created equal" in fact treat their members more equally in practice?

The answer is related to the fact that the egalitarianism in communally oriented societies is often restricted to the homogeneous cultural groups that tend to comprise them and does not extend to other human beings, even if they share their society's dominant cultural beliefs. Moral communities have distinct insiders and outsiders; insiders are treated with a respect and equality that is not extended to outsiders. Indeed, there is an inverse proportion between the solidarity of those inside the community and the hostility, indifference, or intolerance shown to those on the outside. Countries formally "dedicated to the proposition that all men are created equal" must bring together much more disparate peoples who do not necessarily share a set of cultural beliefs or moral standards. In place of moral community, there is law; in place of spontaneous trust, formal equality and due process. If insiders are treated less equally on the basis of a thicket of rules, then outsiders are at least treated with more respect and can hope one day to themselves become insiders.

Since the end of World War II, Germany's communitarian culture has changed to a much greater degree than that of Japan. Reacting to the excesses of the Nazi period, Germany went from being one of the least tolerant European societies to one of the most open. Despite the tightening of the asylum laws and the antiforeigner violence, German cities like Frankfurt and Hamburg remain among the most cosmopolitan in the world. The policy of successive postwar German governments has been to submerge German identity into a broader European one. Older attitudes toward authority, hierarchy, the state, and the nation were rather thoroughly discredited by the war, and a much more individualistic culture is in evidence.[19]

The Japanese postwar transformation was much less thoroughgoing. Although the country accepted a democratic constitution and turned profoundly pacifist, the Japanese, unlike the Germans, never wallowed in their guilt over the war in quite the same way. The differences between the two countries today are evident in the treatment of the war in textbooks and in the way in which respectable Japanese politicians and academics continue to deny responsibility for it.[20] The higher level of conformity in Japan is evident to anyone walking through a large Japanese city; the equivalents of Germany's feminist and environmental movements in contemporary Japan are few and weak, there are no Japanese

Greens or *Autonomen,* no distinct racial or ethnic minorities apart from the small Korean community. As one young German said to a Dutch author writing a book comparing German and Japanese attitudes toward the war, "Please, please don't overdo the similarities. We are very different from the Japanese. We don't sleep in our companies to make them more powerful. We are just people, just normal people."[21] He can be proven right statistically in one respect: the Germans today work, on average, much less hard than the Japanese. Whatever the strength of the traditional German Protestant work ethic celebrated by Max Weber, the average German workweek in manufacturing has fallen to thirty-one hours, compared to forty-two hours for Japan.[22] German workers, it would appear from anecdotal evidence, take their annual vacations with significantly freer consciences than do their Japanese counterparts.

Just as in the case of Japan, the recession of the early 1990s and the general intensification of global competition have and will continue to put a great deal of pressure on German communitarian economic institutions. It is a good principle for companies to say that they will retrain workers rather than laying them off, and the Germans are in a better position to do this than many of their European competitors. But it is not always possible to match skilled labor to high value-added market niches, especially when that labor is as expensive as it is in Germany. It is increasingly possible to find labor with comparable skills at a fraction of the cost in Eastern Europe, Asia, and parts of the Third World. Moreover, many more German communal economic institutions are written into law than in Japan, and more are administered directly by the state. Basing such institutions on law rather than informal moral consensus raises transaction costs and probably adds considerably to the rigidity of the system. The implication is that if Germany is to meet future challenges of global competitiveness, it needs to become not necessarily a less communitarian economy but a less statist one.

CHAPTER 22

The High-Trust Workplace

I f asked to compare the traditional American manufacturing workplace with its high-trust, team-oriented German counterpart, or with
the low-trust, bureaucratically regulated French model, most people
would say it resembled the latter. Frederick Winslow Taylor, after all, was
an American, and the low-trust industrial system he created was regarded
around the world as a uniquely American vision of modernity. The legal-
ism of the Taylorite factory, its pretensions to universality, and the carefully enumerated rights in job control unionism all echo aspects of
American constitutional law. The growing complexity of job classifications
and their ramification throughout the workplace anticipate the spread of
legal relationships in broader American society. The twentieth-century
American system of industrial labor relations, with its periodic massive
layoffs, book-length contracts, and bureaucratic, rule-bound personal interactions, would seem the very model of low-trust social relations.

Yet the Taylorite factory and the job control unionism associated with it have been in rapid decline in the United States over the past couple of decades, replaced by a much more team-oriented form of factory floor organization imported from Japan. A closer look at the history of American mass production indicates that rather than epitomizing the American workplace, Taylorism may have been something of a historic anomaly. Lean manufacturing, in other words, is not an alien cultural practice grafted onto a very different society, but rather has brought American workers back to earlier communal workplace traditions that they lost along the way.

When Taylorism was introduced in the auto industry just after the turn of the century, many of its characteristics, like its cold and formalistic way of treating workers, did not sit well with Americans, and its introduction met considerable resistance. It succeeded, one can argue, only because of the specific conditions of the labor market in Detroit during the first decades of the twentieth century. The new working-class entrants into the auto industry tested the limits of American community as it defined itself at the time. Detroit itself was a new city in many ways; its population exploded from half a million in 1910 to a million one decade later. Few auto workers had any roots in their community. Of a labor force in Detroit estimated at 170,000 in 1911, some 160,000 had been recently recruited from outside the city by the Employer's Association.[1] The vast majority of the new workers attracted to the auto industry were immigrants, primarily from Austria-Hungary, Italy, Russia, and other parts of Eastern Europe. (This was true in other new industries as well; of the 23,337 workers at the Carnegie steel works in Pittsburgh in 1907, two-thirds were immigrants.)[2] A survey of auto workers at Highland Park in 1915 showed that more than fifty languages were spoken there.[3] As remains the case today, it is much easier for employers to exploit immigrants than the native born. Given the ethnic and transitory character of the workforce, it was natural for Ford and other new mass producers not to think of their employees as part of a large, corporate family but rather as strangers who had to be controlled and disciplined through a formal, legalistic set of rules.

Even so, Henry Ford soon implemented a number of paternalistic labor practices that are seldom identified with Taylorism. The nature of work in the new mass production environment was highly stressful and dangerous, and led to a very high rate of labor turnover. Ford reacted negatively to the conditions he saw in his own plant, and himself proposed the most famous innovation: introduction of the $5.00 day in

1914.[4] In doing this, Ford doubled the wage rate of his workers in the midst of a recession. The company subsequently set up a "Sociological Department" that had responsibility for worker welfare. The intrusive department sent investigators to the homes of each worker to examine living conditions, moral behavior, and problems like alcohol abuse; workers would be moved, through inducement or threat, into better housing because Ford did not want to have company slums.[5] The company set up an extensive program of English language training schools and made special efforts to recruit the disabled.[6] There was thus a large gap between theoretical Taylorism and the actual system Henry Ford implemented at Highland Park and later River Rouge.

The auto industry then plunged into the Great Depression, which dried up the market for automobiles and sent labor relations into a tailspin with massive layoffs and violent clashes between militant workers and company police. The infamous battle at the gates of the River Rouge plant in 1932 left four workers killed by gunfire.[7] After World War II and recovery from the depression, the adversarial and legalistic pattern for American labor relations had already been set, and job control unionism proliferated through one industry after another.[8]

The speed with which managements using high-trust Japanese lean production methods have been able to implement them in the United States, and the general enthusiasm of workers employed under this system, indicates that Taylorism and job control unionism are perhaps not as deeply rooted in American culture as it may at first appear. Despite the significantly greater pressures that lean production imposes on workers, the notion of company as family has had considerable appeal to American workers, many of whom have fiercely resisted unionization by the United Auto Workers in nonunionized lean production plants. It is no accident that the Japanese transplants building facilities in the United States have chosen sites in the South or in the rural Midwest, like Honda's plant in Marysville, Ohio. Not only do these areas not have unions and a tradition of union militancy, but they are home to relatively homogeneous communities that hark back in spirit to the small-town America of the early twentieth century.

To understand the revolution in social relations on the factory floor that has been taking place in the United States, we need to understand the nature of lean manufacturing itself.

Lean manufacturing (otherwise known as just-in-time, or *kanban* in Japanese), perfected by the Toyota Motor Corporation, has been an industrial buzzword for a decade and a half now, and the practice has diffused from Japan to North America, Europe, and some parts of the Third World. It has been studied extensively, particularly by the MIT International Motor Vehicle Program, on whose work I will rely heavily here.[9] The fact that it has been implemented in so many different countries suggests to the authors of the MIT study that it is not a culturally determined practice but rather a management technique of universal applicability. This is correct to some extent: high-trust relations can be exported across cultural boundaries. But it is no accident that lean manufacturing was invented in Japan, a country with an extremely high level of generalized social trust. Moreover, it is not clear from the MIT study's own data that this technique can be implemented nearly as well in low-trust countries as in high-trust ones.

Lean production was invented in the 1950s by Toyota's chief production engineer, Taiichi Ono, who was faced with the problem that Toyota's market was too small to support the long production runs, and consequently the highly specialized division of labor, that characterized America's Taylorite mass production auto plants at the time. American manufacturers could afford to purchase specialized machine tools that could be set up once and kept in place over long periods of time, as well as extensive inventories to prevent any disruption of the production line. In trying to find a way around this problem, Ono came up with a system that was cheaper in terms of total capital costs and more productive per unit of capital than Taylorite mass production.[10]

The essence of lean manufacturing is the creation of an extremely taut and fragile manufacturing system that can be easily disrupted by problems anywhere along the line from supply to final assembly.[11] Inventories are kept at a minimal level, and each worker has a cord at his workstation by which he can bring the entire production line to a halt if he sees a problem. If a worker pulls his cord or if a supplier fails to provide the product on the exact schedule expected, the entire assembly line operation will grind to a halt. The very fragility of the lean manufacturing process acts as an information feedback loop that tells the workers or production engineers when there is a problem. Those people operating the line are forced to fix these problems at their source rather than allowing defects to be incorporated into the final product. Thus, for example, in a traditional mass production factory a worker has every incentive to bolt on a door panel even if it is misaligned. In a lean production facility, the line would be stopped until the problem with the door panel was fixed, possibly at the workstation doing the assembly or possibly at the facility of the supplier of the panel itself. The lean production system is very difficult to set up initially, but once working improves product quality substantially. Quality problems are addressed at their source, rather than in the rework shops at the end of the assembly line that characterize most traditional mass production factories.

Ono's lean production system devolves decision-making authority to assembly line workers to an even greater extent than in the German factories described earlier.[12] That is, instead of following the Taylorite prescription for specialized white-collar production engineers to design the plant, the workers who operate the line itself are given substantial responsibility for deciding how best to do so. And rather than being given highly detailed instructions on how to perform a narrow and simple task, an entire team of workers is given broader responsibility to decide collectively how to solve a more complicated production problem. The work groups are given time to discuss the operation of the line and are continually encouraged to make suggestions as to how the production process could proceed more efficiently. The workers' job is not to manipulate a simple operation on a complex machine, as in Adam Smith's pin factory, but to contribute their judgment to help run the production line as a whole. Thus the concept of production teams, and later quality circles, is born.

Delegating responsibility to work teams limits the division of labor: workers are trained to perform a wide number of tasks, so that they can be moved around from one position to another as the need arises. Moreover, using broadly trained workers to do flexibly defined tasks reduces the need for highly specialized machine tools and other expensive capital goods. One of Ono's first innovations was to reorganize the die setup process. Die change times for the large stamping presses used to make auto body parts are reduced from a day to three minutes and could be carried out by production workers themselves rather than by die change specialists. Making parts in small lots improves productivity enormously because it reduces the need to finance large inventories, eliminates requirements for expensive specialized machine tools, and also reveals quality problems before they were replicated in large batches of products.[13] The same assembly line can be used to produce a much broader array of goods using general-purpose tools.

In lean production, the degree of trust shown in the lowliest assembly line worker is extraordinary by Taylorite standards. In a traditional mass production plant, the assembly line is organized to prevent stoppages of the line as a whole at any cost. This is the reason for the buildup of inventories and buffers of spare parts at every workstation; errors are passed down the line, where they are caught either in a rework area at the end of the line or by the final consumer. Stopping the line constitutes a major crisis in the plant, and authority to do so rests only with higher management. In a lean production facility, by contrast, each worker is trusted with a cord to pull to stop the line as a whole if he sees a problem. While the plant was being organized originally, regular cord pulling led to great start-up delays, but with time, the number of stoppages of the line began to decrease dramatically. One can imagine what would happen in a plant with poisonous labor-management relations were every worker in effect given authority to sabotage production as a whole.

For the work team concept to be effective, management has to abandon its Taylorite ambition to compartmentalize the design and control of the production process as a specialized engineering function, instead trusting workers much further down the hierarchy with responsibility for basic production decisions. In the words of the MIT study, "Workers respond only when there exists some sense of reciprocal obligation, a sense that management actually values skilled workers, will make sacrifices to retain them, and is willing to delegate responsibility to the team. Merely changing the organization chart to show 'teams' and introducing quality circles to find ways to improve production processes are unlikely to make much difference."[14]

A downward delegation of authority can come about in lean manufacturing only if workers have a sufficiently broad range of skills to enable them to see the production process as a whole, and not merely one microscopic part of it. The investment in training therefore has to be much higher than in a classic Taylorite factory. This means, in addition, a lower degree of specialization up and down the hierarchy: product engineers are required to work on the assembly line in certain lean facilities to develop familiarity with the production process and are not pigeonholed in narrow professional categories for their entire careers.[15]

In its fully ramified form, the final assembler's entire network of suppliers and subcontractors are drawn into the system as well. Rather than being vertically integrated into the parent company through outright acquisition, the latter are organized into several independent tiers. Suppliers are expected to provide small quantities of product on a tight schedule and to adapt to changes as rapidly as the workers on the final assembly line themselves. Responsibility for product design is devolved to the supplier. Rather than being asked to manufacture to the exact specifications of a blueprint drawn by the final assembler's engineers, the suppliers are given the broad requirements for the part in question and allowed to make their own design decisions. If a quality problem is revealed in the final assembly process, however, the assembler could go back to the supplier and ask that it be solved at its source. At this point the relationship might not be so hands-off: the assembler's engineers might critique the supplier's own manufacturing methods and request changes, in effect forcing the lean production method down the supply chain. The parent company and its suppliers therefore exchange a large volume of information—not just specifications and blueprints but the most intimate details of each other's manufacturing process. Often the exchange of information is accompanied by an exchange of personnel. The whole supplier network is extremely difficult to set up, but when it is finally coordinated, it becomes a vast extension of the lean manufacturing plant itself.

The trust relationship is particularly critical in maintaining the supplier network, and it flourishes in the context of Japanese *keiretsu* relationships. In a purely market-driven assembler-supplier relationship, the purchasing company has an incentive to play its suppliers off against each other in order to get the best price and quality. This in turn creates a gulf of suspicion between the assembler and supplier: the latter will be reluctant to provide the former with data about costs or proprietary manufacturing processes for fear that the information would be used against it. If the supplier develops a process that significantly improves its productivity, it will want to capture the economic returns rather than being forced to pass them on to its clients. The *keiretsu* relationship, on the other hand, is based on a sense of reciprocal obligation between the assembler and supplier: both know that they will be dealing with one another over the long term and will not switch to alternative partners based on a small price differential. Only if there is a high degree of mutual trust will a supplier permit the parent company's engineers to look at cost data and have a voice in how to share the economic returns from productivity improvements.

The lean production system constituted such a powerful boon to productivity that it was soon analyzed and copied by other companies, much as Henry Ford's Highland Park facility was imitated at the beginning of the mass production age. The severe downturn in the American auto industry that followed on the energy crises of the 1970s was the immediate spur to learning on the part of a number of American manufacturers. Introduction of a high-trust production method in what had become an extremely low-trust industrial setting proved extremely difficult, however, since lean production takes aim directly at the job classifications and work rules that are spawned by Taylorite mass production and job control unionism.

General Motors introduced work teams into some of its plants in the early 1980s, in a reform that collapsed a large hierarchy of job classifications into a single production worker category. The GM team system encouraged workers to learn multiple skills through bonuses, to organize some aspects of production, and to form quality circles. The team approach was viewed with extreme suspicion by the United Auto Workers (UAW), however, particularly since GM introduced it first in its southern plants, which were nonunionized at the time.[16] In Japan, workers do not cling to job classifications and written contract guarantees because lean production is embedded in the lifetime employment system, which gives them total job security. The UAW feared that work teams were a means of eroding loyalty to the union, part of a larger antiunion strategy that would encourage workers to give up hard-won work rules without winning anything by way of job security in return. Obligation, in other words, has to be truly reciprocal for lean production to work. And indeed, this particular early effort on GM's part to introduce isolated elements of Japanese lean production did not pan out. The company did not live up to its end of the bargain: while encouraging work teams, it bought robots and continued to lay off workers. It did not help the sense of the company as a team that Roger Smith, GM's chairman, was awarded a $1.5 million bonus on the heels of the bruising 1981–1982 recession.[17]

Other institutional obstacles impeded the introduction of lean production in the United States as well. Much of the work of the officials in union locals around the country was to monitor contracts and administer work rules; if the latter are abolished or given to a team of production workers, these officials are out of a job. Many middle managers, for their part, did not relish giving up their control over the factory floor to production workers. Lean production can be extremely stressful for workers, who must take responsibility for their group's productivity and operate under great pressure to maximize the output of a complex production process.

Many Japanese transplants (factories built by Japanese companies in the United States) overcame the problems of job control unionism by siting themselves in the South or in other areas lacking unionized work forces. When General Motors finally established a lean production facility with direct help from Toyota (the New United Motor Manufacturing Inc. plant in Fremont, California), it did so only by persuading the UAW to drop its thick local work rule agreement in favor of a contract that provided for only two categories of workers.[18]

The problem that lean producers faced with unionized labor was not labor's demands for wages, benefits, or job security (though all employers would naturally like to be able to pay less) but rather the unions' insistence on detailed work rules and job classifications that hampered the introduction of teams and flexible production. Indeed, the implicit bargain that underlies the successful implementation of lean production, in both Japan and the United States, is a trade-off of relaxed work rules for long-term job security. In general, the Ford Motor Company implemented lean production the most comprehensively in its North American plants because it was able to generate a significantly greater sense of trust among its workers that it would live up to its end of the bargain.[19]

The authors of the MIT study argue that lean production is not culturally determined and that under proper management it can be implemented anywhere. To support this view, they make use of their extensive automobile plant productivity data from around the world. These data show that within each region—Japan, North America, Europe, and the Third World—there is considerable variation in the degree of automobile plant productivity, a variation that is greater than the average differences in productivity between regions. This suggests that culture is less of a factor than management in determining auto plant productivity. Lean production did not, after all, spring full-blown out of traditional Japanese culture; it was invented by an engineer at Toyota at a certain historical moment, and that company had a big efficiency advantage over its Japanese rivals until they too adopted the system.[20] Thus, the MIT authors argue, the regional variations in productivity are simply due to the laggard regions' slowness in adopting lean production and moving down the learning curve.[21]

Based on the earlier discussions of culture and trust, we would expect that cultures with a strong propensity for spontaneous sociability, like Japan and Germany, to adopt lean manufacturing the most easily, while familistic cultures, like those of Italy, France, Taiwan, and Hong Kong, would have greater difficulties. The United States is a complicated intermediate case: it is in many ways a traditionally high-trust society but one with a strongly individualistic tradition as well that went in for low-trust in-

TABLE 2

Automobile Assembly Plant Productivity

(units = hours/vehicle)

	BEST	AVERAGE
Japanese in Japan	13.2	16.8
Japanese in North America	18.8	20.9
United States in North America	18.6	24.9
United States & Japan in Europe	22.8	35.3
Europeans in Europe	22.8	35.5
Newly industrializing countries	25.7	41.0

Source: James P. Womack, Daniel T. Jones, and Daniel Roos, *The Machine That Changed the World: The Story of Lean Production* (New York: HarperPerennial, 1991), p. 85.

dustrial solutions at a certain point in its history. It is not obvious that the MIT data, illustrated in table 2, necessarily contradict these predictions.

Anyone looking at the MIT data would have to agree that lean production is a management technique that is exportable across cultural boundaries and that any firm implementing it is likely to see its productivity rise, regardless of where in the world it is situated. But this does not mean that there could not be important cultural factors that impede the successful implementation of lean production in certain countries to a greater degree than in others. For example, although there is considerable productivity variation within countries, both the average productivity and the productivity of the plants using best practice (presumably the lean manufacturers) still vary considerably from region to region. Japan, according to the MIT data, has the highest average and best practice figures, followed by North America, then by Europe as a distant third.[22] (The study also gives data for the Third World, but this is aggregated over so many different countries as not to be helpful for our purposes.) Table 2 indicates that the best Japanese transplants in North America, and the best U.S. manufacturers in North America, both get about the same level of productivity out of their plants, which is still worse than that of the best Japanese plants in Japan.[23]

Given the confrontational character of Korean labor-management relations and the society's more familistic orientation, it should be no surprise that Korean corporations have not been on the cutting edge of lean production. When Korean car makers like Hyundai and Daewoo began entering the North American export market in the 1980s, they did so as low-cost mass producers relying on low wages for their competitive advantage. Although they borrowed Japanese technology heavily (the Hyundai Excel being virtually indistinguishable from the Mitsubishi Colt), they did not import lean production methods, instead remaining a classic mass producer. The Korean automakers did very well initially, but their sales began to collapse in 1988 when labor costs at home started to rise rapidly and when, most important, consumers began to realize that Korean autos did not meet the same quality standards as their Japanese rivals.[24] Lean production methods could be imported later when it became evident that Korea could not compete on the basis of low wages alone, but clearly this method did not come naturally to Korean culture as it did to Japanese.

Not all aspects of the lean manufacturing system have been as successfully exported to the United States as work groups and quality circles. The *keiretsu* relationships that exist between parent companies and their suppliers in Japan have generally not been replicated by automakers in the United States, except where they were physically transported from Japan by the Japanese transplants themselves. American auto companies remain either vertically integrated or else maintain arms-length market relationships with their suppliers. Indeed, some of the innovations introduced into the American auto industry in the 1980s, such as former GM vice president Ignacio Lopez's shakeup of that company's supplier network, sought to use traditional (and often highly adversarial) market discipline to get better prices or quality out of suppliers rather than seeking to build stable, long-term relationships of trust. It is still the case that the assemblers try to play their suppliers off against each other, which makes the latter suspicious and unwilling to share production techniques and cost data.[25] In other cases the problem is more ideological, as when one of GM's Saturn assembly plants, which used lean production methods and tight inventories, was deliberately shut down by one of its supplier's union locals in a muscle-flexing exercise.

The authors of the MIT study argue that since lean manufacturing was exported across the Japanese-U.S. cultural boundary relatively easily, it is not constrained by culture. But the truth of this assertion depends on the assumption, commonly held among people in the competitiveness field, that Japan and the United States stand at opposite poles culturally, with the Japanese as exemplars of groupishness and Americans being highly individualistic. Whether this is in fact the case is open to question, however. It may be that the Taylorite model of industrial organization, invented in America and thence exported to the rest of the world, was actually not a typical or inevitable product of American culture. Taylorism itself may have been something of an aberration in American history, and it could be that its replacement by the more communally oriented lean production model has actually brought the United States back to a different but authentic alternative set of cultural roots. To understand how this may be so, we need to look more closely at America's dual heritage, both individualistic and group oriented.

IV

AMERICAN SOCIETY AND
THE CRISIS OF TRUST

CHAPTER 23

Eagles Don't Flock—or Do They?

From school boards enlarging curricula to include the study of non-Western languages and cultures, to corporations staging "diversity training" seminars to sensitize their employees to subtle forms of discrimination, Americans in the 1990s have become preoccupied—pro or con—with the issue of "multiculturalism." The proponents of multicultural studies have argued that the United States is a diverse society and that Americans need to recognize and better understand the positive contributions of the many cultures, particularly those outside Europe, that make it up. Multicultural proponents argue either that the United States never had a single culture beyond its universalistic political and legal system, or else that the dominant European culture of generations past was oppressive and should not be a model to which all Americans must conform.

No one, of course, can object to the idea of seriously studying other cultures, and in a liberal society it is clearly necessary to learn to tolerate

269

differences among people. It is quite another thing, however, to argue either that the United States never had a dominant culture of its own or that as a matter of principle it *ought not to have* a dominant culture to which diverse groups can assimilate. As this book has documented, a people's ability to maintain a shared "language of good and evil" is critical to the creation of trust, social capital, and all the other positive economic consequences that flow from these attributes. Diversity surely can bring real economic benefits, but past a certain point it erects new barriers to communication and cooperation with potentially devastating economic and political consequences.

Nor is it the case that America was always a highly diverse place, knit together only by a common Constitution and legal system. Beyond America's universalistic political-legal system, there has always been a central cultural tradition that gave coherence to American social institutions and permitted the rise of the United States as a dominant global economic power. That culture, originally the attribute of a particular religious and ethnic group, later became deracinated from those ethnoreligious roots and became a broadly accessible identity for all Americans. In this sense, American culture is very different from European cultures, which are firmly wedded to "blood and soil." What that culture is and where it came from is the subject of considerable misunderstanding on the part of Americans themselves, however, and needs to be elucidated at some length.

Americans typically think of themselves as individualistic, or, harking back to their pioneer days, as rugged individualists. But if Americans were traditionally as individualistic as they think they are, it would be hard to account for the rapid rise of giant corporations in the United States in the nineteenth century. An uninformed visitor, landing in the United States without knowledge of its industrial structure, might assume on being told it was an individualistic society that it would have many small and short-lived firms. Americans would be too headstrong and uncooperative to take orders in large organizations, too independent to build lasting private institutions. Firms would rise, fission, and fall, much as they do in Taiwan or Hong Kong. The observer might assume that Americans would be the opposite in this respect of German and Japanese culture emphasizing authority, hierarchy, and discipline.

And yet the exact opposite was the case: the United States pioneered the development of the modern, hierarchical corporation, and by the end of the nineteenth century it had spawned some of the world's largest organizations. Entrepreneurs were constantly starting new businesses, and Americans did not seem to mind at all working under gigantic bureaucratic hierarchies. This aptitude for organization is not limited to the creation of large firms, however. Today, in an age that calls for downsizing and newer, more flexible forms of business organization like the virtual corporation, Americans are again leading the way. The conventional wisdom that portrays America as the paradigm of individualism is somehow wrong.

Much of the competitiveness literature contrasting Japan and the United States asserts that the United States is the paradigm of an individualistic society in which groups or other larger communities have very little authority. Americans do not work well or naturally in groups, this literature argues, because of their individualistic character. Insistent on their rights, they relate to each other through contract and the legal system when they need to cooperate socially. In the minds of many Asians (in particular, the Japanese), and of Americans who study Asia, American job control unionism is only one symptom of a broadly individualistic culture that in its litigiousness and adversarial character has turned somewhat pathological.

Not only Asians characterize the United States as individualistic. Americans themselves tend to see their own society this way; however, they do not regard individualism as a vice but as an almost unalloyed virtue signifying creativity, initiative, entrepreneurship, and a proud unwillingness to bend to authority. Individualism is therefore often a source of considerable pride, something Americans assume to be one of the most distinctive and appealing aspects of their civilization. In the public discussion of the fall of communism and other authoritarian regimes around the world in the late 1980s, it had become commonplace to assert that dictatorships were undermined by the seduction of American popular culture and its celebration of individual freedom. Part of the reason that independent presidential candidate Ross Perot was so popular with many Americans was that he exemplified for them the best aspects of American individualism. Leaving the computer giant IBM where he felt stifled, he went on to create his own company, Electronic Data Systems, and built a multibillion dollar fortune. Characteristically, Perot's often-repeated slogan is, "Eagles don't flock; you have to find them one at a time."

Whether one takes a positive or negative view of the value of individualism, both Asians and Americans on a popular level seem to agree that America, in contrast to most Asian countries, lies at some sort of individualistic extreme. This popular perception is only half true. In fact, America's cultural heritage is a dual one: alongside the individualistic tendencies, which separate individuals, there has been a powerful propensity to form associations and to participate in other forms of group activity. These supposedly individualistic Americans have also been, historically, hyperactive joiners, creating strong and durable voluntary organizations from Little Leagues and 4H Clubs to the National Rifle Association, the NAACP, and the League of Women Voters.

What is all the more impressive about the high degree of communal solidarity that has existed in the United States is the fact that it has occurred in an ethnically and racially diverse society. Japan and Germany, after all, are racially homogeneous societies whose visible minorities have always been outsiders to the mainstream culture. Although not all homogeneous societies manifest a high degree of spontaneous sociability, ethnic diversity can be a serious obstacle to the development of a common culture, as is evident from the experience of numerous multiethnic societies in Eastern Europe, the Middle East, and South Asia. By contrast, ethnicity has strengthened the cohesiveness of America's small communities, while not (at least, until recently) serving as a barrier to upward mobility and assimilation.

Tocqueville's evaluation of individualism was closer to the Asian than the American view: he regarded it as a vice to which democratic societies were particularly prone. He argued that individualism was a milder form of the vice of selfishness (*egoïsme*), which "disposes each member of the community to sever himself from the mass of his fellows, and to draw apart with his family and his friends, so that after he has thus formed a little circle of his own, he willingly leaves society at large to itself." Individualism arises in democratic societies because the class and other social structures that unite groups of people in aristocratic societies do not exist, leaving people no attachments broader than their families. Hence individualism "at first, only saps the virtues of public life; but in the long run . . . attacks and destroys all others and is at length absorbed in downright selfishness."[1]

Tocqueville believed that the very network of civil associations that he observed in the United States played an important role in combating individualism and limiting its potentially destructive consequences.[2] The weakness of equal individuals in a democratic society induced in them the need to join together to accomplish any end of importance, and cooperation in civil life served as a school of public-spiritedness that drew people out of their natural preoccupation with private self-gratification.[3] In this respect, the United States was very different from France, where despotic governments broke asunder the civil associations that united the citizens, leaving them isolated and more genuinely individualistic.[4]

Tocqueville's concern was not economic but political: he feared that a democratic society's penchant for individualism would lead people to turn away from public life in pursuit of their narrow material interests. With citizens uninterested in public affairs, the way was paved for despotism. But sociability in ordinary civil affairs promotes a vigorous economic life as well, by schooling people in cooperation and self-organization. People good at self-government are also likely to be good at combining for business purposes, enriching themselves to a far greater extent than if they acted alone.

Individualism is deeply embedded in the rights-based political theory underlying the Declaration of Independence and the Constitution, so it is no accident that Americans think of themselves as individualistic. This constitutional-legal structure represents, in Ferdinand Tönnies's phrase, the *Gesellschaft* ("society") of American civilization. But there is an equally old communal tradition in the United States that springs from the country's religious and cultural origins, which constitute the basis of its *Gemeinschaft* ("community"). If the individualistic tradition has been, in many ways, the dominant one, the communal tradition has acted as a moderating force that prevented the individualistic impulses from reaching their logical conclusion. American democracy and the American economy were successful not because of individualism or communitarianism alone but because of the interaction of these two opposing tendencies.

The economic significance of American spontaneous sociability is evident in the rise of corporations in the nineteenth century. As in every other country, all American businesses started out as small family-owned and -managed enterprises. In 1790, some ninety percent of all Americans worked on more-or-less self-sufficient family farms.[5] The scale of the largest enterprises until the 1830s was quite small: Charles Francis Lowell's textile mill in Waltham, Massachusetts, the largest in the country when it was established in 1814, had 300 employees; the largest metalworking establishment at the time was the government-owned Springfield Armory, with 250 workers; and the largest bank, the Second Bank of the United States, had two full-time managers in addition to its president, Nicholas Biddle.[6]

All of this changed with the coming of the railroads in the 1830s. The

actual economic impact of the railroads on U.S. gross domestic product
has been hotly debated by economic historians,[7] but there is little doubt
that they forced a different management style on the organizations that
ran them.[8] Because of their physically dispersed nature, railroads were
the first economic enterprises that could not be practically managed by a
single family, and it was they that gave the impulse to the creation of the
first managerial hierarchies. The railroads grew to enormous size: by
1891, the Pennsylvania Railroad alone had 110,000 employees, dwarfing
the American army of the time.[9] Financing the railroads created requirements for larger financial institutions, and the freight they carried unified
markets over larger and larger areas. Unlike earlier family-run businesses,
managed on a hub-and-spoke system with the founding entrepreneur at
the center, the railroads had to be managed in a more decentralized manner, with layers of middle managers being given substantial authority.
Larger markets increased possibilities for exploiting economies of scale
through a greater division of labor, in both production and marketing. It
became possible to speak of a national market for the first time in the
United States, as grain and beef grown in the Midwest and West were
packed and shipped to consumer markets in the East.

In sharp contrast to Europe, railroads in the United States were
largely financed, owned, and operated privately. In Europe as well, the
railroads constituted the leading edge of large-scale economic organization, but they were almost all promoted by governments that borrowed
organizational and administrative practices from their national bureaucracies.[10] The American state in the 1840s, particularly on the federal
level, was much weaker and less competent than its European counterparts, being plagued by corruption and political intrigue. Hence it is all
the more impressive that Americans created large administrative structures so rapidly, with no obvious models and cadres of trained administrators on which to draw.

After the Civil War, large business enterprises, borrowing the railroads'
rational organizational structure, began to proliferate quickly, first in distribution and then in manufacturing. The period 1887 through 1904 saw
a wave of mergers of epic proportions, led by companies like Standard
Oil and U.S. Steel, the latter being the first American industrial enterprise with a capitalization exceeding $1 billion.[11] By the time of World
War I, the greater part of the American economy's output was being produced by large corporations. These corporations have been remarkably

durable. Some of America's best-known brand names today were created by companies formed in the late nineteenth century, among them General Electric, Westinghouse, Pitney-Bowes, Sears, Roebuck, National Cash Register, and Eastman Kodak. Brand names for mass-market goods were in fact a major innovation of American companies in the second half of the nineteenth century, as distributors took advantage of advances in transportation to reach broader markets. Manufacturers found that they could ensure product quality and reliability in delivery and service only if they obtained control of distribution channels. This kind of forward integration could occur only if the companies themselves were of sufficient scale and durability to develop reputations for quality. This is something that Chinese companies find hard to achieve today, but American companies accomplished readily at a comparable stage of development in the nineteenth century.

There were, of course, any number of factors other than culture to explain the speed and scale by which American companies grew to large size. Most conventional explanations assume, correctly, that there was a natural economic incentive for enterprises to want to exploit the economies of scale created by technological change, especially in view of the large size of the domestic American market and the richness of its natural resources. Property rights and a system of commercial law were in place early in America's industrial history. An open regulatory environment and a market unfettered by artificial internal barriers to trade also helped, as did the rapid spread of universal education and the creation of a first-class system of higher and technical education.

When comparing the United States to societies like France or China, it becomes evident that American culture did not put up the barriers to large organizations that one might have expected from a supposedly individualistic culture. Americans did not, by and large, resist professional management out of distrust of nonkin; they did not seek to keep their businesses in the family when profitable opportunities for expansion came up; and they did not rebel against being herded into large factories or office buildings and working under huge authoritarian, bureaucratic structures. The history of American industrial labor relations in the late nineteenth and early twentieth centuries was, of course, violent and conflictual, as workers established the right to strike, to bargain collectively, and to influence conditions of occupational health and safety. But the labor movement was co-opted into the system after winning these concessions. It never turned to Marxism, anarchosyndicalism, or other radical ideologies in the early twentieth century as did many European trade unions, particularly in southern Europe.

The United States was, in other words, a relatively high-trust society throughout the period of its initial industrialization. This is not to say that Americans were uniformly moral or trustworthy. The great industrialists and financiers of the late nineteenth century, like Andrew Carnegie, Jay Gould, Andrew Mellon, and John D. Rockefeller, all developed reputations for ruthlessness and greed. The history of this period is full of scams and swindles and rapacious business activities unconstrained by the dense regulatory environment of the twentieth century. But for the economic system to have worked as well as it did, there had to be a significant element of generalized social trust.

Consider the transcontinental agricultural commodity trade that developed in the mid-nineteenth century. Shipments moved east through a series of geographically dispersed dealers, each of whom would make advances up the line prior to delivery. In those days, it would be very difficult for a dealer in Chicago to negotiate detailed contracts with another in Abilene or Topeka, much less sue for breach of contract. A great deal of this trade therefore depended on trust. With the development of railroads and telegraphs, a dealer in New York could, by the time of the Civil War, place direct orders for large shipments of grain or cattle with the producers in Kansas or Texas. This cut down the number of advances necessary and hence the risk, but it did not eliminate the need for both parties to believe the word of a partner he had never met at the end of a thousand-mile telegraph line.[12] In other words, Americans could draw on a substantial fund of social capital to reduce the transactions costs of setting up large, complex businesses.

On a political level, Americans expressed substantial distrust of concentrated economic power. The merger wave and the efforts of trusts like Standard Oil to monopolize markets led to the Sherman and Clayton Anti-Trust acts and the trust-busting populism of Theodore Roosevelt. State intervention slowed the merger craze of the turn of the century, and subsequent changes in government policy had profound effects on industrial structure up through the mergers of the Reagan era in the 1980s. But whereas in societies with weak intermediate organizations like France, Italy, or Taiwan, the state had to intervene to develop or sustain large-scale corporations, in the United States the government had to intervene to prevent them from growing too large. The spontaneous tendency in American business was not to fission and collapse for lack of institutionalization, but rather to continue to grow until monopoly power or diseconomies of scale became a problem.

The business elite that created the impressive corporate world that had emerged by the middle of the twentieth century was as homogeneous ethnically, religiously, racially, and in gender terms as those of Japan or Germany. Virtually all of the managers and directors of large American corporations were male, white, Anglo-Saxon Protestants, with an occasional Catholic or non-Anglo-Saxon European thrown in. These directors knew each other through their interlocking directorates, country clubs, schools, churches, and social activities, and they enforced on their managers and employees codes of behavior that reflected the values of their WASP backgrounds. They tried to instill in others their own work ethic and discipline, while ostracizing divorce, adultery, mental illness, alcoholism, not to mention homosexuality and other kinds of unconventional behavior.

While many Americans and even more Asians today argue that America is too individualistic and disparate to be a real community, it is hard to recall that at midcentury most critics of American life characterized U.S. society—and particularly the business community—as *overly* conformist and homogeneous. Two of the major social analyses from this period—William Whyte's *The Organization Man* and David Riesman's *The Lonely Crowd*—pointed to the dangers of a spreading conformism in which individuals anxiously looked over their shoulders at the surrounding community for approval.[13] According to Riesman and his coauthors, the Americans who had built the country in the nineteenth century were inner-directed by religious or spiritual principles, and therefore determined individualists; the contemporary Americans of the 1950s had become other directed, setting their compasses by the least common denominator of mass society.

This period saw the waning of small-town America, under whose constraints people chafed at the time and whose orderliness and familiarity they look back to now with nostalgia. The middle of the century was also the heyday of IBM and its dress code, which required all white-collar employees to wear the same kind of white dress shirt to work. European visitors to the United States often remarked that America seemed much more conformist than their own societies; without its own aristocratic or feudal traditions to lean on, Americans could look only to each other for standards of behavior. The social revolutions that have occurred in the United States since the 1960s—the civil rights movement, sexual libera-

tion, feminism, the hippie movement, and today the gay rights movement—can only be understood as a natural reaction to the often rigid
and stifling homogeneity of mainstream America during the first half of
the century.

The picture of the United States as a hyperindividualistic society
drawn in much of the competitiveness literature often reads like a caricature of this reality. It is as if all American companies showed the same
lack of paternalism as Continental Airlines under Frank Lorenzo, with
management ready to fire longtime employees at the drop of a hat and
the employees itching to flee the moment a higher-paying job came
along. The truth of the matter is that many characteristic Japanese business practices are not uniquely Japanese but have parallels across societies, including America. Noncontractual business relationships, for
example, based not on a legal instrument but on an informal understanding between two businessmen who trust one another, were not uncommon.[14] Nor are purchasing decisions always made on the basis of ruthless
comparisons of price and quality; here, too, relationships of trust between buyers and sellers have a significant impact. There are many specific sectors of the economy that have held down transaction costs
through trust: most stockbrokers, for example, have traditionally exe-
cuted trades on the basis of verbal agreement alone, without requiring
up-front payment. Many American companies have treated their employees paternalistically, particularly smaller family-owned businesses that
function like small communities unto themselves. But even among large
corporations, many like IBM, AT&T, and Kodak practiced what
amounted to lifetime employment and sought to generate worker loyalty
by paying generous benefits. I noted earlier the paternalistic side of
Ford's early mass production facilities. IBM abandoned lifetime employment only in the late 1980s, when it faced a grave crisis and the future of
the company itself was at stake. Most of the large Japanese corporations
with similar employment policies have not yet had to face problems of
this magnitude.

If the United States has had a long-standing tradition oriented toward
group or associational life, how is it that Americans are so convinced of
their thoroughgoing individualism? Part of the problem is semantic. It is
common in American political discourse to present the essential problem
of a liberal society as a dichotomy in which the rights of the individual are
balanced against the authority of the state. But there is no way to refer to
the authority of the welter of intermediate groups between the individual

and the state other than the overly broad and rather academic term *civil society*. It remains true that Americans tend to be antistatist, despite the substantial growth of big government in the United States in the twentieth century. But those same antistatist Americans voluntarily submit to the authority of a variety of intermediate social groups, including families, churches, local communities, workplaces, unions, and professional organizations. Conservatives, who are opposed to the state's delivering certain kinds of welfare services, usually describe themselves as believers in individualism. But such people are often simultaneously in favor of the strengthening of the authority of certain social institutions like the family or the church. In this respect they are not being individualistic at all; rather, they are proponents of a nonstatist form of communitarianism.

A similar linguistic problem can be seen in Seymour Martin Lipset's comparison of the United States and Canada. Lipset argues that Canada has a much more communitarian cultural tradition than the United States, which he characterizes as a highly individualistic nation.[15] By "communitarian" Lipset means primarily statist. Canadians respect the authority of the government (federal or provincial) more than do Americans: they have a larger state sector, pay more taxes, are more law abiding, and tend to defer to government authority more readily than do Americans. What is not clear, however, is whether Canadians are more willing to subordinate their individual interests to those of intermediate social groups. Lipset provides some evidence to indicate they are not: Canadians give substantially less money to charity than do Americans, for example, are less religious, and have a much less vigorous private sector.[16] In these respects, Canada could equally well be spoken of as less communitarian than the United States.

The semantic confusion between individual and community is also apparent in that prototypical act of individualism, the founding of a new religious sect or business. America was born out of sectarianism: the Pilgrims came to Plymouth because they would not accept the authority of the Church of England and were persecuted for their beliefs. The establishment of new religious sects in the United States has occurred continuously since that time, from the original Puritan Congregationalists and Presbyterians, to the Methodists, Baptists, and Mormons of the early nineteenth century, to Pentecostals, Father Divines, and Branch Davidians of the twentieth. The founding of a religious sect is often spoken of as an act of individualism, because members of the new group refuse to accept the authority of some established religious institution. But from another standpoint, the new sect often requires its followers to subordinate their individual interests to the group in a much more disciplined way than the church from which they broke off.

Similarly, the tendency of Americans to leave the companies they work for and start their own businesses is often taken as another example of American individualism. And indeed, when compared to the lifelong loyalty of Japanese employees to their firms, it does appear individualistic. But those new entrepreneurs seldom act purely as individuals; they often leave with others or else quickly establish new organizations with new hierarchies and lines of authority. These new organizations require the same degree of cooperativeness and discipline as the old ones, and if they are economically successful, they can grow to giant size and become very durable. Bill Gates's Microsoft Corporation is a classic example. It is often the case that the person who turns the enterprise into a durable institution is not the same as the founding entrepreneur: the former has to be more group oriented and the latter more individualistic to play their respective roles. But both types have coexisted easily in American culture. For every Joseph Smith, there has been a Brigham Young; for every Steve Jobs, a John Scully. Are the Mormon church and Apple Computers properly seen as examples of American individualism, or American groupism? Although most people would characterize them in the latter way, they in fact represent both tendencies simultaneously.

If we can conceive of a perfectly individualistic society as an "ideal type," it would consist of a group of totally atomized individuals who interact with each other solely out of rational calculations of self-interest and have no ties or obligations to other human beings except the ones that arise out of such calculations. What is usually described as individualism in the United States is actually not individualism in this sense but rather the action of individuals who are embedded in, at a minimum, a family or household. Most Americans do not work to satisfy narrowly selfish ends but also struggle and make considerable sacrifices for the sake of families and households. Some completely atomized individuals do, of course, exist, such as the reclusive millionaire without spouse or children, or the elderly retiree living alone on a pension, or a homeless person in a shelter.

But although most Americans are embedded in families, America has never been a familistic society in the way that China and Italy are. Despite the assertions of some feminists, the patriarchal family has never had the kind of ideological support in the United States that it enjoyed in, say, China or in certain Latin Catholic societies. In the United States, family ties are frequently subordinated to the demands of larger social groups. Indeed, outside certain ethnic communities, kinship has been a relatively small factor promoting sociability in the United States, since there have been so many other bridges to community available. Children are constantly being drawn outside their households by the pull of a religious sect or church, a school or university, the army or a company. Compared to China, where each family behaves like an autonomous unit, the broader community has had substantially more authority for much of American history.

From the moment of its founding up through its rise at the time of World War I as the world's premier industrial power, the United States was anything but an individualistic society. It was, in fact, a society with a high propensity for spontaneous sociability, which enjoyed a widespread degree of generalized social trust and could therefore create large economic organizations in which nonkin could cooperate easily for common economic ends. What bridges to sociability existed in American society that counteracted the effects of the country's inherent individualism and permitted this to happen? The country did not have a feudal past like Japan and Germany, with cultural traditions that could be carried over into the modern industrial era. It did, however, have a religious tradition that was different from that of virtually any country in Europe.

CHAPTER 24

Rugged Conformists

Among the sources of the American penchant for associational life that counterbalanced powerful individualistic tendencies, one of the most important was the sectarian Protestantism that the early immigrants to North America brought with them from Europe.[1] Paradoxically, this same sectarian Protestantism is simultaneously one important source of American individualism; a doctrine subversive of established social institutions at the very same time gave a powerful impetus to the formation of new communities and strong bonds of social solidarity. How Protestantism could be simultaneously the source of individualism and community needs to be explained at greater length.

To comprehend the communal side of American life, we must first understand the origins of its individualism. The United States has undergone a "rights revolution" in the second half of the twentieth century. This revolution has provided a moral and political basis for the promotion of individualistic behavior, with the consequent weakening of many earlier tendencies toward group life. By the 1990s, few people thought of criticizing American society for being too conformist. Rather, problems of an opposite sort were emerging: the nuclear family was disintegrating; institutions were having a great deal of trouble handling ever-increasing diversity; cities and neighborhoods were dying; a sense of social isolation, distrust, and criminality was growing; and many people felt the vague but clear-cut lack of a meaningful sense of community in their lives. It is no accident that the individualistic consequences of the rights revolution played out the way they did in the United States. These ideas did not germinate from alien spores blown to America from some distant continent; they are, in a sense, the logical working out of some tendencies inherent in American liberalism.

In contrast, an Asian ethical system like Confucianism sets forth its moral imperatives as duties rather than rights. That is, an individual is born into the world with a series of obligations to other people: parents, brothers, government officials, the emperor. Being a moral person, or achieving the status of a gentleman-scholar, depends on the extent to which one is able to carry out those duties. Those duties are not derived from prior ethical principles. In this respect, Confucianism is not different from much of the Western philosophical and religious tradition up to the early modern period. Many of the virtues defined in classical political philosophy, such as courage, honor, benevolence, or citizenship, were duties. And God's law for both Judaism and Christianity was almost always enjoined in the form of duties.

Western political thought takes a sharply different turn, however, in the writings of Thomas Hobbes, who stands at the head of the liberal philosophical tradition leading through John Locke to Thomas Jefferson and the drafters of the U.S. Constitution. For Hobbes, man is born not with duties but with rights alone, the most important of which is the right to the preservation of his own life.[2] Whatever duties he takes on, he acquires as a result of his voluntary entry into civil society. Duties, for Hobbes, are entirely derivative of rights and are undertaken only to secure individual rights. Thus, one has an obligation not to do violence to another human being only because to do so would return one to the state of nature, in which one's own right to life would be jeopardized. Whatever the many differences between Hobbes and Locke, and following on Locke the Founding Fathers, all accepted a concept of justice based on the primacy of rights. In the words of the American Declaration of Independence, it is self-evident that "man is endowed with certain inalienable rights" and that governments are instituted among men "to secure these rights." The Constitution's Bill of Rights has thus become the foundation for an imposing edifice of law in the United States, a source of pride for all Americans and a universally accepted starting point for all legitimate political authority.

Confucianism emphasizes duties because its basic image of man is one in which individuals are embedded in a web of existing social relationships. By nature, human beings have obligations to one another. A human being cannot perfect himself in isolation; the highest human virtues, like filial piety and benevolence, must be practiced in relation to another human being. Sociability is not a means to a private end; it constitutes an end of life in itself. Again, this view of human beings as socially embedded is not unique to Confucianism. Aristotle saw man as an inherently political creature: "The city-state is prior in nature to the household and to each of us individually." A totally self-sufficient human being would have to be either a beast or a god.[3]

Again, Anglo-Saxon liberalism takes a very different turn. Not only are duties derivative of rights, but these rights belong to isolated, self-sufficient individuals.[4] The picture drawn of man in the state of nature by Hobbes and Locke is of individuals whose main concern is to take care of themselves and whose primary social contacts are ones of conflict. Social relationships are not natural; they emerge only as a means of securing what individuals in the state of nature wanted but could not obtain on their own. In Rousseau's state of nature, the isolation is even more extreme: not even the family is necessary for human sustenance or happiness. Although the word *individual* does not appear anywhere in the Constitution, the rights bearer as an isolated individual is implicit in the theory on which it is based. Family ties, for example, are nowhere recognized as having a special status, as they do under Confucianism. Chapter 6 of Locke's *Second Treatise of Government* argues that parents and children have mutual obligations of love and respect but that parental authority ends when children are capable of reasoning on their own. Locke's point is, in a way, to argue the exact opposite of Confucianism: paternal authority cannot be the model for political authority; the state derives its just powers from the consent of the governed, and not because it constitutes a kind of "superfamily."[5]

Man in the state of nature for early modern Anglo-Saxon liberal political theorists was the exact counterpart of the economic man of classical economic liberalism. Both were portrayed as isolated individuals, seeking to protect their own basic rights (in the case of political liberalism) or their private "utility" (in the case of economic liberalism). In both cases, social relationships emerged only through contractual relationships in which the rational pursuit of either rights or interests led to cooperation with other human beings.

The other important source of individualism is one that pertains to other Western countries and not just the United States: the Judeo-Christian tradition, especially the way that tradition ultimately evolved into modern Protestantism.[6] Judaism and Christianity posit God as an omnipotent and transcendent lawgiver whose Word is superior to any existing social relationship. Duty to God trumps duty to any social superior, from father to Caesar; Abraham had to be prepared to sacrifice his own son at God's command. God's law is a universal standard by which any set of positive laws established by man can be judged.

The mere existence of a transcendental law does not in itself necessarily lay the groundwork for individualism, since the question of who interprets that law remains open. The Catholic church, of course, established itself as a mediator between God's will and His people and declared that its own interpretation would be authoritative. In this role it sanctioned over the years any number of other social institutions as embodying, or at any rate not being inconsistent with, God's will, from the family to the state to a wide variety of priests, officials, rulers, and notables in between. Indeed, the church itself became a major source of community in Catholic countries, one that established a stability of moral standards as it guarded its role as gatekeeper between man and God.

The Protestant Reformation reopened the prospect of an individual's unmediated relationship to God. Grace now did not depend on good works or the fulfillment of a certain set of social obligations; it could be given to the most fallen sinner out of the latter's faith. The fact that individualism has positive rather than negative connotations in the West arises historically more than anything else from the prototypical act of Christian conscience, the rejection of an unjust law or command in the name of God's higher law. Martin Luther's nailing of his ninety-five Theses to the cathedral door at Wittenberg in 1517 was just the first of many individualistic acts in the Protestant tradition. In the long run, the individual's ability to have a direct relationship with God had extremely subversive consequences for all social relationships, because it gave individuals a moral ground to rebel against even the most broadly established traditions and social conventions.

The perspective of Confucianism is entirely different. Its ethical guideposts stem from societal institutions—the family, lineage, emperor, Mandarinate—and invests them with moral significance. There is no higher ground from which one can criticize these basic institutions. Under this ethical system, the grounds are much weaker for an individual to decide as a matter of private conscience that the obligations imposed by a father or a government official contradicted a higher law and therefore had to be rejected. Confucianism, moreover, does not try to abstract its own moral principles and make them apply to all human beings as such. It is no surprise, then, that the issue of human rights has been such an irritant in America's relationship with China and other Asian countries. Contemporary advocates of human rights are frequently not Christians, but they share the Christian belief in the validity of a single, higher universal standard of ethical conduct that applies to people *qua* human beings, regardless of their particular cultural background.

Asian folk religions like Taoism and Shinto do not legitimate individualism. These pantheistic religions worship many gods or spirits, residing in rocks, trees, streams, even computer chips. None is all-powerful like the Judeo-Christian God, and none powerful enough to legitimate, for example, a son's defiance of his father or a political uprising against the constituted authorities. The only Asian religion that does legitimate individualism to any extent is Buddhism, which, while not monotheistic, teaches rejection of all worldly things. Buddhism was powerful enough to make sons leave their families to become monks and priests, and for this reason Buddhism was frequently regarded as inimical to Confucian values.[7] In Japan, Buddhism has displayed a Protestant-like tendency to spawn new sects. For the most part, they made their peace with existing Japanese social institutions, though they have at times been a source of irritation to the political authorities because of their independence.[8]

Hobbes and Locke did not write from a Christian perspective, but they shared the Christian view that the individual had a right to judge the adequacy of the laws and social institutions surrounding him based on higher principles. Where the Protestant could judge them on the basis of his interpretation of God's will as expressed in the Bible, man in the state of nature for Hobbes or Locke had knowledge of his natural rights and the rationality to be the best judge of his own interests. In a country like the United States, both currents—Protestant and Enlightenment—have served as sources of support for individualism.

What, then, were the specific mechanisms by which Protestantism shaped the American penchant for association? Much of the answer has to do with the sectarian nature of Protestantism in the United States.

The U.S. Constitution prohibits the federal government from establishing a national religion, though it does not prohibit the states from doing so. Some individual states like Massachusetts had established religions as late as the 1830s but the principle of the separation of church and state is an old and venerable one. One would think that the establishment of a national church, as in a number of European countries, would promote a strong sense of community, since it would bind national to religious identity and give citizens a common culture beyond the political system. In fact, something of the opposite tends to happen. In countries with established churches, where religious identity is ascribed rather than voluntary, people frequently tend toward secularism and in many cases become openly anticlerical. Countries without established churches, on the other hand, often experience a higher degree of genuine religious observance. Thus, the United States, with no established church and an increasingly secular public life, continues to enjoy a far higher degree of religiosity than virtually all European countries with national churches. This is true by almost any measure of religious feeling: church attendance, the number of people who assert that they believe in God, or the level of private charitable donations to religious organizations.[9] By contrast, Catholic countries like France, Italy, and many Latin American nations have given birth to militantly anticlerical movements— in the twentieth century, often Marxist—intent on the thorough elimination of religious influence from social life. Lutheranism was the established church in Sweden; in the nineteenth century, it enforced its monopoly to the point where many Swedish Baptists were forced to emigrate. In reaction to this earlier orthodoxy, the Social Democratic party, which came to power in the twentieth century, became strongly anticlerical, and today Sweden is one of the most secular countries in Europe.[10] What kept alive religious feeling, it would appear, was less the specific doctrine of the church (e.g., Catholic or Protestant), so much as whether the church was established or voluntary.

The reason for this apparent paradox is that when religious identity is mandatory, it often begins to feel like an unwanted burden. The greater the insistence is on religious observance by the state, the more religion is resented and burdened with all of the other grievances that people have against the authorities in general. But in a country where religious observance is voluntary, no one even joins a church unless he or she is interested in spiritual things in the first place. The church to which one belongs, rather than becoming a lightning rod for complaints against the state or the larger society, can itself become a vehicle for protest. While voluntary sects, like all other voluntary organizations, can break up more easily than ascriptive ones, they can also generate a much higher degree of genuine commitment. The higher degree of religiosity in America than in Europe is due, therefore, to what Roger Finke and Rodney Stark have called the "free market" in religions in the United States, in which people have a wide choice of religious affiliation.[11]

The voluntary and entrepreneurial character of American religious life explains further how religious commitment could be renewed over long periods of time against the broader forces of secularization. Older, established churches whose ministries had become routinized and whose doctrines grew more latitudinarian were constantly being challenged by new fundamentalist sects with higher entrance requirements for joining. When membership in a church extracts a high price in terms of emotional commitment and changes in lifestyle, it creates a strong sense of moral community among its members. Just as the Marine Corps, with its strict discipline and demanding basic training, engenders greater loyalty and esprit de corps than the Army, so the fundamentalist churches develop more passionately committed members than do the easy-going mainline Protestant denominations.

The United States has gone through a number of periods of fundamentalist renewal. The sociologist David Martin points to three major waves: the original Puritanism of the colonial settlers, the Methodist (and also Baptist) revival of the first half of the nineteenth century, and the Pentecostal evangelical movement of the twentieth century, which is still ongoing.[12] The early Puritans (Congregationalists, Presbyterians, Quakers, and so on) were the Dissenting churches of England that came to North America in search of religious freedom. By the early nineteenth century, they (and the Episcopalians in the South) had become the churches of the older Federalist establishment, and were challenged by a broad evangelical movement, led by Methodists and Baptists, that appealed to the lower classes enfranchised in the Jackson era.[13] (It may surprise today's Methodists to learn that their early forebears, much like contemporary Pentecostals, staged all-night revival meetings, complete with shouting, praying, and falling down on the floor.) By the end of the nineteenth century, the Methodists and Baptists, now part of the establishment and largely Republican,[14] were challenged in turn by the Pentecostals and other fundamentalist groups that appealed to poor whites, blacks, and other people excluded from or ignored by the mainstream denominations. In each case the older, established churches looked down on the newer ones with distaste as uneducated, lower-class organizations, while steadily losing membership to them. Today in the United States the original New England Puritan churches are nearly empty, while the Assemblies of God and other evangelical churches continue to grow at an astonishing pace.

The sectarian, as opposed to established, character of Protestantism in the United States, and its resulting vigor, would appear to be crucial for understanding the continuing strength of associational life in American society. The voluntary character of religion in the United States is often interpreted as a manifestation of American individualism. But sectarian Protestantism, renewed periodically by fundamentalist revivals, in fact fostered a tremendously vigorous community life by uniting its members around a common moral code. Though he does not cite a figure, it is likely that a very high percentage of the civil associations that Tocqueville observed when he visited the United States in the 1830s, and whose existence he believed so crucial to the success of American democracy, were religious in character: temperance societies, choral groups, charitable associations, Bible studies, abolitionist organizations, schools, universities, hospitals, and others. Max Weber too observed the importance of the Protestant sects in promoting community and trust when he visited the United States at the end of the nineteenth century; he believed that these characteristics had promoted economic exchange.

The relationship between the voluntary, sectarian character of American religious life, and the propensity for spontaneous sociability, is perhaps best illustrated by the Mormon church. The Church of Jesus Christ of Latter-Day Saints is a perfect example of a community united around shared moral values. The Mormons do not consider themselves Protestants; they have their own unique (and, to non-Mormons, bizarre) theology based on the revelation of the Angel Moroni to Joseph Smith in 1823. They also have their own history of martyrdom and struggle, with the murder of Joseph Smith in Illinois in 1844 and the long trek across the great western desert that led to the founding of Salt Lake City. Finally, they have their own strict moral code. Like Weber's early Puritans, the Mormons forbid drinking alcohol, smoking, premarital sex, drugs, and homosexuality. They value discipline and hard work, and many individual Mormons have adopted a somewhat materialistic attitude toward worldly achievement.[15] Despite the early practice of polygamy (banned by the church in 1890), the Mormons encourage large families, stay-at-home wives, and otherwise strong, traditional family values.[16] Contemporary Mormons, in other words, exemplify many of the original Puritan virtues, now regarded as intolerably repressive by the rest of American society. In addition to having to abide by this moral code, the entry costs for being a Mormon are extremely high by contemporary American standards: all Mormon young people at the age of nineteen are encouraged to spend two years on mission, proselytizing for their religion abroad, and must thereafter tithe to the church.[17]

The result of these high entry costs is a remarkably strong sense of community. Brigham Young was a genius at organization, and of the Mormon church one turn-of-the century cleric said, "No other organization is as perfect . . . except for the German Army."[18] Today it receives what amounts to over $8 billion a year in revenues and disposes of multibillion dollar investment and real estate portfolios. The church manages an extensive hierarchy to look after the needs of the nearly 9 million Mormons worldwide.[19] Young Mormon boys are put under great pressure to develop administrative skills through church-related activities like running Boy Scout troops or organizing charitable events.[20]

Despite their social conservatism and political anticommunism, the Mormons throughout their history have supported each other through quasi-socialist kinds of institutions. Settling in the Utah desert, the Mormons built an extensive irrigation system under highly adverse conditions, with water resources remaining community property.[21] In one of Joseph Smith's early revelations, God commanded his people to "take care of the poor." Over the years the Mormons set up a number of social welfare programs, including the Law of Consecration and the fast offering, under which each member of the community was expected to donate a part of his or her income to support the poor—not the poor in general but those less fortunate within their own community.[22] The Welfare Services Program, established during the Great Depression and still in place today, provides aid to those in the community who cannot take care of themselves and have no family to rely on. Because this program operates inside a community with a high degree of moral consensus, it is able to make demands that a federal program like Aid to Families with Dependent Children cannot. Welfare support from the church is coupled with a requirement that recipients work in return, and the latter are encouraged to look after themselves as soon as possible. There is an intrusive early-detection system that tries to prevent individual families from sliding into poverty.[23] Like the Jews, Chinese, and other ethnic groups in the United States, the Mormons' strong sense of community has allowed them to take care of their own. Although the Mormons, like other parts of American society, have experienced poverty and family breakdown, their rate of welfare dependency is significantly below the national average.

Again, like the early Puritans, the Mormons have been extremely successful economically, consequences of their classic Puritan work ethic and the fact that they are, as a group, better educated than the American population as a whole. In the United States, 47 percent of Mormon households have incomes over $25,000, compared to 39.5 percent nationally, and 9 percent have incomes over $50,000, compared to a national figure of 6 percent.[24] In recent years, the Mormons have been very successful in high-tech industries. Both the WordPerfect Corporation (now owned by Novell) and Novell itself, the nation's leading networking software company, were started and initially staffed by Mormons.[25] The story is told of Novell's CEO, Ray Noorda—one of the richest men in the United States—that a potential business partner once went to meet a Novell executive in a dingy hotel in Austin, Texas, and could not find the executive's name in the register. He examined the list of guests registered and found the name Noorda listed; Noorda was sharing a room because he did not want to pay for two rooms.[26] Despite a difficult business climate in the 1980s due to turndowns in mining and steel, Utah has emerged as a center of high-tech development in large measure because of Mormon entrepreneurship.[27]

Just as in the case of the Japanese, the Germans, and all other communities that have sharply defined insides and outsides, the downside of this extremely strong Mormon sense of community is hostility to outsiders. The Mormon church openly discriminated against African-Americans until 1978, not permitting them to become members of the priesthood, and was frequently (though wrongly) accused of evangelizing only in European countries to preserve the racial character of the Mormons.[28] Although the Mormon community has expanded enormously in the Third World in recent years, Mormons in their home base in Utah are anything but diverse in the contemporary American sense: there are few openly gay people, feminists, blacks, or other minorities.[29]

The Mormons, then, exemplify the strange paradox of American individualism and communitarianism. From one perspective, they are highly individualistic, rejecting all established churches and denominations in favor of a new and strange faith, and suffering all the persecution and rejection of apostates in the process. Yet from another perspective, they are highly communitarian, drawing their members out of exclusive preoccupation with their private lives (Mormons devote an average of over fourteen hours a week to church-related activities), taking care of the weak and poorer members of their community, and establishing an astonishing variety of enduring social institutions.

The Mormons' degree of self-organization and communal self-help is extraordinary by any standard and is much more extensive than for most Protestant sects. But in less extreme ways, other denominations have promoted similar sorts of communal institutions, setting up schools, hospitals, charities, and other social welfare organizations. The cult of Father Divine in Harlem in the 1930s is one example. The fact that they were sectarian—that is, they were formed by breaking away from a larger, more established institution, usually on the basis of a stricter or more fundamentalist interpretation of Christianity—renewed their spiritual energy and gave new impulse to the formation of strong community.

The significance of Protestant sectarianism goes far beyond the people who actually belong to them. This type of Protestantism was the mold within which American culture as such was cast in the nineteenth century, and other religious groups like Catholics and Jews who had no experience of voluntaristic religion in Europe gradually came to share similar qualities. Sectarian religious life served as a school for social self-organization and permitted the formation of a kind of social capital that could be useful in a variety of nonreligious settings. America's Anglo-Saxon Protestant culture was, in other words, not limited to WASPs. As other ethnic and religious groups entered the country and went through the Protestant-controlled public school system, they assimilated the same value system. Protestants themselves retained an ability to organize and cooperate, even as their denominations turned more mainline and became more secular. The art of association became, in other words, a general American national characteristic rather than a specifically Protestant one.

Sectarian Protestantism is thus paradoxically the source of both individualism and community in the United States. Many people have argued, with considerable justice, that in the end the individualistic impulse would ultimately win out over the communitarian one.[30] That is, while revolt against an established church and the setting up of a new sect promotes community within that sect over the short run, the long-term impact of this habit of mind is to weaken respect for authority per se, and not just of the older institution. In the long run, with the broad secularization of society, the habits of sociability would fade away as the social capital accumulated by the original converts was spent. Religiosity might renew itself periodically through new waves of fundamentalism and sect formation. But overall, the final legacy of American Protestantism would be an individualistic cast of mind that was unable to accept stable authority or social consensus for any length of time. The sociability it created, in other words, became gradually self-undermining.

CHAPTER 25

Blacks and Asians in America

W hen African-American community activists like New York's Reverend Al Sharpton organize boycotts of Jewish and Korean businesses and urge their followers to buy from black-owned businesses, many white Americans grow resentful and complain of "reverse racism." The racial and ethnic balkanization of the United States is, of course, not something to be welcomed or encouraged. But while whites complain that blacks are too race conscious, the African-American problem has been, in a way, that blacks have never been race conscious enough to stick together in tightly knit economic organizations. The frequent efforts of black community leaders to encourage their members to "buy black" is testimony not to the natural solidarity of the African-American community but rather to its weakness. Other ethnic groups, from Jews and Italians to Chinese and Koreans, bought from their coethnics not because they were encouraged to do so by their political leadership but because they felt safer and more comfortable dealing with each other rather than with outsiders. Although blacks do not enjoy having to buy from whites or Asians, and often may not have the opportunity to buy from other blacks, there are not the same traditions of trust and solidarity linking black merchants with their customers as in America's ethnic communities. Not only are blacks mistrusted by the surrounding white community, but, for reasons we shall discuss, they mistrust one another. This lack of internal social cohesiveness has nothing to do with African cultures, since most of the latter are pervaded by a variety of strong social groups. But today's native-born African-Americans are descended from people who, as slaves, were deracinated from their native cultures. This deculturation has been one of the key factors impeding the economic advancement of the African-American community in the United States.

Besides the sectarian character of religion in America, ethnicity has been the second major source of community that has moderated the inherent individualism of the political system in the twentieth century. Many of the large number of immigrants who arrived in the United States in the decades before and after the turn of the nineteenth century carried with them strong communal traditions and structures from their native countries. Like the tight communities formed by the early Protestant sects, these ethnic enclaves could be self-supporting in a manner no longer achievable by the surrounding mainstream culture. Most of these immigrants suffered from the absence of individualism in the traditional societies from which they came, being rigidly locked into castes, classes, or other communal structures that prevented mobility, innovation, or entrepreneurship. Once in the United States, however, they found it possible to synthesize community and individualism: they were liberated from the constraints of their traditional cultures, while retaining enough of their former cultures to avoid the atomizing pitfalls of American society.

There was a considerable degree of variance, as one might expect, in the degree of spontaneous sociability exhibited by different ethnic groups, based on the nature of social traditions in their countries of origin. Many of the latter were not helpful to upward economic mobility. The Irish, for example, brought with them from Ireland little tradition of higher education and tended to segregate their children in a separate parochial school system in order to preserve their religious identities.[1] There were similar obstacles to Italian advance in the early twentieth century: given their extremely strong emphasis on the family, higher education was often seen as a threat to family cohesion and income, and children, particularly girls, were discouraged from going off to school.[2]

The importance of ethnicity as a source of spontaneous sociability, and of sociability to economic betterment, becomes clearly evident if we look at the striking contrast in the trajectories of Asian- and African-Americans. Chinese, Japanese, Korean, and other Asian immigrant groups have on the whole been extraordinarily successful economically, moving past many of their European counterparts in terms of per capita income, education, participation in the professions, and virtually every other standard of socioeconomic performance. African-Americans, on the other hand, have made progress only slowly and painfully, and since the beginning of the civil rights era in the 1960s, a significant segment of the black community has lost ground.

This contrast is particularly evident in business ownership. Small-business ownership constitutes one clear-cut route toward upward social mobility, particularly when a group has recently arrived in America or is excluded from participation in mainstream economic institutions.[3] Many Asian groups have had high rates of self-employment and small-business ownership. In 1920, more than 50 percent of all Chinese males in the United States were employed or self-employed in ethnic businesses like restaurants and laundries, and in 1940 there was a comparable rate of 40 percent self-employment among Japanese males.[4] One 1973 study put the percentage of Korean families in business at 25 percent,[5] and another found the rate of self-employment among Korean-American males has been 23.5 percent, compared to a rate of 7 percent for the American population as a whole.[6]

The African-American community, by contrast, has a lower-than-average rate of self-employment and small-business ownership,[7] and the lack of a black entrepreneurial class has for long been a staple of the sociological literature.[8] At the turn of the century both Booker T. Washington and W. E. B. du Bois felt obliged to call for blacks to go into business to remedy this situation. In most American inner cities, local businesses have tended for decades to be owned not by blacks but by people outside the African-American community. Through the early postwar period, many ghetto business owners were Jews; in the past generation the latter have been replaced by Koreans, Vietnamese, and other Asian proprietors. African-Americans have had some business success in banking and have managed to prosper in certain limited sectors, such as beauty parlors,

barber shops, and undertaking. But despite a couple of decades of minority set-asides and subsidies by various government agencies, there are
few signs of a strong, emerging black entrepreneurial class.

The failure of African-Americans to control businesses in their own
neighborhoods has been the source of enormous resentment and conflict.
The Watts riots of 1965, the Detroit riots of 1967, and the Los Angeles
riots of 1992 were all occasions for inner-city residents to attack businesses
in their neighborhoods owned by nonblacks. Indeed, in the Los Angeles
riots there was what appears to have been deliberate and systematic efforts
on the part of some rioters to target Korean businesses, an enormous number of which were destroyed or damaged.[9] Popular resentments against
nonblack business owners run high, spawning conspiracy theories about
how outsiders have plotted to exploit African-Americans economically. We
have seen how, in Chinese and Korean culture, trust runs high within families but is much lower when dealing with nonkin, while Japanese have similar problems dealing with non-Japanese. This flinty attitude toward
strangers is reflected in the frequent complaints by blacks that Asian proprietors are often rude and show little interest in their customers or the
surrounding community.

In the scholarly literature, the reasons for differences in economic performance between groups have been no less controversial. One common
explanation for the relatively poor performance of blacks in small business
has to do with external environment. Many hold that it is misguided to
compare African-Americans to ethnic groups like Chinese or Koreans because the degree of prejudice faced by the former is incomparably greater.
Blacks, unlike other ethnic groups, were brought to the United States in-
voluntarily, were brutalized by slavery, and suffered a significantly higher
level of discrimination because of their racial distinctiveness.[10] One vari-
ant of this hypothesis, using the terminology of dependency theory, maintains that there is a "dual" economy in the United States that relegates
blacks and other minorities to the "peripheral" economy, which in contrast to the white-dominated "core" is doomed to small scale, low technology, and excessive competition. A somewhat different and more specific
form of the environmental argument is that African-Americans have not
been able to start businesses because they have been denied credit by the
white banking system. It is argued that blacks have not received credit either out of simple racism or because their impoverished backgrounds and
the small scale of their enterprises make them poor credit risks and therefore doom them to a continuing cycle of poverty.

A second explanation of black performance is related to consumer demand: in contrast to other ethnic groups, blacks had no special needs that only they could supply. Whereas whites could not compete against Chinese in the Chinese restaurant business, they could compete against blacks in providing food to other blacks.[11] Others have made a related argument that blacks were not suppliers of distinctive commodities; African-American cuisine, for example, was never popular in the larger community the way other types of ethnic cuisine were.[12] The only areas where black businesses have succeeded are those uniquely catering to the restricted number of uniquely African-American needs, for example, barber shops and beauty parlors.[13]

Neither of these explanations for African-American weakness in small business is ultimately persuasive, however.[14] The hostility of the external environment may explain why blacks are underrepresented in corporate boardrooms or as employees of white-owned businesses, but it can hardly explain why they are not self-employed. There is an important category of "outsider" theories in the sociological literature that argue that it is precisely the prejudice and hostility of the external environment that causes many minority groups to fall back on themselves, creating businesses employing fellow ethnics and catering to the demands of their own community.[15] Indeed, inability to find employment in the white community was one of the reasons for the high levels of Chinese and Japanese self-employment in the first decades of this century.[16] It is certainly the case that blacks have endured the greatest degree of prejudice of any other racial or ethnic group in the United States, and that although Asian immigrants have faced racial hostility not experienced by European ethnic groups, they have been accepted by the dominant community to a significantly greater extent than blacks. But all of this is irrelevant in explaining why there are so few African-Americans selling to other African-Americans, or why many blacks themselves appear to prefer to buy from nonblacks. Not only do African-Americans do poorly in the "core" economy (if such a thing actually exists), but they do poorly in the "peripheral" economy as well. This is true when blacks are compared to Hispanics, who are also said to participate in the peripheral economy and suffer from similar discrimination.[17]

The explanation that there has been insufficient consumer demand for products best supplied by black businesses does not suffer from this weakness. But as the sociologist Ivan Light has shown, this argument as well does not stand up to scrutiny. That is, while Asians may have had a captive market of coethnics, they were also quite successful in selling to whites outside their community in a way that African-Americans were not. For example, the cash value of Asian commerce with non-Asians in California in 1929 was more than all of retail business transacted by blacks in Illinois, despite the fact that the black population was three and a half times larger.[18] This suggests that Asian success was the result of a much more generalized marketing ability that did not exist in the black community.

If we look more closely at the question of bank credit, we begin to see the beginnings of an explanation for the differences in group performance that has little to do with external environment but a great deal to do with the group's internal cohesiveness. Lack of access to bank credit has been a major African-American grievance for many generations and has been the focus of federal investigations as recently as the Clinton administration. But while there has undoubtedly been bias in lending toward blacks, particularly in loans for residential housing, such discrimination is largely irrelevant in explaining the different rates of black versus Asian entrepreneurship. In the first place, very few small businesses in the United States have ever been established with bank credit; the great majority are started out of personal savings.[19] There was, moreover, a period in the mid-nineteenth century when African-Americans established a number of commercial banks and were ready to lend to other African-Americans. These banks foundered, however, because of insufficient demand for credit from black businesses, indicating that the supply shortfall lay not in credit but in black entrepreneurs.[20] Finally, when many Chinese and Japanese were setting up family businesses in the first decades of the twentieth century, they too were denied access to the white-run banking system. If access to credit were the key to small-business success, then it is hard to see why Asians should have been overrepresented in this category relative to whites.

The reason that lack of bank credit was not more of a stumbling block for Asians was that the Chinese, Japanese, and Koreans brought with them from their native cultures a dense network of community organizations, one of which was the rotating credit association. These associations were means by which coethnics pooled their savings and used them to establish one or another of their members in business.[21] The forms of these rotating credit associations differed between the Chinese and Japanese in characteristic ways. The Chinese *hui* was based on kinship, organized among people from the same village or lineage or with the same surname in China. By contrast, the Japanese *tanomoshi* included unrelated people from the same district or prefecture in Japan.[22] (A similar institution exists in Korea, known as the *kye*.) Both had a similar structure: a small number of people would contribute an equal share of money to a common pool, which would then be allocated to a single member through lottery or auction. As these associations turned larger and more sophisticated, they grew into quasi-credit unions, paying interest on deposits and lending out money.

The *hui* and *tanomoshi* had no legal backing and sometimes even lacked formal rules. It was entirely possible for the winner of an early lottery to abscond with the savings of the entire group. There was no legal sanction for fraud or free riding, apart from the moral sanction that could be imposed within the tightly knit Chinese and Japanese communities. If an individual defaulted, his family was required to make restitution. For such an informal system to work, there had to be a high degree of trust among the association's members, which in turn was the result of preexisting social ties based on kinship or geographic residence in the native country.

The existence of a high level of trust within the Chinese and Japanese communities was probably just as important as consumer demand for specific ethnic products in explaining why members of the community patronized businesses run by their coethnics. The radius of trust was not necessarily community-wide; among Chinese, for example, it often did not extend beyond one's lineage or village, and rival lineage associations frequently clashed with one another. The level of trust among coethnics was also likely to be higher in the United States, where they faced a common hostile outside environment, than in their native countries. Nonetheless, these groups benefited enormously from the fact that their cultures gave them a common moral structure in which they could cooperate with one another.

The rotating credit associations were just one of a number of social institutions created spontaneously within the Chinese and Japanese communities. Many Chinese arrived in the United States during the nineteenth century as single male workers, typically from a single region of southern China.[23] These immigrants founded lineage or surname associations, whose local branches grouped themselves into larger federations (the most famous were the Six Companies in San Francisco).[24] These lineage associations provided a range of welfare services, such that those seeking employment or falling on hard times generally did not have to go outside their own community for help. A number of Chinese organizations did not play so beneficent a role: the infamous Chinese *tongs* were criminal gangs that ran gambling, prostitution, and protection rackets within their local communities.

Again, the Japanese equivalents of the Chinese lineage or surname associations were not based so much on kinship as on geographic origin: the *kai* linked those who had emigrated from the same prefecture in Japan and provided a similar range of welfare services. These organizations helped people find work, took care of those not able to care for themselves, and were the reason for the extraordinarily low rate of Japanese-American dependence on government welfare services.[25] Such communal institutions frequently dealt with problems of delinquency through group pressure before they reached the police or the criminal justice system. The family alone was therefore not the only instrument of socialization; it was supplemented by larger organizations that bolstered the family's influences.[26]

Rotating credit associations played an important role in Chinese and Japanese economic development only for the first couple of generations of immigrants. Thereafter, other kinds of cultural factors took over. The Confucian emphasis on education and greater acceptance by the dominant white community allowed subsequent generations to assimilate and to achieve significant upward mobility outside the ethnic enclave. The lineage and prefectural associations gradually lost their central roles and were replaced by more modern voluntary organizations like the Japanese-American Citizens' League, which today function like any other interest group in a democracy. But there is no question that the culturally based credit associations played a significant role historically in promoting small-business entrepreneurship within these Asian ethnic communities.

There is nothing comparable to the Chinese or Japanese rotating credit associations in the experience of African-Americans after slavery. Black entrepreneurs usually had to face the world alone, with their own savings and little by way of help from extended family or friends. This is not, as Ivan Light points out, because of the absence of such institutions in African culture. Rotating credit associations of various sorts are virtually a cultural universal in traditional societies, including those parts of West Africa from which many North American slaves were abducted. In Nigeria, an institution similar to the *hui* or *tanomoshi* was known as the *esusu*. Light argues that such institutions were brought with the slaves to the New World, but in the United States the slaves were, in effect, decultured. Indeed, he speculates that one of the reasons for the superior economic performance of black immigrants from the British West Indies in the United States is that the form of plantation slavery practiced there was less disruptive of these traditional African cultural patterns.[27] Jamaicans and Trinidadians coming to New York in the early decades of the twentieth century thus had a significantly higher degree of social cohesiveness than blacks descended from slaves. In other words, slavery in the United States did more than rob African-Americans of their individual dignity; it robbed them of their social cohesiveness as well by discouraging cooperative behavior. North American slavery provided no incentives for thrift, money management, or enterprise. British slavery in the West Indies, although extremely harsh, left much more of the Africans' native culture intact and failed to atomize existing social groups to the extent that its American counterpart did.[28]

Lack of spontaneous sociability becomes more pronounced the poorer one gets, as one would expect given the causal linkage between inability to cohere socially and poverty. The urban poor are notoriously hard to organize into groups of any sort, even for short-term economic goals like rent strikes. As one moves down the income ladder, not only do social groups beyond the family become rare, but families themselves begin to disintegrate rather rapidly. The contemporary black underclass in America today represents what is perhaps one of the most thoroughly atomized societies that has existed in human history. It is a culture in which individuals find it extremely difficult to work together for any purpose, from raising children to making money to petitioning city hall. If individualism means the unwillingness or inability to subordinate one's individual inclinations to larger groups, then the underclass is one of the most individualistic segments of American society.

It would be a mistake to portray poor African-Americans as uniformly isolated and atomized individuals. The terrain has been relieved by a number of organizations. Among the most important historically have been various black churches and religious groups, which have provided an important counterweight to the atomizing forces to which the community was subject. In certain periods, African-Americans have been able to organize relatively strong small- to medium-sized business enterprises, like the black banks and insurance companies that appeared in the middle of the nineteenth century.[29] Middle-class blacks have always been relatively well organized in modern voluntary organizations like the Southern Christian Leadership Conference and the National Association for the Advancement of Colored People; indeed, there is evidence that middle-class blacks participate in such voluntary organizations at a higher rate than do whites.[30] In many African-

American neighborhoods, there are what amount to informal associations, in which relatives and friends pool funds to help each other out in hard times through gifts or loans.[31] And finally, among poor blacks there are the delinquent communities of street gangs like Los Angeles's notorious Bloods and Crips and the Blackstone Rangers in Chicago.[32] Like the Irish before them, however, organizations within the African-American community have been much better at pursuing political power than at creating large numbers of viable economic organizations within their own community.

African-Americans and Asian-Americans constitute contrasting poles in economic performance, and in the propensity for spontaneous social cohesion as well. Their differences mirror in a more extreme form those between European groups like Jews and Irish. There is a broad correlation between the degree of cohesiveness within a particular ethnic community and the rate at which it advanced economically and assimilated into the broader society. The Jewish community was notable for the degree to which it spawned new organizations designed to take care of its own. There were numerous organizations like the German-Jewish United Hebrew Charities, which in 1900 boasted of having taken care of every impoverished Jew in its community, or the Educational Alliance, or the contemporary B'nai B'rith and American Jewish Congress. Self-help and charitable organizations provided life insurance, sickness benefits, and funeral costs.[33]

The Jewish proclivity for spontaneous community contrasts in some measure with the Irish experience, which in certain ways prefigured that of African-Americans in the twentieth century. Irish social advancement tended to come not through self-employment in small businesses but rather through capture or influence over large, centralized institutions such as city governments or the Catholic church. Irish domination of the political machines in big cities like New York, Boston, Chicago, Buffalo, and Milwaukee by the early twentieth century is legendary, and with that political control came a host of patronage jobs in police departments and city bureaucracies that provided a substantial degree of Irish-American employment. The Irish depended on a single social organization, the Catholic church, to meet many of their welfare needs. Unlike Italians and immigrants from Latin countries, they were much less anticlerical because of the church's role in supporting Irish national identity and fighting British rule back home. Much of the energy that in Protestant or Jewish communities would have gone into building up smaller local congregations went into the American Catholic church, which was dominated for many years by Irish priests. On the other hand, the Irish were substantially underrepresented in small business: in 1909, despite the fact that the Boston Irish had higher incomes than Jews, Jews were nine times more heavily represented in small businesses.[34]

The Italians, who advanced more rapidly than the Irish but less rapidly than the Jews, fell somewhere in between the two in terms of community self-organization. A number of mutual aid societies were created by workers and shopkeepers, but the Italian community never spawned large, community-wide charitable or welfare organizations like the B'nai B'rith. Although there was Italian charitable giving, much of it went into noble gestures like monuments rather than into durable social institutions.[35]

Of course, many other factors besides sociability account for the different speeds with which ethnic groups advanced in the United States, the most important of which was probably attitudes toward education. The existence of Italian, Irish, Chinese, African-American, and other criminal gangs indicates that sociability in itself is not necessarily conducive to economic efficiency. Sociability must be combined with other factors like honesty, a high propensity to save, entrepreneurial energy and talent, and interest in education to lead to economically productive activities.

The main problem facing immigrant communities was to change the sort of sociability they practiced from an ascriptive to a voluntary form. That is, the traditional social structures they brought with them were based on family, ethnicity, geographic origin, or some other characteristic with which they were born. For the first generation that landed in the United States, they created the trust necessary for revolving credit associations, family restaurants, laundries, and grocery stores. But in subsequent generations they could become a constraint, narrowing the range of business opportunities and keeping descendants in ethnic ghettoes. For the most successful ethnic groups, the sons and daughters of first-generation immigrants had to learn a broader kind of sociability that would get them jobs in the mainstream business world or in the professions.

The speed with which immigrants could make the transition from a member of an ethnic enclave to assimilated mainstream American explains how the United States could be both ethnically diverse and strongly disposed to community at the same time. In many other societies, the descendants of immigrants were never permitted to leave their ethnic ghetto. Although solidarity within the ethnic enclave remained high, the society as a whole was balkanized and conflicted. Diversity can have clear benefits for a society, but is better taken in small sips than in large gulps. It is easily possible to have too diverse a society, in which people not only fail to share higher values and aspirations but even fail to speak the same language. The possibilities for spontaneous sociability then begin to flow only within the cleavage lines established by race, ethnicity, language, and the like. Assimilation through language policy and education must balance ethnicity if broader community is to be possible.

The United States presents a mixed and changing picture. If we take into account factors like America's religious culture and ethnicity, there are ample grounds for categorizing it simultaneously as both an individualistic and a group-oriented society. Those who see only the individualism are ignoring a critical part of American social history. Yet the balance has been shifting toward individualism rapidly in the last couple of decades, so it is perhaps no accident that Asians and others see it as the epitome of an individualistic society. This shift has created numerous problems for the United States, many of which will play themselves out in the economic sphere.

CHAPTER 26

The Vanishing Middle

The United States is heir to two distinct traditions, the first highly
individualistic, and the second much more group and community
oriented. The second tradition has moderated the individualistic
tendencies inherent in the country's ideology and constitutional-legal system, and the coexistence of the two has contributed to the overall success
of American democracy. And yet both strains have been the source of
problems in American society as well. The challenge for the United States
is to bring these tendencies into better balance.

No one can deny that American individualism has brought enormous
benefits to American society, not the least in the economic sphere. Despite the self-doubts felt in the 1980s concerning Japanese competition,
the American economy has emerged in the 1990s as the clear global
leader in a host of critical high-value-added sectors: computers and semiconductors, aerospace, software, telecommunications and networking, financial services, capital goods, and biotechnology.[1] It continues to be the

case that major changes in technology and organization have originated in the United States rather than in Europe or Japan. Helped by a weak dollar, American exports have risen sharply in the past decade, particularly if one considers nonmerchandise trade. Indeed, if one looks at the trade balance of American-owned parent companies, regardless of the country in which they are located, rather than the more usual merchandise trade balance, a large deficit turns into an equally large global surplus.[2]

Much of this competitive edge stems from the great innovativeness and entrepreneurial energy of American companies, which in turn is fueled by American reluctance to obey traditional sources of authority. In this respect, diversity is a great boon. America's high continuing levels of immigration, though strongly decried by some as a threat to American jobs and culture, has provided the United States with a critical source of human capital.[3] Consider the roster of CEOs of major technology companies: Intel's Andrew Grove was born in Hungary; 3COM's (a leading networking company) Eric A. Benhamou was born in Algeria; Philippe Kahn of Borland was a Jew born in France who immigrated illegally to the United States. All of them found much more fertile ground for their entrepreneurial energies and talents in the United States than they did in their countries of origin.

Americans are so used to celebrating their own individualism and diversity, however, that they sometimes forget that there can be too much of a good thing. Both American democracy and American business have been successful because they partook of individualism and community simultaneously. Those foreign-born entrepreneurs could not have been successful if their exclusive talent, besides their technical genius, was their ability to defy authority. They also needed to be good organizers and company men who could establish and motivate large organizations. But it is possible to have too much diversity and arrive at a situation in which people in a society have nothing in common besides the legal system—no shared values, consequently no basis for trust, indeed no common language in which to communicate.

The balance between individualism and community has shifted dramatically in the United States over the past fifty years. The moral communities that made up American civil society at midcentury, from the family to neighborhoods to churches to workplaces, have been under assault, and a number of indicators suggest that the degree of general sociability has declined.

The most noticeable deterioration in community life is the breakdown of the family, with the steady rise of the rates of divorce and single-parent families since the late 1960s. This trend has had clear-cut economic consequences: a sharp rise in poverty associated with single motherhood. Strictly speaking, family is different from community; as we have seen, familism that is too strong can weaken the bonds among people who are not related to one another and prevent the emergence of associational life based on something other than kinship. The American family has always been weaker in many respects than its counterparts in China and Italy, and in many respects this has been an economic advantage rather than a liability. But American family life has not been deteriorating because other forms of associational life are growing stronger. All are declining in tandem, and the importance of family increases with the deterioration of other forms of sociability because it becomes the only remaining opportunity for moral community of any sort.

Robert Putnam has compiled data that point to a striking decline in sociability in the United States.[4] Since the 1950s, membership in voluntary associations has dropped. Although America remains far more religious than other industrialized countries, net church attendance has fallen by approximately one-sixth; union membership has declined from 32.5 to 15.8 percent; participation in parent-teacher associations has plummeted from 12 million in 1964 to 7 million today; fraternal organizations like the Lions, Elks, Masons, and Jaycees have lost from an eighth to nearly half of their memberships in the past twenty years. Similar declines are reported in organizations from the Boy Scouts to the American Red Cross.[5]

On the other hand, there continues to be a steady proliferation of interest groups of all sorts in American public life: lobbying organizations, professional associations, trade organizations, and the like, whose purpose is to protect particular economic interests in the political marketplace. Although many of these organizations, like the American Association of Retired Persons and the Sierra Club, boast large memberships, their members seldom interact beyond paying dues and receiving newsletters.[6] It is, as always, possible for Americans to relate to one another through the legal system, building organizations on the basis of contract, law, or bureaucratic authority. But communities of shared values, whose members are willing to subordinate their private interests for the sake of larger goals of the community as such, have become rarer. And it is these moral communities alone that can generate the kind of social trust that is critical to organizational efficiency.

Perhaps even more striking than the decline of participation in associations by Americans are changes in the general attitudes Americans express toward one another. In one longitudinal survey, Americans were asked whether they felt "most people" could be trusted. The number answering affirmatively fell from fifty-eight percent in 1960 to only thirty-seven percent in 1993. In another survey that asked how often the respondent spent a social evening with a neighbor, the proportion answering "more than once a year" declined from seventy-two percent in 1974 to sixty-one percent in 1993.[7]

Apart from opinion surveys, the decline of social trust is evident on both sides of the law, in both the rise of crime and civil litigation. Both reflect the decreasing trustworthiness of some Americans, and produce greater suspiciousness on the part of those who would normally be trusting and trustworthy themselves. As has been noted by innumerable observers, crime rates in the United States are substantially higher than in any other developed country and have mounted steadily over the past couple of generations.[8] Crime in the United States is relatively concentrated in poor inner-city areas; the affluent have largely been able to shield themselves from its direct effects by moving to suburbs or otherwise walling themselves off from it. But the indirect effects of crime are perhaps more corrosive of a sense of community than the direct ones. American cities have divided themselves into black inner cores and white suburbs; the kind of cultured and sophisticated urban life that still exists in Europe has disappeared from the United States as downtown areas empty out after work. In the suburbs themselves, houses with front porches opening onto the street have given way to walled security communities with guards at the front gate as a prevalent new style of housing. Parents teach their children to be suspicious rather than trusting of strangers as a matter of self-protection, even in isolated rural communities.

The incident that took place in Louisiana in 1992, in which a Japanese exchange student, Yoshihiro Hattori, was shot to death by Rodney Peairs when he mistakenly appeared at his front door on the way to a party, attracted considerable attention in both the United States and Japan. Many Japanese (as well as Americans) were shocked by the absence of gun control in America.[9] But the real issue was fear: the home owner, holed up in his private fortress and so distrustful of the outside world that he was ready to shoot a neighborhood teenager who came to his front door, is the very image of social isolation.

The increase in litigation in America has been remarked on almost as often as crime. The United States has always been a "nation of lawyers," but the readiness of people to sue has jumped in the second half of the twentieth century. It is hard to know whether Americans are defrauding each other at a higher rate than previously, but they certainly seem to behave as if this were true. The increase in litigation means that fewer disputes are capable of being resolved informally, through negotiation or third-party arbitration. For negotiation to work, each party must have some degree of belief in the other's good intentions and a willingness not to stand on his or her rights at all costs. They must accept at face value assertions that a manufacturer tried to produce a safe product, that the doctor or hospital used best judgment in treatment, or that a business partner was not out to cheat or defraud deliberately. The rise in litigation reflects, by contrast, a decreased willingness to accept the authority of existing social structures and to work things out under the environment they provide.

Besides the direct costs of lawyers, the decline of trust imposes substantial indirect costs on the society as well. In recent years, for example, many American businesses have stopped writing recommendations for employees wanting to move on to different jobs. This came about because employers had been successfully sued by employees unhappy with the quality of the recommendations they had received. Since writing a recommendation for a former employee is of no direct benefit to the employer, most have found it safer not to write recommendations at all. The efficacy of the earlier system was based entirely on trust: employees had confidence that employers would write honest evaluations and were willing to accept the consequences if the latter came out unfavorably. While there were undoubtedly cases where employers would set out to damage the job prospects of former employees intentionally and maliciously, the assumption was that this situation would be quite rare and that any occasional damage would be outweighed by the benefits of a frank system of evaluation. This informal, trust-based system was moved progressively into the legal arena, however, and it collapsed. Subjective personal judgments are replaced by impersonal bureaucratic rules, which, like job control unionism, are less effective and more costly to implement.

The causes of the growth of American individualism at the expense of community are numerous. A primary one is capitalism itself.[10] Modern capitalism is, as Joseph Schumpeter explained, a process of continual "creative destruction." As the technological frontier moves outward, markets expand, and new forms of organization emerge. In the process, older forms of social solidarity are ruthlessly crushed underfoot. The original industrial revolution destroyed guilds, townships, extended families, cottage industries, and peasant communities. Today's continuing capitalist revolution undermines local communities as jobs are moved overseas or to wherever else capital can earn its highest return; families are uprooted; and loyal workers are laid off in the name of downsizing. The intensification of global competition in the 1980s and 1990s has undoubtedly accelerated this process. Many American companies like IBM and Kodak that practiced a form of corporate paternalism with generous benefits and job security were forced to lay off workers. (This phenomenon is not limited to the United States, of course; paternalistic labor practices in both Japan and Germany came under severe pressure during the recession of the early 1990s as well.) Americans have seen a familiar story play itself out over the past decades, as a small family business with strong internal bonds is bought out by a larger company. Unsmiling new managers with reputations for ruthlessness are brought in; long-time employees are fired or fear for their jobs, and the former atmosphere of trust gives way to one of suspicion. The strong traditional communities of the midwestern rust belt were devastated over the past generation by chronic unemployment and out-migration to the West or South in search of jobs. Loss of low-skill jobs in manufacturing and meatpacking contributed significantly to the descent of part of the postwar urban black population into its current underclass hell of drugs, violence, and poverty.

The negative consequences of capitalism for community life are only part of the story, however, and in many ways not the most important one. Capitalism has been uprooting Americans for most of their national history; in many ways, the social changes brought about by industrialization between the years 1850 and 1895 were greater than those that have occurred since 1950.[11] One of the conclusions implicit in this book is that there are many more degrees of freedom in how capitalist societies can be organized than is often realized. To be sure, technology dictates the broad features of industrial society at any given time. No one can undo the larger consequences of the railroad or telephone or microprocessor, but within these general constraints, the demands of efficiency do not necessarily dictate rigidly a certain form of industrial organization. The societies we have investigated differ from one another less in level of development and technology than in overall industrial structure and in the way that workers and managers relate to one another.

Capitalism can create as many new communities as it destroys; witness the postwar Japanese *kaisha,* which constitutes a source of social solidarity stronger in many ways than even the family and stronger than the forms of economic organization that it replaced in prewar Japan. During the so-called "decade of greed" of the 1980s, when some American corporations were ruthlessly laying off workers and undermining communities, many other American corporations were simultaneously introducing lean production, work teams, incentive systems requiring evaluation in small groups, quality circles, and a host of other workplace innovations. The aim of these innovations was to break down the walls of social isolation created by the Taylorite mass production factory and the job control unionism that it spawned. The enterprises that submitted to the logic of these changes became simultaneously more productive and more community oriented.

There were other important reasons for the growth of American individualism at the expense of community in the second half of the twentieth century besides the nature of capitalism. The first arose as an unintended consequence of a number of liberal reforms of the 1960s and 1970s. Slum clearance uprooted and destroyed many of the social networks that existed in poor neighborhoods, replacing them with an anonymous and increasingly dangerous existence in high-rise public housing units. "Good government" drives eliminated the political machines that at one time governed most large American cities. The old, ethnically based machines were often highly corrupt, but they served as a source of local empowerment and community for their clients. In subsequent years, the most important political action would take place not in the local community but at higher and higher levels of state and federal government.

A second factor had to do with the expansion of the welfare state from the New Deal on, which tended to make federal, state, and local governments responsible for many social welfare functions that had previously been under the purview of civil society. The original argument for the expansion of state responsibilities to include social security, welfare, unemployment insurance, training, and the like was that the organic communities of preindustrial society that had previously provided these services were no longer capable of doing so as a result of industrialization, urbanization, decline of extended families, and related phenomena. But it proved to be the case that the growth of the welfare state accelerated the decline of those very communal institutions that it was designed to supplement. Welfare dependency in the United States is only the most prominent example: Aid to

Families with Dependent Children, the depression-era legislation that was designed to help widows and single mothers over the transition as they reestablished their lives and families, became the mechanism that permitted entire inner-city populations to raise children without the benefit of fathers.

The rise of the welfare state cannot be more than a partial explanation for the decline of community, however. Many European societies have much more extensive welfare states than the United States; while nuclear families have broken down there as well, there is a much lower level of extreme social pathology. A more serious threat to community has come, it would seem, from the vast expansion in the number and scope of rights to which Americans believe they are entitled, and the "rights culture" this produces.

Rights-based individualism is deeply embedded in American political theory and constitutional law. One might argue, in fact, that the fundamental tendency of American institutions is to promote an ever-increasing degree of individualism. We have seen repeatedly that communities tend to be intolerant of outsiders in proportion to their internal cohesiveness, because the very strength of the principles that bind members together exclude those that do not share them. Many of the strong communal structures in the United States at midcentury discriminated in a variety of ways: country clubs that served as networking sites for business executives did not allow Jews, blacks, or women to join; church-run schools that taught strong moral values did not permit children of other denominations to enroll; charitable organizations provided services for only certain groups of people and tried to impose intrusive rules of behavior on their clients. The exclusiveness of these communities conflicted with the principle of equal rights, and the state increasingly took the side of those excluded against these communal organizations.

The chief injustice that began the rights revolution from the 1960s onward was racial discrimination. One of the great and necessary victories of American liberalism was the ending of legal discrimination with passage of the Civil Rights Act of 1964 and the Voting Rights Act of 1965, as well as the courts' vigorous enforcement of the Fourteenth Amendment's equal protection clause. The success of the civil rights movement in using the courts to open up public institutions, and then private organizations serving the public, made it the strategy of choice for subsequent excluded minorities, including people accused of crimes, women, the disabled, homosexuals, and more recent immigrant groups like Hispanics. Over the second half of the century, this drive to include the formerly excluded led to increasingly broad interpretations of the individual rights defined by the Constitution. Although each of the individual steps taken could be justified in terms of the country's basic egalitarian principles, the cumulative and unintended effect was for the state to become an enemy of many communal institutions. Virtually all communities saw their authority weakened: towns were less able to control the spread of pornography; public housing authorities were forbidden from denying housing to tenants with criminal or drug abuse records; police departments were enjoined from even such innocuous activities as setting up sobriety checkpoints.

As an example of the difficulties that communal institutions face, consider the Boy Scouts, an organization founded as a Christian group intended to inculcate "manly" virtues like courage, self-reliance, and fortitude in boys. In subsequent times, it has been sued by Jews for excluding non-Christians, by women for admitting only boys, and by gay rights groups for excluding homosexual scout masters. The organization, as a result, has become fairer and less exclusive, but in the process of becoming as diverse as the American population, it has also lost those features that made it a strong moral community.

Americans have developed a "culture" of rights that is quite distinctive among other modern liberal democracies. The constitutional scholar Mary Ann Glendon has pointed out that although most other modern democracies have adopted American-style bills of rights since World War II, there remains a unique character to the American "language of rights."[12] For Americans, rights have an absolute character that is not balanced or moderated by constitutional language outlining duties to the community or responsibilities to other people. The constitutions or basic laws of most European countries contain, in addition to enumerated rights, language similar to that of the Universal Declaration of Human Rights to the effect that "everyone has duties to the community."[13] American law does not support any kind of duty to rescue or otherwise enjoin citizens to do good to strangers in need. A Good Samaritan in the United States is much more likely to be sued for administering the wrong kind of help than rewarded for his or her troubles.[14]

As Glendon points out, the American language of rights gives political discourse in the United States an absolute and uncompromising character that it need not have. This is a characteristic that pertains to Americans on both the right and the left. Liberals are extremely vigilant against any effort to curtail pornography as an abridgment of the First Amendment's freedom of speech; conservatives are equally vehement about gun control, citing the Second Amendment's right to bear arms. In fact, neither right has ever been exercised unconditionally; the television networks are no more able to broadcast hard-core pornography during prime time than private citizens are allowed to own shoulder-fired anti-aircraft missiles. Yet proponents of these rights talk as if exercise of that particular freedom were an end in itself, regardless of consequences for the larger community, and they fiercely resist the slightest abridgment for fear of a slippery slope that somehow quickly ends in tyranny and a total loss of rights.

The uncompromising character of American rights discourse is based on the belief that the end of government is to protect the sphere of autonomy in which self-sufficient individuals can enjoy their natural rights, free of pressures, constraints, or obligations to those around them. That sphere of autonomy has grown substantially over the past decades. The right to privacy, for example, was originally designed to protect celebrities and other prominent people from the prying eyes of photographers and cranks. It has subsequently evolved into a much broader protection of individual behavior that makes unconstitutional, among other things, restrictions on abortion.[15] What is particularly insidious about the American culture of rights is that it dignifies with high moral purpose what often amount to low private interests or desires. The debate over pornography, for example, would sound very different if it were couched in terms of the "interests" of pornographers versus local communities, rather than one involving "freedom of speech" in the abstract, and gun control would be much easier to achieve if the conflict were seen as one satisfying the "interests" of gun owners rather than their "right" to bear arms. Rights, which should be the noble attribute of free and public-spirited citizens, instead tend to become a kind of cover for selfish individuals to pursue their private aims without any regard for the surrounding community.

A final explanation for the rise of individualism at the expense of community has to do with electronic technology. While proponents of the Internet have argued that the computer opens up broad new possibilities for "virtual communities" not dependent on geographic proximity, it would appear that many technological innovations since World War II have had a privatizing effect. Movies and television, unlike earlier entertainments such as fairs, meetings of people with similar interests, or simple conversation, involve one-way communication with no opportunity for direct social interaction. Moreover, the ways in which they are delivered—over the airwaves, by videocassette or cable—means that they can increasingly be enjoyed at home without recourse to even the limited public space represented by a movie theater. Although there may be some countervailing trends in the newer networking technologies, it remains to be seen whether virtual communities will be an adequate substitute for face-to-face ones.[16]

What are the implications of this shift in American culture in the direction of an increasingly pure rights-based individualism for American society, and for the policymakers, executives, and workers who have to operate within it?

When it comes to the policies of individual companies, managers need to recognize that they may have a good deal more freedom to experiment with work relationships and labor policies than they may believe. Lean manufacturing is a case in point; by the 1970s, American automobile companies had become fat and happy in their belief that the Taylorite factory was the only available model for organizing a modern, mass production enterprise. They fiercely resisted the devolution of managerial responsibilities and functions to the shop floor and were complicit with the unions in wanting to preserve a rigid but familiar job classification system. It was only when the productivity gains from lean production become too obvious to ignore that the practice was copied and spread. For more than a decade now, work teams, productivity-related bonuses, broadbanding (the collapsing of multiple job categories into one or fewer), quality circles, and the like have been the rage in American industry and have clearly helped Americans to close the productivity gap with the Japanese.

Despite these innovations, many American managers still have not comprehended the ethical bargain that is at the root of lean production and a communally oriented workplace. When they look at Japan, they see a country with weak labor unions (as well as companies that try to hire nonunionized labor for their plants in North America), a docile workforce, and substantial managerial autonomy. They often miss the other half of the equation: paternalistic companies that guarantee their workers job security, training, and a relatively high level of benefits in return for loyalty, hard work, and above all flexibility. In a more legalistic form, this is also the bargain that exists in Germany: in return for workers who are willing to learn new skills and occupations, employers provide a high standard of living and the training that allows the unneeded worker to move into a different job where he or she can be productive.

Obligation is a two-way street, and those managers who hope to get loyalty, flexibility, and cooperativeness out of their workers without giving
anything in return, whether in the form of security, benefits, or training,
are being exploitative.

It is important to note that the propensity for spontaneous sociability
need not be tied permanently to one organizational form like the quality
circle or lean manufacturing. Indeed, the reason that the art of association
is an important economic virtue is that it is inherently flexible: people who
trust each other and are good at working with one another can adapt easily to new conditions and create appropriate new organizational forms.
Networking and other modern communications technologies are changing the way that large corporations do business quite dramatically, for instance, by eliminating the need for layers of middle managers.
Globalization of the world economy has created new modes of marketing
and production that have very different organizational requirements. No
one at this point knows what the corporation of the early twenty-first century will look like. Whatever that form of organization turns out to be,
however, will be discovered most quickly by societies that have a strong
tradition of social cooperation. Conversely, societies that are riven with
barriers of distrust, based on class, ethnicity, kinship, or other factors, will
face extra roadblocks in their adoption of new organizational forms.

Like all stories about culture, there are limits to the degree to which
government policy can be deployed to change habits and practices. Although the Federal Reserve Board can modify monetary aggregates and
Congress can decree spending, it is much harder for government agencies to make people more willing to take risks, be sociable, or be inclined
to trust one another. Thus, a first order of business might be to say that
government policy should seek to do no harm, and in particular should
not seek to undermine existing communal institutions in the pursuit of
abstract diversity or openness.

One area in which the state needs to do less harm is in the question of
assimilation of new Americans. Immigrants have been extremely important to the United States, but they have been valuable because the diversity they bring to the table has been harnessed to central American
institutions. As this book should have indicated by now, the more one is
familiar with different cultures, the more one understands that they are
not all created equal. An honest multiculturalism would recognize that
some cultural traits are not helpful in the sustenance of a healthy democratic political system and capitalist economy. This should not be the

grounds for barring certain peoples with cultures deemed unacceptable but, rather, grounds for the assertion of positive aspects of American culture like the work ethic, sociability, and citizenship as immigrants move through the educational system.

Given the close relationship between religion and community in American history, Americans need to be more tolerant of religion and aware of its potential social benefits. Many educated people have a distaste for certain forms of religiosity, particularly that of Christian fundamentalists, and believe themselves above such dogmas. But they need to look to religion's social consequences in terms of promoting the American art of association.[17] In the words of the historian William McNeill,

> Scornful Marxists and impatient liberals looked on old-fashioned religion [as a weakness] in the recent past. Why rely on individuals and private moral reformation when it was social institutions and property rights that were at fault? But twentieth-century efforts to transform social institutions and to abolish or modify property rights so as to guarantee everyone the material basis for a good life have fallen far short of expectations. All too obviously, bureaucratic schemes for distribution and redistribution of goods have either created or been unable to prevent acute social ills. This casts considerable doubt on both liberal and communist programs for the reform of society. Perhaps, therefore, the slower, individualized, and from-the-bottom-up approach of religious reformation is preferable. Perhaps moral communities of fellow believers are necessary for social well-being. Perhaps only when such moral communities have come to terms with the dictates of market behavior can humanity at large expect to reap more fully the advantages of specialization and productive efficiency that economists so plausibly portray as the rational goal of economic development.[18]

This is not an argument for the promotion of religion in public life; recall that religious belief in the United States has been stronger because it was not established. It is, however, an argument for tolerance of religion as a source of culture.

Understanding genuine cultural differences is vitally important, but also particularly difficult for Americans. Large and for many years close to self-sufficient economically, the United States was never forced to pay attention to foreign cultures as a matter of survival. The assumption until recently of many Americans, including a large number of sophisticated social scientists, was that American culture was a universal one that would ultimately come to be shared by all societies as they modernized. In making this assumption, they were mistaking institutions for culture. It is indeed the case that many countries around the globe today share the liberal democratic political system and market-oriented economy of the United States. But American *culture* is more than the sum of its political and economic institutions. While the democratic nature of those institutions has shaped American culture profoundly, they have been sustained by a culture that had other sources like religion and ethnicity. Not to understand one's own cultural roots makes it more difficult to conceive of the way one is different from others.

The ability of Americans to understand the nature of other cultures is harmed rather than helped by recent calls for multicultural studies. The purpose of multicultural curricula in American classrooms today is not to confront and understand cultural differences squarely. If that were all there were to it, no one could possibly object to this kind of broadening of horizons. The problem with multiculturalism as it is practiced in the American educational system is that its underlying objective is not to understand but to validate the non-Western cultures of America's various ethnic and racial minorities. Arriving at a positive evaluation of these cultures is far more important than being accurate about them. In some cases, the underlying message is an ecumenical but false one that all cultures ultimately uphold the same decent, liberal values as the writers of the multicultural curriculum itself; in other cases, foreign cultures are held to be superior to that of the United States. This dogma serves to retard, not enhance, our understanding of them.

Americans need to understand that theirs is not simply an individualistic tradition and that historically people have come together, cooperated, and deferred to the authority of a myriad of larger communities. While the state, particularly at the federal level, may not be the appropriate locus of this sense of community for many purposes, the ability to obey communal authority is key to the success of the society.[19] This has implications for both the left and the right. American liberals need to understand that they cannot take organic cohesion of American society for granted as they attempt to use the law to extend an equality of rights and recognition throughout society. American conservatives, for their part, have to understand that before they cut back the role of the state in society, they should have some idea about how to regenerate civil society and find alternative ways of taking care of its weaker members.

From the perspective of the middle of the last decade of the twentieth century, the economic prospects of the United States look very good indeed. After a bruising recession earlier in the decade, the country has emerged with highly productive corporations in positions of technological leadership in any number of key sectors. A new phase of postindustrial history is being written primarily by American firms involved in one way or another with information technology. Although the budget deficit and an aging population remain as serious economic concerns for the future, there have been few other periods in recent decades when American economic prospects looked brighter.

Under these circumstances, it may seem odd to sound an alarm, however modest, about the economic consequences of a decline in American social capital. Unlike other types of economic pathology, the causal relationship between social capital and economic performance is indirect and attenuated. If the savings rate falls suddenly or the money supply is inflated, the consequences in terms of interest rates or inflation are felt within years or even months but social capital can be spent slowly over a prolonged period of time without any realization that the fund is drying up. People born with the habit of cooperating do not lose it easily, even if the basis for trust has started to disappear. The art of association may thus appear quite healthy today, with new groups, associations, and communities springing up all the time. But interest groups in the political arena or "virtual" communities in cyberspace are not likely to replace older moral communities of shared value in their impact on ethical habit. And as the cases of the low-trust societies that we have examined indicate, once social capital has been spent, it may take centuries to replenish, if it can be replenished at all.

V

ENRICHING TRUST

*Combining Traditional Culture and
Modern Institutions in the Twenty-first Century*

CHAPTER 27

Late Developers

U p to this point, I have argued that a society's endowment of social capital is critical to understanding its industrial structure, and hence its place in the global capitalist division of labor. Important as these issues are, social capital has implications that go well beyond the economy. Sociability is also a vital support for self-governing political institutions and is, in many respects, an end in itself. Social capital, which is practiced as a matter of arational habit and has its origins in "irrational" phenomena like religion and traditional ethics, would appear to be necessary to permit the proper functioning of rational modern economic and political institutions—a fact that has interesting implications for the nature of the modernization process as a whole.

Before turning to these issues in the final chapters of this book, however, we need to consider whether industrial structure—the scale of businesses, their overall distribution in the economy, and the way individual firms are organized—indeed has cultural roots, or whether there are other noncultural factors that explain more efficiently the differences among societies described in the preceding pages. Given the dramatic shift in perceptions of the impact of Confucian culture on Chinese economic growth from hindrance[1] to competitive advantage,[2] we need to be cautious about the role of culture if more parsimonious explanations exist.[3]

There are at least five alternative interpretations for the relatively small scale of private firms in Taiwan, Hong Kong, Italy, and France, compared to the much larger corporations in Japan, Germany, and the United States: first, that small scale can be explained by the size of national markets; second, that it can be explained by the level of a society's economic development; third, that it can be explained by late development; fourth, that it is due to a lack of legal, commercial, and financial institutions needed to support large economic organizations; and fifth, that the chief determinant of scale is not culture but the behavior of the state. The most important of these factors is the last, which must therefore be considered in conjunction with social capital as part of a complete explanation.

The first argument holds that scale and industrial structure are driven ultimately by the size of a country's national market, in conjunction with technology.[4] The level of technology for a given manufacturing process dictates the minimum efficient scale at which it can operate. Minimum efficient scale is relatively small for sectors like apparel or furniture but tends to be rather large for more complicated, technology-driven processes like semiconductors and automobiles. At the level of technology of the mid-1970s, for example, it was hard to operate an integrated steel plant efficiently that produced less than 6 million tons per year, requiring a minimum of three 250-ton oxygen furnaces.[5] Similarly, it is hard to produce refrigerators or automatic transmissions efficiently in lots smaller than 800,000 and 450,000 per year, respectively.[6]

The importance of market size was captured in Adam Smith's famous dictum, "The division of labour is limited by the extent of the market." That is, scale economies can be exploited only if demand is sufficiently large to take advantage of minimum efficient scale. A small company will not invest in an expensive custom-designed machine tool to mill a particular part unless it knows it can cover its costs through a large number of unit sales. Moreover, marketing costs like advertising and the fielding of a sales force are lower if they can be spread over a large national market.[7] This means that the size of firms in a national economy will be correlated to a large extent with their absolute gross domestic product (GDP); larger economies will produce larger firms.

There is obviously some correlation between level of development and firm size, but it tends to break down for the cases we have studied. The lack of correlation between absolute GDP and firm size is evident from table 3. Taiwan's GDP is 67 percent as large as South Korea's, and yet that country's ten largest firms are only 17 percent as large as Korea's ten largest firms. Similarly, Taiwan's economy is 5 percent the size of Japan's, while its ten largest private firms are just under 2 percent as big. By contrast, Korea's economy is 8.5 percent as large as Japan's while its ten largest firms are at 11 percent the size of Japan's top ten, indicating a much higher level of industrial concentration.

A similar lack of correlation between absolute GDP and firm size is evident in Europe (see table 3). Italy has an absolute GDP that is 68 percent the size of Germany, and yet the ten largest private firms in Italy are only 33 percent as large as the ten largest German firms. These differences become even more pronounced for several of Europe's smaller economies, which are far more concentrated than Germany's: Dutch

TABLE 3

Ten Largest Private Companies: Revenues versus GDP

(US$ billions, 1992)

	TOP TEN	GDP
United States	755.2	6,039
Japan	551.2	3,663
Germany	414.3	1,789
France	233.3	1,322
Italy	137.9	1,223
Korea	61.2	308
Taiwan	10.7	207
Hong Kong	24.7	86

Source: *International Financial Statistics 1994 Yearbook* (Washington: International Monetary Fund, 1994); "Country Profile: Taiwan," *Economist Intelligence Unit* (London: Economist, 1994); and *World Factbook, 1993* (Washington: Central Intelligence Agency, 1993).

GDP is only 18 percent as large as Germany's, and yet in terms of employment, Holland's ten largest firms employ 48 percent as many people as Germany's top ten.[8] Similarly, the ten largest firms in Sweden, with an economy only 14 percent the size of Germany's, employ 27 percent as many people as the top ten of Germany.

The problem with relating firm size to national markets is that many smaller economies pursued export orientation at an early stage; the size of their national markets was unimportant because they were producing for broader global markets. Thus, Korea could become a major manufacturer and exporter of television sets at a time when government policy was deliberately holding down domestic TV sales by keeping their prices high. International markets are similarly important for the smaller European countries with large companies like Holland, Switzerland, and Sweden.

A second alternative explanation for firm size, related to the first, is that it is the product not of national market size but of the overall level of economic development; that is, it is correlated with per capita rather than absolute GDP. Societies dominated by small-scale firms are on the same trajectory as those with large firms but have not yet had time to evolve modern corporate structures. The early phases of American and German economic development were dominated by family businesses as well; it was only in the late nineteenth century that the modern corporate form of organization evolved. National economies in the early stages of production will have abundant (and therefore relatively cheap) labor but scarce capital. As they grow, capital accumulates, allowing businesses to invest in more capital- and technology-intensive processes. At the same time, wages rise and labor becomes more scarce relative to capital, increasing incentives to replace labor with capital. Businesses now must move into more capital-intensive manufacturing sectors, which in turn require larger plants and larger organizations to operate them. Hence firm size should be determined first by the overall level of economic development, which in turn dictates the scale of its leading industries.[9] According to this interpretation, there will be eventual convergence: by the time the per capita incomes of Taiwan or Hong Kong reach the level of those of Japan or the United States, their industrial structures will no longer be dominated by small-scale family businesses but by modern corporations as well.[10]

The problem with this explanation is that the United States and Japan were already moving to professional management in the late nineteenth century, when their per capita incomes were well below levels achieved by Taiwan and Hong Kong during the 1980s. Indeed, the Japanese had a tradition of professional management well before the Meiji Restoration—before, that is, the country had even embarked on the industrialization process. The larger family-owned and -managed enterprises in Hong Kong, Taiwan, and Singapore are all extremely modern in most aspects of their operations, including the level of education of their family managers and the kinds of technologies they employ. They have been interacting with Japanese, American, and European companies for many years, so it can hardly be argued that they do not have the example of modern corporate management before them. Thus, their failure to adopt similar organizational and management techniques cannot simply be due to an immature level of development on their part.[11]

The level-of-development argument falls on its face if we compare Taiwan and Korea. Taiwan's per capita income has been consistently higher than Korea's throughout this period and has been held by most economists to be slightly in advance in its overall level of economic development. Yet the statistics set out in table 3 indicate that South Korean industry is far more concentrated than its Taiwanese counterpart. While there is only 1 Chinese company in the largest 150 Pacific Rim companies surveyed by *Fortune,* there are 11 from South Korea.[12] Similarly in Europe, Germany in the nineteenth century came from a lower level of per capita income than France and, by building modern corporations at an earlier point, surpassed it over the course of two or three generations. The regional differences in industrial structure in Italy cannot be explained by level of development, since the North, with relatively larger firms, was less urbanized than was the South when industrialization took off in the 1870s. These cases suggest that to the extent that there is a correlation between firm size and either per capita or absolute GDP, the causal relationship may work in the opposite direction. That is, the culturally based ability to create large firms leads to larger markets and faster per capita GDP growth, rather than vice versa.

A third alternative explanation for the distinctive features of the Japanese and German economies is what social scientists have labeled "late development."[13] In contrast to the preceding argument, which asserts that all countries follow an essentially similar development path, this one holds that countries industrializing later can take advantage of lessons learned by the early developers and therefore follow a very different evolutionary path. Late development, it has been argued, accounts for the distinctive characteristics of the Japanese and German economies: the heavy role of the state in promoting development, their concentrated industrial structure with bank-centered finance, and their paternalistic worker-management relationships.

Like the level-of-development argument, the late-development argument falls on its face—at least in terms of phenomena like firm size and workplace organization—simply by contrasting Germany and Japan to countries that developed even later than they, including Italy, Taiwan, Korea, and Hong Kong. Industrial structure, labor practices, and workplace organization vary as much among the late developers as between the late developers and the early developers. It is much more likely that the similarities between Japan and Germany arose out of fortuitously similar cultural factors like the prevalence of high-trust social relationships than because they industrialized at roughly the same time.

A fourth alternative explanation is that small firm size is due to inadequate institutional and legal structures for creating large, professionally managed corporations. Many societies have been relatively slow in developing systems of property rights, commercial law, and financial institutions. In contrast to the United States, which has had a stock market since 1792, Chinese equity markets are of recent vintage and relatively immature. Businesses controlled by families often prefer to raise capital through borrowing or retained earnings; equity financing increases reporting requirements, dilutes ownership, and raises the specter of external takeovers. Once all of these institutions are in place, by this argument, businesses will expand beyond the family, just as they did in the United States.

The lack of formal institutions applies most fully to the People's Republic of China, where Maoist ideology was responsible for delaying the introduction of "bourgeois" commercial law. To this day, entrepreneurs in China face a highly arbitrary legal environment, in which property rights can be tenuous, levels of taxation variable according to which provincial government one is dealing with, and bribery a way of life in dealing with government officials.

But modern commercial law has been established for a much longer period in overseas Chinese settlements like Hong Kong, Taiwan, and Singapore. Hong Kong, after all, has operated under British law from the start, and it is very difficult to attribute its *falling* enterprise size to an absence of institutions.

The immaturity of equity markets in Chinese societies has probably constrained nonfamily forms of ownership to some extent. But here again, comparison of Chinese societies with their Asian neighbors indicates that equity market development is not key to understanding industrial concentration because there is no correlation in Asia between development of equity markets and scale of enterprise.[14] Korea, whose firms are far more concentrated than those of Taiwan, has a stock market that is, if anything, less developed than that of Taiwan.[15] The Korea Stock Exchange was established in 1956; the Korean government deliberately restricted its development in order to limit foreign access, and subsequently it has played only a minor role in raising capital for Korean corporations.[16] By contrast, one of Asia's oldest stock exchanges is not in Japan but in Hong Kong, whose average firm size has declined since the end of World War II. (Asia's oldest equity market is that of Bombay, which opened in 1873.) Share trading in the Crown Colony dates back to 1866, and the Hong Kong Stock Exchange, the oldest of Hong Kong's four exchanges, was founded in 1891.[17] As of 1992, the total market capitalization of Hong Kong's markets totaled $80 billion, which was dwarfed by the Japanese market's $2.6 trillion capitalization. But as a percentage of GNP, Hong Kong's market capitalization was larger than Japan's (140 percent versus 90 percent).[18] Hong Kong's market also plays an important international role as a trading center for European bonds and other assets from around the Pacific Rim.

Equity markets in general have played a relatively minor role throughout Asia because most Asian companies are highly leveraged, financing their expansion through debt rather than equity. This is no less true of Japan than other Asian nations; whereas Japan may have a relatively well-developed stock market, most large Japanese corporations have historically relied on bank borrowing to a much greater extent than their American counterparts. Japan's prewar *zaibatsu* were industrial groups centered around a bank or other financial institution that served as the group's main source of capital. Just as in Germany during the same period, such financial institutions were perfectly adequate to allow the *zaibatsu* to grow to enormous size and to take on many of the attributes of modern, professionally managed corporations. Even in the absence of a mature equity market, the Japanese had already separated family ownership from family management, whereas the relatively well-developed Hong Kong equity market disguises the fact that many large publicly listed Hong Kong companies continue to be family-managed at their upper levels. In Taiwan and Korea, it would seem fairer to say that their stock markets are underdeveloped *because* of the preference for familistic management, not that they retain familistic management because the equity market is underdeveloped. Despite government efforts to increase participation in the stock market, family enterprises have been very reluctant to go public due to a fear of losing control of their companies and because of the reporting and disclosure requirements. The preference of many family businesses is to keep everything in the family.[19]

It is true that the Japanese *keiretsu* system, whose function is in part to secure the scale economies achieved by vertical integration, is dependent on cross-shareholding and therefore on the existence of a developed equity market. But the cross-shareholding would seem to be a reflection of the de facto relationships between *keiretsu* members rather than a financially necessary precondition for those relationships to exist in the first place.[20]

The argument that firm size is determined by government policy is valid to some extent. Governments everywhere can affect firm size in the private sector through their taxation and procurement policies, by their antitrust laws, and by the degree to which they enforce the latter.[21] It is clear that German, as opposed to American, law favored the development of cartels and other large concentrations of economic power. The governments of Japan and particularly Korea deliberately encouraged the formation of large companies by giving them preferential treatment, particularly through preferential access to credit. By contrast, the Nationalist government on Taiwan deliberately sought to discourage large private corporations to prevent the emergence of political competitors. In Korea, the state sought deliberately to imitate Japan and its *zaibatsu,* and therefore subsidized large private corporations in a variety of ways. As a result, the Korean state's industrial policy completely swamped cultural factors. Korea's family structure, being much more similar to that of China than Japan, should have dictated small average firm size and low levels of industrial concentration. But Korea after 1961 was determined to push Korean economic development rapidly using Japan as a model, and part of that model was Japan's large corporations and their *keiretsu* networks.

Certainly there is no direct correlation between the degree of government intervention in the economy and private sector firm size. Both Hong Kong and Taiwan have a small average firm size, and yet the Taiwanese government has been as interventionist as the Korean government in the financial sector. In Taiwan as in Korea (but in contrast to the laissez-faire British colonial administration of Hong Kong), all of the major banks that were responsible for capitalizing Taiwan's businesses were state owned, and they remained state owned longer than Korea's.[22]

Both Taiwan and Korea controlled interest rates, exchange rates, and capital flows rather rigidly, strictly limiting the number of foreign financial institutions that could operate within their countries. Both countries allocated credits to "strategic" sectors. The chief difference between them was that Korea was much more selective in its credit allocation and directed resources at the large *chaebol* conglomerates, whereas the Taiwanese state (outside of the public sector) did not show a comparable favoritism to large companies.[23]

State policy, then, played an important role in determining firm size and industrial structure in Korea. In Japan, it encouraged a tendency toward large firm size that was in the culture to begin with. In Taiwan, government policy affected many aspects of industrial development but not firm size, such that cultural factors remained important determinants. And in Hong Kong, state action influenced industrial structure hardly at all. Hong Kong therefore is the purest example of Chinese economic culture, undistorted by deliberate state manipulation.

Hence a multiplicity of factors besides culture can affect industrial structure. But the role of culture, and particularly spontaneous sociability, has been greatly underestimated by conventional economic analysis in explaining the large variations among societies that are otherwise at a similar level of development.

CHAPTER 28

Returns to Scale

I
n this book we have examined a variety of societies from the standpoint of one specific aspect of culture as it relates to economic life:
the ability to create new associations. All of the cases treated in
depth here have been economically successful ones. A good deal of the
book's focus has been on Asia, because much of Asia is in the process of
moving up from Third to First World status, and culture is commonly
said to be an important element of Asian success. Certainly many other
cultures around the world could have been included in this study, but
every comparative study must make a trade-off between breadth and
depth. In any event, the general analytical framework for understanding
the various bridges to economic sociability has been established and can
be applied to other societies.

That framework and its supporting hypotheses may be described briefly
as follows. Virtually all economic activity in the contemporary world is car-

ried out not by individuals but by organizations that require a high degree of social cooperation. Property rights, contracts, and commercial law are all indispensable institutions for creating a modern market-oriented economic system, but it is possible to economize substantially on transaction costs if such institutions are supplemented by social capital and trust. Trust, in turn, is the product of preexisting communities of shared moral norms or values. These communities, at least as they are lived and experienced by their most recent members, are not the product of rational choice in the economists' sense of the term.

Among the numerous forms of social capital that enable people to trust one another and build economic organizations, the most obvious and natural one is the family, with the consequence that the vast majority of businesses, both historically and now, are family businesses. Family structure affects the nature of family businesses: the large extended families of southern China and central Italy have become the basis for rather large-scale and dynamic enterprises. Beyond the family, there are kinship ties like the lineages in China and Korea that serve to expand the radius of trust outward.

Families, however, are a mixed blessing with regard to their impact on economic development. If familism is not accompanied by the strong emphasis on education that exists, for example, in Confucian or Jewish cultures, then it can lead to a stifling morass of nepotism and inbred stagnation. Familism that is too strong, moreover, can come at the expense of other forms of sociability. Hence the distrust that exists between nonkin in strongly familistic societies like those of China and southern Italy limits the ability of strangers to cooperate in economic ventures. In most cultures, there is something of a trade-off between the strength of family ties and the strength of nonkinship bonds. The ability to enter into associations readily with nonkin means necessarily that the family does not constitute an all-encompassing social horizon.

In other societies, however, there have been other forms of social capital besides family and kinship. Well before it modernized, Japan was host to a wide variety of social groups not based on kinship, whose permissive condition was a family structure that permitted the easy incorporation of biological outsiders into the household. In Germany, a variety of nonkinship-based structures like the guilds remained from that country's feudal period, and in the United States, sociability was the product of a sectarian Protestant religious culture. There is, in other words, no single bridge to sociability beyond the family that spans all cultures exhibiting a high degree of trust and spontaneous sociability.

There is, however, a common condition that applies to many familistic societies experiencing a low degree of trust between nonkin. China, France, southern Italy, and other low-trust societies all went through a period of strong political centralization, when an absolute emperor, monarch, or state deliberately set out to eliminate competitors for power. In such societies, the social capital that existed in the period before absolutist centralization was depleted, and social structures like the French guilds were placed in the service of the state. By contrast, the societies experiencing a high degree of social trust, such as Japan, Germany, and the United States, never experienced a prolonged period of centralized state power. With political power more dispersed—as in the Japanese and German feudal periods or as a deliberate result of constitutional structure in the United States—a rich profusion of social organizations could flourish without interference and become the basis for economic cooperation.

Although we did not consider cases in this category, it is also possible to have a society that has neither strong families nor strong associations outside of kinship—societies, in other words, that are deficient in social capital across the board. The cases that we touched upon that came closest to this description were the extremely poor peasants described by Edward Banfield in southern Italy, whose families were nuclear, small, and weak, and the black underclass in contemporary American inner cities, where single-parent families have become the norm. There are likely other cases as well. The Russian countryside, for example, does not have a rich associational life outside of the state-run *kolkhozi* and *sovkhozi* (collectivized state farms), and the Russian peasant family is troubled and weak. It would appear that in many contemporary African cities, older tribal structures and family ties have broken down with rapid urbanization and have not been replaced by strong voluntary associations outside of kinship. This kind of atomized society does not provide fertile ground for economic activity, supporting neither large organizations nor family businesses. One interesting thread that runs through such societies, however, is that of delinquent community: the community structures that do exist are criminal organizations. It is as if there is a natural, universal human impulse toward sociability, which if blocked from expressing itself through legitimate social structures like the family or voluntary organizations, appears in pathological forms like criminal gangs. And indeed, "mafias" have appeared as one of the strongest forms of social organization precisely in places like southern Italy, the American inner city, Russia, and many sub-Saharan African cities.

One of the most immediate consequences of a culture with a high propensity for spontaneous sociability is the ability to form large, modern corporations. The emergence of large, professionally managed corporations was driven, of course, by a host of technological and market-size factors as producers and distributors sought optimum scale efficiencies. But the development of large organizations able to exploit such efficiencies was greatly facilitated by the prior existence of a culture inclined to spontaneous social organization. It would appear to be no accident that three high-trust societies, Japan, Germany, and the United States, pioneered the development of large-scale, professionally managed enterprises. Low-trust societies like France, Italy, and noncommunist Chinese states including Taiwan and Hong Kong, by contrast, were relatively late in moving beyond large family businesses to modern corporations.

In the absence of a wide radius of trust and an inclination for spontaneous association, a society has two options for building large-scale economic organizations. The first is one that has been exploited from time immemorial: use of the state as a promoter of economic development, often directly in the form of state-owned and -managed enterprises. Many familistic societies with strong states wishing to have large-scale enterprises have followed this route, including France, Italy, and Taiwan. Korea falls in this category as well; though its large corporations are theoretically part of the private sector, they owe their dominance to the prolonged favoritism shown them by the Korean state.

A second option exists for building large organizations in a low-trust society: foreign direct investment or joint ventures with large foreign partners. This route, which I have not discussed at any length in this book, has been the one taken by many of the fast-developing states of Southeast Asia. The countries we have studied in this book have, by and large, eschewed massive direct foreign investment, choosing rather to create large corporations with indigenous talent (though frequently with foreign capital). A list of the largest companies for countries like Singapore, Malaysia, or Thailand will often include, besides state-owned companies, local subsidiaries of major multinational corporations. This pattern is also true in much of Latin America and seems to be developing in parts of the former communist world as well.

One might argue that since the failure to generate large-scale economic organizations in the private sector can be overcome by either the intervention of the state or foreign investment, the whole issue of spontaneous sociability is not important in the long run. In some sense this is true. France, despite the weakness of its private sector, has still managed to achieve front-rank status as a technologically advanced power through its state-owned and -subsidized companies. There are, however, important caveats to this line of argument. State-run companies are generally less efficient than their private counterparts: managements are constantly tempted to base decisions on political rather than market criteria, and the entire direction of strategic state investment may be misdirected because of simple miscalculation. It is true that in some cultures state-run companies can be better managed than in others and that mechanisms exist to shield them from political pressures. But although parastatals in Korea and Taiwan may have managed better than those of Brazil or Mexico, they still tend to be less efficient and dynamic than their private sector counterparts.

Foreign direct investment causes problems of a different sort. Ultimately, the technology and management skills brought in by foreign multinationals diffuse into the local economy, but that can take many years. In the meantime, countries whose leading companies are subsidiaries of foreign corporations face problems starting competitive businesses owned and managed by locals. Many of the fast modernizers in Asia, like Japan, Korea, and Taiwan, permitted inflows of foreign capital but constrained direct investment by foreign multinationals in order to give native businesses a chance to ramp up to global standards. Direct investment brings in technology and skills immediately, but it may delay the infrastructural and educational investments needed to create a strong group of local engineers, entrepreneurs, and managers. And like other forms of dependence, foreign direct investment often creates resentments and jealousies that may spill over into the political arena.

Cultural factors like spontaneous sociability are simply one of several factors contributing to aggregate GDP growth, and not always the most important. The kinds of issues studied by mainstream economists—macroeconomic policies, both fiscal and monetary; institutions; international conditions; barriers to trade; and the like—remain the principal determinants of long-term GDP growth. The primary impact of spontaneous sociability would appear to be on industrial structure—that is, the number and importance of large versus small corporations in a national economy, the ways in which they interact with one another, the presence of networks, and so forth. Culture inhibits the growth of large companies in some societies, permits it in others, and stimulates the emergence of new forms of economic enterprise, such as the Japanese network organization, in others.

Industrial structure determines, in turn, the sector of the global economy in which a country participates. The purpose of large corporations is to exploit economies of scale in sectors that are highly capital intensive, involve highly complex manufacturing processes, or require extensive distribution networks. Small companies, on the other hand, tend to be better at organizing more labor-intensive activities and in sectors demanding flexibility, innovativeness, and speed in decision making. A society hosting giant corporations will gravitate toward automobiles, semiconductors, aerospace, and the like, while those inclined toward small businesses will tend to concentrate in apparel, design, machine tools, and furniture. It is important to note that until now, there has been no obvious correlation between average scale and aggregate GDP growth. Societies have been able to become quite wealthy via either the large- or small-company route. Taiwan is no poorer than Korea for having companies of a smaller average size, and Italy grew faster than Germany in the 1980s. What small companies give up in terms of financial clout, technological resources, and staying power, they gain in flexibility, speed of decision-making, lack of bureaucracy, and innovativeness.

The relative prestige of large versus small companies has changed with the times. In the first half of the century, most people associated the highest levels of industrial modernity with very large scale; it became a fashion all over the world for governments to encourage the development of large-scale heavy industries of the sort that had propelled the United States and Germany to the front rank of industrial powers in the second half of the nineteenth century.

More recently, the trend has swung over far in the opposite direction. Public policy in the United States and Europe has been shaped in recent years by the perception that small companies are more innovative and create greater employment. Most corporations are today trying to downsize, decentralize, and become more flexible. Everyone has in mind the example of the computer industry, where Steve Jobs and Steve Wozniak, working out of their garage, invented the personal computer and started a technological revolution that within a decade undermined the behemoth IBM. The argument is also made that improvements in communications technology make possible industries that are far more decentralized and deconcentrated than before, leveling the playing field between small companies and their larger rivals.

This current mania for small companies may be no better founded than the earlier fashionableness of large ones.[1] In many sectors, important scale economies dictate a certain minimum efficient scale. Today it costs well over a billion dollars to set up a state-of-the-art silicon wafer fabrication facility, and the price tag has been rising steadily over the past decade. Continuing mergers and acquisitions in sectors from health care to telecommunications are testimony to the fact that the executives who make investment decisions still believe there are important economies of scale and scope to be exploited. Indeed, the cottage industry image of software production, where an enterprising individual working out of a garage could write pathbreaking applications, is hardly characteristic of other high-tech fields. Today, even the writing of competitive software programs is a bureaucratized and increasingly large-scale operation.[2] Creating a new operating system may not be as capital intensive as building an integrated steel mill, but it is an activity that nonetheless can benefit from important economies of scope. It is no accident that the American software industry has become increasingly dominated by a single large player, Microsoft, and that small start-up companies are all consolidating, being acquired, or going out of business.

The relative importance of scale, and consequently small versus large companies, may well change in the future, and in unpredictable ways. Future scale economies will depend on technological developments that have not yet occurred and are therefore impossible to predict. No one could have known ahead of time that IBM's massive R&D advantage would be undermined by its slowness in making decisions or that the development of continuous casting steelmaking technology would make possible mini-mills that could steal market share from the traditional large, integrated producers. It is possible that scale economies will increase in some sectors and decrease in others at the same time, such that no general overall pattern will emerge.

In the light of these kinds of uncertainties, it is possible to argue that in the future the optimal form of industrial organization will be neither small companies nor large ones but network structures that share the advantages of both. Network organizations can take advantage of scale economies while avoiding the overhead and agency costs of large, centralized organizations. If this will in fact be the case, then societies with a high degree of social trust will have a natural advantage. Networks can save on transaction costs substantially if their members follow an informal set of rules that require little or no overhead to negotiate, adjudicate, and enforce. The moment that trust breaks down among members of a business network, relations have to be spelled out in detail, unwritten rules codified, and third parties brought in to resolve differences. At this point the network ceases to look like a network and begins to resemble, depending on the degree of integration among network members, either a market relationship or an old-fashioned hierarchical corporation.

Lean manufacturing is perhaps the clearest example of the efficiency gains that can come about from the proliferation of network structures in the context of a high-trust society. Lean production decentralizes decision-making authority down to the lowest level of the factory floor and replaces centralized, rule-based cooperation with a more informal sense of workplace community. It also tends to flatten compensation rates throughout an organization (though paradoxically increasing individual incentives by making possible the elimination of seniority-based hiring and promotion). Whatever is lost in terms of individual carrot-and-stick rewards and punishments is more than compensated for by a higher degree of group effort, loyalty, and solidarity. The impact of the productivity gains made possible through this form of organization are measurable and large and have already been ramifying throughout the marketplace.

The impact of spontaneous sociability on economic life is significant. It affects the overall structure of national economies, the sectoral distribution of industries, the role that the state is tempted to play, and the day-to-day conditions under which workers relate to managers and to one another. It may also have an important impact on aggregate GDP as well. It is possible to imagine futures in which large, complex, and sophisticated corporations take the lead in creating wealth, as well as futures dominated by small, nimble, and innovative ones. Since we cannot predict future directions in technology, we cannot know which of these futures will materialize. What we can say is that the impact of cultural differences in the propensity for sociability will have a large, but at the moment indeterminate, impact on economic life.

CHAPTER 29

Many Miracles

It should be obvious by now that there is neither a single Asian model of economic development nor a unified "Confucian challenge" to the West.

Of course, some aspects of culture are common to virtually all East Asian societies. Among these is respect for education, which has been shared equally by Japanese, Chinese, Koreans, and the other cultures touched by Confucianism in a significant way. A culturally induced respect for learning may not have made economic sense fifty or a hundred years ago, when the returns to higher education were relatively small, but in today's technological world, the returns to skills and education have increased dramatically. While the market itself creates an incentive to invest in education, it helps greatly if parents push their children to do well in school and governments create the educational institutions to allow them to do so as a matter of habit.

Similarly, all East Asian cultures share a similar work ethic, though with somewhat different origins depending on the country. In Japan, it tends to grow more out of Buddhism, while in Korea and China it seems to come from Confucianism.[1] All of these societies have come to terms with the legitimacy of worldly labor; aristocratic or religious values disdaining commerce, moneymaking, or the dignity of everyday work have largely disappeared.

Finally, in most Asian societies, the state has played a rather large and active role in shaping the direction of economic development. This is far from a universal characteristic of Asian development, however. There is a wide degree of variation in the extent and nature of state intervention throughout East Asia, from the hyperactivity of the Korean state in the Park Chung Hee period, to the almost totally laissez-faire administration of the British colonial government in Hong Kong. State intervention and industrial policy are taken to be the essence of the Asian "economic miracle" by writers like Chalmers Johnson and James Fallows, but economic success does not correlate very well with the degree of state intervention among the countries in East Asia, suggesting that industrial policy per se is not the key determinant of growth. What may be culturally distinctive about East Asia is the fact that those states in the region that do seek to be interventionist are much more successful at pulling it off without deleterious consequences.

In terms of sociability, however, there are major differences among Japan, China, and Korea, differences that have resulted in their distinct industrial structures, management practices, and forms of organization. Many Americans and Europeans tend to see Asia as more homogeneous than it actually is, with Taiwan, Singapore, the PRC, and other states in Southeast Asia rising fast and following the same development trajectory as Japan, only on a later schedule. This view has been reinforced by promoters of the concept of a Confucian challenge from East Asia.

The reality, however, is that Asian countries have been segmented into different sectors of the global economy and are likely to stay there for some time. Japan and Korea, with their large corporations, have moved into areas like automobiles, consumer electronics, and semiconductors that are directly competitive with large North American and European industries. This is not, however, a natural strength of most Chinese societies, which do better in sectors where flexibility rather than scale is important. There are in fact two rival economic cultures arising in Asia— one Japanese and the other Chinese. Each is unified in a literal sense by large network organizations based, characteristically, on generalized social trust in the Japanese case and on family and kinship in the Chinese. These networks obviously interact with each other at many points, but their internal wiring diagrams proceed along very distinct paths.

The difficulties experienced by Chinese societies in establishing large, private, professionally managed corporations will in the future pose a dilemma for them that is more political than economic. It is not clear that the absence of large, professionally managed corporations is a particular obstacle to rapid aggregate GDP growth. Those who argued that Chinese familism would impede economic modernization were simply wrong, and will continue to be in the absence of technological developments favoring large organizations. Indeed, it is equally likely that small Chinese family businesses will prosper better than large Japanese corporations in an era of rapid corporate restructuring and downsizing. If the only objective of these societies is the maximization of aggregate wealth, then they have no particular need to move beyond relatively small-scale family businesses. Canada, New Zealand, and Denmark all grew wealthy through agriculture, raw materials, and other relatively low-tech industries. It is not obvious that they are less happy because they do not have powerful domestic semiconductor and aerospace industries.

On the other hand, many countries believe that the acquisition of industries in certain key strategic sectors is a good thing in itself, either because they believe that they know better than the market where the best long-run returns will be or because they are seeking noneconomic ends like international prestige or national security. France and Korea are prime examples of countries whose economic decision making was very much colored by noneconomic goals.

It is for this kind of society that lack of a spontaneous tendency toward large organizations may create the greatest pitfalls. If the private sector is unable to generate strategic industries on its own, then the state will be strongly tempted to step in and encourage development in that direction. Industrial development that is directly sponsored by the state brings with it all sorts of risks not associated with market-driven investment.

State-driven economic development will be a particular problem for the People's Republic of China. The Chinese economy is bifurcated between an old, inefficient, and declining state sector (that boasts, among other things, the world's least efficient automobile manufacturing operation) and a new market sector composed mostly of small family businesses or joint ventures with foreign partners. What does not exist in China today is a modern, efficient, indigenous, private large-company sector. China's astounding rate of aggregate growth in recent years (reaching some thirteen percent annually in 1992 and 1993) has been fueled largely by the capitalist small-business sector and by foreign investment. These rates of growth have been made possible by the introduction of market incentives into a hugely inefficient command economy. At the moment, China is too poor to worry about the sectoral distribution of its industries; everyone is grateful enough that they are growing at such an astounding rate. There are many basic problems that have yet to be worked out in the Chinese economy, such as establishment of a stable system of property rights and commercial law.

But China will face major problems if and when it catches up to the current per capita income levels of Taiwan or Hong Kong in the next generation or two. China watchers are familiar with a litany of potential problems that may brake the country's future growth, such as inflationary pressures, absent infrastructure and bottlenecks from too rapid a pace of development, vast disparities in per capita income between the coastal provinces and the hinterland, and a large number of environmental time bombs now being planted that eventually will explode. In addition, China will also face the issue of developing large, modern, professionally managed corporations. A Hong Kong or Taiwan might be willing to leave certain high-prestige forms of manufacturing to others while they grow faster along more market-directed lines, but the same is unlikely to be true for mainland China, in part because China as a great power is not going to want to be left out of the high end of industrial modernity. China's very size also dictates that it eventually develop a balanced economy, including both capital- and labor-intensive sectors; it cannot expect to reach a high level of overall development as a niche player like the small states of East Asia.

But the shift from family business to modern corporation will be much more problematic for the PRC than it was for Japan or the United States, and the state will have to play a much larger role. China needs, at a minimum, political stability born out of a basic legitimacy of its political institutions and a competent state structure prone neither to excessive corruption nor to outside political influence. China's communist political structure, however, lacks both legitimacy and, increasingly, competence. It is not at all clear to most observers whether China's political institutions will survive the enormous socioeconomic pressures created by its headlong industrialization, or whether there will even be a unitary state by the twenty-first century. An unstable China, or a China ruled by a nervous and capricious government, will not be a propitious environment for wise economic policymaking.

The contrast between Japanese and Chinese economic culture has important implications for Japan as well. With the rise of Japan as an economic superpower, there has been talk among certain Japanese of a "Japanese model" that should be followed by the other nations of Asia, if not by other parts of the world more generally.[2] And indeed the Japanese have a great deal to teach other nations of Asia (not to mention competitors in North America and Europe) that have already greatly benefited from Japanese technology and management skills in the recent past.

In terms of industrial structure, however, there is a wide gap between Japan and other Asian cultures, and some reason for thinking that it will be very difficult for Sinitic societies to adopt Japanese practices. The *keiretsu* system, for example, would seem to be very difficult to export to a Chinese society. Chinese firms and entrepreneurs would seem to be too individualistic to cooperate in that fashion and in any case have their own kinship-based networks. And the returns are not yet in on whether lean manufacturing can be implemented as successfully in a Chinese society as in Japan or North America. The Chinese, in other words, may well have to find their own organizational route to modernity.

CHAPTER 30

After the End of Social Engineering

The worldwide convergence in basic institutions around liberal democracy and market economics forces us to confront the question of whether we have reached an "end of history," in which the broad process of human historical evolution culminates not, as in the Marxist version, in socialism but rather in the Hegelian vision of a bourgeois liberal democratic society.[1]

Some readers of this book might think it takes a very different and contradictory position, because they believe it argues against a purely liberal economic order in favor of one that is both traditional and communitarian. This interpretation could not be further from the truth.[2] Not one of the traditional cultures studied in this book—not that of Japan, China, Korea, or any of the older Catholic-authoritarian cultures of Europe—was capable of producing the modern capitalist economic order. Max Weber is frequently criticized for arguing that Confucian societies like Japan and China could not become successful capitalist ones. But he

349

was actually speaking to a somewhat narrower point: he wanted to understand why modern capitalism, as well as other aspects of the modern world like natural science and the rational mastery of nature, arose in Protestant Europe and not in traditional China, Japan, Korea, or India.[3] And on this point, he was absolutely correct when he asserted that aspects of these traditional cultures were hostile to economic modernity. Only when the latter was introduced from the outside, as a consequence of China and Japan's contact with the West, did capitalist development begin to take off. This confrontation with the technological and social prowess of the West forced these societies to drop many key elements of their traditional cultures. China had to eliminate "political Confucianism," the entire imperial system with its class of gentlemen-scholars; Japan and Korea had do away with their traditional class divisions, and the former had to redirect the *samurai* warrior ethic.

None of the Asian societies that has prospered economically in the past few generations could have done so without incorporating important elements of economic liberalism into their indigenous cultural systems, including property rights, contract, commercial law, and the entire confluence of Western ideas concerning rationality, science, innovation, and abstraction. The work of Joseph Needham and others has shown that the Chinese level of technology in the year 1500 was higher than that prevailing in Europe.[4] What China did not have, however, and what Europe subsequently developed, was a scientific method that permitted the progressive conquest of nature through empirical observation and experiment. The scientific method itself was made possible by a cast of mind that sought to understand higher-level causality through abstract reasoning about underlying physical principles, something alien to the polytheistic religious cultures of Asia.[5]

It is understandable that the Chinese societies that were the first to industrialize and prosper were those that fell under the control or influence of Western powers like Britain or the United States, including Hong Kong, Singapore, and Taiwan. And it is no accident that immigrants from traditional societies to liberal countries like the United States, Canada, and Britain did much better than their countrymen at home. In all of these cases, the framework of a liberal society constituted a liberation from the constraints of a traditional culture that inhibited the development of entrepreneurship and constrained the open-ended accumulation of material wealth.

On the other hand, most thoughtful observers and theorists of political liberalism have understood that the doctrine, at least in its Hobbesean-Lockean form, is not self-sustaining and needs the support of aspects of traditional culture that do not themselves arise out of liberalism. That is, a society built entirely out of rational individuals who come together on the basis of a social contract for the sake of the satisfaction of their wants cannot form a society that would be viable over any length of time. In a criticism frequently leveled at Hobbes, such a society can provide no motive for any citizen to risk his or her life in defense of the larger community, since the purpose of the community was to preserve the individual's life. More broadly, if individuals formed communities only on the basis of rational long-term self-interest, there would be little in the way of public spiritedness, self-sacrifice, pride, charity, or any of the other virtues that make communities livable.[6] Indeed, one could hardly imagine a meaningful family life if families were essentially contracts between rational, self-interested individuals.[7] While liberalism arose historically out of an effort to exclude religion from public life, most liberal theorists have thought that religious belief could not, and should not, be eliminated from social life. While not necessarily believers themselves, virtually all of the American Founding Fathers believed that a vigorous religious life, with its belief in divine rewards and punishments, was important to the success of American democracy.

A parallel argument can be made with respect to economic liberalism. That modern economies arise out of the interactions of rational, utility-maximizing individuals in markets is incontestable. But rational utility maximization is not enough to give a full or satisfying account of why successful economies prosper or unsuccessful ones stagnate and decline. The degree to which people value work over leisure, their respect for education, attitudes toward the family, and the degree of trust they show toward their fellows all have a direct impact on economic life and yet cannot be adequately explained in terms of the economists' basic model of man. Just as liberal democracy works best as a political system when its individualism is moderated by public spirit, so too is capitalism facilitated when its individualism is balanced by a readiness to associate.

If democracy and capitalism work best when they are leavened with cultural traditions that arise from nonliberal sources, then it should be clear that modernity and tradition can coexist in a stable equilibrium for extended periods of time. The process of economic rationalization and development is an extremely powerful social force that compels societies to modernize along certain uniform lines. In this respect, there is clearly such a thing as "History" in the Marxist-Hegelian sense that homogenizes disparate cultures and pushes them in the direction of "modernity." But since there are limits to the effectiveness of contract and economic rationality, the character of that modernity will never be completely uniform. For example, certain societies can save substantially on transaction costs because economic agents trust one another in their interactions and therefore can be more efficient than low-trust societies, which require detailed contracts and enforcement mechanisms. This trust is not the consequence of rational calculation; it arises from sources like religion or ethical habit that have nothing to do with modernity. The most successful forms of modernity, in other words, are not completely modern; that is, they are not based on the universal proliferation of liberal economic and political principles throughout the society.

This conundrum can be expressed in a different way. Not only have grand ideological projects like communism failed, but even the more modest efforts at social engineering—the sort attempted by moderate democratic governments—have reached a dead end at the conclusion of the twentieth century. The French Revolution ushered in a period of incredibly rapid social change. Over the next two hundred years, all European societies and many of those outside Europe were transformed beyond recognition from poor, uneducated, rural, agricultural, authoritarian ones to urban, industrialized, wealthy democracies. In the course of these transformations, governments played a major role in precipitating or facilitating change (and in some cases, trying to stop it). They abolished entire social classes, engaging in land reform and the disbanding of large estates; they introduced modern legislation guaranteeing equality of rights for ever-larger circles of the population; they built cities and encouraged urbanization; they educated entire populations and provided the infrastructure for modern, complex, information-intensive societies.

There have been increasing indications over the past generation, however, that the kinds of results achievable through this sort of large-scale social engineering have been subject to diminishing marginal returns. In 1964, the Civil Rights Act laid to rest at the stroke of a pen legally sanctioned racial inequalities in the United States. In subsequent years, however, abolishing substantive inequality for African-Americans has proven a much more difficult problem. The solution that seemed so obvious in the 1930s and 1940s was the steady expansion of the welfare state through income redistribution or job creation and the opening to minorities of health, education, employment, and other social benefits. By the end of the century, these solutions not only seem ineffective, but in many cases are seen as contributing to the very problems they sought to solve. A generation or more ago, there would have been a broad consensus among social scientists of a largely one-way causal relationship between poverty and family breakdown, flowing from the former to the latter. Today people are much less certain, and few believe that the problems of the contemporary American family can be fixed simply through the equalization of incomes. It is easy to see how government policies can encourage the breakdown of families, as when they subsidize single motherhood; what is less obvious is how government policy can restore family structure once it has been broken.

The collapse of communism and the end the cold war have not, as many commentators have asserted, led to a global upsurge of tribalism, a revival of nineteenth-century nationalist rivalries,[8] or a breakdown of civilization into anomic violence.[9] Liberal democracy and capitalism remain the essential, indeed the only, framework for the political and economic organization of modern societies. Rapid economic modernization is closing the gap between many former Third World countries and the industrialized North. With European integration and North American free trade, the web of economic ties within each region will thicken, and sharp cultural boundaries will become increasingly fuzzy. Implementation of the free trade regime of the Uruguay Round of the General Agreement on Tariffs and Trade (GATT) will further erode interregional boundaries. Increased global competition has forced companies across cultural boundaries to try to adopt "best-practice" techniques like lean manufacturing from whatever source they come from. The worldwide recession of the 1990s has put great pressure on Japanese and German companies to scale back their culturally distinctive and paternalistic labor policies in favor of a more purely liberal model. The modern communications revolution abets this convergence by facilitating economic globalization and by propagating the spread of ideas at enormous speed.

But in our age, there can be substantial pressures for cultural differentiation even as the world homogenizes in other respects. Modern liberal political and economic institutions not only coexist with religion and other traditional elements of culture but many actually work better in conjunction with them. If many of the most important remaining social problems are essentially cultural in nature and if the chief differences among societies are not political, ideological, or even institutional but rather cultural, it stands to reason that societies will hang on to these areas of cultural distinctiveness and that the latter will become all the more salient and important in the years to come.

Awareness of cultural difference will be abetted, paradoxically, by the same communications technology that has made the global village possible. There is a strong liberal faith that people around the world are basically similar under the surface and that greater communications will bring deeper understanding and cooperation. In many instances, unfortunately, that familiarity breeds contempt rather than sympathy. Something like this process has been going on between the United States and Asia in the past decade. Americans have come to realize that Japan is not simply a fellow capitalist democracy but has rather different ways of practicing both capitalism and democracy. One result, among others, is sthe emergence of the revisionist school among specialists on Japan, who are less sympathetic to Tokyo and argue for tougher trade policies. And Asians are made vividly aware through the media of crime, drugs, family breakdown, and other American social problems, and many have decided that the United States is not such an attractive model after all. Lee Kwan Yew, former prime minister of Singapore, has emerged as a spokesman for a kind of Asian revisionism on the United States, which argues that liberal democracy is not an appropriate political model for the Confucian societies.[10] The very convergence of major institutions makes peoples all the more intent on preserving those elements of distinctiveness they continue to possess.

If these differences cannot be reconciled, they can at least be confronted squarely. Obviously, one cannot begin any serious study of foreign cultures by evaluating them from the standpoint of one's own. On the other hand, one of the biggest obstacles to a serious comparative study of culture in the United States is the assumption, made for political reasons, that all cultures are inherently equal. Any such study requires the exploration of differences among cultures against some standard, which in this book has been economic performance. The desire for economic prosperity is itself not culturally determined but almost universally shared. It is hard, in this context, not to come to some judgments about the relative strengths and weaknesses of different societies. It is not sufficient to say that everyone eventually arrives at the same goal but by different paths. *How* a society arrives and the speed with which it does so affect the happiness of its people, and some never arrive at all.

CHAPTER 31

The Spiritualization of Economic Life

Social capital is critical to prosperity and to what has come to be called competitiveness, but its more important consequences may not be felt in the economy so much as in social and political life. Spontaneous sociability has consequences that are not easy to capture in aggregate income statistics. Human beings are at the same time narrowly selfish individuals and creatures with a social side who shun isolation and enjoy the support and recognition of other human beings. There are, of course, some individuals who prefer working in a low-trust Taylorite mass production factory because it defines the minimum of work they need to do to earn their paychecks and otherwise makes few claims on them. But on the whole, workers do not want to be treated like cogs in a large machine, isolated from managers and fellow workers, with little pride in their skills or their organization, and trusted with a minimal amount of authority and control over the work they do for a living. Any number of empirical studies from Elton Mayo on have indicated that workers are happier in group-oriented organizations than in more individualistic ones. Thus, even if productivity was equal between low- and high-trust factories and offices, the latter are more humanly satisfying places in which to work.

Furthermore, a successful capitalist economy is clearly very important as a support for stable liberal democracy. It is, of course, possible for a capitalist economy to coexist with an authoritarian political system, as in the PRC today or as previously existed in Germany, Japan, South Korea, Taiwan, and Spain. But in the long run, the industrialization process itself necessitates a more highly educated population and a more complex division of labor, both of which tend to be supportive of democratic political institutions. As a consequence, there are today virtually no wealthy capitalist countries that are not also stable liberal democracies.[1] One of the great problems of Poland, Hungary, Russia, Ukraine, and other former communist states is that they have tried to establish democratic political institutions without the benefit of functioning capitalist economies. The lack of firms, entrepreneurs, markets, and competition not only perpetuates poverty, it fails to provide critical forms of social support for the proper functioning of democratic institutions.

It has been argued that the market itself constitutes a school for sociability, by providing the opportunity and incentive for people to cooperate with one another for the sake of mutual enrichment. But while the market does impose its own socializing discipline to some degree, the larger theme of this book is that sociability does not simply emerge spontaneously once the state retreats. The ability to cooperate socially is dependent on prior habits, traditions, and norms, which themselves serve to structure the market. Hence it is more likely that a successful market economy, rather than being the cause of stable democracy, is codetermined by the prior factor of social capital. If the latter is abundant, then both markets and democratic politics will thrive, and the market can in fact play a role as a school of sociability that reinforces democratic institutions. This is particularly true in newly industrializing countries with authoritarian governments, where people can learn new forms of sociability in the workplace before applying the lessons to politics.

The concept of social capital makes clear why capitalism and democracy are so closely related. A healthy capitalist economy is one in which there will be sufficient social capital in the underlying society to permit businesses, corporations, networks, and the like to be self-organizing. In default of this self-organizing capability, the state can step in to promote key firms and sectors, but markets almost always work more efficiently when private actors are making the decisions.

That self-organizing proclivity is exactly what is necessary to make democratic political institutions work as well. It is law based on popular sovereignty that converts a system of liberty into one of ordered liberty. But no such system can come into being on the basis of a mass of unorganized, isolated individuals, able to make their own views and preferences known only at election time. Their weakness and atomization would not permit them to express their views properly, even when those views were held by a majority, and would be an open invitation to despotism and demagogy. In any meaningful democracy, the interests and wishes of the different members of society have to be articulated and represented through political parties and other kinds of organized political groups. And a stable party structure can come about only if people with common interests are able to work with one another for common ends—an ability that rests, in the end, on social capital.

The same propensity for spontaneous sociability that is key to building durable businesses is also indispensable for putting together effective political organizations. In default of real political parties, political groupings come to be based on changeable personalities or patron-client relationships; they fracture easily and fail to work together for common purposes even when they have a strong incentive to do so. One should expect countries with small, weak, private firms also to have fragmented and unstable party systems. This is in fact the case if we compare the United States and Germany to France and Italy. Both private companies and political parties are weak or nonexistent in postcommunist societies like Russia and Ukraine, and elections lurch between extremes defined around individuals rather than coherent political programs. The "democrats" in Russia all believe in democracy and markets on an intellectual level, but they lack the social habits necessary to create a unified political organization.

A liberal state is ultimately a limited state, with government activity strictly bounded by a sphere of individual liberty. If such a society is not to become anarchic or otherwise ungovernable, then it must be capable of self-government at levels of social organization below the state. Such a system depends ultimately not just on law but on the self-restraint of individuals. If they are not tolerant and respectful of each other or do not abide by the laws they set for themselves, they will require a strong and coercive state to keep each other in line. If they cannot cohere for common purposes, then they will need an intrusive state to provide the organization they cannot provide themselves. Conversely, the "withering away of the state" Karl Marx envisioned could conceivably arise only in a society with an extraordinarily high degree of spontaneous sociability, where restraint and norm-based behavior would flow from within rather than having to be imposed from without. A low social capital country is not only likely to have small, weak, and inefficient companies; it will also suffer from pervasive corruption of its public officials and ineffective public administration. This situation is painfully evident in Italy, where there is a direct relationship between social atomization and corruption as one moves from the North and center to the South.

A dynamic and prosperous capitalist economy is crucial to stable democracy in an even more fundamental way, one that is related to the ultimate end of all human activity. In *The End of History and the Last Man,* I argued that the human historical process could be understood as the interplay between two large forces.[2] The first was that of rational desire, in which human beings sought to satisfy their material needs through the accumulation of wealth. The second, equally important motor of the historical process was what Hegel called the "struggle for recognition," that is, the desire of all human beings to have their essence as free, moral beings recognized by other human beings.[3]

Rational desire corresponds, more or less, to the rational utility maximization of neoclassical economics: the endless accumulation of material possessions to satisfy an ever-increasing set of wants and needs. The desire for recognition, on the other hand, has no material object but seeks only a just evaluation of one's worth on the part of another human consciousness. All human beings believe they have a certain inherent worth or dignity. When that worth is not recognized adequately by others, they feel anger; when they do not live up to others' evaluation, they feel shame; and when they are evaluated appropriately, they feel pride. The desire for recognition is an extraordinarily powerful part of the human psyche; the emotions of anger, pride, and shame are the basis of most political passions and motivate much that goes on in political life. The desire for recognition can be manifest in any number of contexts: in the anger of an employee who quits the company because she feels her contribution has not been adequately recognized; in the indignation of a nationalist who wants his country recognized as an equal of others; in the rage of the antiabortion crusader who feels that innocent life has not been equally protected; and in the passion of feminist or gay rights activists who demand that members of their group be treated with equal respect by the larger society. The passions engendered by the desire for recognition often work at cross purposes with the desire for rational accumulation, as when a man risks his liberty and possessions to take revenge on someone who has wronged him or when a nation goes to war for the sake of national dignity.

In the earlier book, I argued at some length that what usually passes as economic motivation is in fact not a matter of rational desire but a manifestation of the desire for recognition. Natural wants and needs are few in number and rather easily satisfied, particularly in the context of a modern industrial economy. Our motivation in working and earning money is much more closely related to the recognition that such activity affords us, where money becomes a symbol not for material goods but for social status or recognition. Adam Smith explained in the *Theory of Moral Sentiments,* "It is the vanity, not the ease or the pleasure, which interests us."[4] The worker who strikes for higher wages does not do so simply because he is greedy and wants all the material comforts he can get; instead, he seeks economic justice in which his labor is compensated fairly in relation to others—in other words, that it be recognized for its true worth. Similarly, the entrepreneurs who create business empires do not do so because they want to spend the hundreds of millions of dollars they will earn; rather, they want to be recognized as the creators of a new technology or service.

If we understand, then, that economic life is pursued not simply for the sake of accumulating the greatest number of material goods possible but also for the sake of recognition, then the critical interdependence of capitalism and liberal democracy becomes clearer. Prior to modern liberal democracy, the struggle for recognition was carried on by ambitious princes who sought primacy over each other through war and conquest. Indeed, Hegel's account of the human historical process began with a primordial "bloody battle" in which two combatants sought to be recognized by the other, leading one ultimately to enslave the other. Conflicts based on religious or nationalist passion are much more intelligible if understood as manifestations of the desire for recognition rather than rational desire or "utility maximization." Modern liberal democracy seeks to satisfy this desire for recognition by basing the political order on the principle of universal and equal recognition. But in practice, liberal democracy works because the struggle for recognition that formerly had been carried out on a military, religious, or nationalist plane is now pursued on an economic one. Where formerly princes sought to vanquish each other by risking their lives in bloody battles, they now risk their capital through the building of industrial empires. The underlying psychological need is the same, only the desire for recognition is satisfied through the production of wealth rather than the destruction of material values.

In *The Passions and the Interests,* the economist Albert Hirshman sought to explain the rise of the modern bourgeois world in terms of an ethical revolution that sought to replace the "passion" for glory that characterized aristocratic societies, with the "interest" in material gain that was the hallmark of the new bourgeois.[5] Early political economists of the Scottish Enlightenment like Adam Ferguson, Adam Smith, and James Steuart all hoped that the destructive energies of a warrior culture would be channeled into the safer pursuits of a commercial society, with a corresponding softening of manners. Indeed, this substitution was also very much in the mind of the first liberal political theorist, Thomas Hobbes, who conceived of civil society as the deliberate subordination of the desire for glory, whether fueled by religious passion or aristocratic vanity, to the pursuit of rational accumulation.

Whatever the expectations of these early modern theorists, it seems that what has happened in the modern world is not simply the embourgeoisement of warrior cultures and the replacement of passions by interests but also as the spiritualization of economic life and the endowment of the latter with the same competitive energies that formerly fueled political life. Human beings frequently do not act like rational utility maximizers in any narrow sense of the term utility, but they invest economic activity with many of the moral values of their broader social lives. In Japan, this happened directly as the *samurai* or warrior class was capitalized in what amounted to a buyout of their social status, and turned toward business, which they approached with much of their *bushido* warrior ethic still intact. This process has occurred in virtually all other industrialized societies as well, where the opportunities of entrepreneurship became the outlet for the energies of countless ambitious people who in earlier ages could have been "recognized" only by starting a war or revolution.

The role that a capitalist economy plays in channeling recognition struggles in a peaceful direction, and its consequent importance to democratic stability, is evident in postcommunist Eastern Europe. The totalitarian project envisioned the destruction of an independent civil society and the creation of a new socialist community centered exclusively around the state. When the latter, highly artificial community collapsed, there were virtually no alternative forms of community beyond those of family and ethnic group, or else in the delinquent communities constituted by criminal gangs. In the absence of a layer of voluntary associations, individuals clung to their ascriptive identities all the more fiercely. Ethnicity provided an easy form of community by which they could avoid feeling atomized, weak, and victimized by the larger historical forces swirling around them. In developed capitalist societies with strong civil societies, by contrast, the economy itself is the locus of a substantial part of social life. When one works for Motorola, Siemens, Toyota, or even a small family dry-cleaning business, one is part of a moral network that absorbs a large part of one's energies and ambitions. The Eastern European countries that appear to have the greatest chances for success as democracies are Hungary, Poland, and the Czech Republic, which retained nascent civil societies throughout the communist period and were able to generate capitalist private sectors in relatively short order. There is no lack of divisive ethnic conflicts in these places, whether over competing Polish and Lithuanian claims to Vilnius or Hungarian irredenta vis-à-vis neighbors. But they have not flared up into violent conflicts yet because the economy has been sufficiently vigorous to provide an alternative source of social identity and belonging.

The mutual dependence of economy and polity is not limited to democratizing states in the former communist world. In a way, the loss of social capital in the United States has more immediate consequences for American democracy than for the American economy. Democratic political institutions no less than businesses depend on trust for effective operation, and the reduction of trust in a society will require a more intrusive, rule-making government to regulate social relations.

Many of the cases covered in this book stand as a cautionary tale against overcentralized political authority. More than former communist countries suffer from weak or damaged civil societies. Familistic societies with a low degree of generalized trust in China, France, and southern Italy were all products of centralizing monarchies in times past (and, in the French case, Republican governments) that undercut the autonomy of intermediate social institutions in their quest for exclusive power. Conversely, societies exhibiting a relatively high degree of generalized trust, like Japan and Germany, lived under relatively decentralized political authority for much of their late premodern existences. In the United States, the weakening authority of civil associations has been connected with the rise of a strong state, through both the courts and the executive.

Social capital is like a ratchet that is more easily turned in one direction than another; it can be dissipated by the actions of governments much more readily than those governments can build it up again. Now that the question of ideology and institutions has been settled, the preservation and accumulation of social capital will occupy center stage.

NOTES

CHAPTER 1. ON THE HUMAN SITUATION AT THE END OF HISTORY

1. See Francis Fukuyama, *The End of History and the Last Man* (New York: Free Press, 1992).
2. For an excellent discussion of the origins of civil society and its relationship to democracy, see Ernest Gellner, *Conditions and Liberty: Civil Society and Its Rivals* (London: Hamish Hamilton, 1994).
3. For a more detailed discussion of this point, see Francis Fukuyama, "The Primacy of Culture," *Journal of Democracy* 6 (1995): 7–14.
4. Samuel P. Huntington, "The Clash of Civilizations?" *Foreign Affairs* 72 (1994): 22–49.
5. According to Durkheim, "Society is not alone in its interest in the formation of special groups to regulate their own activity, developing within them what otherwise would become anarchic; but the individual, on his part, finds joy in it, for anarchy is painful to him. He also suffers from pain and disorder produced whenever inter-individual relations are not submitted to some regulatory influence." *The Division of Labor in Society* (New York: Macmillan, 1933), p. 15.
6. See Fukuyama (1992), particularly chap. 21, "The Thymotic Origins of Work."
7. For a readable account of Nucor's rise as a steel company, see Richard Preston, *American Steel* (New York: Avon Books, 1991).
8. James S. Coleman, "Social Capital in the Creation of Human Capital," *American Journal of Sociology* 94 (1988): S95–S120. See also Robert D. Putnam, "The Prosperous Community: Social Capital and Public Life," *American Prospect* 13 (1993): 35–42; and Putnam, "Bowling Alone," *Journal of Democracy* 6 (1995):

65–78. According to Putnam, the first use of the term *social capital* was by Jane Jacobs, in *The Death and Life of Great American Cities* (New York: Random House, 1961), p. 138.

9. Gary S. Becker, *Human Capital: A Theoretical and Empirical Analysis,* 2d ed. (New York: National Bureau of Economic Research, 1975).

CHAPTER 2. THE TWENTY PERCENT SOLUTION

1. On this aspect of Adam Smith, see Jerry Z. Muller, *Adam Smith in His Time and Ours* (New York: Free Press, 1992).

2. The neomercantilists share with earlier Marxist and Keynesian critics an emphasis on the importance of the state as an economic actor. Nonetheless, their critique is a pale shadow of these earlier attacks on orthodox free market economics. The Marxists argued for more or less total state control of the economy, with outright government ownership of the "commanding heights" of the economic system. Their intention was nothing less than the ending of "the exploitation of man by man." The Keynesians, by contrast, accepted the need for a strong private sector but argued for massive government intervention through public spending in order to maintain full employment and other social welfare goals. The neomercantilist wave focuses on more modest objectives like the promotion of high-technology industries in a highly competitive and interdependent global market. The neomercantilists would concede that global competition produces beneficial economic efficiencies and that economies should be export oriented and outward looking, and for the most part they believe that welfare goals like full employment or equitable income distribution can be achieved only indirectly. They would argue the more modest point that the market alone is insufficient to produce technological leadership and hence rapid long-term growth.

3. James Fallows, *Looking at the Sun: The Rise of the New East Asian Economic and Political System* (New York: Pantheon Books, 1994).

4. For examples of this genre, see Chalmers Johnson, *MITI and the Japanese Miracle* (Stanford: Stanford University Press, 1982); James Fallows, "Containing Japan," *Atlantic Monthly* 263, no. 5 (1989): 40–54; "Looking at the Sun," *Atlantic Monthly* 272, no. 5 (1993): 69–100; "How the World Works," *Atlantic Monthly* 272, no. 6 (1993): 61–87; Chalmers Johnson, Laura D'Andrea Tyson, and John Zysman, *The Politics of Productivity* (Cambridge, Mass.: Ballinger Books, 1989); Laura D'Andrea Tyson, *Who's Bashing Whom? Trade Conflicts in High-Technology Industries* (Washington, D.C.: Institute for International Economics, 1993); Karl van Wolferen, *The Enigma of Japanese Power: People and Politics in a Stateless Nation* (London: Macmillan, 1989); Clyde V. Prestowitz, Jr., *Trading Places: How We Allowed Japan to Take the Lead* (New York: Basic Books, 1988).

5. Paul Krugman has recently gone so far as to argue that the "Asian miracle" is actually not a miracle at all but simply represents the mobilization of unused resources in relatively undeveloped economies comparable to high-growth periods in early phases of European and American economic development. See "The Myth of Asia's Miracle," *Foreign Affairs* 73 (1994): 28–44.

6. James C. Abegglen and George Stalk, Jr., *Kaisha: The Japanese Corporation*

(New York: Basic Books, 1985), pp. 20–23.

7. Gary Becker argues that economics ought not to be thought of as a specific subject of study (e.g., the study of money or wealth) but as a method that can be applied to a wide range of human behavior. See Becker, *The Economic Approach to Human Behavior* (Chicago: University of Chicago Press, 1976), pp. 3–14.

8. For critiques of the rational choice school, see Donald P. Green and Ian Shapiro, *Pathologies of Rational Choice Theory: A Critique of Applications in Political Science* (New Haven: Yale University Press, 1994), and Chalmers Johnson and E. B. Keehn, "A Disaster in the Making: Rational Choice and Asian Studies," *National Interest,* no. 36 (1994): 14–22.

9. For a fascinating interchange on the limits of the ability of economics to give an account of politics, see the dialogue among James Buchanan, Viktor Vanberg, and Allan Bloom in James Nichols and Colin Wright, eds., *From Political Economy to Economics . . . and Back?* (San Francisco: Institute for Contemporary Studies, 1990), pp. 193–206.

10. In the words of Gordon Tullock, a collaborator of James Buchanan and one of the founding members of the "public choice" school, "Most economists having observed the functioning of the market and government for some time tend to think that most people, most of the time, have a demand curve, the overwhelmingly largest component of which is their own selfish desires." Quoted in Steven E. Rhoads, "Do Economists Overemphasize Monetary Benefits?" *Public Administration Review* 45 (1985): 815–820. This article contains considerable evidence that, despite their theoretical openness to other forms of motivation, neoclassical economists believe in the fundamental power of material self-interest.

11. Rhoads (1985), p. 816.

12. For a critique of the neoclassical model that runs along similar lines, see Amitai Etzioni, *The Moral Dimension: Toward a New Economics* (New York: Free Press, 1988), pp. 1–27; Etzioni, "A New Kind of Socioeconomics (vs. Neoclassical Economics)," *Challenge* 33 (1990): 31–32; and Steven E. Rhoads, "Economists on Tastes and Preferences," in Nichols and Wright (1990), pp. 79–98. See also Neil J. Smelser and Richard Swedberg, "The Sociological Perspective on the Economy," in Smelser and Swedberg, eds., *The Handbook of Economic Sociology* (Princeton: Princeton University Press, 1994), as well as several of the other articles in this collection.

13. For a different kind of critique of the concept of "utility," see Joseph Cropsey, "What Is Welfare Economics?" *Ethics* 65 (1955): 116–125.

14. On this point, see Steven Kelman, "'Public Choice' and Public Spirit," *Public Interest* no. 87 (1987): 80–94.

15. Gary Becker, for example, argues that "the economic approach I refer to does not assume that individuals are motivated solely by selfishness or material gain. . . . I have tried to pry economists away from narrow assumptions about self-interest. Behavior is driven by a much richer set of values and preferences." See his "Nobel Lecture: The Economic Way of Looking at Things," *Journal of Political Economy* 101 (1993): 385–409.

16. Amartya Sen criticizes the concept of revealed preference because the preference supposedly revealed is actually ambiguous. For example, a person may ac-

tually prefer to throw away glass bottles rather than recycle them but feels a strong moral compulsion to do the latter or simply wants to do so for the sake of appearances. Behavior by itself does not tell an outside observer which is the real motive. Sen further argues that users of the revealed-preference concept make use of a hidden assumption that preferences are self-interested, whereas people in reality also have a social side and typically act out of mixed motives. See "Behaviour and the Concept of Preference," *Economics* 40 (1973): 214–259.

17. F. Y. Edgeworth, as quoted by Amartya Sen in "Rational Fools: A Critique of the Behavioral Foundations of Economic Theory," *Philosophy and Public Affairs* 6 (1977): 317–344.

18. See Kenneth Arrow's critique of the assumption of many economists that consumers are rational in their choices. Arrow, "Risk Perception in Psychology and Economics," *Economic Inquiry* 20 (1982): 1–9.

19. Hence, for example, we decide to buy a brand name like Kellogg's Corn Flakes rather than the store brand because we assume, in the absence of detailed research, that it is of higher quality.

20. See Becker (1976), p. 11.

21. Mark Granovetter, "Economic Action and Social Structure: The Problem of Embeddedness," *American Journal of Sociology* 91 (1985): 481–510.

22. See World Bank, *The East Asian Miracle* (Oxford: Oxford University Press, 1993), pp. 304–316.

CHAPTER 3. SCALE AND TRUST

1. See, for example, Alvin Toffler and Heidi Toffler, *War and Anti-War: Survival at the Dawn of the 21st Century* (Boston: Little, Brown, 1993); Peter W. Huber, *Orwell's Revenge: The 1984 Palimpsest* (New York: Free Press, 1994).

2. Scott Shane, *Dismantling Utopia: How Information Ended the Soviet Union* (Chicago: Ivan Dee, 1994); Gladys D. Ganley, "Power to the People via Personal Electronic Media," *Washington Quarterly* (Spring 1991): 5–22.

3. William H. Davidow and Michael S. Malone, *The Virtual Corporation: Structuring and Revitalizing the Corporation for the 21st Century* (New York: Harper-Collins, 1992).

4. Huber (1994), pp. 177–181, 193.

5. This argument is made by Peter Huber himself. See Peter W. Huber, Michael K. Kellogg, and John Thorne, *The Geodesic Network II: 1993 Report on Competition in the Telephone Industry* (Washington, D.C.: Geodesic Co., 1992), chap. 3.

6. It is not sufficient that members of the community expect regular behavior. There are many societies in which there is the expectation that other people will regularly cheat their fellows; behavior is regular but dishonest, and leads to a deficit of trust.

7. Emile Durkheim, *The Division of Labor in Society* (New York: Macmillan 1933), pp. 181–182. On the insufficiency of contract to produce organic solidarity, see p. 183.

8. Lester Thurow, *Head to Head: The Coming Economic Battle among Japan, Europe, and America* (New York: Warner Books, 1993), p. 32.
9. See, for example, Ronald P. Dore, *British Factory, Japanese Factory* (London: Allen and Unwin, 1973), pp. 375–376; James Fallows, *More Like Us: Making America Great Again* (Boston: Houghton Mifflin, 1989), p. 48; Seymour Martin Lipset, "Pacific Divide: American Exceptionalism—Japanese Uniqueness," in *Power Shifts and Value Changes in the Post Cold War World*, Proceedings of the Joint Symposium of the International Sociological Association's Research Committees: Comparative Sociology and Sociology of Organizations (Japan: Kibi International University, Institute of International Relations of Sophia University, and Social Science Research Institute of International Christian University, 1992), pp. 41–84.
10. The following list contains the revenues (in US$ millions) of the ten, twenty, and forty largest private, nonforeign companies in eight economies:

	Top Ten	Top Twenty	Top Forty
United States	755,202	1,144,477	1,580,411
Japan	551,227	826,049	1,224,294
Germany	414,332	629,520	869,326
France	233,350	366,547	544,919
Italy	137,918	178,669	259,595
Korea	61,229	86,460	107,889
Hong Kong	24,725	30,633	35,515
Taiwan	10,705	N.A.	N.A.

Sources: *Hoover's Handbook of American Business 1994* (Austin, Tex.: The Reference Press, 1994); *Moody's International Company Data, May 1994;* Korea Trade Center of Los Angeles; *Germany's Top 300, 1993/94 Edition* (Austin, Tex.: The Reference Press, 1994).

This table is based on data from the 100 largest companies in each of the eight listed economies, excluding firms that are publicly owned or are subsidiaries of foreign multinationals. There is some ambiguity about the ownership of certain firms; they may be only partially publicly or foreign owned, or true ownership is hidden through holding companies or cross-shareholding.

A number of problems are associated with comparative measurements of the size of large companies in different economies. It is possible to measure the size of firms by revenues, value-added (i.e., pretax earnings), employment, or total market capitalization. Value-added is perhaps the best all-around measure of a company's size in any particular year, though market capitalization would measure expectations of future earnings. Revenues as a measure do not take into account profit margins and future expectations; they are used here because of the difficulty of obtaining firm-level earnings data and capitalization data on all of the countries and companies.

This table does not present concentration ratios because they tend to be somewhat misleading as to the relative scale of corporations in or economy. A concentration ratio for a single sector of an economy is calculated by measuring the total value-added, employment, or market capitalization for the top X number of firms (where X is, typically, three to ten firms for individual sectors), and dividing this total by the value-added, employment, or market capitalization for that sector. Hence a three-firm concentration ratio for the U.S. steel industry will show how much of total U.S. steel output is produced by the three largest producers. This ratio is commonly used as a measure of monopoly or oligopoly in a particular sector. This kind of analysis can be extended to national economies as well, by expanding the concentration ratios to the top ten, twenty, or more largest firms in the economy as a whole. Table 1 in chapter 14 presents such data, based on employment, for a selected group of countries.

One might be tempted to think that the concentration ratio is a better measure than the absolute size of a nation's largest companies, since it is easy to imagine that there is some relationship between a country's gross domestic product, population, and the size of firms it is able to support (see Chapter 27). On the other hand, a number of small European countries have been hosts to extremely large corporations. Switzerland, Sweden, and Holland all have ten-firm concentration ratios higher than the United States, Japan, or Germany. Past a certain minimum population, as well as a certain level of overall economic development, the correlation between an economy's absolute size and its ability to produce large companies would appear to be weak.

Nor is average size of firms in a national economy a good measure of the ability to generate large companies. In addition to hosting extremely large corporations, Japan's economy has produced a very large number of very small firms. Based simply on average firm size, one would be led to conclude that Japanese companies were smaller than their Taiwanese counterparts. (See note 4 in chapter 8.)

The data in the table above on Japan exclude the revenues of the first six general trading companies, since in my view they for the most part represent not new net sales but what in the United States would be accounted as intracompany transfers.

11. To take just one example, there are many fewer large banks in the American economy than in, say, the Japanese or Italian ones. This has entirely to do with the American law on interstate banking; with this law's abolition in 1994, the size of American banks is likely to grow substantially.

CHAPTER 4. LANGUAGES OF GOOD AND EVIL

1. Clifford Geertz, *The Interpretation of Cultures* (New York: Basic Books, 1973), pp. 4–5.
2. Ian Jamieson, *Capitalism and Culture: A Comparative Analysis of British and American Manufacturing Organizations* (London: Gower, 1980), p. 9.
3. Geertz in fact goes further than this and asserts that there is no such thing as "human nature," that is, a set of characteristics common to all human beings. He argues that human beings developed cultures before they had stopped

evolving biologically, so what human beings are "by nature" is in good measure determined by the cultures they adopt. Geertz (1973), pp. 34–35; 49.

4. Geertz (1973), p. 89.

5. For a discussion of cows in India, see Gunnar Myrdal, *Asian Drama: An Inquiry into the Poverty of Nations* (New York: Twentieth Century Fund, 1968), 1: 89–91.

6. *Nichomachean Ethics* Book II i.8. Aristotle explains that for people to be truly virtuous, they must habituate themselves to virtuous behavior such that it becomes a kind of second nature that is pleasurable in itself, or if not pleasurable something that the virtuous man takes pride in. See *Nichomachean Ethics* Book II iii.2.

7. George Stigler and Gary Becker take issue with John Stuart Mill's assertion that custom and tradition require a modification of economic theory, because habitual action may often be the least costly alternative: "The making of decisions is costly, and not simply because it is an activity which some people find unpleasant. In order to make a decision one requires information, and the information must be analyzed. The costs of searching for information and of applying the information to a new situation are such that habit is often a more efficient way to deal with moderate or temporary changes in the environment than would be a full, apparently utility-maximizing decision." From "De Gustibus Non Est Disputandum," *American Economic Review* 67 (1977): 76–90.

8. Aaron Wildavsky and Karl Dake, "Theories of Risk Perception: Who Fears What and Why," *Daedalus* 199 (1990): 41–60. See also Aaron Wildavsky, "Choosing Preferences by Constructing Institutions: A Cultural Theory of Preference Formation," *American Political Science Review* 81 (1987): 3–21; and Harry Eckstein, "Political Culture and Political Change," *American Political Science Review* 84 (1990): 253–259.

9. Max Weber, *The Protestant Ethic and the Spirit of Capitalism* (London: Allen and Unwin, 1930).

10. For an example, see Leonard Goodwin, "Welfare Mothers and the Work Ethic," *Monthly Labor Review* 95 (1972): 35–37.

11. For an early discussion of this issue, see Alan J. Winter, *The Poor: A Culture of Poverty, or a Poverty of Culture?* (Grand Rapids, Mich.: William B. Eerdmans, 1971).

12. According to Tocqueville, "In the fourteenth century the principle of 'No taxation without the people's consent' seemed as well established in France as in England herself. It was often cited; to override it was always regarded as a tyrannical gesture, and to abide by it as the due observance of an immemorial right. Indeed, at that time the political institutions in France and England were very similar. Subsequently, however, there was a parting of the ways, and as time went on, the two nations became ever more dissimilar. Thus two lines starting out from practically the same point but given slightly different directions diverge more and more, the more they are prolonged." *The Old Regime and the French Revolution* (Garden City, N.Y.: Doubleday Anchor, 1955), p. 98.

13. This is, of course, a greatly oversimplified account of the differences between

France and England. Another highly significant factor was the victory of the Reformation in England, which also played a role in the strengthening of associational life there.

14. Michael Novak, *The Catholic Ethic and the Spirit of Capitalism* (New York, Free Press, 1993), describes the evolution of official Catholic thought toward modern capitalism. See in particular his discussion of Amintore Fanfani's critique of capitalism, published in 1935.

15. Novak (1993), pp. 115–143, points in particular to Pope John Paul II's encyclical *Centesimus Annus* as marking a break with earlier Vatican positions on capitalism.

16. These included Spain, Portugal, virtually all countries in Latin America, as well as Hungary, Poland, and Lithuania. See Samuel Huntington, *The Third Wave* (Oklahoma City: University of Oklahoma Press, 1991), pp. 74–85.

17. Among the places where the fit is less than perfect is the tradition of liberation theology in Latin America, which is overtly hostile to capitalism and often ambivalent about liberal democracy.

18. James Q. Wilson has documented at length that this moral side has a natural basis that is evident even in infants and young children who have not yet been "socialized." See Wilson, *The Moral Sense* (New York: Free Press, 1993), pp. 121–140.

CHAPTER 5. THE SOCIAL VIRTUES

1. The classic discussions and elaborations of the Weber hypothesis are to be found in R. H. Tawney, *Religion and the Rise of Capitalism* (New York: Harcourt, Brace and World, 1962); Ernst Troeltsch, *The Social Teaching of the Christian Churches,* 2 vols. (New York: Macmillan, 1950); H. H. Robertson, *Aspects of the Rise of Economic Individualism* (Cambridge: Cambridge University Press, 1933); and Kemper Fullerton, "Calvinism and Capitalism," *Harvard Theological Review* 21 (1928): 163–191. For a short survey of the Weber debate, see Robert W. Green, *Protestantism and Capitalism: The Weber Thesis and Its Critics* (Lexington, Mass.: D. C. Heath, 1973).

2. For an example of the latter written in the 1960s, see Kurt Samuelsson, *Religion and Economic Action* (Stockholm: Svenska Bokforlaget, 1961).

3. The Afrikaners were a predominantly agricultural population up until the aftermath of the World War II, when the National party gained power and began using its control over the state as a means of economic advancement. The 1970s and 1980s, however, saw an increasing convergence between the English-speaking and Afrikaner populations in terms of the latter's participation in the private sector. See Irving Hexham, "Dutch Calvinism and the Development of Afrikaner Nationalism," *African Affairs* 79 (1980): 197–202; André Du Toit, "No Chosen People," *American Historical Review* 88 (1983): 920–952; and Randall G. Stokes, "The Afrikaner Industrial Entrepreneur and Afrikaner Nationalism," *Economic Development and Cultural Change* 22 (1975): 557–559.

4. See Reinhard Bendix, "The Protestant Ethic—Revisited," *Comparative Studies in Society and History* 9 (1967): 266–273.

5. Michael Novak, *The Catholic Ethic and the Spirit of Capitalism* (New York: Free Press 1993), pp. 17–35.

6. S. N. Eisenstadt, "The Protestant Ethic Thesis in an Analytical and Comparative Framework," in S. N. Eisenstadt, ed., *The Protestant Ethic and Modernization: A Comparative View* (New York: Basic Books, 1968).

7. David Martin, *Tongues of Fire: The Explosion of Protestantism in Latin America* (Oxford: Basil Blackwell, 1990), pp. 50–51.

8. In addition to Martin (1992), see Emilio Willems, *Followers of the New Faiths: Culture, Change and the Rise of Protestantism in Brazil and Chile* (Nashville, Tenn.: Vanderbilt University Press, 1967); Willems, "Protestantism as a Factor of Culture Change in Brazil," *Economic Development and Cultural Change* 3 (1955): 321–333; Willems, "Culture Change and the Rise of Protestantism in Brazil and Chile," in Eisenstadt, ed. (1968); Paul Turner, "Religious Conversions and Community Development," *Journal for the Scientific Study of Religion* 18 (1979): 252–260; James Sexton, "Protestantism and Modernization in Two Guatemalan Towns," *American Ethnologist* 5 (1978): 280–302; Bryan R. Roberts, "Protestant Groups and Coping with Urban Life in Guatemala," *American Journal of Sociology* 6 (1968): 753–767; Bernard Rosen, "The Achievement Syndrome and Economic Growth in Brazil," *Social Forces* 42 (1964): 341–354; and Jorge E. Maldonado, "Building 'Fundamentalism' from the Family in Latin America," in Martin E. Marty and R. Scott Appleby, *Fundamentalisms and Society: Reclaiming the Sciences, the Family, and Education* (Chicago: University of Chicago Press, 1992). For a critical view of the role of Protestant evangelicals in Latin America, see David Stoll, *Is Latin America Turning Protestant? The Politics of Evangelical Growth* (Berkeley: University of California Press, 1990); and Stoll, "'Jesus Is Lord of Guatemala': Evangelical Reform in a Death-Squad State," in Marty and Appleby, eds., *Accounting for Fundamentalisms: The Dynamic Character of Movements* (Chicago: University of Chicago Press, 1994).

9. For an effort to measure the impact of a work ethic quantitatively, see Roger D. Congleton, "The Economic Role of a Work Ethic," *Journal of Economic Behavior and Organization* 15 (1991): 365–385.

10. On the industriousness of the traditional Chinese peasant, see Maurice Freedman, *The Study of Chinese Society* (Stanford: Stanford University Press, 1979), p. 22; see also Marion J. Levy, *The Family Revolution in Modern China* (Cambridge: Harvard University Press, 1949), p. 217. On the contemporary American work ethic, see Ann Howard and James A. Wilson, "Leadership in a Declining Work Ethic," *California Management Review* 24 (1982): 33–46.

11. Some have pointed out that while peasants work extremely hard in certain seasons like spring planting and the harvest, they have long periods of slack as well. Thus the regularity of modern factory work, while less "hard" in certain respects, requires a different sort of work ethic than does peasant life.

12. For a series of penetrating vignettes on the cultural obstacles to development in traditional Third World societies, see the writings of Robert E. Klitgaard, a former World Bank official, including *Tropical Gangsters* (New York: Basic Books, 1990).

13. This essay is reprinted in *From Max Weber: Essays in Sociology,* trans. and ed. H. H. Gerth and C. Wright Mills (New York: Oxford University Press, 1946), pp. 302–322.
14. Weber (1946), p. 303.
15. Quoted in Seymour Martin Lipset, "Culture and Economic Behavior: A Commentary," *Journal of Labor Economics* 11 (1993): S330–347. See also Lipset, *Continental Divide: The Values and Institutions of the United States and Canada* (New York: Routledge, 1990), and "Values and Entrepreneurship in the Americas," in *Revolution and Counterrevolution* (New York: Basic Books, 1968).
16. Lipset (1993), pp. S336-S343.
17. Douglass C. North and Robert Paul Thomas, *The Rise of the Western World* (Cambridge: Cambridge University Press, 1973), p. 1.
18. On this accident, see Alfred D. Chandler, *The Visible Hand: The Managerial Revolution in American Business* (Cambridge: Harvard University Press, 1977), p. 96.
19. See, for example, David J. Cherrington, *The Work Ethic: Working Values and Values That Work* (New York: Amacom, 1980); Seymour Martin Lipset, "The Work Ethic: Then and Now," *Journal of Labor Research* 13 (1992): 45–54; and the various works of Adrian Furnham, including *The Protestant Work Ethic: The Psychology of Work-Related Beliefs and Behaviours* (London: Routledge and Kegan Paul, 1990); "The Protestant Work Ethic: A Review of the Psychological Literature," *European Journal of Social Psychology* 14 (1984): 87–104; and "The Protestant Work Ethic and Attitudes towards Unemployment," *Journal of Occupational Psychology* 55 (1982): 277–285. See also Thomas Li-ping Tang and Jen Yann Tzeng, "Demographic Correlates of the Protestant Work Ethic," *Journal of Psychology* 126 (1991): 163–170.

CHAPTER 6. THE ART OF ASSOCIATION AROUND THE WORLD

1. According to Tocqueville, "Americans of all ages, all conditions, and all dispositions constantly form associations. They have not only commercial and manufacturing companies, in which all take part, but associations of a thousand other kinds, religious, moral, serious, futile, general or restricted, enormous or diminutive. The Americans make associations to give entertainments, to found seminaries, to build inns, to construct churches, to diffuse books, to send missionaries to the antipodes; in this manner they found hospitals, prisons, and schools. If it is proposed to inculcate some truth or to foster some feeling by the encouragement of a great example, they form a society. Wherever at the head of a great undertaking you see the government in France, or a man of rank in England, in the United States you will be sure to find an association." *Democracy in America* (New York: Vintage Books, 1945), 2: p. 114.
2. Max Weber, "The Protestant Sects and the Spirit of Capitalism," in *From Max Weber: Essays in Sociology,* ed. and trans. by C. Wright Mills and Hans Gerth (New York: Oxford University Press, 1946), p. 310.
3. For comparative figures on welfare spending within the Organization for Eco-

nomic Cooperation and Development, see Vincent A. Mahler and Claudio Katz, "Social Benefits in Advanced Capitalist Countries," *Comparative Politics* 21 (1988): 37–51.

4. See Seymour Martin Lipset, *Pacific Divide: American Exceptionalism—Japanese Uniqueness* (Tokyo: Kibi International University, Sophia University, 1992), p. 42.

5. While distrust of "big government" is frequently thought of as an attitude held by the right in the United States, there are actually right- and left-wing versions of it. The right distrusts state intervention in economic affairs and rails against excessive regulation. The left abhors state interference in personal lifestyles and a host of other individual liberties, while attacking the "national security state" and large corporations. Both left and right in America have their own versions of liberal individualism.

6. Gerschenkron argued that a strong state is typical of all late developers, not just Japan. See *Economic Backwardness in Historical Perspective* (Cambridge: Harvard University Press, 1962). See also Chalmers Johnson, *MITI and the Japanese Miracle* (Stanford: Stanford University Press, 1982); "The State and Japanese Grand Strategy," in R. Rosecrance and A. Stein, eds., *The Domestic Bases of Grand Strategy* (Ithaca, N.Y.: Cornell University Press, 1993), pp. 201–223; "The People Who Invented the Mechanical Nightingale," *Daedalus* 119 (1990): 71–90.

7. Many would argue that the large U.S. postwar defense budget was in effect an industrial policy with important implications for certain sectors of the civilian economy like aerospace.

8. In the early years after 1868, the Japanese government founded and operated numerous industries, particularly in transportation, mining, engineering, and weapons manufacture, just as many Third World countries are doing in the twentieth century. Many of these enterprises lost money; almost all were quickly sold off (often at bargain-basement prices) and later became the basis of some of the large, private fortunes in later decades. The Japanese government in effect engaged in what amounted to a broad-ranging privatization program a hundred years before this became the fashion in Europe and Latin America. See William W. Lockwood, *The Economic Development of Japan: Growth and Structural Change, 1868–1938* (Princeton: Princeton University Press, 1954), p. 15.

9. Mahler and Katz (1988), p. 38.

10. Yasuzo Horie, for example, argues that early entrepreneurs like Masatatsu Ishikawa and Takato Oshima were infused with a national consciousness and intent on building national wealth. See "Business Pioneers of Modern Japan," *Kyoto University Economic Review* 30 (1960): 1–16; and "Confucian Concept of State in Tokugawa Japan," *Kyoto University Economic Review* 32 (1962): 26–38.

11. On the historical importance of small businesses in Japan, see Lockwood (1954), pp. 201–213; and David Friedman, *The Misunderstood Miracle* (Ithaca: Cornell University Press, 1988), pp. 9–11.

12. Lockwood (1954), pp. 578, 588.

13. See Winston Davis, "Japanese Religious Affiliations: Motives and Obligations," *Sociological Analysis* 44 (1983): 131–146.

14. For an argument—not entirely convincing—that there are signs of greater individualism in Japan, see Kuniko Miyanaga, *The Creative Edge: Emerging Individualism in Japan* (New Brunswick, N.J.: Transaction Publishers, 1991).
15. Alexis de Tocqueville, *The Old Regime and the French Revolution* (New York: Doubleday Anchor, 1955), p. 206.
16. Edward C. Banfield, *The Moral Basis of a Backward Society* (Glencoe, Ill.: Free Press, 1958).
17. Lawrence Harrison, *Who Prospers?* (New York: Basic Books, 1992), p. 55.

CHAPTER 7. PATHS AND DETOURS TO SOCIABILITY

1. James Q. Wilson, "The Family-Values Debate," *Commentary* 95 (1992): 24–31.
2. For documentation see U.S. Bureau of the Census, *Studies in Marriage and the Family*, P-23, no. 162; *Changes in American Family Life*, P-23, no. 163; *Family Disruption and Economic Hardship: The Short-Run Picture for Children* (Survey of Income and Program Participation), p-70, no. 23; and *Poverty in the United States*, P-60, no. 163 (Washington, D.C.: US Government Printing Office, 1991).
3. See my article, "Immigrants and Family Values," *Commentary* 95 (1992): 26–32.
4. For a general description of the evolution of American family businesses, see W. Gibb Dyers, Jr., *Cultural Change in Family Firms: Anticipating and Managing Business and Family Transitions* (San Francisco: Jossey-Bass Publishers, 1986).
5. Dyers (1986).
6. On Campbell Soup and other large, durable American family businesses, see Philip Scranton, "Understanding the Strategies and Dynamics of Long-lived Family Firms," *Business and Economic History*, 2d ser. 21 (1992): 219–227.
7. Oliver Williamson, "The Vertical Integration of Production: Market Failure Considerations," *American Economic Review* 61 (1971): 112–123.
8. Adolph A. Berle and Gardner C. Means, *The Modern Corporation and Private Property* (New York: Macmillan, 1932); see also Means, *Power Without Property: A New Development in American Political Economy* (New York: Harcourt, Brace 1959).
9. Alfred D. Chandler, *The Visible Hand: The Managerial Revolution in American Business* (Cambridge: Harvard University Press, 1977).
10. Clark Kerr, John T. Dunlop, F. Harbison, and C. A. Myers, *Industrialism and Industrial Man* (Harmondsworth: Pelican Books, 1973), p. 94.
11. On negative views of the Chinese family, see Brigitte Berger, "The Culture of Modern Entrepreneurship," in Brigitte Berger, ed., *The Culture of Entrepreneurship* (San Francisco: Institute for Contemporary Studies, 1991), p. 24.
12. See Alexander Gerschenkron, *Economic Backwardness in Historical Perspective* (Cambridge: Harvard University Press, 1962).
13. Conversely, it should be pointed out that large-scale, professionally managed, rationally organized state enterprises have existed since time immemorial, such as the giant Chinese porcelain factory at Jingdezhen that employed thousands of workers. Such state enterprises anticipated the form and functions of mod-

ern private corporations, in a preindustrial society without institutionalized property rights.

14. Tamara Hareven, "The History of the Family and the Complexity of Social Change," *American Historical Review* 96 (1991): 95–122; Hareven, "A Complex Relationship: Family Strategies and the Processes of Economic and Social Change," in Roger Friedland and A. F. Robinson, eds., *Beyond the Marketplace: Rethinking Economy and Society* (New York: Aldine de Gruyter, 1990). See also William J. Goode, *World Revolution and Family Patterns* (Glencoe, Ill.: Free Press, 1959), pp. 23–24, who notes that many of the characteristics of the "modern" Western family actually predated the industrial revolution.

CHAPTER 8. A LOOSE TRAY OF SAND

1. Charles C. Kenney, "Fall of the House of Wang," *Computerworld* 26 (1992): 67–69; see also Donna Brown, "Race for the Corporate Throne," *Management Review* 78 (1989): 26–27.
2. Daniel Cohen, "The Fall of the House of Wang," *Business Month* 135 (1990): 22–31.
3. Cohen (1990), p. 24.
4. Gary Hamilton and Kao Cheng-shu argue that the axiomatic assumption of small firm size in Taiwan compared to Japan and Korea is not borne out by the facts and that Taiwan actually has fewer firms with fewer than 30 workers as a percentage of all manufacturing firms than its Asian neighbors. However, by their statistics, Taiwan also has more large firms with over 300 workers than Japan, which is highly misleading. The problem is that the number of firms of a given size as a percentage of the number of all firms is not the best measure of their importance in an economy; a much more significant measure would be the total value-added as a percentage of gross national product. It would then be obvious that the giant firms of Japan and Korea play a much larger role in their respective economies than do those of Taiwan. Hamilton and Kao, "The Institutional Foundations of Chinese Business: The Family Firm in Taiwan," *Comparative Social Research: Business Institutions* 12 (1990): 135–151. See also Samuel P. S. Ho, *Small-Scale Enterprises in Korea and Taiwan* (Washington: World Bank Staff Working Paper 384, April 1980).
5. Ramon H. Myers, "The Economic Development of the Republic of China on Taiwan, 1965–1981," in Lawrence J. Lau, *Models of Development: A Comparative Study of Economic Growth in South Korea and Taiwan* (San Francisco: Institute for Contemporary Studies, 1986), p. 29.
6. Tibor Scitovsky, "Economic Development in Taiwan and South Korea, 1965–1981," in Lau (1986), p. 146.
7. Myers in Lau (1986), p. 54. See also Ramon H. Myers, "The Economic Transformation of the Republic of China on Taiwan," *China Quarterly* 99 (1984): 500–528.
8. Simon Tam, "Centrifugal versus Centripetal Growth Processes: Contrasting Ideal Types for Conceptualizing the Developmental Patterns of Chinese and

Japanese Firms," in Stewart R. Clegg and S. Gordon Redding, eds., *Capitalism in Contrasting Cultures* (Berlin: De Gruyter, 1990), p. 161.

9. John C. Pelzel, "Factory Life in Japan and China Today," in Albert M. Craig, *Japan: A Comparative View* (Princeton: Princeton University Press, 1979), p. 379.

10. G. L. Hicks and S. Gordon Redding, "Culture and Corporate Performance in the Philippines: The Chinese Puzzle," in R. M. Bautista and E. M. Perina, eds., *Essays in Development Economics in Honor of Harry T. Oshima* (Manila: Philippine Institute for Development Studies, 1982), p. 212.

11. That company, Chinese Petroleum Company, is the forty-first largest corporation on the Pacific Rim, with $8 billion in 1989 sales. "The Pac Rim 150," *Fortune* 122 (Fall 1990): 102–106.

12. Gustav Ranis, "Industrial Development," in Walter Galenson, ed., *Economic Growth and Structural Change in Taiwan: The Postwar Experience of the Republic of China* (Ithaca, N.Y.: Cornell University Press, 1979), p. 228.

13. Justin D. Niehoff, "The Villager as Industrialist: Ideologies of Household Manufacturing in Rural Taiwan," *Modern China* 13 (1987): 278–309.

14. Alice Amsden, "The State and Taiwan's Economic Development," in Peter B. Evans, Dietrich Rueschmeyer, and Theda Skocpol, eds., *Bringing the State Back In* (Cambridge: Cambridge University Press, 1985), pp. 78–106. By Amsden's own figures, the share of total industrial output accounted for by state-owned companies fell from fifty-seven percent in 1952 to eighteen percent in 1980.

15. Robert H. Silin, *Leadership and Values: The Organization of Large-Scale Taiwanese Enterprises* (Cambridge: Harvard University Press, 1976), p. 16.

16. On Asian network organizations in general, see Gary G. Hamilton, William Zeile, and Wan-Jin Kim, "The Network Structures of East Asian Economies," in Clegg and Redding (1990), pp. 105–129.

17. Michael L. Gerlach, *Alliance Capitalism: The Social Organization of Japanese Business* (Berkeley: University of California Press, 1992), p. 82.

18. Hamilton and Kao (1990), pp. 140–142.

19. Robert Wade, "East Asian Financial Systems as a Challenge to Economics: Lessons from Taiwan," *California Management Review* 27 (1985): 106–127.

20. Hamilton and Kao (1990), pp. 145–146. See also Joel Kotkin, *Tribes* (New York: Random House, 1993), pp. 165–200.

21. S. Gordon Redding, *The Spirit of Chinese Capitalism* (Berlin: De Gruyter, 1990), p. 3.

22. Many publicly listed companies on the Hong Kong stock exchange are actually controlled by families. One observer reports that half of the larger cotton-spinning mills in Hong Kong were family owned but that this actually understated the true number because family ownership did not have to be disclosed in corporate filings. Siu-lun Wong, "The Chinese Family Firm: A Model," *British Journal of Sociology* 36 (1985): 58–72.

23. On the career of Y. K. Pao, see Robin Hutcheon, *First Sea Lord: The Life and Work of Sir Y. K. Pao* (Hong Kong: Chinese University Press, 1990).

24. Redding (1990), p. 151.
25. Robert Heller, "How the Chinese Manage to Keep It All In the Family," *Management Today* (November 1991): 31–34.
26. Heller (1991), p. 34; "The Overseas Chinese," *Economist,* July 18, 1992, pp. 21–24.
27. "The Overseas Chinese," p. 24.
28. Richard D. Whitley, "Eastern Asian Enterprise Structures and the Comparative Analysis of Forms of Business Organization," *Organization Studies* 11 (1990): 47–74.
29. For revealing studies of particular Chinese firms, see Wellington K. K. Chan, "The Organizational Structure of the Traditional Chinese Firm and Its Modern Reform," *Business History Review* 56 (1982): 218–235, and *Merchants, Mandarins and Modern Enterprise in Late Ch'ing China* (Cambridge: East Asian Research Center, 1977).
30. On this point, see Richard Whitley, "The Social Construction of Business Systems in East Asia," *Organization Studies* 12 (1991): 1–28.
31. Redding (1990), p. 66.
32. Redding (1990), p. 36.
33. The Chinese equivalent of the *banto* is the *zhanggui,* a professional manager who ran the business for owners who, in some cases, did not want their ownership role to be known. The *banto* was much more common in Japanese culture than the *zhanggui* in Chinese, however. I am grateful to Wellington Chan for pointing this out to me.
34. Siu-lun Wong, "The Applicability of Asian Family Values to Other Sociocultural Settings," in Peter L. Berger and Hsin-Huang Michael Hsiao, *In Search of an East Asia Development Model* (New Brunswick, N.J.: Transaction Books, 1988), p. 143.
35. Gary G. Hamilton and Nicole Woolsey Biggart, "Market, Culture, and Authority: A Comparative Analysis of Management and Organization in the Far East," *American Journal of Sociology* 94 Supplement (1988): S52–94.
36. Francis L. K. Hsu, *Iemoto: The Heart of Japan* (New York: Schenkman Publishing Co., 1975), p. 15.
37. Quoted by Wong in Berger and Hsiao (1988), p. 136.
38. For descriptions of this evolution, see Wong in Berger and Hsiao (1988), pp. 140–142; and Redding (1990), pp. 104–106.
39. John Kao, "The Worldwide Web of Chinese Business," *Harvard Business Review* 71 (1993): 24–34.
40. Whitley (1990), p. 64.
41. Wong in Berger and Hsiao (1988), p. 139.
42. Brown (1989), pp. 22–29
43. Albert Feuerwerker, *China's Early Industrialization* (Cambridge: Harvard University Press, 1958), pp. 84–85.
44. This point is made in Redding (1990), p. 5.
45. Redding (1990), p. 229.
46. Japanese semiconductor firms have not been successful in competing with the

likes of Intel and Motorola to produce leading-edge microprocessors and other logic circuits; they have been much more successful in memories and at the commodity end of the semiconductor business. Nonetheless, their level of sophistication is far higher than that of any other Asian country.

47. W. J. F. Jenner, *The Tyranny of History: The Roots of China's Crisis* (London: Allen Lane/Penguin, 1992), p. 81.

48. These *kuan-tu shang-pan* industries were extremely inefficient. The officials appointed to oversee them regarded themselves primarily as tax farmers. As in the private sector, advancement came about on the basis of kinship ties rather than universalistic criteria; the officials running these businesses were noted for their lack of initiative. In contrast to the Japanese state, which sold off comparable industries early on, the government of Qing China (as well as various regional and local governments) did not privatize these industries but relied on them as a source of tax revenue. Feuerwerker (1958), pp. 9–11, 22–23.

CHAPTER 9. THE "BUDDENBROOKS" PHENOMENON

1. On the problems the one-child policy created for peasant households, see Elisabeth Croll, "Some Implications of the Rural Economic Reforms for the Chinese Peasant Household," in Ashwani Saith, ed., *The Re-emergence of the Chinese Peasantry: Aspects of Rural Decollectivization* (London: Croom Helm, 1987), pp. 122–123.

2. On the religious dimensions of Confucianism, see C. K. Yang, *Religion in Chinese Society: A Study of Contemporary Social Functions of Religion and Some of Their Historical Factors* (Berkeley: University of California Press, 1961), pp. 244–277.

3. On this Confucian ideal, see Gilbert Rozman, "The East Asia Region in Comparative Perspective," in Rozman, ed., *The East Asian Region: Confucian Heritage and Its Modern Adaptation* (Princeton: Princeton University Press, 1991), p. 24.

4. For a discussion of merchants in traditional Chinese society, see Michael R. Godley, *The Mandarin Capitalists from Nanyang: Overseas Chinese Enterprise in the Modernization of China* (Cambridge: Cambridge University Press, 1981), pp. 34–37.

5. This is not to say that there were no class distinctions within the overseas Chinese communities. Many Chinese emigrated as coolie laborers, who obviously constituted a class distinct from the merchants and businessmen; but there was no gentry class and no bureaucracy, these positions being reserved throughout Southeast Asia for local elites. See Godley (1981), p. 38.

6. On the Confucian virtues, see Michio Morishima, *Why Has Japan "Succeeded"? Western Technology and the Japanese Ethos* (Cambridge: Cambridge University Press, 1982), pp. 3–4.

7. On the differences between Western and other families, see William J. Goode, *World Revolution and Family Patterns* (Glencoe, Ill.: Free Press, 1963), p. 22.

8. Marion J. Levy, *The Rise of the Modern Chinese Business Class* (New York: Institute of Pacific Relations, 1949, hereafter 1949I), p. 1.

9. Margery Wolf, *The House of Lim: A Study of a Chinese Farm Family* (Englewood Cliffs, N.J.: Prentice-Hall, 1968), p. 23.

10. Marion J. Levy, *The Family Revolution in Modern China* (Cambridge: Harvard University Press, 1949, hereafter 1949II), pp. 208–209.

11. Kyung-sup Chang, "The Peasant Family in the Transition from Maoist to Lewisian Rural Industrialization," *Journal of Development Studies* 29 (1993): 220–244.

12. Levy (1949II), pp. 213–216.

13. From the standpoint of property rights, the fact that the tax burden was arbitrarily set was more important than that it was high in absolute terms. There is in fact evidence that the tax burden decreased on average in Qing times. Albert Feuerwerker, "The State and the Economy in Late Imperial China," *Theory and Society* 13 (1984): 297–326.

14. W. J. F. Jenner, *The Tyranny of History: The Roots of China's Crisis* (London: Allen Lane/Penguin, 1992), p. 4.

15. On the Chinese practice of equal inheritance, see Hugh Baker, *Chinese Family and Kinship* (New York: Columbia University Press, 1979), p. 12; Siu-lun Wong, "The Applicability of Asian Family Values to Other Sociocultural Settings," in Peter Berger and Hsin-Huang Michael Hsiao, *In Search of an East Asian Development Model* (New Brunswick, N.J.: Transaction Books, 1988), p. 139; Jenner (1992), p. 89; and Gordon S. Redding, *The Spirit of Chinese Capitalism* (Berlin: De Gruyter, 1990), p. 134.

16. In addition, the plot often consisted of noncontiguous strips of land that were difficult to farm. Albert Feuerwerker, *The Chinese Economy ca. 1870–1911* (Ann Arbor: University of Michigan Press, 1969), p. 15.

17. For an account of adoption in traditional Chinese society, see James L. Watson, "Agnates and Outsiders: Adoption in a Chinese Lineage," *Man* 10 (1975): 293–306.

18. There were elaborate rules for who could be adopted: a sonless man would look first to adopt one of his brother's sons; the oldest brother generally had privileged access to the sons of his younger brothers in such circumstances. If none was available, he would go to other descendants of his grandfather (i.e., cousins), and if this failed, he could turn to the larger lineage or clan, and so on in ever-widening circles of kinship. Only in extreme cases, a man could buy a son from a poor outsider.

19. The following is an account of an adoption ceremony: "The initiation [of a nonkin adopted son] takes place during an elaborate banquet. . . . Unlike wedding banquets, the guests do not bring gifts of money to compensate the host for his hospitality. The whole tone of the banquet is different because the adopting father must compensate his fellow lineage members for accepting an outsider into their midst. The guests try their best to humiliate the host by shouting insults about this inability to produce his own heirs. During the banquet any guest may seek out the host and borrow money on the spot. This is done with full knowledge that the lender will never ask for repayment, for it would only be an embarrassing reminder of the initiation. . . . As they leave the

hall, the guests berate the host for defiling the lineage and complain about the miserable food." Watson (1975), p. 298. See also James L. Watson, "Chinese Kinship Reconsidered: Anthropological Perspectives on Historical Research," *China Quarterly* 92 (1982): 589–627.

20. Francis Hsu gives an account of the reasons that some families rose while others fell. See *Under the Ancestors' Shadow: Kinship, Personality, and Social Mobility in Village China* (Garden City, N.Y.: Anchor Books, 1967), pp. 5–7.

21. Baker (1979), p. 131.

22. Baker (1979), pp. 133–134.

23. Jenner (1992), pp. 119–120.

24. For general works on the Chinese family, see Hsu (1967); Maurice Freedman, *The Study of Chinese Society* (Stanford: Stanford University Press, 1979); Baker (1979); and Paul Chao, *Chinese Kinship* (London: Kegan Paul International, 1979). For an analysis of the contrast between Hsu's and Freedman's interpretations of the Chinese family and lineage, see Siu-lun Wong, "The Applicability of Asian Family Values to Other Sociocultural Settings," in Berger and Hsiao (1988), p. 145.

25. For categorization of types of Chinese families, see Maurice Freedman, *Chinese Lineage and Society: Fukien and Kwangtung* (London: Athlone Press, 1971), pp. 43–67.

26. Tamara Hareven, "Reflections on Family Research in the People's Republic of China," *Social Research* 54 (1987): 663–689.

27. See Shu Ching Lee, "China's Traditional Family, Its Characteristics and Disintegration," *American Sociological Review* 18 (1953): 272–280; Francis Hsu, "A Hypothesis on Kinship and Culture," in Hsu, ed., *Kinship and Culture* (Chicago: Aldine Publishing Co., 1971), p. 7.

28. Baker (1979), pp. 21–22. The common practice of polygamy among the wealthy created special problems for inheritance. The principle of equal inheritance applied only to the sons of a particular wife, but her sons' total allocation depended on her rank within the family. The sons of a third or fourth wife, or of a concubine, would have steadily diminishing claims. These heirs often needed to resort to complicated strategies to extract their shares from the more senior sons and their mothers. A lower-ranking wife, for example, had more leverage over the husband dead (i.e., as a ghost) than alive; the problem was how to make him fear her vengeful spirit without actually having to commit suicide.

29. Baker (1979), p. 49. In a traditional Chinese family, a woman's status is lower than that of her sons; she consequently has no authority to punish them but must refer them to their father. Lee (1953), p. 275.

30. Watson (1982), p. 394. See also Baker (1979), p. 49.

31. Redding (1990), pp. 54–55.

32. Baker (1979), p. 67.

33. Hui-chen Wang Liu, "An Analysis of Chinese Clan Rules: Confucian Theories in Action," in David S. Nivison and Arthur F. Wright, *Confucianism in Action* (Stanford: Stanford University Press, 1959), pp. 63–96.

34. Freedman (1979), p. 241.

35. P. Steven Sangren, "Traditional Chinese Corporations: Beyond Kinship," *Journal of Asian Studies* 43 (1984): 391–415.
36. In Chinese society, there have been some traditional organizations not based on kinship. The secret societies and *tongs,* or criminal gangs, for example, operating among Chinese immigrant communities in the United States, required their members to break their kinship ties and swear what amounted to a blood oath to their new "families." See Baker (1979), p. 170; and Ivan Light, *Ethnic Enterprise in America* (Berkeley: University of California Press, 1972), pp. 94–98.
37. Such a doctrine was taught by Confucius's rival, Mo Di, a century later, but the doctrines of Mohism have always been treated as a dangerous heresy by orthodox Confucians. See Jenner (1992), p. 113.
38. The lack of universal ethical principles in Confucianism clearly lies at the heart of the current debate between Americans and Asians over human rights. The Christian God is both unitary and jealous; he lays down a set of moral principles that apply to all human beings without distinction. The liberal political teachings of Locke and the American founders are similarly universalistic and egalitarian, and the contemporary human rights movement in the United States is extending these principles to societies that do not have a similar sense of universal obligation.
39. Barrington Moore, *Social Origins of Dictatorship and Democracy: Lord and Peasant in the Making of the Modern World* (Boston: Beacon Press, 1966), p. 208.
40. See Redding (1990), p. 188; also Lucian W. Pye, *Asian Power and Politics: The Cultural Dimensions of Authority* (Cambridge: Harvard University Press, 1985), p. 292.
41. For an overview of research on changes in the Chinese family, see Wei Zhangling, "The Family and Family Research in Contemporary China," *International Social Science Journal* 126 (1986): 493–509; Hareven (1987); Ming Tsui, "Changes in Chinese Urban Family Structure," *Journal of Marriage and the Family* 51 (1989): 737–747; Arland Thornton and Thomas E. Fricke, "Social Change and the Family: Comparative Perspectives from the West, China, and South Asia," *Sociological Forum* 2 (1987): 746–779; Janet W. Salaff, *Working Daughters of Hong Kong: Filial Piety or Power in the Family?* (Cambridge: Cambridge University Press, 1981).
42. Lee (1953), p. 279; Goode (1959), p. 6.
43. Jack M. Potter, *Capitalism and the Chinese Peasant* (Berkeley: University of California Press, 1968), p. 161.
44. See especially Hareven (1987), and Bernard Gallin, "Rural to Urban Migration in Taiwan: Its Impact on Chinese Family and Kinship," in David C. Buxbaum, ed., *Chinese Family Law and Social Change in Historical and Comparative Perspective* (Seattle: University of Washington Press, 1978). For an overview of some of the complexities of the new family patterns established since decollectivization, see Martin King Whyte, "Rural Economic Reforms and Chinese Family Patterns," *China Quarterly,* no. 130 (1992): 316–322.
45. Jenner (1992), p. 128. This point is also made in Oded Shenkar and Simcha Ronen, "The Cultural Context of Negotiations: The Implications of the Chi-

nese Interpersonal Norms," *Journal of Applied Behavioral Science* 23 (1987): 263–275.

46. Victor Nee, "The Peasant Household Individualism," in William L. Parish, ed., *Chinese Rural Development: The Great Transformation* (Armonk, N.Y.: M. E. Sharpe, 1985), p. 185; Victor Nee, "Peasant Household Economy and Decollectivization in China," *Journal of Asian and African Studies* 21 (1986): 185–203; Victor Nee and Su Sijin, "Institutional Change and Economic Growth in China: The View from the Villages," *Journal of Asian Studies* 49 (1990): 3–25; and Victor Nee and Frank W. Young, "Peasant Entrepreneurs in China's 'Second Economy': An Institutional Analysis," *Economic Development and Cultural Change* 39 (1991): 293–310. Elsewhere Nee argues that rural cadres continue to play important middleman functions. See "Peasant Entrepreneurship in China," in Nee and David Stark, eds., *Remaking the Economic Institutions of Socialism: China and Eastern Europe* (Stanford: Stanford University Press, 1989), pp. 171–172.

47. Jenner (1992), p. 13.

CHAPTER 10. ITALIAN CONFUCIANISM

1. The name "Montegrano" was fictitious, but the town was not; its real name was Chiaromonte. Edward C. Banfield, *The Moral Basis of a Backward Society* (Glencoe, Ill.: Free Press, 1958), pp. 107, 115–116.

2. Banfield (1958), p. 85.

3. Banfield (1958), p. 7.

4. Banfield (1958), p. 88.

5. Robert D. Putnam, *Making Democracy Work: Civic Traditions in Modern Italy* (Princeton: Princeton University Press, 1993), pp. 91–92. Putnam also provides broader data on other kinds of organizations that show the same sort of North-South distribution.

6. Putnam (1993), p. 97.

7. Putnam (1993), p. 111.

8. Putnam (1993), p. 107.

9. Putnam (1993), p. 139.

10. Bevilacqua, as quoted by Paul Ginsburg and requoted by Putnam (1993), p. 143.

11. This term was coined by Jesse Pitts in reference to France. See Jesse R. Pitts, "Continuity and Change in Bourgeois France," in Stanley Hoffmann and Charles Kindleberger, eds., *In Search of France* (Cambridge: Harvard University Press, 1963).

12. On this point, see Putnam (1993), p. 146.

13. See the map of the relative density of civic community given in Putnam (1993), p. 97.

14. Italy in 1992 had a gross domestic product of $1,223 billion; those of Holland, Sweden, and Switzerland were $320, $247, and $241 billion, respectively. *International Financial Statistics 1994 Yearbook* (Washington, D.C.: International Monetary Fund, 1994).

15. The original concept of a "Third Italy" was articulated by Arnoldo Bagnasco, *Tre Italie: la problematica territoriale dello sviluppo italiano* (Bologna: Il Mulino, 1977). Other works on small-scale industrialization in Italy are Arnoldo Bagnasco and Rosella Pini, "Sviluppo economico e trasformazioni sociopolitiche nei sistemi territoriali e economia diffus: Economia e struttura sociale," *Quaderni di Fondazione Giangiacomo Feltrimelli* no. 14 (1975); Giorgio Fua and Carlo Zacchia, *Industrilizzazione sensa fratture* (Bologna: Il Mulino 1983).

16. Michael J. Piore and Charles F. Sabel, *The Second Industrial Divide: Possibilities for Prosperity* (New York: Basic Books, 1984), p. 227.

17. Sebastiano Brusco, "Small Firms and Industrial Districts: The Experience of Italy," in David Keeble and Robert Wever, *New Firms and Regional Development in Europe* (London: Croom Helm, 1982), pp. 192–193. Machine tools are, by their very nature, inherently low-volume products whose manufacturers tend to be small scale regardless of country.

18. Julia Bamford, "The Development of Small Firms, the Traditional Family and Agrarian Patterns in Italy," in Robert Goffee and Richard Scase, eds., *Entrepreneurship in Europe: The Social Processes* (London: Croom Helm, 1987), p. 8.

19. There is a third company, Versace, which as of 1994 was planning to go public. *New York Times,* June 13, 1994, pp. D1-D2.

20. The flexible specialization paradigm and the argument about the role of small firms in modern economies is developed in Piore and Sabel (1984); Charles Sabel, *Work and Politics: The Division of Labor in Society* (Cambridge: Cambridge University Press, 1981); Michael J. Piore and Suzanne Berger, *Dualism and Discontinuity in Industrial Societies* (Cambridge: Cambridge University Press, 1980); Charles Sabel and Jonathan Zeitlin, "Historical Alternatives to Mass Production: Politics, Markets and Technology in Nineteenth-Century Industrialization," *Past and Present* 108 (1985): 133–176.

21. Employment in small- and medium-size enterprises has not grown so much as shrunk less quickly. See Richard D. Whitley, "The Revival of Small Business in Europe," in Brigitte Berger, ed., *The Culture of Entrepreneurship* (San Francisco: Institute for Contemporary Studies, 1991), p. 162.

22. Growth in small-business employment has been most significant in Italy, Spain, Portugal, Greece, the Netherlands, and Denmark. Whitley in Berger (1991), p. 170.

23. Putnam (1993), pp. 156–157.

24. On these points, see Putnam (1993), pp. 158–159.

25. The scholar chiefly responsible for this revision is Peter N. Laslett. See his edited volume *Household and Family in Past Time* (Cambridge: Cambridge University Press, 1972); and "The Comparative History of Household and Family," in Michael Gordon, ed., *American Family in Social-Historical Perspective* (New York: St. Martin's Press, 1973).

26. Bamford in Goffee and Scase (1978), p. 16. For a detailed description of extended families in the community of Bertalia and in the sharecropping regions of central Italy generally, see David I. Kertzer, *Family Life in Central Italy, 1880–1910* (New Brunswick, N.J.: Rutgers University Press, 1984). See also

David I. Kertzer and Richard P. Saller, eds., *The Family in Italy from Antiquity to the Present* (New Haven: Yale University Press, 1991).

27. Bamford in Goffee and Scase (1987), p. 17.
28. The importance of the extended family is noted also in Piore and Sabel (1984), pp. 227–228.
29. Banfield (1958), pp. 118–119.
30. Bamford in Goffee and Scase (1978), pp. 17–19; Kertzer (1984), pp. 32–35.
31. Bamford in Goffee and Scase (1978), pp. 19–20.
32. Putnam (1993), p. 130.
33. Putnam (1993), pp. 159–160. The role of local governments in this scenario is to provide infrastructural support to business networks, such as training and information services.
34. This will be discussed at much greater length in the chapters on Japan.
35. Santo Versace, as quoted in *New York Times,* June 13, 1994, p. D2.
36. Michael L. Blim, *Made in Italy: Small-Scale Industrialization and Its Consequences* (New York: Praeger, 1990), p. 258.
37. According to Blim (1990), pp. 162–165, in the area of the Marche that he studied, only one owner of a shoe factory out of twenty-five refused to go along with the *lavoro nero.*
38. Whitley in Berger (1991), p. 168.

CHAPTER 11. FACE-TO-FACE IN FRANCE

1. In the protracted disputes between the United States and the European Airbus consortium over government subsidization, the Europeans always argue that American private companies like Boeing have benefitted tremendously from the large military business they do, which amounts to a covert subsidy. These arguments doubtless have some validity; this does not affect my argument about French weaknesses in creating private large-scale organizations, however.
2. Eli Noam, *Telecommunications in Europe* (New York: Oxford University Press, 1992), pp. 160–161.
3. Quoted in Noam (1992), p. 147.
4. David S. Landes, "French Entrepreneurship and Industrial Growth in the Nineteenth Century," *Journal of Economic History* 9 (1949): 45–61. For a detailed account of one entrepreneurial family, see Landes, "Religion and Enterprise: The Case of the French Textile Industry," in Edward C. Carter II, Robert Forster, and Joseph N. Moody, eds., *Enterprise and Entrepreneurs in Nineteenth- and Twentieth-Century France* (Baltimore: Johns Hopkins University Press, 1976). For an in-depth study of one family firm in the metalworking industry, see Robert J. Smith, "Family Dynamics and the Trajectory of a Family Firm: Bouchayer Enterprise of Grenoble (1868–1972)" (unpublished paper, 1994).
5. Landes (1949), p. 50.
6. Jesse R. Pitts, "Continuity and Change in Bourgeois France," in Stanley Hoffmann and Charles Kindleberger, eds., *In Search of France* (Cambridge: Harvard University Press, 1963), pp. 239–246.

7. This point was later admitted by Landes himself. See "New-Model Entrepreneurship in France and Problems of Historical Explanation," *Explorations in Entrepreneurial History,* 2d ser. 1 (1963): 56–75.

8. Patrick O'Brien and Caglar Keyder argue that labor productivity grew at comparable rates until the 1870s and were higher in France than in Britain until the 1890s. See *Economic Growth in Britain and France 1780–1914: Two Paths to the Twentieth Century* (London: Allen and Unwin, 1978), pp. 192–193. See also Jean Bouvier, "Libres propos autour d'une démarche révisionniste," in Patrick Fridenson and André Straus, eds., *Le Capitalisme français XIXe–XXe siècle: Blocages et dynamismes d'une croissance* (Paris: Fayard, 1987); François Crouzet, "Encore la croissance française au XIX siècle," *Revue du nord* 54 (1972): 271–288. Crouzet (p. 274) indicates that between 1870 and 1913, French per capita production and productivity, while somewhat behind that of Germany, were higher than in England and exactly equal to the average for ten European countries.

9. See Louis Bergeron, *Les Capitalistes en France (1780–1914)* (Paris: Gallimard, 1978).

10. On the development of Bon Marché, see Michael B. Miller, *The Bon Marché: Bourgeois Culture and the Department Store, 1869–1920* (Princeton: Princeton University Press, 1981).

11. Maurice Levy-Leboyer, "The Large Family Firm in the French Manufacturing Industry," in Akio Okochi and Shigeaki Yasuoka, eds., *Family Business in the Era of Industrial Growth* (Tokyo: University of Tokyo Press, 1984), pp. 222–223.

12. Levy-Leboyer in Okochi and Yasuoka (1984), pp. 216–217.

13. Pitts in Hoffmann and Kindleberger (1963), pp. 274–277.

14. This is true even of historians who would argue, contra Landes, that there has been no general retardation of French economic development. See Jean-Charles Asselain, *Histoire économique de la France du XVIIIe siècle à nos jours,* vol. 1: *De l'Ancien Régime à la Première Guerre mondiale* (Paris: Editions du Seuil, 1984), pp. 13–19.

15. On this point, see Charles Kindleberger, "The Postwar Resurgence of the French Economy," in Hoffmann and Kindelberger (1963), p. 120.

16. Kindleberger in Hoffmann and Kindelberger (1963), p. 136.

17. On the issue of adoption, see Rhoda Metraux and Margaret Mead, *Themes in French Culture: A Preface to a Study of French Community* (Stanford: Stanford University Press, 1954), pp. 3–4, 69–84.

18. Michel Crozier, *The Bureaucratic Phenomenon* (Chicago: University of Chicago Press, 1964), pp. 213–214.

19. Crozier (1964), p. 216.

20. Crozier (1964), p. 217.

21. On this phenomenon, see Stanley Hoffmann, *Decline or Renewal? France Since the 1930s* (New York: Viking Press, 1974), pp. 69–70, 121.

22. Crozier (1964), p. 222.

23. As the work of the historian Maurice Agulhon has demonstrated, the degree of isolation and distrust in French social life has never been as complete as in southern Italy or as in a contemporary former socialist society. But many of the

spontaneous social groups that have sprung up have tended to be what Jesse Pitts calls "delinquent communities," that is, communities whose purpose is not ethically sanctioned by the larger society. See Maurice Agulhon and Maryvonne Bodiguel, *Les Associations au village* (Le Paradou: Actes Sud, 1981); and Agulhon, *Le Cercle dans la France bourgeoise, 1810–1848, étude d'une mutation de sociabilité* (Paris: A. Colin, 1977); and Pitts in Hoffmann and Kindleberger (1964), pp. 256–262.

24. On the military origins of the modern European state, see Bruce Porter, *War and the Rise of the Nation-State* (New York: Free Press, 1993).
25. Alexis de Tocqueville, *The Old Regime and the French Revolution* (Garden City, N.Y.: Doubleday, 1955), p. 51.
26. Tocqueville (1955), p. 88.
27. Douglass C. North and Robert P. Thomas, *The Rise of the Western World* (London: Cambridge University Press, 1973), p. 122.
28. Tocqueville (1955), p. 91.
29. Tocqueville (1955), pp. 94–95.
30. Hoffmann (1974), p. 123.
31. Hoffmann (1974), pp. 68–76.
32. Kindleberger in Hoffmann and Kindleberger (1963), pp. 136–137.
33. North and Thomas (1973), p. 126.
34. Quoted in Werner Sombart, *The Quintessence of Capitalism* (New York: Dutton and Co., 1915), p. 138.
35. Tocqueville (1955), p. 70.
36. See Michel Bauer and Elie Cohen, "Le Politique, l'administratif, et l'exercice du pouvoir industriel," *Sociologie du travail* 27 (1985): 324–327.
37. Tocqueville (1955), pp. 65–66.
38. While in office during the 1980s, the Socialists plowed some $5 billion into nationalized industries. See Vivien Schmidt, "Industrial Management Under the Socialists in France: Decentralized Dirigisme at the National and Local Levels," *Comparative Politics* 21 (1988): 53–72.
39. "The Bank That Couldn't Say No," *Economist*, April 9, 1994, pp. 21–24. Of course, this kind of poor judgment on the part of banks and other financial institutions is by no means limited to public sector companies, as is evident from the periodic crises in the American and Japanese banking industries. In the Crédit Lyonnais case, however, a certain number of key loans appear to have been made for political motives, which presumably would not exist for a private sector bank.
40. Tocqueville (1955), p. 61.
41. Kindleberger in Hoffmann and Kindleberger (1955), p. 157.

CHAPTER 12. KOREA: THE CHINESE COMPANY WITHIN

1. Young Ki Lee, "Conglomeration and Business Concentration in Korea," in Jene K. Kwon, ed., *Korean Economic Development* (Westport, Conn.: Greenwood Press, 1989), p. 328.

2. Byong-Nak Song, *The Rise of the Korean Economy* (Hong Kong: Oxford University Press, 1990), p. 114.

3. Alice H. Amsden, *Asia's Next Giant: South Korea and Late Industrialization* (New York: Oxford University Press, 1989), p. 116.

4. Song (1990), pp. 112–113.

5. Gary G. Hamilton and Nicole Woolsey Biggart, "Market, Culture, and Authority: A Comparative Analysis of Management and Organization in the Far East," *American Journal of Sociology* 94, Supplement (1988): S52-S94.

6. For a background on this period, see Nicole Woolsey Biggart, "Institutionalized Patrimonialism in Korean Business," in Craig Calhoun, ed., *Comparative Social Research: Business Institutions,* vol. 12 (Greenwich, Conn.: JAI Press, 1990), pp. 119–120.

7. See, for example, the account of the Korean entrepreneur Yon-su Kim in Dennis L. McNamara, "Entrepreneurship in Colonial Korea: Kim Yon-su," *Modern Asian Studies* 22 (1988): 165–177; and Dennis L. McNamara, *The Colonial Origins of Korean Enterprise, 1910–1945* (Cambridge: Cambridge University Press, 1990).

8. Lee in Kwon, ed. (1989), p. 329.

9. Richard D. Whitley, "Eastern Asian Enterprise Structures and the Comparative Analysis of Forms of Business Organization," *Organization Studies* 11 (1990): 47–74.

10. Hitachi, for example, is a member of the Presidents' Councils of the Fuyo, Sanwa, and Dai-Ichi Kangyo *keiretsu,* while Kobe Steel is a member of the Sanwa and Dai-Ichi Kangyo groups. See Michael L. Gerlach, *Alliance Capitalism: The Social Organization of Japanese Business* (Berkeley: University of California Press, 1992), pp. 82–84.

11. Tamio Hattori, "The Relationship between Zaibatsu and Family Structure: The Korean Case," in Akio Okochi and Shigeaki Yasuoka, *Family Business in the Era of Industrial Growth* (Tokyo: University of Tokyo Press, 1984), p. 132.

12. Clark Sorenson, "Farm Labor and Family Cycle in Traditional Korea and Japan," *Journal of Anthropological Research* 40 (1984): 306–323.

13. Hattori in Okochi and Yasuoka, eds. (1984), p. 133.

14. Sorenson (1984), p. 310.

15. Choong Soon Kim, *The Culture of Korean Industry: An Ethnography of Poongsan Corporation* (Tucson: University of Arizona Press, 1992), p. 13.

16. On the importance of family ties in Korea, see B. C. A. Walraven, "Symbolic Expressions of Family Cohesion in Korean Tradition," *Korea Journal* 29 (1989): 4–11.

17. On this point, see Richard M. Steers, Yoo Keun Shin, and Gerardo R. Ungson, *The Chaebol: Korea's New Industrial Might* (New York: Harper & Row, 1989), pp. 17, 135.

18. On these points, see Song (1990), pp. 31–34.

19. Mutsuhiko Shima, "In Quest of Social Recognition: A Retrospective View on the Development of Korean Lineage Organization," *Harvard Journal of Asiatic Studies* 50 (1990): 87–192.

20. Not all those Kims and Parks claim ancestry from the same lineage; the sur-name *Kim,* for example, is shared among seven or eight large lineages.
21. Roger L. Janelli and Dawn-hee Yim Janelli, "Lineage Organization and Social Differentiation in Korea," *Man* 13 (1978): 272–289.
22. Kwang Chung Kim and Shin Kim, "Kinship Group and Patrimonial Executives in a Developing Nation: A Case Study of Korea," *Journal of Developing Areas* 24 (1989): 27–46.
23. Sang M. Lee and Sangjin Yoo, "The K-Type Management: A Driving Force of Korean Prosperity," *Management International Review* 27 (1987): 68–77.
24. Chan Sup Chang, "Chaebol: The South Korean Conglomerates," *Business Horizons* 31 (1988): 51–57.
25. Steers, Shin, and Ungson (1989), pp. 37–38.
26. C. Kim (1992), p. 77.
27. C. Kim (1992), p. 66.
28. Chang (1988), p. 53.
29. Hattori in Okochi and Yasuoka, eds. (1984), pp. 137–139.
30. Hattori in Okochi and Yasuoka, eds. (1984), p. 134.
31. Steers, Shin, and Ungson (1989), pp. 38–39; and Lee and Yoo (1987), p. 75. It is argued, however, that while top family managers make decisions autocrati-cally, most decisions are not made at the top. See Alice Amsden, "The Rise of Salaried Management," in Kwon, ed. (1989), p. 363.
32. From *Dong An Ilbo,* as quoted in Steers, Shin, and Ungson (1989), p. 39.
33. Steers, Shin, and Ungson (1989), p. 47.
34. Steers, Shin, and Ungson (1989), p. 123.
35. Steers, Shin, and Ungson (1989), pp. 91–92. See also C. Kim (1992), p. 134.
36. Song (1990), p. 199. Song goes on to say that the cultural roots of this greater Korean individualism are not clear to him. From the preceding discussion, it should be clear that it arises out of the nature of Korean familism.
37. Lee and Yoo (1987), p. 74.
38. C. Kim (1992), p. 151. Another in-depth study of a single Korean corporation reports a significant degree of suspicion and distrust among workers in revealing their opinions or in opening up to outsiders about their social relations within the firm. See Roger L. Janelli and Dawn-hee Yim [Janelli], *Making Capitalism: The Social and Cultural Construction of a South Korean Conglomerate* (Stanford: Stanford University Press, 1993), pp. 3–12.
39. Song (1990), pp. 199–200.
40. As of the late 1980s, some seventy-two percent of the over-sixty-five population were totally dependent on their children for support. David I. Steinberg, "Sociopolitical Factors and Korea's Future Economic Policies," *World Development* 16 (1988): 19–34.
41. Labor unions became politically active in the turmoil that followed the assassi-nation of President Park Chung Hee in 1979 and again in the agitation against the military regime of President Chun Doo Hwan in 1987. The Korean labor movement initiated some 3,000 strikes in the summer of 1987, which had an important effect in inducing the Democratic Justice party's candidate, Roh Tae

Woo, to break with Chun and accept calls for direct elections for the presidency. With liberalization of labor legislation and the calling of the first relatively free elections in 1988, it was only natural that pent-up labor demands suddenly exploded. Strikes took place throughout Korean industry in the late 1980s, and wages rose some thirty-seven percent in the two years 1987–1988 alone. Steers, Shin, and Ungson (1989), pp. 126–127.

42. I am grateful to Kongdan Oh for this point.

43. Kim and Kim (1989), p. 41; Susan De Vos and Yean-Ju Lee, "Change in Extended Family Living Among Elderly People in South Korea, 1970–1980," *Economic Development and Cultural Change* 41 (1993): 377–393; Myung-hye Kim, "Transformation of Family Ideology in Upper-Middle-Class Families in Urban South Korea," *Ethnology* 32 (1993): 69–85.

44. That is, it would be costly in cases where Korean companies had developed brand-name recognition for consumer or other products. As will be seen below, however, it is not clear that large size and conglomeration are particularly valuable from an efficiency point of view; a breakup of many Korean *chaebol* (whether for familistic or other reasons) may actually improve efficiency.

45. Leroy P. Jones and Il Sakong, *Government, Business, and Entrepreneurship in Economic Development: The Korean Case* (Cambridge: Harvard University Press, 1980), p. 148.

46. Song (1990), p. 129.

47. Edward S. Mason, ed., *The Economic and Social Modernization of the Republic of Korea* (Cambridge: Harvard University Press, 1980), pp. 336–337.

48. Song (1990), p. 161; see also Robert Wade, "East Asian Financial Systems as a Challenge to Economics: Lessons from Taiwan," *California Management Review* 27 (1985): 106–127.

49. Quoted in Alice H. Amsden, *Asia's Next Giant: South Korea and Late Industrialization* (New York: Oxford University Press, 1989), p. 2.

50. Richard D. Whitley, "The Social Construction of Business Systems in East Asia," *Organization Studies* 12 (1991): 1–28.

51. It may have been that the early *chaebol* were the first enterprises to have generalized modern management skills and therefore had a competitive advantage in running many parts of the traditional Korean economy. Having money to invest at negative interest rates gives a firm a powerful incentive to purchase assets of virtually any sort, however.

52. Mark L. Clifford, *Troubled Tiger: Businessmen, Bureaucrats and Generals in South Korea* (Armonk, N.Y.: M. E. Sharpe, 1994), chap. 9.

53. Eun Mee Kim, "From Dominance to Symbiosis: State and *Chaebol* in Korea," *Pacific Focus* 3 (1988): 105–121.

54. Amsden (1989), p. 17.

55. Song (1990), pp. 98–100.

56. Whitley (1991), p. 18.

57. Amsden (1989), p. 72; Wade (1985), p. 122.

58. In 1979, when the Yolsan *chaebol* flirted with an opposition political leader, the government used its control over credit to drive the company out of business.

Bruce Cumings, "The Origins and Development of the Northeast Asian Political Economy: Industrial Sectors, Product Cycles, and Political Consequences," *International Organization* 38 (1984): 1–40.

59. Clifford (1994), chap. 9.

60. Clifford (1994), chap. 9.

61. On the question of regionalism in Korean business, see Jones and Sakong (1980), pp. 208–219. Regionalism has also been an important factor in Korean politics; the 1988 presidential election among Roh Tae Woo, Kim Dae Jung, and Kim Young Sam reflected a regional as well as an ideological split, since Kim Dae Jung came from Cholla province and Kim Young Sam and Roh Tae Woo represented southern and northern Kyongsang province, respectively.

62. Kim and Kim (1989), pp. 42–43.

63. Chan Sup Chang, "Chaebol: The South Korean Conglomerates," *Business Horizons* 31 (1988): 51–57.

64. Song (1990), p. 46.

65. Jones and Sakong (1980), pp. 212–219.

66. David Martin, *Tongues of Fire: The Explosion of Protestantism in Latin America* (Oxford: Basil Blackwell, 1990), p. 143.

67. Jones and Sakong (1980), pp. 221–222.

68. Jones and Sakong (1980), p. 222; Martin (1990), p. 154.

69. David Martin argues that Protestantism may have played an indirect role in promoting economic growth by inducing a kind of political quietism that prevented the system from blowing up as it was industrializing. The only problem with this interpretation is that Korea's Confucian culture would probably have had a similar effect had there been no Protestant conversions. Christians, for their part, were quite active in opposition political circles, even if this did not end up destabilizing Korea in an economically harmful way. See Martin (1990), pp. 154–155.

70. Amsden (1989), p. 129.

71. According to one story, the relationship between Park and Chung Ju Yung of Hyundai was cemented when the former paid a surprise dawn inspection visit by helicopter at a work site and found the latter already hard at work. See Clifford (1994), chap. 9.

72. "Innovate, Not Imitate," *Far Eastern Economic Review,* May 13, 1994, pp. 64–68.

73. "Breaking Up Is Hard to Do," *Far Eastern Economic Review,* September 29, 1988, p. 103.

74. "Paralysis in South Korea," *Business Week,* June 8, 1992, pp. 48–49.

CHAPTER 13. FRICTION-FREE ECONOMIES

1. This was, of course, the view of most social scientists in this century. See Max Weber, *General Economic History* (New Brunswick, N.J.: Transaction Books, 1981), pp. 277, 338–351.

2. In addition, there is the cost of setting up the institutions that make possible these sorts of transactions, which is usually borne by the society as a whole.

3. Kenneth J. Arrow, *The Limits of Organization* (New York: Norton, 1974), p. 23.

4. These include crash development projects like the Polaris submarine launched ballistic missile and the U-2 spy plane.

5. For a description of this process of overregulation, see *Integrating Commercial and Military Technologies for National Strength: An Agenda for Change,* Report of the CSIS Steering Committee on Security and Technology (Washington, D.C.: Center for Strategic and International Studies, 1991); and Jacques Gansler, *Affording Defense* (Cambridge: MIT Press, 1991), pp. 141–214.

6. For example, a purchasing agent working for a commercial company will not solicit bids from all suppliers theoretically capable of providing a given good or service; he or she will usually choose from the top three or four that, on the basis of past experience, have reputations for quality, reliability, or price. Government purchasing agents, by contrast, are required to open bids to all potential suppliers, and parties making losing bids have an unlimited right of recusal. The purpose of such a regulation is to prevent "favoritism."

7. Nathan Rosenberg and L. E. Birdzell, Jr., *How the West Grew Rich: The Economic Transformation of the Industrial World* (New York: Basic Books, 1986), p. 114. On this point, see also James R. Beniger, *The Control Revolution: Technological and Economic Origins of the Information Society* (Cambridge: Harvard University Press, 1986), pp. 126–127.

8. See Mancur Olson, *The Logic of Collective Action: Public Goods and the Theory of Collective Action* (Cambridge: Harvard University Press, 1965). There is by now an enormous literature on the free rider problem, which has become one of the central issues for the "rational choice" school. See, for example, the summaries in Russell Hardin, *Collective Action* (Baltimore: Johns Hopkins University Press, 1982); and Todd Sandler, *Collective Action: Theory and Applications* (Ann Arbor: University of Michigan Press 1992).

9. The other classic group behavior problem is the prisoner's dilemma, in which two prisoners, held in separate cells without being able to communicate, face a choice in which they can benefit only if *both* pick a cooperative option, without, however, knowing which choice each will make. It would appear that a culture that inculcated a strong sense of reciprocal obligation among its members would more easily find a solution to the prisoner's dilemma than one that legitimized greater individualism.

10. Victor Nee, "The Peasant Household Economy and Decollectivization in China," *Journal of Asian and African Studies* 21 (1986): 185–203. Elsewhere, Nee notes, "Peasant rational calculation tended to focus on maximizing individual household advantage over the interests of the collective economy. This manifested itself in a persistent problem, according to Yangbei cadres, in the complaint that villagers lacked genuine enthusiasm when working on the collective fields, by contrast to the effort displayed in the course of work on household private plots, sidelines, and household chores. This disparity between productivity in the collective and in private sectors points to the heart of the problem of collective farming in Yangbei. Simply stated, if all households benefited from the team economy performing well, then those who worked harder worried that their additional effort, though ultimately benefiting their own

household, also might be subsidizing those who worked less hard. . . . This is the classic 'free rider' dilemma." Nee, "Peasant Household Individualism," in William L. Parrish, ed., *Chinese Rural Development: The Great Transformation* (Armonk, N.Y.: M. E. Sharpe, 1985), p. 172.

11. For a critique of the role of professional associations in general, see James Fallows, *More Like Us: Making America Great Again* (Boston: Houghton Mifflin, 1989), pp. 132–146

12. Mancur Olson, *The Rise and Decline of Nations: Economic Growth, Stagflation, and Social Rigidities* (New Haven: Yale University Press, 1982).

13. Olson (1982).

14. See Jonathan Rauch, *Demosclerosis: The Silent Killer of American Government* (New York: Times Books, 1994).

15. Ian Jamieson, *Capitalism and Culture: A Comparative Analysis of British and American Manufacturing Organizations* (London: Gower, 1980), pp. 56–57.

16. Ronald P. Dore, *British Factory, Japanese Factory* (London: Allen and Unwin, 1973), p. 140.

CHAPTER 14. A BLOCK OF GRANITE

1. Masaru Yoshimori, "Source of Japanese Competitiveness, Part I," *Management Japan* 25 (1992): 18–23.

2. Richard E. Caves and Masu Uekusa, *Industrial Organization in Japan* (Washington, D.C.: Brookings Institution, 1976), p. 60.

3. "The Japanese Economy: From Miracle to Mid-Life Crisis," *Economist,* March 6, 1993, pp. 3–13. On this general point, see also Kuniyasu Sakai, "The Feudal World of Japanese Manufacturing," *Harvard Business Review* 68 (1990): 38–47. For background on *keiretsu* relationships in the Japanese auto industry, see Koichi Shimokawa, "Japan's Keiretsu System: The Case of the Automobile Industry," *Japanese Economic Studies* 13 (1985): 3–31.

4. James P. Womack, Daniel T. Jones, and Daniel Roos, *The Machine That Changed the World: The Story of Lean Production* (New York: Harper Perennial, 1991), p. 83. This figure overstates Toyota's overall productivity advantage, because the Framingham plant was one of GM's worst performers.

5. William W. Lockwood, *The Economic Development of Japan* (Princeton: Princeton University Press, 1954), pp. 207, 110–111.

6. Lockwood (1954), p. 206.

7. David Friedman, *The Misunderstood Miracle* (Ithaca: Cornell University Press, 1988), p. 10.

8. Caves and Uekusa (1976), p. 3.

9. Friedman (1988) bases his broad argument on a detailed analysis of the Japanese machine tool industry. Machine tools are unrepresentative of manufacturing as a whole, however, because they lend themselves to craft production techniques, short production runs, and small scale.

10. "Founder of Hal Computers Resigns to Be Fujitsu Consultant," *New York Times,* July 16, 1993, p. D4.

11. See "Japan, US Firms Enter Microprocessor Pacts," *Nikkei Weekly,* May 2, 1994, pp. 1, 19.
12. Lockwood (1954), p. 215.
13. Lockwood (1954), p. 215. See also Shigeaki Yasuoka, "Capital Ownership in Family Companies: Japanese Firms Compared with Those in Other Countries," in Akio Okochi and Shigeaki Yasuoka, eds., *Family Business in the Era of Industrial Growth* (Tokyo: University of Tokyo Press, 1984), p. 2.
14. Yasuoka in Okochi and Yasuoka (1984), p. 9.
15. Ronald P. Dore, *British Factory, Japanese Factory* (London: Allen and Unwin, 1973), p. 270; see also James C. Abegglen, *The Japanese Factory: Aspects of Its Social Organization* (Glencoe, Ill.: Free Press, 1958), p. 17.
16. The pact not to let the sons into the business was made together with Honda's second in command, Takeo Fujisawa. Fujisawa himself was a *banto,* having been hired by Honda early on to take care of the purely business side of the company. Saburo Shiroyama, "A Tribute to Honda Soichiro," *Japan Echo* (Winter 1991): 82–85.
17. See the comments by Hidesasa Morkiawa in Okochi and Yasuoka (1984), p. 36.
18. Hence the titular president of Sumitomo Goshigaisha at the time that its headquarters was formed into a limited partnership was the head of the Sumitomo household, Kichizeamon Sumitomo, but the latter delegated operational authority to a professional manager, Masaya Suzuki. The professional managers of the Sumitomo *zaibatsu* also served on its board. Michael L. Gerlach, *Alliance Capitalism: The Social Organization of Japanese Business* (Berkeley: University of California Press, 1992), pp. 98–99.
19. Yasuoka in Okochi and Yasuoka (1984), pp. 9–10.
20. Yasuoka in Okochi and Yasuoka (1984), pp. 17–18.
21. For a historical account of this process by someone who participated in it, see Eleanor Hadley, *Antitrust in Japan* (Princeton: Princeton University Press, 1970).
22. Yoshimori (1992), p. 19.
23. Yoshimori (1992), p. 20. Yoshimori presents a table, partially reproduced here, seeking to compare the rates of family ownership in Japan with those of the United States, Britain, West Germany, and France, in which Japan ranks the lowest.

Corporate Ownership in Five Countries

Ownership structure	*Japan (% of firms)*	*United States (% of market cap)*	*United Kingdon (% of sales)*	*Federal Republic of Germany (% of firms)*	*France (% of firms)*
Family and individuals	14	28.5	56.25	48.0	44.3
Managerial or other control	86	71.5	43.75	52.0	55.7

The author admits, however, that his data come from disparate sources and are not really comparable. For example, his ownership category "Family and Individuals" appears to refer to all noninstitutional investors and not necessarily owners of family businesses. The percentages of ownership also refer to different measures in different countries.

24. Abegglen (1958), p. 84.
25. For an account of this competition from an American perspective, see Clyde V. Prestowitz, Jr., *Trading Places: How We Allowed Japan to Take the Lead* (New York: Basic Books, 1988), pp. 26–70.

CHAPTER 15. SONS AND STRANGERS

1. For a discussion of common elements of Chinese and Japanese family life and ideology, see Francis L. K. Hsu, *Iemoto: The Heart of Japan* (New York: Schenkman Publishing Co., 1975), pp. 25–27.
2. James I. Nakamura and Matao Miyomoto, "Social Structure and Population Change: A Comparative Study of Tokugawa Japan and Ch'ing China," *Economic Development and Cultural Change* 30 (1982): 229–269.
3. Chie Nakane, *Kinship and Economic Organization in Rural Japan* (London: Althone Press, 1967), p. 4.
4. Nakane (1967), p. 9. See also Hironobu Kitaoji, "The Structure of the Japanese Family," *American Anthropologist* 73 (1971): 1036–1057.
5. Martin Collcutt, "The Legacy of Confucianism in Japan," in Gilbert Rozman, ed., *The East Asian Region: Confucian Heritage and Its Modern Adaptation* (Princeton: Princeton University Press, 1991), pp. 122–123.
6. Hsu (1975), p. 39.
7. Jane M. Bachnik, "Recruitment Strategies for Household Succession: Rethinking Japanese Household Organization," *Man* 18 (1983): 160–182; and John C. Pelzel, "Japanese Kinship: A Comparison," in Maurice Freedman, ed., *Family and Kinship in Chinese Society* (Stanford: Stanford University Press, 1970).
8. One exception is the imperial family, into which males may not be adopted. Shichihei Yamamoto, *The Spirit of Japanese Capitalism and Selected Essays* (Lanham, Md.: Madison Books, 1992), p. 24. See also Nakamura and Miyamoto (1982), p. 254.
9. Takie Sugiyama Lebra, "Adoption Among the Hereditary Elite of Japan: Status Preservation Through Mobility," *Ethnology* 28 (1989): 218.
10. Hsu (1975), p. 38.
11. Yamamoto (1992), pp. 24–25.
12. R. A. Moore, "Adoption and Samurai Mobility in Tokugawa Japan," *Journal of Asian Studies* 29 (1970): 617–632.
13. Joseph M. Kitagawa, *Religion in Japanese History* (New York: Columbia University Press, 1966), p. 98.
14. Nakane (1967), p. 6.
15. Hsu (1975), pp. 29–30.
16. Nakane (1967), p. 5.

17. Hsu (1975), pp. 32–33.
18. Hsu (1975), p. 36.
19. Yamamoto (1992), pp. 27–28.
20. Thus, for example, one of the leaders of the Choshu clique who played a key role establishing the Meiji regime and went on to be a major statesman, Aritomo Yamagata, could not pass on his position to his son. Yamamoto (1992), p. 28.
21. In the words of Francis Hsu (1975, p. 44), "What we have in the Japanese *ie* and especially in the *dozoku* is a degree of voluntary association of human beings not found in the Chinese *chia* [*jia* or family] and *tsu* [clan]. Human beings cannot choose their parents, children uncles, or aunts. But they certainly have greater room for maneuvering when they can adopt adults to whom they are not related into their *ie* and *dozoku*. In other words, they enjoy more liberalized criteria for recruitment."
22. Nakane (1967), p. 21. She adds, "The son's attitude towards the retired aged parent was particularly out of keeping with that of the Chinese."
23. On changes in the contemporary Japanese family, see Fumie Kumagai, "Modernization and the Family in Japan," *Journal of Family History* 2 (1986): 371–382; Kiyomi Morioka, "Demographic Family Changes in Contemporary Japan," *International Social Science Journal* 126 (1990): 511–522; and S. Philip Morgan and Kiyosi Hiroshima, "The Persistence of Extended Family Residence in Japan: Anachronism or Alternative Strategy?" *American Sociological Review* 48 (1983): 269–281.
24. This is the central thesis of Chie Nakane's well-known book *Japanese Society* (Berkeley: University of California Press, 1970).
25. Francis Hsu calls this relationship "kin-tract," to indicate that *iemoto* organizations partake of the characteristics of both kinship groups and modern associations based on contract. Hsu (1975), p. 62.
26. Hsu (1975), p. 69.
27. Hsu (1975), p. 69; Winston Davis, "Japanese Religious Affiliations: Motives and Obligations," *Sociological Analysis* 44 (1983): 131–146.
28. See Sepp Linhart, "The Family As Constitutive Element of Japanese Civilization," in Tadao Umesao, Harumi Befu, and Josef Kreiner, eds., *Japanese Civilization in the Modern World: Life and Society, Senri Ethnological Studies* 16 (1984): pp. 51–58.
29. For a history of the spread of Confucianism in Japan, see Collcutt in Rozman (1991).
30. See, for example, Yasuzo Horie, "Confucian Concept of State in Tokugawa Japan," *Kyoto University Economic Review* 32 (1962): 26–38, which asserts that nationalism was "systematically and logically advocated by Confucianism." See also Yoshio Abe, "The Basis of Japanese Culture and Confucianism," *Asian Culture Quarterly* 2 (1974): 21–28.
31. In orthodox Confucianism, this benevolence is not supposed to be limited to the family, however, but should be extended to nonkin as well.
32. Michio Morishima, *Why Has Japan "Succeeded"? Western Technology and the Japanese Ethos* (Cambridge: Cambridge University Press, 1982), p. 4; see also Morishima, "Confucius and Capitalism," *UNESCO Courier* (December 1987): 34–37.

33. Morishima (1982), p. 6.
34. See Morishima (1982), pp. 6–7, who argues that "the meaning of loyalty (Ch. *chung,* Jap. *chu*) was not the same in both China and Japan. . . . In China loyalty meant being true to one's own conscience. In Japan, although it was also used in this same sense, its normal meaning was essentially a sincerity that aimed at total devotion to one's lord, i.e., service to one's lord to the point of sacrificing oneself. Consequently Confucius' words 'act with loyalty in the service of one's lord' were interpreted by the Chinese to mean 'Retainers must serve their lord with a sincerity which does not conflict with their own consciences', whereas the Japanese interpreted the same words as 'Retainers must devote their whole lives to their lord.' "
35. Morishima (1982), p. 8; see also Lucian W. Pye, *Asian Power and Politics: The Cultural Dimensions of Authority* (Cambridge: Harvard University Press, 1985), pp. 56–57.
36. For another discussion of the relative positions of loyalty and filial piety in China and Japan, see Warren W. Smith, Jr., *Confucianism in Modern Japan: A Study of Conservatism in Japanese Intellectual History* (Tokyo: Hokuseido Press, 1959), p. 230.
37. According to one source, "The Japanese recount with awe and admiration stories of dutiful samurai who lived up to this code [*bushido*], unflinchingly allowing their whole families to be slaughtered by the enemy rather than utter a word that might compromise the safety of the lord." Johannes Hirschmeier, *The Origins of Entrepreneurship in Meiji Japan* (Cambridge: Harvard University Press, 1964), p. 48.
38. Collcutt in Rozman (1991), p. 33; I. J. McMullen, "Rulers or Fathers? A Casuistical Problem in Early Modern Japan," *Past and Present* 116 (1987): 56–97.
39. Ronald P. Dore, *British Factory, Japanese Factory* (London: Allen and Unwin, 1973), p. 396.
40. Collcutt in Rozman (1991), pp. 147–151.
41. Morishima (1982), p. 105.
42. Chalmers Johnson, *MITI and the Japanese Miracle* (Stanford: Stanford University Press, 1982), pp. 11–12.
43. "Inside the Charmed Circle," *Economist,* January 5, 1991, p. 54.
44. On the operations of Japanese multinationals in the United States, see James R. Lincoln, Jon Olson, and Mitsuyo Hanada, "Cultural Effects on Organizational Structure: The Case of Japanese Firms in the United States," *American Sociological Review* 43 (1978): 829–847.
45. Deng Xiaoping is something of an exception to this. Since 1981 his nominal position has been head of the Military Commission, while he nonetheless had supreme authority over the government and the Communist party. This kind of indirect power, however, has not been the rule in Chinese history.
46. See Saburo Shiroyama, "A Tribute to Honda Soichiro," *Japan Echo* (Winter 1991): 82–85.
47. See, for example, Barrington Moore, Jr., *Social Origins of Dictatorship and Democracy* (Boston: Beacon Press, 1966).

48. Norman Jacobs, *The Origins of Modern Capitalism in Eastern Asia* (Hong Kong: Hong Kong University Press, 1958), p. 29.
49. Richard D. Whitley, "The Social Construction of Business Systems in East Asia," *Organization Studies* 12 (1991): 1–28.
50. On the role of Osaka as a commercial center, see Hirschmeier (1964), pp. 14–28.
51. Robert N. Bellah, *Tokugawa Religion* (Boston: Beacon Press, 1957); Bellah, *Religion and Progress in Modern Asia* (Glencoe, Ill.: Free Press, 1965); and Yamamoto (1992).
52. For an account of the training and Buddhist teaching that lies behind such skills, see Eugen Herrigel, *Zen in the Art of Archery* (New York: Pantheon Books, 1953); and Soetsu Yanagi, *The Unknown Craftsman: A Japanese Insight into Beauty* (Tokyo: Kodansha International, 1989). See also Francis Fukuyama, "Great Planes," *New Republic,* September 6, 1993. For a point of view questioning the degree to which Buddhist doctrine can be properly used as a tool to enhance performance in the martial arts, see Brian Bocking, "Neo-Confucian Spirituality and the Samurai Ethic," *Religion* 10 (1980): 1–15.
53. In fact, there is a relationship between perfectionism in craft skills and social organization. These skills are kept alive and transmitted from generation to generation through *iemoto*-type organizations, in which a master passes on his knowledge, often in a nonverbal fashion, to a series of disciples. While quality control in modern organizations can be taught adequately in modern American business schools, there is perhaps an extra element of quality consciousness that is imparted through the *iemoto* system.

CHAPTER 16. JOB OF A LIFETIME

1. Reciprocal moral obligation is similar to the concept of social exchange as defined by Yasusuke Murakami and Thomas P. Rohlen: "Social-Exchange Aspects of the Japanese Political Economy: Culture, Efficiency, and Change," in Shumpei Kumon and Henry Rosovsky, eds., *The Political Economy of Japan, vol. 2: Cultural and Social Dynamics* (Stanford: Stanford University Press, 1992), pp. 73–77.
2. One of the first Western observers to describe the Japanese postwar lifetime employment system was James C. Abegglen, *The Japanese Factory: Aspects of Its Social Organization* (Glencoe, Ill.: Free Press, 1958), (p. 67.) Abegglen's interpretation has been challenged by later writers, both Western and Japanese, for among other things ignoring the Japanese small-business sector, where lifetime employment is not the rule.
3. Shichihei Yamamoto, *The Spirit of Japanese Capitalism and Selected Essays* (Lanham, Md.: Madison Books, 1992), p. 9.
4. Michio Morishima, *Why Has Japan "Succeeded"? Western Technology and the Japanese Ethos* (Cambridge: Cambridge University Press, 1982), p. 174.
5. Abegglen (1958), pp. 116–117.
6. Ronald P. Dore, "Industrial Relations in Japan and Elsewhere," in Albert M.

Craig, ed., *Japan: A Comparative View* (Princeton: Princeton University Press, 1979), p. 340.

7. The Japanese labor market is in fact a good deal more flexible than it might at first seem. Although large companies take on a lifetime employment obligation, workers within a company are not rigidly tied to a particular job description. Indeed, professionalism is much less a source of identity, and consequently less of a constraint, in Japan than it is in the United States or Britain. Japanese engineers, for example, tend to take less pride in their engineering qualifications than in the particular company they work for, and therefore they are more willing to shift specializations or even to move out of engineering altogether. Companies have a great deal of flexibility in being able to move workers around and take on the responsibility for retraining. Hence the process of layoff, retraining, and rehiring takes place in Japan just as in the United States but within the enterprise, with the company taking responsibility for moving the worker from one sector to another. The Japanese steelmaker NKK, for example, when faced with declining employment in its core steel business, moved foundry workers into a consumer goods subsidiary. See "Deep Cutbacks in Japan, Too," *New York Times,* March 11, 1993, p. D5.

   A further escape hatch is the dual structure of the Japanese labor market. Lifetime employment is a privilege only of large companies and is not nearly as widely practiced among small companies. Many big companies can cut their own employment by pushing unneeded workers onto their subsidiaries, where they can be paid less and ultimately be fired. The threat of dropping out of the large-company employment pool is also a very live sanction motivating employees to work hard.

8. Ronald P. Dore, *British Factory, Japanese Factory* (London: Allen and Unwin, 1973), p. 208; Abegglen (1958), p. 97.

9. Dore (1973), p. 220.

10. Abegglen (1958), p. 99.

11. Abegglen (1958), p. 94.

12. Seymour Martin Lipset, "Pacific Divide: American Exceptionalism—Japanese Uniqueness," in *Power Shifts and Value Changes in the Post Cold War World,* Proceedings of the Joint Symposium of the International Sociological Association's Research Committee: Comparative Sociology and Sociology of Organizations (Japan: Kibi International University, Sophia University, and International Christian University, 1992), p. 57.

13. Dore (1973), p. 140. Dore notes that although some British trade unionists accept the fact that the health of their industry is of importance to them, more militant ones hope that their industry will do poorly so as to expedite the collapse of the capitalist system as a whole.

14. See Dore (1973), p. 154.

15. This is particularly true of Abegglen (1958; see esp. p. 100); also see Solomon B. Levine, *Industrial Relations in Postwar Japan* (Urbana, Ill.: University of Illinois Press, 1958).

16. For an example of the misapplication of cultural factors, see Dominique V.

Turpin, "The Strategic Persistence of the Japanese Firm," *Journal of Business Strategy* (January–February 1992): 49–52, who argues that Japanese firms' interest in market share over profits springs from the importance of the value of persistence in Japanese culture. This does not explain why the Japanese did not persist in other sectors, like textiles and shipbuilding.

17. John C. Pelzel, "Factory Life in Japan and China Today," in Craig (1979), p. 390.
18. Sanford Jacoby, "The Origins of Internal Labor Markets in Japan," *Industrial Relations* 18 (1979): 184–196.
19. Dore (1974), p. 388.
20. According to Chalmers Johnson, "The elite develops and propagates ideologies to try to convince the public that the social conditions in their country are the result of anything—culture, history, language, national character, climate, and so forth—other than politics." From "The People Who Invented the Mechanical Nightingale," *Daedalus* 119 (1990): 71–90; see also Johnson, *MITI and the Japanese Miracle* (Stanford: Stanford University Press, 1982), p. 8.
21. For a discussion of the relative merits of cultural versus structural explanations for business organization in East Asia, see Gary G. Hamilton and Nicole Woolsey Biggart, "Market, Culture, and Authority: A Comparative Analysis of Management and Organization in the Far East," *American Journal of Sociology* 94 (1988): S52–S94.
22. See *New York Times,* June 25, 1994, p. D1.
23. "Decline in Recruiting Slows to 10% Drop," *Nikkei Weekly,* June 6, 1994, p. 3.
24. On the general question of the future of the Japanese economic model, see Peter F. Drucker, "The End of Japan, Inc.?" *Foreign Affairs* 72 (1993): 10–15.

CHAPTER 17. THE MONEY CLIQUE

1. In other words, it is a network in the sense of Shumpei Kumon, defined later in this chapter as "consensus/inducement-based exchange."
2. The problem was finally solved when their Internet service provider cancelled their account because of the high volume of hate e-mail they received.
3. For further background on the history and functions of the *keiretsu,* see Richard E. Caves and Masu Uekusa, *Industrial Organization in Japan* (Washington, D.C.: Brookings Institution, 1976), pp. 63–70; Chalmers Johnson, "*Keiretsu:* An Outsider's View," *International Economic Insights* 1 (1992): 15–17; Masaru Yoshitomi, "Keiretsu: An Insider's Guide to Japan's Conglomerates," *International Economic Insights* 1 (1992): 10–14; Maruyama Yoshinari, "The Big Six Horizontal Keiretsu," *Japan Quarterly* 39 (1992): 186–198; Robert L. Cutts, "Capitalism in Japan: Cartels and Keiretsu," *Harvard Business Review* 70 (1992): 48–55; James R. Lincoln, Michael L. Gerlach, and Peggy Takahashi, "Keiretsu Networks in the Japanese Economy: A Dyad Analysis of Intercorporate Ties," *American Sociological Review* 57 (1992): 561–585; Marco Orrù, Gary G. Hamilton, and Mariko Suzuki, "Patterns of Inter-Firm Control in Japanese Business," *Organization Studies* 10 (1989): 549–574; Ken-ichi Imai, "Japan's

Corporate Networks," in Shumpei Kumon and Henry Rosovsky, eds., *The Political Economy of Japan. vol. 3: Cultural and Social Dynamics* (Stanford: Stanford University Press, 1992),

4. For a discussion of networks in developing countries, see Nathaniel H. Leff, "Industrial Organization and Entrepreneurship in the Developing Countries: The Economic Groups, *Economic Development and Cultural Change* 26 (1978): 661–675.

5. Michael L. Gerlach, *Alliance Capitalism: The Social Organization of Japanese Business* (Berkeley: University of California Press, 1992), p. 82.

6. Gerlach (1992), p. 85.

7. The failure of the *zaibatsu* to seek or achieve monopoly positions is of very long standing; see William W. Lockwood, *The Economic Development of Japan* (Princeton: Princeton University Press, 1954), p. 223.

8. For evidence, see Gerlach (1992), pp. 137–149.

9. Richard D. Whitley, "East Asian Enterprise Structures and the Comparative Analysis of Forms of Business Organization," *Organization Studies* 11 (1990): 47–74.

10. For an account, see Masaru Yoshimori, "Source of Japanese Competitiveness, Part I," *Management Japan* 25 (1992): 18–23.

11. Ronald H. Coase, "The Nature of the Firm," *Economica* 4 (1937): 386–405.

12. See inter alia Oliver E. Williamson, "The Economics of Organization: The Transaction Cost Approach," *American Journal of Sociology* 87 (1981, hereafter 1981a): 548–577; *The Nature of the Firm: Origins, Evolution, and Development* (Oxford: Oxford University Press, 1993); and "The Vertical Integration of Production: Market Failure Considerations," *American Economic Review* 61 (1971): 112–123.

13. Oliver Williamson, "The Modern Corporation: Origins, Evolution, Attributes," *Journal of Economic Literature* 19 (1981, hereafter 1981b): 1537–1568.

14. According to Williamson, "The human agents that populate the firms and markets with which I am concerned differ from economic man (or at least the common caricature thereof) in that they are less competent in calculation and *less trustworthy* and reliable in action. A condition of bounded rationality is responsible for the computational limits of organization man. A proclivity for (at least some) economic agents to behave opportunistically is responsible for their unreliability. . . . Ubiquitous, albeit incomplete, contracting would nevertheless be feasible if economic agents were completely *trustworthy*" (Williamson 1981b, p. 1545; italics added).

15. Armen A. Alchian and Harold Demsetz, "Production, Information Costs, and Economic Organization," *American Economic Review* 62 (1972): 777–795.

16. Oliver E. Williamson, *Corporate Control and Business Behavior* (Englewood Cliffs, N.J.: Prentice-Hall, 1970), p. 175.

17. Ronald P. Dore, "Goodwill and the Spirit of Market Capitalism," *British Journal of Sociology* 34 (1983): 459–482.

18. This argument is made in Masanori Hashimoto, *The Japanese Labor Market in a Comparative Perspective with the United States* (Kalamazoo, Mich.: W. E. Upjohn

Institute for Employment Research, 1990), p. 66, and also by Dore (1983), p. 463.

19. On the inter-*keiretsu* "beer wars," see Gerlach (1992), pp. xx–xxi.

20. Whitley (1990), pp. 55–56.

21. The mechanism of overloaning is described in Chalmers Johnson, *MITI and the Japanese Miracle* (Stanford: Stanford University Press, 1982), pp. 203–204.

22. See Ken'ichi Imai, "The Corporate Network in Japan," *Japanese Economic Studies* 16 (1987–1988): 3–37.

23. For reasons that this should be so, see F. M. Scherer and David Ross, *Industrial Market Structure and Economic Performance, 3d ed.* (Boston: Houghton Mifflin, 1990), pp. 126–130.

24. On this general point, see Dennis J. Encarnation, *Rivals Beyond Trade: American versus Japan in Global Competition* (Ithaca, N.Y.: Cornell University Press, 1992).

25. Mark Mason, *American Multinationals and Japan: The Political Economy of Japanese Capital Controls, 1899–1980* (Cambridge: Council on East Asian Studies, Harvard University, 1992), pp. 205–207.

26. Shumpei Kumon, "Japan as a Network Society," in Kumon and Rosovsky (1992), p. 121.

27. One member of a large automaker's *keiretsu* network was told to cut prices for parts by fifteen percent over three years, or the parent firm could seek other suppliers. "Small Manufacturers Face Survival Fight," *Nikkei Weekly,* June 13, 1994, pp. 1, 8.

28. Thus, Nippon Steel sold $9.6 billion in holdings of various banks, and Matsushita Electric and Nissan sharply reduced their holdings of each other's share. The total percentage of cross-held shares dipped to just under forty percent of all outstanding equity. These changes have not affected core *keiretsu* relations, however. See "Recession Forces Firms to Dump Shares of Allies," *Nikkei Weekly,* May 2, 1994, pp. 1, 12.

29. It does not, *pace* James Fallows, extend necessarily to the nation as a whole. See Fallows, *More Like Us: Making America Great Again* (Boston: Houghton Mifflin, 1989), pp. 25–26.

CHAPTER 18. GERMAN GIANTS

1. They are shared, however, by other Central European countries like Austria and Switzerland.

2. A draft antitrust law was introduced in 1952, but industry opposition delayed it until 1957, when it was passed as the Law against Restraints of Competition (*Gesetz gegen Wettbewerbsbeschraenkungen*). See Hans-Joachim Braun, *The German Economy in the Twentieth Century* (London: Routledge, 1990), p. 180.

3. Alfred D. Chandler, *Scale and Scope: The Dynamics of Industrial Capitalism* (Cambridge, Mass.: Belknap Press & Harvard University Press, 1990), pp. 464–465.

4. Chandler (1990), p. 469.
5. Chandler (1990), pp. 276–277.
6. Chandler (1990), p. 399.
7. Alan S. Milward and S. B. Saul, *The Development of the Economies of Continental Europe, 1780–1870* (London: George Allen and Unwin, 1977), p. 425.
8. Chandler (1990), pp. 417–418.
9. Of course, whether that long-term perspective makes sense depends on one's expectations of future real discount rates; if they are low, it is better to take profits in the short-run.
10. Martin J. Wiener, *English Culture and the Decline of the Industrial Spirit, 1850–1980* (Cambridge: Cambridge University Press, 1981), pp. 128–129.
11. Chandler (1990), p. 423.
12. Chandler (1990), pp. 500–501.
13. Christopher S. Allen, "Germany: Competing Communitarianisms," in George C. Lodge and Ezra F. Vogel, eds., *Ideology and National Competitiveness* (Boston: Harvard Business School Press, 1987), p. 88.
14. The law in question was the *Gesetz über die Investitionshilfe der gewerblichen Wirtschaft.* Braun (1990), p. 179.
15. Ernst Zander, "Collective Bargaining," in E. Grochla and E. Gaugler, eds., *Handbook of German Business Management,* vol.2 (Stuttgart: C. E. Poeschel Verlag, 1990), p.430.
16. On this legislation, see A. J. P. Taylor, *Bismarck: The Man and the Statesman* (New York: Vintage Books, 1967), pp. 202–203.
17. Braun (1990), p. 54.
18. See Klaus Chmielewicz, "Codetermination," in *Handbook of German Business Management,* Vol. 2 (199), pp. 412–438.
19. Peter Schwerdtner, "Trade Unions in the German Economic and Social Order," *Zeitschrift für die gesamte Staatswissenschaft* 135 (1979): 455–473.
20. On this general point, see Allen in Lodge and Vogel, eds. (1987), pp. 79–80.
21. James Fallows and others have made a great deal of the importance of Friedrich List, asserting that the latter's *National System of Political Economy* has been a better guide to both German and Asian economic growth than Adam Smith's *Wealth of Nations.* List, however, simply repeats many of the mercantilist dicta about the centrality of national power and the subordination of economic means to strategic ends that was the staple of mercantilists from earlier centuries like Colbert or Turgot. Adam Smith would have found nothing in List's arguments that he would have considered a decisive critique; indeed, *The Wealth of Nations* was itself written as a critique of List's mercantilist predecessors. Fallows, moreover, vastly overstates the importance of List to German economic thought and practice. See Fallows, *Looking at the Sun: The Rise of the New East Asian Economic and Political System* (New York: Pantheon Books, 1994), pp. 189–190.
22. Tomas Riha, "German Political Economy: History of Alternative Economics," *International Journal of Social Economics* 12 (1985): 192–209.
23. Allen in Lodge and Vogel, eds. (1987), pp. 176–177.
24. On the establishment of the *Technische Hochschule,* see Peter Mathias and M.

M. Postan, *The Cambridge Economic History of Europe, vol. 7: The Industrial Economies: Capital, Labour, and Enterprise. Part I: Britain, France, Germany, and Scandinavia* (London: Cambridge University Press, 1978), pp. 458–459.

25. The degree to which the economy operated independent of the state during the National Socialist period has been debated at great length. See the discussion in Braun (1990), p. 82.

26. There is a long-standing argument, made originally by Alexander Gerschenkron, that heavy state involvement in the promotion of economic development is a general characteristic of late-developing societies. Although there is clearly some merit to this argument, there is also obviously a great deal of variance in state behavior—with regard to both the extent and the competence with which it is implemented—between different late-developing societies.

CHAPTER 19. WEBER AND TAYLOR

1. On the nature of charismatic authority, see Max Weber, *From Max Weber: Essays in Sociology* (New York: Oxford University Press, 1946), p. 245.

2. Or what Weber called "instrumental" rationality, which is divorced from the rationality of ends. See the discussion of the intimate connection between rationality and the rise of the modern Western world in the introduction to *The Protestant Ethic and the Spirit of Capitalism* (London: Allen and Unwin, 1930), pp. 13–16.

3. Weber (1946), p. 196.

4. According to Weber, "The authority to give the commands . . . is distributed in a stable way and is strictly delimited by rules concerning the coercive means, physical, sacerdotal, or otherwise, which may be placed at the disposal of officials." Weber (1946), p. 196.

5. On the pervasiveness of the bureaucratic form in modern life, see Charles Lindblom, *Politics and Markets: The World's Political-Economic Systems* (New York: Basic Books, 1977), pp. 27–28.

6. Max Weber, *Economy and Society: An Outline of Interpretive Sociology* (Berkeley: University of California Press, 1978), 2: 668–681.

7. Weber (1978), p. 669.

8. The family might serve as another example of a group that works better because trust has not been displaced by law and contract. In most modern societies, the state does not closely regulate the relationships between parents and their children. That is, it does not lay down detailed guidelines as to the quantity and quality of time that parents should devote to their children's upbringing, how they should educate them, and what values they should teach. While family disputes are submitted to the courts if they involve breach of the marriage contract or criminal offenses, in other areas families are left to settle their own disputes. This happens because it is assumed that parents have a natural sense of responsibility to their children. Things could, of course, be otherwise; already in the United States there is talk of "children's rights," civil suits involving parents and children, and other attempts to extend the legal system into family relations.

9. On this point, see Alan Fox, *Beyond Contract: Work, Power and Trust Relationships* (London: Faber and Faber, 1974), pp. 30–31.

10. On this shift in paradigms, see Maria Hirszowicz, *Industrial Sociology: An Introduction* (New York: St. Martin's Press, 1982), pp. 28–32.

11. Charles Sabel, *Work and Politics* (Cambridge: Cambridge University Press, 1981), pp. 31–33.

12. Joan Campbell, *Joy in Work, German Work: The National Debate, 1800–1945* (Princeton: Princeton University Press, 1989), pp. 131–132; Hans-Joachim Braun, *The German Economy in the Twentieth Century* (London: Routledge, 1990), p. 50.

13. Frederick Winslow Taylor, *The Principles of Scientific Management* (New York: Harper Brothers, 1911). Taylor gave his first lecture on scientific management in 1895. See Alfred D. Chandler, *The Visible Hand: The Managerial Revolution in American Business* (Cambridge: Harvard University Press, 1977), p. 275.

14. For an overview of Taylor and his later critics, see Hirszowicz (1982), p. 53.

15. Fox (1974), p. 23.

16. For a description of labor-management relations in the wake of the spread of mass production, see William Lazonick, *Competitive Advantage on the Shop Floor* (Cambridge: Harvard University Press, 1990), pp. 270–280.

17. Alvin W. Gouldner, "The Norm of Reciprocity: A Preliminary Statement," *American Sociological Review* 25 (1960): 161–278; see also Fox (1974), p. 67.

18. Harry C. Katz, *Shifting Gears: Changing Labor Relations in the U.S. Automobile Industry* (Cambridge: MIT Press, 1985), p. 13.

19. Katz (1985), pp. 38–39.

20. Katz (1985), pp. 39–40, 44.

21. This is the view taken in Clark Kerr, John Dunlop, Charles Myers, and F. H. Harbison, *Industrialism and Industrial Man: The Problems of Labor and Management in Economic Growth* (Cambridge: Harvard University Press, 1960); see also Dunlop et al., *Industrialism Reconsidered: Some Perspectives on a Study over Two Decades of the Problems of Labor* (Princeton, N.J.: Inter-University Study of Human Resources, 1975); and Clark Kerr, *The Future of Industrial Societies: Convergence or Diversity?* (Cambridge: Cambridge University Press, 1983).

22. Adam Smith's description of the progressive division of labor in the pin factory into tasks of smaller and simpler scope at the beginning of *The Wealth of Nations* is actually the locus classicus for this line of criticism of modern industrial society. See *An Enquiry in the Nature and Causes of the Wealth of Nations* (Indianapolis: Liberty Classics, 1981), pp. 14–15.

23. On the Judeo-Christian tradition, see the chapter by Jaroslav Pelikan in Jaroslav J. Pelikan et al., *Comparative Work Ethics: Christian, Buddhist, Islamic* (Washington, D.C.: Library of Congress, 1985). See also Michael Novak, "Camels and Needles, Talents and Treasure: American Catholicism and the Capitalist Ethic," in Peter L. Berger, *The Capitalist Spirit: Toward a Religious Ethic of Wealth Creation* (San Francisco: Institute for Contemporary Studies, 1990).

24. Robert Blauner argues that there is an inverted U-curve of alienation from work. Alienation increases as traditional craft industries are replaced by mass produc-

tion factories but then decreases again as automation increases and workers require new skills to operate these highly complicated machines. Robert Blauner, *Alienation and Freedom* (Chicago: University of Chicago Press, 1973).

25. Sabel (1981), pp. 64–67.
26. See, for example, the findings of Robert Blauner in "Work Satisfaction and Industrial Trends," in Walter Galenson and Seymour Martin Lipset, eds., *Labor and Trade Unionism* (New York: Wiley, 1960). One study that surveyed the views of workers in four countries found that skilled workers were concerned with having jobs that were intrinsically interesting or fulfilling, while unskilled workers were more interested in income. Many new entrants and low-skill workers, moreover, believed that having a factory job in the first place conferred significant social status. William H. Form, "Auto Workers and Their Machines: A Study of Work, Factory, and Job Satisfaction in Four Countries," *Social Forces* 52 (1973): 1–15.
27. On the Hawthorne experiments, see Hirszowicz (1982), pp. 52–54.
28. See Elton Mayo, *The Human Problems of an Industrial Civilization* (New York: Macmillan, 1933), and *The Social Problems of an Industrialized Civilization* (London: Routledge and Kegan Paul, 1962).
29. Ian Jamieson, "Some Observations on Socio-Cultural Explanations of Economic Behaviour," *Sociological Review* 26 (1978): 777–805. For a summary of studies on the culture-bound nature of American management practices, see A. R. Negandhi and B. D. Estafen, "A Research Model to Determine the Applicability of American Management Know-How in Differing Cultures and/or Environments," *Academy of Management Journal* 8 (1965): 309–318.

CHAPTER 20. TRUST IN TEAMS

1. Joan Campbell, *Joy in Work, German Work: The National Debate, 1800–1945* (Princeton: Princeton University Press, 1989), p. 133.
2. Campbell (1989), pp. 137–141.
3. The councils were regarded suspiciously by management, which wanted to preserve its prerogatives, by the socialist parties and trade unions, which sought transformation of the capitalist system itself, and even by the Christian trade unions. The only workers' associations to give the concept unqualified support in this period were those connected with the antidemocratic *Wirtschaftsfriedliche* movement. Campbell (1989), p. 163.
4. Marc Maurice, François Sellier, and Jean-Jacques Silvestre, *The Social Foundations of Industrial Power: A Comparison of France and Germany* (Cambridge: MIT Press, 1986), pp. 68–69, 72–73.
5. Maurice, Sellier, and Silvestre (1986), pp. 74, 128–129.
6. Maurice, Sellier, and Silvestre (1986), p. 173.
7. Maurice, Sellier, and Silvestre (1986), p. 111.
8. Arndt Sorge and Malcolm Warner, *Comparative Factory Organization: An Anglo-German Comparison on Manufacturing, Management, and Manpower* (Aldershot: Gower, 1986), p. 100.

9. Sorge and Warner (1986), p. 150. As noted in the previous chapter, a skilled machinist who can also program usually gets better productivity out of his NC equipment.

10. Maurice, Sellier, and Silvestre (1986), pp. 12–13.

11. Maurice, Sellier, and Silvestre (1986), pp. 51–52.

12. Maurice, Sellier, and Silvestre (1986), p. 132.

13. Maurice, Sellier, and Silvestre (1986), pp. 14–16.

14. For an overview, see Bernard Casey, "The Dual Apprenticeship System and the Recruitment and Retention of Young Persons in West Germany," *British Journal of Industrial Relations* 24 (1986): 63–81.

15. Bernard Casey, *Recent Developments in West Germany's Apprenticeship Training System* (London: Policy Studies Institute, 1991), p. vii.

16. See "German View: 'You Americans Work Too Hard—and for What?" *Wall Street Journal,* July 14, 1994, pp. B1, B6.

17. Casey (1991), p. 67. Other studies show that fifty-five percent of graduates leave their company after one year, rising to eighty percent after five years. Maurice, Sellier, and Silvestre (1986), p. 44.

18. For an attempt to reconcile the apprenticeship system with Gary Becker's human capital model, see David Soskice, *Reconciling Markets and Institutions: The German Apprenticeship System,* (Wissenschaftszentrum Berlin and Oxford University, Institute of Economics and Statistics, 1992).

19. Soskice (1992), pp. 13–14. In addition, Soskice notes that the long-term outlook fostered by German bank financing tends to support the apprenticeship system, since employers can afford to take a longer-term perspective on their labor-market investments.

20. According to Soskice (1992, p. 17), "We note the low *distrust transactions costs* to companies arising from the advice and monitoring activities of in-company training by unions and works councils. These activities complement those of business associations, particularly in medium and large companies. They are necessary to provide a guarantee to apprentices on the quality and marketability of the training. The low distrust is a consequence of the generally close and high trust relations between company management and the works council, and the fact that most of the monitoring activities are carried out by the works council rather than by the union."

21. In the manual trades (unskilled workers and agricultural workers), only five percent enter *Gymnasia* and less than two percent complete it. Maurice, Sellier, and Silvestre (1986), pp. 30–31.

22. Maurice, Sellier, and Silvestre (1986), pp. 31–32.

23. Maurice, Sellier, and Silvestre (1987), p. 39.

24. Casey (1991), pp. 6–9.

25. Alternatively, it could be argued that no standardized training system is necessary at all: there is no system of certification for obtaining employment in the dynamic American computer industry, and many feel it would be worse off if there were. Some of the industry's most innovative entrepreneurs, like Mi-

crosoft's Bill Gates and Sun Microsystems' Scott McNeely, had little or no formal training in their business whatsoever.

26. Charles Sabel, *Work and Politics* (Cambridge: Cambridge University Press, 1981), p. 23.

CHAPTER 21. INSIDERS AND OUTSIDERS

1. E. E. Rich and C. H. Wilson, eds., *The Economic Organization of Early Modern Europe,* The Cambridge Economic History of Europe, vol. 5 (Cambridge: Cambridge University Press, 1977), p. 466; C. Gross, *The Guild Merchant* (Oxford: Clarendon Press, 1890).

2. The guilds, for example, were responsible for developing trademarks, seals, and the like as types of early brand names. A. B. Hibbert, "The Gilds," in M. M. Postan, E. E. Rich, and Edward Miller, eds., *Cambridge Economic History of Europe,* (Cambridge: Cambridge University Press, 1963), 3: 230–280.

3. See Charles Hickson and Earl E. Thompson, "A New Theory of Guilds and European Economic Development," *Explorations in Economic History* 28 (1991): 127–168; for representative complaints against the guilds, see Johannes Hanssen, *History of the German People After the Close of the Middle Ages* (New York: AMS Press, 1909), p. 108.

4. Arndt Sorge and Malcolm Warner, *Comparative Factory Organization: An Anglo-German Comparison on Manufacturing, Management, and Manpower* (Aldershot: Gower, 1986), p. 184.

5. Alan S. Milward and S. B. Saul, *The Development of the Economies of Continental Europe, 1780–1870* (London: George Allen and Unwin, 1977), p. 414.

6. Milward and Saul (1977), p. 415; see also Sorge and Warner (1986), p. 184.

7. Peter Rütger Wossidlo, "Trade and Craft," in E. Grochla and E. Gaugler, eds., *Handbook of German Business Management,* (Stuttgart: C. E. Poeschel Verlag, 1990), 2: 2368–2376.

8. Sorge and Warner (1986), p. 185.

9. Wossidlo in Grochla and Gaugler, eds. (1990).

10. Sorge and Warner (1986), p. 185.

11. Sorge and Warner (1986), p. 187.

12. For two classic analyses of this problem, see Fritz Stern, *The Politics of Cultural Despair: A Study in the Rise of German Ideology* (Berkeley: University of California Press, 1974); and Ralf Dahrendorf, *Society and Democracy in Germany* (Garden City, N.Y.: Doubleday, 1969).

13. It is hard to date the major milestones in American public and higher education because these were done on a state-by-state basis. Compulsory public education was introduced in Massachusetts in 1852 and was adopted by virtually all states by World War I. In Britain, by contrast, universal public education was not introduced until 1880 and was not made free until 1891.

14. On contrasts in U.S. and British work attitudes, see Richard Scott, "British Immigrants and the American Work Ethic," *Labor History* 26 (1985): 87–102.

15. Martin J. Wiener, *English Culture and the Decline of the Industrial Spirit* (Cambridge: Cambridge University Press, 1981), pp. 13–14.

16. Wiener (1981), pp. 146–147.

17. Quoted in Wiener (1981), p. 136.

18. Alfred Chandler links the British failure to exploit entrepreneurial opportunities in key industries of the second industrial revolution (e.g., chemicals, metalworking, electrical equipment) to the family-oriented nature of British business. See *Scale and Scope: The Dynamics of Industrial Capitalism* (Cambridge: Belknap Press of Harvard University Press, 1990), pp. 286–287.

19. There continues to be controversy over exactly how much German culture has in fact changed since the war. Suspicions about the dark side of German communitarianism—the closed and intolerant character of German society—still abound and have been stoked by skinhead violence since the fall of communism. Skeptics will argue that while postwar Germany has had liberal asylum laws, it remains extremely difficult to become a German citizen. Turks living in Germany for generations would never be considered real Germans, and there is no German equivalent of Léopold Senghor, the Senegalese-born poet who was admitted to the Académie française. There is also a fanatic character to left-wing German politics, evident among Greens who argue that Germany needs to be deindustrialized, or supporters of the Palestinians who readily compare the Israelis to the Nazis. This suggests that something of the hardness of the Germans' old Protestant culture has not yet disappeared.

20. Until the apology for the war given by reformist prime minister Masuhiro Hosokawa in 1993, no Japanese prime minister had apologized formally for Japan's role in the war, and it is safe to say that no Japanese politician has yet made Willy Brandt's gesture of falling to his hands and knees in contrition for the Holocaust. Although there are revisionists in Germany who deny the Holocaust ever happened, they are regarded as part of a crackpot fringe; in Japan, by contrast, respectable politicians like Shintaro Ishihara and academics like Soiichi Watanabe can still deny that the Nanking Massacre was an atrocity.

21. Ian Buruma, *The Wages of Guilt: Memories of War in Germany and Japan* (New York: Farrar Straus Giroux, 1994), p. 31.

22. This is based on average annual hours of 1,604 for Germany and 2,197 for Japan. Data taken from David Finegold, K. Brendley, R. Lempert et. al., *The Decline of the U.S. Machine-Tool Industry and Prospects for its Sustainable Recovery* (Santa Monica, Ca.: RAND Corporation MR-479/1-OSTP, 1994), p. 23.

CHAPTER 22. THE HIGH-TRUST WORKPLACE

1. Allan Nevins, with Frank E. Hill, *Ford: The Times, the Man, the Company* (New York: Scribner's, 1954), p. 517.

2. Nevins (1954), p. 553.

3. James P. Womack, Daniel T. Jones, and Daniel Roos, *The Machine That Changed the World: The Story of Lean Production* (New York: HarperPerennial, 1991), p. 31.

4. David A. Hounshell, *From the American System to Mass Production, 1800–1932* (Baltimore: Johns Hopkins University Press, 1984), pp. 258–259.

5. Nevins (1954), p. 558.

6. Nevins (1954), pp. 561–562. This system is also described in Allan Nevins and Frank E. Hill, *Ford: Expansion and Challenge, 1915–1933* (New York: Scribner's, 1954).

7. Allan Nevins and Frank E. Hill, *Ford: Decline and Rebirth, 1933–1962* (New York: Scribner's, 1962), pp. 32–33.

8. On this period, see William Lazonick, *Competitive Advantage on the Shop Floor* (Cambridge: Harvard University Press, 1990), pp. 240–251.

9. For a summary of that program's findings, see Womack, Jones, and Roos, (1991).

10. That is, less of a company's capital is tied up financing inventories, while the remaining capital is more productive. For a description of this system from the perspective of a chief financial officer, see Shawn Tully, "Raiding a Company's Hidden Cash," *Fortune,* August 22, 1994, pp. 82–89.

11. The authors of the MIT study also describe lean marketing as practiced in Japan, which unlike the manufacturing process appears to be significantly less efficient than American practices.

12. On this point, see Lazonick (1990), pp. 288–290.

13. Womack, Jones, and Roos (1991), pp. 52–53.

14. Womack, Jones, and Roos (1991), p. 99.

15. Womack, Jones, and Roos (1991), p. 129.

16. Harry Katz, *Shifting Gears: Changing Labor Relations in the U.S. Automobile Industry* (Cambridge: MIT Press, 1985), p. 89.

17. Katz (1985), p. 175.

18. Womack, Jones, and Roos (1991), p. 83.

19. Womack, Jones, and Roos (1991), pp. 99–100.

20. Indeed, one of the reforms that Mazda's *keiretsu* backers insisted on during its reorganization in the early 1970s was that it adopt the Toyota lean production system. It did, and saw its productivity climb substantially.

21. Womack, Jones, and Roos (1991), pp. 84–88.

22. The European data are not disaggregated by country; we would expect large differences in the success of implementation of lean production among different countries in Europe.

23. It is also possible that there could be increasing resistance to lean production in certain countries as the method proliferates across the manufacturing sector. Those companies that are the first to implement the method, particularly if they are foreign transplants, often have the option of siting their facilities optimally in terms of areas without a history of union militancy, or where unemployment makes workers particularly docile. Hence the good early reception of the technique; as it spreads to older industrial districts, however, it may encounter significantly stronger cultural resistance.

24. Womack, Jones, and Roos (1991), pp. 261–263.

25. Womack, Jones, and Roos (1991), pp. 144–146.

CHAPTER 23. EAGLES DON'T FLOCK—OR DO THEY?

1. Alexis de Tocqueville, *Democracy in America* (New York: Vintage Books, 1945), 2: 104.
2. Tocqueville argued that there were also two other factors that moderated individualism in the United States: the existence of free political institutions, which allowed citizens to participate in public affairs, and the principle of "self-interest rightly understood," which caused people to calculate that cooperation with their fellows was in their own enlightened self-interest.
3. Tocqueville (1945), pp. 114–118.
4. See the discussions of Tocqueville's arguments in *The Old Regime and the French Revolution* in chapter 15.
5. Alfred D. Chandler, Jr., *The Visible Hand: The Managerial Revolution in American Business* (Cambridge: Belknap Press of Harvard University Press, 1977), p. 51.
6. Chandler (1977), pp. 43, 58, 72. There were also a small number of plantations with as many as a thousand slaves.
7. See particularly Robert W. Fogel, *Railroads and Economic Growth* (Baltimore: Johns Hopkins University Press, 1964).
8. Chandler (1977), pp. 79, 188.
9. The total number of men under arms at that time was 39,492. Chandler (1977), pp. 204–205.
10. Chandler (1977), p. 205; Alan S. Milward and S. B. Saul, *The Development of the Economies of Continental Europe, 1780–1870* (London: George Allen and Unwin, 1977), pp. 378–380.
11. F. M. Scherer and David Ross, *Industrial Market Structure and Economic Performance,* 3d ed. (Boston: Houghton Mifflin, 1990), p. 155.
12. Chandler (1977), p. 210.
13. William H. Whyte, *The Organization Man* (New York: Simon & Schuster, 1956); David Riesman, with Reuel Denny and Nathan Glazer, *The Lonely Crowd: A Study of the Changing American Character* (New Haven: Yale University Press, 1950).
14. See Stewart Macaulay, "Non-Contractual Relations in Business: A Preliminary Study," *American Sociological Review* 28 (1963): 55–69.
15. Seymour Martin Lipset, *Continental Divide: The Values and Institutions of the United States and Canada* (New York: Routledge, 1990), pp. 3–10.
16. Lipset (1990), p. 46–56.

CHAPTER 24. RUGGED CONFORMISTS

1. A number of other factors have been cited as causes for the American proclivity for association, such as the frontier, which forced early settlers to rely on each other. Clearly, the nature of American federalism promotes local self-government as well.
2. For a discussion, see Leo Strauss, *The Political Philosophy of Thomas Hobbes: Its*

Basis and Genesis (Chicago: University of Chicago Press, 1952); see also my discussion of this issue in *The End of History and the Last Man* (New York: Free Press, 1992), pp. 153–161.

3. Aristotle, *Politics* I i.11–12.
4. On this point, see Mary Ann Glendon, *Rights Talk: The Impoverishment of Political Discourse* (New York: Free Press, 1991), pp. 67–69.
5. John Locke, *The Second Treatise of Government* (Indianapolis: Bobbs-Merrill, 1952), pp. 30–44.
6. On this general topic, see Louis Dumont, "A Modified View of Our Origins: The Christian Beginnings of Modern Individualism," *Religion* 12 (1982): 1–27; also Robert N. Bellah et al., "Responses to Louis Dumont's 'A Modified View of Our Origins'" *Religion* 12 (1982): 83–91.
7. This was particularly true at the height of the Buddhist cultural invasion of China in the sixth century. See W. J. F. Jenner, *The Tyranny of History: The Roots of China's Crisis* (London: Allen Lane/Penguin, 1992), pp. 113–114.
8. See Joseph M. Kitagawa, *Religion in Japanese History* (New York: Columbia University Press, 1966), pp. 100–130.
9. See, inter alia, Seymour Martin Lipset and Jeff Hayes, "Individualism: A Double-Edged Sword," *Responsive Community* 4 (1993–1994): 69–81.
10. David Martin, *Tongues of Fire: The Explosion of Protestantism in Latin America* (Oxford: Basil Blackwell, 1990), p. 14.
11. This is the familiar thesis in Roger Finke and Rodney Stark, "How the Upstart Sects Won America: 1776–1850," *Journal for the Scientific Study of Religion* 28 (1989): 27–44.
12. Martin (1990), p. 20.
13. Seymour Martin Lipset, "Religion and Politics in America, Past and Present," in *Revolution and Counterrevolution* (New York: Basic Books, 1968), pp. 309–312.
14. Lipset (1968), p. 314.
15. Thomas F. O'Dea, *The Mormons* (Chicago: University of Chicago Press, 1957), pp. 143, 150. According to the Mormon historian Leonard J. Arrington, 88 of Joseph Smith's 112 revelations dealt with economic matters. Strictly speaking, there are many aspects of Mormon doctrine eschewing wealth and promoting economic equality—as in the case of Weber's early Puritans.
16. The average number of children among Mormons is 4.61, or twice the US national average. The rate of illegitimate teenage births in Utah is less than one-third the national average: 48 per 1,000 live births, compared to 155. Darwin L. Thomas, "Family in the Mormon Experience," in William V. Antonio and Joan Aldous, eds., *Families and Religions: Conflict and Change in Modern Society* (Beverly Hills, Calif.: Sage Publications, 1983), p. 276; and H. M. Bahr, ed., *Utah in Demographic Perspective: Regional and National Contrasts* (Provo, Utah: Family and Demographic Research Institute, Brigham Young University, 1981), p. 72.
17. In practice, only half of young Mormon men, and a smaller percentage of women, go on mission.
18. Quoted in "Mormon Conquest," *Forbes,* December 7, 1992, p. 78.
19. "Building on Financial Success," *Arizona Republic* July 13, 1991.

20. Malise Ruthven, "The Mormon's Progress," *Wilson Quarterly* 15 (1991): 23–47.
21. Bryce Nelson, "The Mormon Way," *Geo* 4 (May 1982): 79–80.
22. Albert L. Fisher, "Mormon Welfare Programs: Past and Present," *Social Science Journal* 15 (1978): 75–99. The fast offering, which ultimately proved unworkable, required church members to donate the whole of their incomes to the church, which would return a portion of it as it saw fit. This still remains something of an ideal in the Mormon community.
23. Tucker Carlson, "Holy Dolers: The Secular Lessons of Mormon Charity," *Policy Review*, no. 59 (Winter 1992): 25–31.
24. Ruthven (1991), pp. 36–37.
25. The fact that Mormons have been highly entrepreneurial does not necessarily mean that they always do well. WordPerfect was sold by its private owners to Novell in part because they had been unable to implement a modern financial system. Noorda, for his part, was initially unable to get any banks in Salt Lake City to loan him money, when he first tried to turn Novell around, because of the Mormon practice of avoiding debt. "Mormon Conquest," p. 80.
26. Gary Poole, "'Never Play Poker with This Man,'" *UnixWorld* 10 (August 1993): 46–54.
27. On the turndown in the 1980s, see Greg Critser, "On the Road: Salt Lake City, Utah," *Inc.* (January 1986): 23–24; on newer technological development, see Sally B. Donnelly, "Mixing Business with Faith," *Time,* July 29, 1991, pp. 22–24.
28. This practice has changed considerably in recent years, as Mormon missions in the Third World have increased.
29. The Mormons expect that by the year 2000, there will be more Spanish- than English-speaking Mormons; among the large non-European Mormon communities are ones in Polynesia, the Philippines, and Africa. Mormons in Utah constitute only one million out of the nine million worldwide.
30. According to one author, "Personal mobility—social or geographic—is supported in sectarian groups that offer the kind of social interaction and personal formation usually experienced in the family, along with a demand for conversion that burns bridges between former periods of one's life and the new loyalties. While authority and social cohesion are high in the sects, their final impact is to reinforce individualism over group loyalty." Barbara Hargrove, "The Church, the Family, and the Modernization Process," in Antonio and Aldous, eds. (1983), p. 25.

Chapter 25. Blacks and Asians in America

1. It has been noted by a number of authors that Ireland was the only European country that did not create a great university during the Middle Ages. See Nathan Glazer and Daniel Patrick Moynihan, *Beyond the Melting Pot: The Negroes, Puerto Ricans, Jews, Italians, and Irish of New York City,* 2d ed. (Cambridge: MIT Press, 1970), p. 232.
2. Glazer and Moynihan (1970), p. 197.
3. The rate of immigrant self-employment in the United States is 7.2 percent,

compared to 7.0 percent for the native born; of immigrants in the country since 1980, the rate is 8.4 percent. Michael Fix and Jeffrey S. Passel, *Immigration and Immigrants: Setting the Record Straight* (Washington, D.C.: Urban Institute, 1994), p. 53.

4. These individuals include employees of ethnic businesses and not simply proprietors. Ivan H. Light, *Ethnic Enterprise in America: Business and Welfare Among Chinese, Japanese, and Blacks* (Berkeley: University of California Press, 1972), pp. 7, 10.

5. Pyong Gap Min and Charles Jaret, "Ethnic Business Success: The Case of Korean Small Business in Atlanta," *Sociology and Social Research* 69 (1985): 412–435.

6. Eui-hang Shin and Shin-kap Han, "Korean Immigrant Small Business in Chicago: An Analysis of the Resource Mobilization Processes," *Amerasia* 16 (1990): 39–60. For similar data see Ivan Light and Edna Bonacich, *Immigrant Entrepreneurs: Koreans in Los Angeles, 1965–1982* (Berkeley: University of California Press, 1988), p. 1.

7. Light (1972), p. 3.

8. See, for example, Robert H. Kinzer and Edward Sagarin, *The Negro in American Business* (New York: Greenberg, 1950); E. Franklin Frazier, *Black Bourgeoisie* (New York: Collier Books, 1962); James Q. Wilson, *Negro Politics: The Search for Leadership* (Glencoe, Ill.: Free Press, 1960); Glazer and Moynihan (1970), pp. 24–44.

9. On black-Asian tensions, see Light and Bonacich (1988), pp. 318–320.

10. On this controversy, see Nathan Glazer, "Blacks and Ethnic Groups: The Difference, and the Political Difference It Makes," *Social Problems* 18 (1971): 444–461.

11. Kinzer and Sagarin (1950), pp. 144–145.

12. John Sibley Butler, *Entrepreneurship and Self-Help Among Black Americans: A Reconsideration of Race and Economics* (Albany, N.Y.: State University of New York, 1991), p. 147.

13. Butler (1991) seeks to refute arguments about the weak tradition of African-American entrepreneurship by contesting its empirical basis; there has consistently been a strong and underestimated entrepreneurial tradition within the black community, which he seeks to document. However, while it is true that this tradition has received less attention than it deserves, the individual cases he cites of successful black entrepreneurship remain anecdotal and do not explain away the broader statistical data indicating the weakness of the black business class relative to other groups.

14. For a broad-based critique of "environmental" explanations. see Thomas Sowell, *Race and Culture* (New York: Basic Books, 1994).

15. For examples of such theories, see Werner Sombart, *The Quintessence of Capitalism* (New York: Dutton, 1915), pp. 302–303; Everett E. Hagen, *On the Theory of Social Change: How Economic Growth Begins* (Homewood, Ill.: Dorsey Press, 1962); Edna Bonacich, "A Theory of Middleman Minorities," *American Sociological Review* 38 (1972): 583–594; and Jonathan H. Turner and Edna

Bonacich, "Toward a Composite Theory of Middleman Minorities," *Ethnicity* 7 (1980): 144–158.

16. Light (1972), p. 7.

17. Kenneth L. Wilson and Alejandro Portes, "Immigrant Enclaves: An Analysis of the Labor Market Experiences of Cubans in Miami," *American Journal of Sociology* 86 (1980): 295–319; and Kenneth L. Wilson and W. A. Martin, "Ethnic Enclaves: A Comparison of the Cuban and Black Economies in Miami," *American Journal of Sociology* 88 (1982): 138–159.

18. Light (1972), pp. 15–18.

19. Light (1972), p. 19.

20. Light (1972), pp. 55–57.

21. On rotating credit associations, see Light (1972), pp. 19–44; also see William Peterson, "Chinese Americans and Japanese Americans," in Thomas Sowell, *Essays and Data on American Ethnic Groups* (Washington, D.C.: Urban Institute, 1978), pp. 80–81.

22. Light (1972), pp. 27–30.

23. Victor Nee and Herbert Y. Wong, "Asian-American Socioeconomic Achievement: The Strength of the Family Bond," *Sociological Perspectives* 28 (1985): 281–306.

24. Peterson in Sowell (1978), p. 79.

25. The Chinese and Japanese consumed a much lower level of relief funds during the Great Depression than either blacks or whites did. A federal welfare agency trying to help Japanese families affected by the wartime relocation found, even under these circumstances, very few takers. Peterson in Sowell (1978), pp. 79–80.

26. Peterson in Sowell (1978), p. 93.

27. Thomas Sowell, "Three Black Histories," *Wilson Quarterly* (Winter 1979): 96–106.

28. Light (1972), pp. 30–44.

29. See Butler (1992), pp. 124–126, and Light (1972), pp. 47–58.

30. For an early account of civil associations in the African-American community, see James Q. Wilson, *Negro Politics: The Search for Leadership* (New York: Free Press, 1960), pp. 295–315.

31. See the reference to the work of Carol Stack in Andrew J. Cherlin, *Marriage, Divorce, Remarriage* (Cambridge: Harvard University Press, 1981), p. 108. In contrast to a rotating credit association, these groups sometimes function more as rotating consumption associations because the money is used not for productive investment in a business but to meet day-to-day consumption needs (which, for poor people, are obviously pressing). The moral generosity implicit in such organizations can have the perverse effect of deconcentrating savings and making more difficult the kind of simple capital accumulation needed to establish small businesses.

32. The question of why black-organized criminal gangs could not be turned to productive purposes is investigated in the books reviewed by Nathan Glazer in "The Street Gangs and Ethnic Enterprise," *Public Interest*, no. 28 (1972):

82–89. Part of the answer may be that these gangs are not very effective even as criminal organizations; unlike the Chinese *tongs,* or Italian *mafia,* and other ethnic criminal groups, they do not encourage a strong sense of criminal honor and are themselves riven with internal distrust. The books recounted by Glazer give pathetic examples of efforts at black underclass attempts at self-organization.

33. Kessler-Harris and Virginia Yans-McLaughlin in Sowell (1978), pp. 122–123.

34. Thomas Sowell, *Ethnic America: A History* (New York: Basic Books, 1981), pp. 35–36.

35. Glazer and Moynihan (1970), pp. 192–194; also Kessler-Harris and Yans-McLaughlin in Sowell (1978), p. 121.

CHAPTER 26. THE VANISHING MIDDLE

1. For one small example, taken from enterprise networking, see "High-Tech Edge Gives US Firms Global Lead in Computer Networks," *Wall Street Journal,* September 9, 1994, pp. A1, A10.

2. See Dennis Encarnation, *Rivals Beyond Trade: America Versus Japan in Global Competition* (Ithaca, N.Y.: Cornell University Press, 1992), pp. 190–197; also DeAnne Julius, *Global Companies and Public Policy: The Growing Challenge of Foreign Direct Investment* (London: Royal Institute of International Affairs, 1990).

3. See Jagdish Bhagwati and Milind Rao, "Foreign Students Spur US Brain Gain," *Wall Street Journal,* August 31, 1994, p. A12.

4. Robert D. Putnam, "Bowling Alone," *Journal of Democracy* 6 (1995): 65–78.

5. Putnam (1995), pp. 69–70.

6. The AARP, whose membership stood at 33 million in 1993, is the world's largest private organization after the Catholic church. Putnam (1995), p. 71.

7. Putnam (1995), p. 73.

8. The tapering off of growth and, in some cases, decline in violent crime in some urban areas in the late 1980s and early 1990s was viewed by certain observers as evidence that the problem is not as serious as the American public thinks. These trends do little, however, to affect the overall magnitude of the level of crime in the United States when compared with other developed countries.

9. For an account of the reaction, see *New York Times,* May 28, 1993, p. B7.

10. This critique is more prevalent on the left, where many would point to the specific policies of the Reagan and Bush years as exacerbating this problem. For an example of this line of argument, see Barry Schwartz, *The Costs of Living: How Market Freedom Erodes the Best Things of Life* (New York: Norton, 1994).

11. In the mid-nineteenth century, a great majority of Americans still lived on farms; by the end of the century, a majority had moved to cities and were in some way involved in the industrial economy. The country's overall level of education, its ethnic and religious mix, even styles of dress, had changed dramatically. Despite a universally shared impression that the rate of change has steadily accelerated in the twentieth century, the shifts that have taken place a hundred years later are arguably much less dramatic.

12. Mary Ann Glendon, *Rights Talk: The Impoverishment of Political Discourse* (New York: Free Press, 1991).
13. Glendon (1991), p. 13.
14. Glendon (1991), pp. 76–89.
15. Glendon (1991), pp. 48–61.
16. A similar point is made by Putnam (1995), p. 75.
17. Outside the United States, a case in point is Latin America. From all of the available empirical data, however, it would appear that the North American Protestant fundamentalists are creating the social basis for the missing democratic-capitalist center, much as Max Weber argued they did in Europe during the sixteenth and seventeenth centuries. While the policies of leftist governments can and have been reversed overnight, the slow, massive conversion of Latin America to Protestantism promises to bring about long-term social changes much more profound than any that can be achieved through political revolution.
18. William H. McNeill, "Fundamentalism and the World of the 1990s," in Martin E. Marty and R. Scott Appleby, eds., *Fundamentalisms and Society: Reclaiming the Sciences, the Family, and Education* (Chicago: University of Chicago Press, 1993), p. 568.
19. For some purposes, it obviously is; to wit, war.

CHAPTER 27. LATE DEVELOPERS

1. For the first two-thirds of the twentieth century, there was an almost unanimous consensus among Sinologists and other students of East Asia that Chinese Confucianism was an enormous obstacle to capitalism and to economic modernization. Perhaps the most famous book arguing this point was Max Weber's work on China, originally written in 1919 and published in English as *The Religion of China: Confucianism and Taoism.* Weber asserted that although Confucianism was a "rational" ethical system like Protestantism, its rationality resulted not in "the truly endless task ethically and rationally subduing and mastering the given world," as Protestantism did, but in "adjustment to the world," that is, the preservation of tradition. A Confucian society, in other words, could not innovate or adapt sufficiently to bring about the enormous social changes required by capitalist industrialization.

The general assessment of the economic impact of Confucianism had changed dramatically by the 1990s. It was perhaps natural for Weber, writing at the beginning of a period of decay and warlordism in Chinese history, to have been pessimistic about that country's economic prospects. But more than seventy years later the People's Republic of China had the world's fastest growing economy, and virtually all culturally Chinese societies outside the PRC had experienced two generations of extremely rapid economic growth. Today the conventional wisdom is that Confucianism is somehow at the root of the East Asian "economic miracle," and an enormous body of literature details the "Confucian challenge" to the West. Contemporary observers, looking at different aspects of

Confucianism, such as its emphasis on education or the so-called Confucian work ethic, argue that this system of beliefs has been critical to economic dynamism. Indeed, in many cases commentators have pointed to the Chinese family, which Weber regarded as the central obstacle to economic progress, as a source of Chinese strength.

For discussions of *The Religion of China,* see Mark Elvin, "Why China Failed to Create an Endogenous Industrial Capitalism: A Critique of Max Weber's Explanation," *Theory and Society* 13 (1984): 379–391; and Gary G. Hamilton and Cheng-shu Kao, "Max Weber and the Analysis of East Asian Industrialization," *International Sociology* 2 (1987): 289–300. For some representative discussions of cultural limits to Chinese development, see Joseph Needham, *Science and Civilization in China,* particularly vol. 1: *Introductory Orientations* (Cambridge: Cambridge University Press, 1954); Mark Elvin, *The Pattern of the Chinese Past: A Social and Economic Interpretation* (Stanford: Stanford University Press, 1973); Michael R. Godley, *The Mandarin Capitalists from Nanyang: Overseas Chinese Enterprise in the Modernization of China* (Cambridge: Cambridge University Press, 1981), esp. pp. 37–38; and Marie-Claire Bergère, "On the Historical Origins of Chinese Underdevelopment," *Theory and Society* 13 (1984): 327–337.

2. For examples of the literature on the "Confucian challenge," see Roderick McFarquhar, "The Post-Confucian Challenge," *Economist* (1980): 67–72; Roy Hofheinz, Jr., and Kent E. Calder, *The Eastasia Edge* (New York: Basic Books, 1982); Peter L. Berger and Hsin-huang Michael Hsiao, *In Search of an East Asian Development Model* (New Brunswick, N.J.: Transaction Books, 1988); Michael H. Bond and Geert Hofstede, "The Cash Value of Confucian Values," *Human Systems Management* 8 (1989): 195–200; Bond and Hofstede, "The Confucius Connection: From Cultural Roots to Economic Growth," *Organizational Dynamics* (1988): 5–21. For a positive assessment of the role of the Chinese family in Chinese business, see Joel Kotkin, *Tribes: How Race, Religion, and Identity Determine Success in the New Global Economy* (New York: Random House, 1993), p. 188.

3. For a skeptical view of the importance of cultural explanations, particularly for the study of Japan, see Winston Davis's chapter in Samuel P. Huntington and Myron Weiner, eds., *Understanding Political Development* (Boston: Little, Brown, 1987).

4. See Richard Caves, "International Differences in Industrial Organization," in Richard Schmalensee and Robert D. Willig, eds., *Handbook of Industrial Organization* (Amsterdam: Elsevier Science Publishers, 1989), p. 1233. I am grateful to Henry Rowen for this reference.

5. Frederick M. Scherer and David Ross, *Industrial Market Structure and Economic Performance,* 3d ed. (Boston: Houghton Mifflin, 1990), p. 102.

6. Scherer and Ross (1990), p. 109.

7. In addition, large corporations tend to enjoy lower capital costs due to perceptions of lower risk on the part of investors. Scherer and Ross (1990), pp. 126–130.

8. These numbers are derived using the employment statistics in table 1 in chapter 14.

9. In highly developed economies like that of the United States, this explanation is complicated by certain anomalies—for example, that American companies in many sectors are actually larger than one would expect based on considerations of optimal scale alone. See table 4.6 in Scherer and Ross (1990), p. 140, which indicates that the average market share of the three largest firms exceeds that dictated by considerations of minimum efficient scale in cigarettes, fabric weaving, paints, shoes, steel, storage batteries, and other products.

   One explanation for this anomaly given by Scherer and Ross is that market structure is determined by sheer historical chance. That is, an industry that starts out with firms of equal size in any given time period can expect to produce firms of widely differing sizes as time goes on from purely chance factors. This explanation would obviously be insufficient to explain why industrial concentration varied so consistently across different societies. See Scherer and Ross (1990), pp. 141–146.

10. Caves in Schmalensee and Willig, eds. (1989), p. 1234, notes that similar industries produce similar levels of industrial concentration in different countries, implying that industrial structures will become more homogeneous as countries move up the technological-developmental ladder. While this is doubtless true, the thrust of the argument in this book has been that different societies will excel in different sectors, dependent not on their level of development but rather on each society's ability to generate large-scale organizations.

11. This point is also made by S. Gordon Redding, *The Spirit of Chinese Capitalism* (Berlin: De Gruyter, 1990), p. 4.

12. "The Pac Rim 150," *Fortune* 122 (Fall 1990): 102–106.

13. The late development hypothesis has been argued by many people, including Alexander Gerschenkron, *Economic Backwardness in Historical Perspective* (Cambridge: Harvard University Press, 1962); Ronald Dore, "Industrial Relations in Japan and Elsewhere" in Albert M. Craig, ed., *Japan: A Comparative View* (Princeton: Princeton University Press, 1979), pp. 325–335; and Chalmers Johnson, *MITI and the Japanese Miracle* (Stanford: Stanford University Press, 1982), p. 19.

14. Japan has a relatively well-developed stock market. The Tokyo Stock Exchange was founded in 1878, briefly closed during World War II, and opened again in 1949 under the American occupation. See *Tokyo Stock Exchange 1994 Fact Book,* (Tokyo: Tokyo Stock Exchange, 1994), p. 89.

15. The Taiwan Stock Exchange, which was founded in 1961, grew very slowly, with only 102 companies listed by 1980. Ching-ing Hou Liang and Michael Skully, "Financial Institutions and Markets in Taiwan" in Michael T. Skully, ed., *Financial Institutions and Markets in the Far East: A Study of China, Hong Kong, Japan, South Korea, and Taiwan* (New York: St. Martin's Press, 1982), pp. 191–192.

16. Sang-woo Nam and Yung-chul Park, "Financial Institutions and Markets in South Korea," in Skully (1982), pp. 160–161.

17. Michael T. Skully, "Financial Institutions and Markets in Hong Kong," in Skully (1982), p. 63.

18. Matthew Montagu-Pollack, "Stocks: Hong Kong, Indonesia, Japan, Malaysia, the

Philippines, Singapore, South Korea, Taiwan, Thailand," *Asian Business* 28 (1992): 56–65. This was, of course, after the Tokyo stock market's crash of 1989–1991, which reduced that market's total valuation by approximately sixty percent.

19. Nam and Park in Skully (1982), p. 160.

20. This is suggested, inter alia, by the fact that the level of cross–shareholding increased substantially in the 1960s only after the Japanese government, bowing to foreign pressure, agreed to liberalize the rules concerning direct foreign investment. The cross–shareholding, in other words, was a defensive mechanism to prevent *foreign* takeover; it was not necessary for the *keiretsu* to maintain their integrity as network organizations and achieve scale economies.

21. See Scherer and Ross (1990), pp. 146–151.

22. Most South Korean banks were denationalized between 1980 and 1983. See Robert Wade, "East Asian Financial Systems as a Challenge to Economics: Lessons from Taiwan," *California Management Review* 27 (1985): 106–127.

23. Wade (1985), p. 121.

CHAPTER 28. RETURNS TO SCALE

1. See Gary Stix and Paul Wallich, "Is Bigger Still Better?" *Scientific American* 271 (March 1994): 109.

2. The production of software is not, however, nearly as systematized as other engineering fields. See W. Wayt Gibbs, "Software's Chronic Crisis," *Scientific American* 271 (September 1994): 86–95.

CHAPTER 29. MANY MIRACLES

1. See also Winston L. King, "A Christian and a Japanese-Buddhist Work-Ethic Compared," *Religion* 11 (1981): 207–226.

2. Japanese commentators alternate between arguing that Japanese culture and institutions are totally unique and unexportable and saying that they could potentially be a model for other parts of Asia. For a hostile Western account of the literature on Japanese uniqueness, or *nihonjinron,* see Peter N. Dale, *The Myth of Japanese Uniqueness* (New York: St. Martin's Press, 1986).

CHAPTER 30. AFTER THE END OF SOCIAL ENGINEERING

1. See Francis Fukuyama, *The End of History and the Last Man* (New York: Free Press, 1992).

2. In addition, virtually all of the central themes of this book concerning the importance of culture to economic behavior were anticipated in my earlier work. See Fukuyama (1992), chaps. 20, 21; and "The End of History?" *National Interest,* no. 16 (Summer 1989): 3–18, where I discuss the Weber hypothesis and the impact of culture.

3. This point is argued in David Gellner, "Max Weber: Capitalism and the Religion of India," *Sociology* 16 (1982): 526–543.

4. Joseph Needham, *Science and Civilization in China* (Cambridge: Cambridge University Press, 1958), vol 1.
5. This point is made in Ernest Gellner, *Plough, Sword, and Book: The Structure of Human History* (Chicago: University of Chicago Press, 1988), pp. 39–69. See also Robert K. Merton, "Science, Religion, and Technology in Seventeenth Century England," *Osiris* 4 (1938): 360–632.
6. This is, in essence, the central problem with politics understood as "rational choice." See Steven Kelman, "'Public Choice' and Public Spirit," *Public Interest,* no. 87 (1987): 80–94.
7. That family life can in fact be understood in these terms is the theme of Gary S. Becker's *A Treatise on the Family* (Cambridge: Harvard University Press, 1981).
8. John J. Mearsheimer, "Back to the Future: Instability in Europe After the Cold War," *International Security* 15 (Summer 1990): 5–56.
9. See Robert Kaplan, "The Anarchy," *Atlantic* 273 (February 1994): 44–81; and Hans Magnus Enzenberger, *Civil Wars: From L.A. to Bosnia* (New York: New Press, 1994).
10. See, for example, Lee's interview with Fareed Zakaria in *Foreign Affairs* 73 (1994): 109–127.

CHAPTER 31. THE SPIRITUALIZATION OF ECONOMIC LIFE

1. The correlation between democracy and development is explored by Seymour Martin Lipset, "Some Social Requisites of Democracy: Economic Development and Political Legitimacy," *American Political Science Review* 53 (1959): 69–105. For a review of the literature on the Lipset hypothesis that largely confirms this point, see Larry Diamond, "Economic Development and Democracy Reconsidered," *American Behavioral Scientist* 15 (March–June 1992): 450–499.
2. For a summary of this argument, see Francis Fukuyama, *The End of History and the Last Man* (New York: Free Press, 1992), pp. xi–xxiii.
3. This is described on pp. 143–180 of Fukuyama (1992).
4. Adam Smith, *The Theory of Moral Sentiments* (Indianapolis: Liberty Classics, 1982), p. 50.
5. Albert O. Hirschman, *The Passions and the Interests: Political Arguments for Capitalism Before Its Triumph* (Princeton: Princeton University Press, 1977).

BIBLIOGRAPHY

Abe, Yoshio, "The Basis of Japanese Culture and Confucianism (2)," *Asian Culture Quarterly* 2 (1974): 21–28.

Abegglen, James C., *The Japanese Factory: Aspects of Its Social Organization* (Glencoe, Ill.: Free Press, 1958).

Abegglen, James C. and Stalk, George Jr., *Kaisha: The Japanese Corporation* (New York: Basic Books, 1985).

Agulhon, Maurice, *Le Cercle dans la France bourgeoise: 1810–1848: étude d'une mutation de sociabilité* (Paris: A. Colin, 1977).

Agulhon, Maurice and Bodiguel, Maryvonne, *Les associations au village* (Le Paradou: Actes Sud, 1981).

Alchian, A. A. and Demsetz, H., "Production, Information Costs, and Economic Organization," *American Economic Review* 62 (1972).

Amsden, Alice H., *Asia's Next Giant: South Korea and Late Industrialization* (New York/Oxford: Oxford University Press, 1989).

Arrow, Kenneth J., "Risk Perception in Psychology and Economics," *Economic Inquiry* (1982): 1–9.

_____,*The Limits of Organization* (New York: W. W. Norton, 1974).

Ashton, T. S., *The Industrial Revolution, 1760–1830* (London: Oxford University Press, 1948).

Asselain, Jean-Charles, *Histoire économique de la France du XVIIIe siècle a nos jours* (Paris: Editions du Seuil, 1984).

Bachnik, Jane M., "Recruitment Strategies for Household Succession: Rethinking Japanese Household Organization," *Man* 18 (1983): 160–182.

Bagnasco, Arnoldo, *Tre Italie: la problematica territoriale dello sviluppo italiano* (Bologna: Il Mulino, 1977)

Bagnasco, Arnoldo, and Pini, R., "Sviluppo economico e trasformazioni sociopolitche dei sistemi territoriali a economia diffus: Economia e struttura sociale," *Quaderni Fondazione Feltrinelli* no 14 (1975).

Bahr, H. M., ed., *Utah in Demographic Perspective: Regional and National Contrasts* (Provo, Utah: Brigham Young University, 1981).

Baker, Hugh, *Chinese Family and Kinship* (New York: Columbia University Press, 1979).

Banfield, Edward C., *The Moral Basis of a Backward Society* (Glencoe, Ill.: Free Press, 1958).

Bauer, Michel and Cohen, Elie, "Le politique, l'administratif, et l'exercice du pouvoir industriel," *Sociologie du Travail* 27 (1985): 324–327.

Bautista, R. M. and Perina, E. M., eds., *Essays in Development Economics in Honor of Harry T. Oshima* (Manila: Philippine Institute for Development Studies, 1982).

Becker, Gary S., *A Treatise on the Family* (Cambridge: Harvard University Press, 1981).

_____, *Human Capital: A Theoretical and Empirical Analysis,* second edition (New York: National Bureau of Economic Research, 1975).

_____, "Nobel Lecture: The Economic Way of Looking at Behavior," *Journal of Political Economy* 101 (1993): 385–409.

_____, *The Economic Approach to Human Behavior* (Chicago: University of Chicago Press, 1976).

Bellah, Robert N., *Religion and Progress in Modern Asia* (Glencoe, Ill.: Free Press, 1965)

_____, "Responses to Louis Dumont's 'A Modified View of Our Origins, The Christian Beginnings of Modern Individualism,'" *Religion* 12 (1982): 83–91.

_____, *Tokugawa Religion* (Boston: Beacon Press, 1957).

Bendix, Reinhard, "The Protestant Ethic—Revisited," *Comparative Studies in Society and History* 9 (1967): 266–273.

Beniger, James R., *The Control Revolution: Technological and Economic Origins of the Information Society* (Cambridge: Harvard University Press, 1986).

Berger, Brigitte, ed., *The Culture of Entrepreneurship* (San Francisco: Institute for Contemporary Studies, 1991).

Berger, Peter L., *The Capitalist Spirit: Toward a Religious Ethic of Wealth Creation* (San Francisco: Institute for Contemporary Studies, 1990).

Berger, Peter L. and Hsiao, Hsin-Huang Michael, *In Search of an East Asian Development Model* (New Brunswick, N.J.: Transaction Books, 1988).

Bergère, Marie-Claire, "On the Historical Origins of Chinese Underdevelopment," *Theory and Society* 13 (1984): 327–337.

Bergeron, Louis, *Les capitalistes en France (1780–1914)* (Paris: Gallimard, 1978).

Berle, Adolph A., *Power without Property: A New Development in American Political Economy* (New York: Harcourt, Brace, 1959).

Berle, Adolph A. and Means, Gardner C., *The Modern Corporation and Private Property* (New York: Macmillan, 1932).

Blauner, Robert, *Alienation and Freedom* (Chicago: University of Chicago Press, 1973).

Blim, Michael L., *Made In Italy: Small-Scale Industrialization and Its Consequences* (New York: Praeger, 1990).

Bocking, Brian, "Neo-Confucian Spirituality and the Samurai Ethic," *Religion* 10 (1980): 1–15.

Bonacich, Edna, "A Theory of Middleman Minorities," *American Sociological Review* 38 (1972): 583–594.

Bond, Michael H. and Hofstede, Geert, "The Cash Value of Confucian Values," *Human Systems Management* 8 (1989): 195–200.

Braun, Hans-Joachim, *The German Economy in the Twentieth Century* (London and New York: Routledge, 1990).

Brown, Donna, "Race for the Corporate Throne," *Management Review* 78 (1989): 22–29.

Buruma, Ian, *The Wages of Guilt: Memories of War in Germany and Japan* (New York: Farrar, Straus, Giroux, 1994).

Butler, John Sibley, *Entrepreneurship and Self-Help Among Black Americans: A Reconsideration of Race and Economics* (Albany, N.Y.: State University of New York, 1991).

Buxbaum, David C., ed., *Chinese Family Law and Social Change in Historical and Comparative Perspective* (Seattle: University of Washington Press, 1978).

Calhoun, Craig, ed., *Comparative Social Research: Business Institutions* 12 (Greenwich, Conn.: JAI Press,1990).

Campbell, Joan, *Joy in Work, German Work. The National Debate, 1800–1945* (Princeton: Princeton University Press, 1989).

Carlson, Tucker, "Holy Dolers: The Secular Lessons of Mormon Charity," *Policy Review* 59 (1992): 25–31.

Carter, Edward, Forster, Robert and Moody, Joseph N., eds., *Enterprise and Entrepreneurs in Nineteenth- and Twentieth-Century France* (Baltimore: Johns Hopkins University Press, 1976).

Casey, Bernard, *Recent Developments in West Germany's Apprenticeship Training System* (London: Policy Studies Institute, 1991).

_____, "The Dual Apprenticeship System and the Recruitment and Retention of Young Persons in West Germany," *British Journal of Industrial Relations* 24 (1986): 63–81.

Caves, Richard E. and Uekusa, Masu, *Industrial Organization in Japan* (Washington, D.C.: Brookings Institution, 1976).

Center for Strategic and International Studies, *Integrating Commercial and Military Technologies for National Strength: An Agenda for Change.* Report of the CSIS Steering Committee on Security and Technology (Washington, D.C.: Center for Strategic and International Studies, 1991).

Chan, Wellington K. K., *Merchants, Mandarins and Modern Enterprise in Late Ch'ing China* (Cambridge: Harvard East Asian Research Center, 1977).

_____, "The Organizational Structure of the Traditional Chinese Firm and Its Modern Reform," *Business History Review* 56 (1982): 218–235.

Chandler, Alfred D., *Scale and Scope: The Dynamics of Industrial Capitalism* (Cambridge: Harvard University Press/Belknap, 1990).

_____, The Visible Hand: The Managerial Revolution in American Business (Cambridge: Harvard University Press, 1977).

Chang, Chan Sup, "Chaebol: The South Korea Conglomorates," Business Horizons 31 (1988): 51–57.

Chang, Kyung-sup, "The Peasant Family in the Transition from Maoist to Lewisian Rural Indistrialization," Journal of Development Studies 29 (1993): 220–244.

Chao, Paul, Chinese Kinship (London: Kegan Paul International, 1983).

Cherlin, Andrew J., Marriage, Divorce, Remarriage (Cambridge: Harvard University Press, 1981).

Cherrington, David J., The Work Ethic: Working Values and Values that Work (New York: Amacom, 1980).

Clegg, Stewart R. and Redding, S. Gordon, Capitalism in Contrasting Cultures (Berlin: Walter de Gruyter, 1990).

Clifford, Mark L., Troubled Tiger: Businessmen, Bureaucrats and Generals in South Korea (Armonk, N.Y.: M. E. Sharpe, 1994).

Coase, Ronald H., "The Nature of the Firm," Economica 6 (1937): 386–405.

Cohen, Daniel, "The Fall of the House of Wang," Business Month 135 (1990): 22–31.

Coleman, James S., "Social Capital in the Creation of Human Capital," American Journal of Sociology, 94 Supplement (1988): S95-S120.

Congleton, Roger D., "The Economic Role of a Work Ethic," Journal of Economic Behavior and Organization 15 (1991): 365–385.

Conroy, Hilary and Wray, Harry, eds., Japan Examined: Perspectives on Modern Japanese History (Honolulu: University of Hawaii Press, 1983).

Craig, Albert M., ed. Japan: A Comparative View (Princeton: Princeton University Press, 1979).

Critser, Greg, "On the Road: Salt Lake City, Utah," Inc. (January 1986).

Cropsey, Joseph, "What is Welfare Economics?" Ethics 65 (1955): 116–125 .

Crouzet, François, "Encore la croissance française au XIX siècle," Revue du nord 54 (1972): 271–288.

Crozier, Michel, The Bureaucratic Phenomenon (Chicago: University of Chicago Press, 1964).

Cumings, Bruce, "The Origins and Development of the Northeast Asian Political Economy: Industrial Sectors, Product Cycles, and Political Consequences," International Organization 38 (1984): 1–40.

Cutts, Robert L., "Capitalism in Japan: Cartels and Keiretsu," Harvard Business Review 70 (1992): 48–55.

D'Antonio, William V. and Aldous, Joan, eds., Families and Religions: Conflict and Change in Modern Society (Beverly Hills, Ca.: Sage Publications, 1983).

Dahrendorf, Ralf, Society and Democracy in Germany (Garden City, N.Y.: Doubleday, 1969).

Dale, Peter N., The Myth of Japanese Uniqueness (New York: St. Martin's Press, 1986).

Davidow, William H. and Malone, Michael S., The Virtual Corporation: Structuring and Revitalizing the Corporation for the 21st Century (New York: HarperCollins, 1992).

Davis, Winston, "Japanese Religious Affiliations: Motives and Obligations," *Sociological Analysis* 44 (1983): 131–146.

De Vos, Susan and Lee, Yean-Ju, "Change in Extended Family Living Among Elderly People in South Korea," *Economic Development and Cultural Change* (1993): 377–393.

Diamond, Larry, "Economic Development and Democracy Reconsidered," *American Behavioral Scientist* 15 (1992): 450–499.

Dore, Ronald P., *British Factory, Japanese Factory* (London: Allen and Unwin, 1973).

_____, "Goodwill and the Spirit of Market Capitalism," *British Journal of Sociology* 34 (1983): 459–482.

Drucker, Peter F., "The End of Japan, Inc.?" *Foreign Affairs* 72 (1993): 10–15.

Du Toit, Andre, "No Chosen People," *American Historical Review* 88 (1983).

Dumont, Louis, "A Modified View of Our Origins: The Christian Beginnings of Modern Individualism," *Religion* 12 (1982): 1–27.

Dunlop, John, Harbison, F. et. al., *Industrialism Reconsidered: Some Perspectives on a Study over Two Decades of the Problems of Labor* (Princeton: Inter-University Study for Human Resources, 1975).

Durkheim, Emile, *The Division of Labor in Society* (New York: Macmillan, 1933).

Dyer, W. Gibb, *Cultural Change in Family Firms: Anticipating and Managing Business and Family Transitions* (San Francisco: Jossey-Bass Publishers, 1986).

Eckstein, Harry, "Political Culture and Political Change," *American Political Science Review* 84 (1990): 253–259.

Eisenstadt, S. N., ed., *The Protestant Ethic and Modernization: A Comparative View* (New York: Basic Books, 1968).

Elvin, Mark, *The Pattern of the Chinese Past: A Social and Economic Interpretation* (Stanford: Stanford University Press, 1973).

_____, "Why China Failed to Create an Endogenous Industrial Capitalism: A Critique of Max Weber's Explanation," *Theory and Society* 13 (1984): 379–391.

Encarnation, Dennis, *Rivals Beyond Trade: American v. Japan in Global Competition* (Ithaca, N.Y.: Cornell University Press, 1992).

Enzenberger, Hans Magnus, *Civil Wars: From L.A. to Bosnia* (New York: New Press, 1994).

Etzioni, Amitai, "A New Kind of Socioeconomics (vs. Neoclassical Economics)," *Challenge* 33 (1990): 31–32.

_____, *The Moral Dimension: Toward a New Economics* (New York: Free Press, 1988).

Fallows, James, *Looking at the Sun: The Rise of the New East Asian Economic and Political System* (New York: Pantheon Books, 1994).

_____, *More Like Us: Making America Great Again* (Boston: Houghton Mifflin, 1989).

Feingold, David, Brendley, K., Lempert, R., et. al., *The Decline of the US Machine-Tool Industry and Prospects for its Sustainable Recovery* (Santa Monica, Ca.: RAND Corporation MR-479/1-OSTP, 1994).

Feuerwerker, Albert, *China's Early Industrialization* (Cambridge: Harvard University Press, 1958).

_____, *The Chinese Economy ca. 1870–1911* (Ann Arbor, Mich.: University of Michigan Press, 1969).

_____, "The State and the Economy in Late Imperial China," *Theory and Society* 13 (1984): 297–326.

Fisher, Albert L., "Mormon Welfare Programs," *Social Science Journal* 25 (1978): 75–99.

Fix, Michael and Passel, Jeffrey S., *Immigration and Immigrants* (Washington, D.C.: Urban Institute, 1994).

Fogel, Robert W., *Railroads and Economic Growth* (Baltimore: Johns Hopkins University Press, 1964).

Form, W. H., "Auto Workers and their Machines: A Study of Work, Factory, and Job Statisfaction in Four Countries," *Social Forces* 52 (1973): 1–15.

Fox, Alan, *Beyond Contract: Work, Power and Trust Relationships* (London: Faber and Faber, 1974).

Frazier, E. Franklin, *Black Bourgeoisie* (New York: Collier Books, 1962).

Freedman, Maurice, *Chinese Lineage and Society: Fujian and Guangdong* (London: Althone, 1966).

_____, Maurice, *The Study of Chinese Society* (Stanford: Stanford University Press, 1979).

_____, *Family and Kinship in Chinese Society* (Stanford: Stanford University Press, 1970).

Fricke, Thomas E. and Thornton, Arland, "Social Change and the Family: Comparative Perspectives from the West, China, and South Asia," *Sociological Forum* 2 (1987): 746–779.

Fridenson, Patrick and Straus, André, *Le Capitalism français 19e-20e siècles: blocages et dynamismes d'une croissance* (Paris: Fayard, 1987).

Friedland, Roger and Robertson, A. F., *Beyond the Marketplace: Rethinking Economy and Society* (New York: Aldine de Gruyter, 1990).

Friedman, David, *The Misunderstood Miracle* (Ithaca, N.Y.: Cornell University Press, 1988).

Fua, Giorgio and Zacchia, Carlo, *Industrilizzazione senza fratture* (Bologna: Il Mulino, 1983).

Fukuyama, Francis, *The End of History and the Last Man* (New York: Free Press, 1992).

_____, "The End of History?" *National Interest* (1989): 3–18.

_____, "Great Planes," *New Republic* (1993): 10–11.

_____, "Immigrants and Family Values," *Commentary* 95 (1993): 26–32.

_____, "The Primacy of Culture," *Journal of Democracy* 6 (1995): 7–14.

Fullerton, Kemper, "Calvinism and Capitalism," *Harvard Theological Review* 21 (1928): 163–191.

Furnham, Adrian, *The Protestant Work Ethic: The Psychology of Work-Related Beliefs and Behaviors* (London: Routledge and Kegan Paul, 1990).

_____, "The Protestant Work Ethic and Attitudes Towards Unemployment," *Journal of Occupational Psychology* 55 (1982): 277–285.

_____, "The Protestant Work Ethic: A Review of the Psychological Literature," *European Journal of Social Psychology* 14 (1984): 87–104.

Galenson, Walter, ed., *Economic Growth and Structural Change in Taiwan* (Ithaca, N.Y.: Cornell University Press, 1979).

Galenson, Walter, and Lipset, Seymour Martin, eds., *Labor and Trade Unionism* (New York: Wiley, 1960).

Ganley, Gladys D., "Power to the People via Personal Electronic Media," *Washington Quarterly* (1991): 5–22.

Gansler, Jacques, *Affording Defense* (Cambridge: MIT Press, 1991).

Geertz, Clifford, *The Interpretation of Cultures* (New York: Basic Books, 1973).

Gellner, David, "Max Weber: Capitalism and the Religion of India," *Sociology* 16 (1982): 526–543.

Gellner, Ernest, *Conditions of Liberty: Civil Society and its Rivals* (London: Hamish Hamilton, 1994).

_____, *Plough, Sword, and Book: The Structure of Human History* (Chicago: University of Chicago Press, 1988).

Gerlach, Michael L., *Alliance Capitalism: The Social Organization of Japanese Business* (Berkeley: University of California Press, 1992).

Gerschenkron, Alexander, *Economic Backwardness in Historical Perspective* (Cambridge: Harvard University Press, 1962).

Gibbs, W. Wayt, "Software's Chronic Crisis," *Scientific American* 271 (1994): 86–95.

Glazer, Nathan, "Black and Ethnic Groups: The Difference and the Political Difference It Makes," *Social Problems* 18 (1971): 444–461.

_____, "The Street Gangs and Ethnic Enterprise," *Public Interest* (1972): 82–89.

Glendon, Mary Ann, *Rights Talk: The Impoverishment of Political Discourse* (New York: Free Press, 1991).

Godley, Michael R., *The Mandarin Capitalists from Nanyang: Overseas Chinese Enterprise in the modernization of China 189* (Cambridge: Cambridge University Press, 1981).

Goffee, Robert and Scase, Richard, eds., *Entrepreneurship in Europe: The Social Processes* (London: Croom Helm, 1987).

Goode, William, *World Revolution and Family Patterns* (Glencoe, Ill.: Free Press, 1963).

Goodwin, Leonard, "Wefare Mothers and the Work Ethic," *Monthly Labor Review* 95 (1972): 35–37.

Gordon, Michael, ed., *American Family in Social-Historical Perspective* (New York: St. Martin's Press, 1973).

Gouldner, Alvin W., "The Norm of Reciprocity: A Preliminary Statement," *American Sociological Review* 25 (1960): 161–178.

Granovetter, Mark, "Economic Action and Social Structure: The Problem of Embeddedness," *American Journal of Sociology* 91 (1985): 481–510.

Green, Donald, and Shapiro, Ian, *Pathologies of Rational Choice Theory: A Critique of Applications in Political Science* (New Haven: Yale University Press, 1994).

Green, Robert W., *Protestantism, Capitalism, and Social Science: The Weber Thesis Controversy* (Lexington, Mass.: D. C. Heath, 1973).

Grochla E., and Gaugler, E., eds., *Handbook of German Business Management,* (Stuttgart: C. E. Poeschel Verlag, 1990).

Gross, C., *The Guild Merchant* (Oxford: Clarendon Press, 1980).

Hadley, Eleanor, *Antitrust in Japan* (Princeton: Princeton University Press, 1970).

Hagen, Everett E., *On the Theory of Social Change: How Economic Growth Begins* (Homewood, Ill.: Dorsey Press, 1962).

Hamilton, Gary G. and Biggart, Nicole W., "Market, Culture, and Authority: A Comparative Analysis of Mangement and Organization in the Far East," *American Journal of Sociology* 94 (1988): S52–S94.

Hamilton, Gary G. and Kao, Cheng-shu, "The Institutional Foundations of Chinese Business: The Family Firm in Taiwan," *Comparative Social Research* 12 (1990): 135–151.

_____, "Max Weber and the Analysis of East Asian Industrialization," *International Sociology* 2 (1987): 289–300.

Hanssen, Johannes, *History of the German People After the Close of the Middle Ages* (New York: AMS Press, 1909).

Hardin, Russell, *Collective Action* (Baltimore: Johns Hopkins University Press, 1982).

Hareven, Tamara K., "The History of the Family and the Complexity of Social Change," *American Historical Review* 96 (1991): 95–122.

_____, "Reflections on Family Research in the People's Republic of China," *Social Research* 54 (1): 663–689.

Harrison, Lawrence E., *Who Prospers? How Cultural Values Shape Economic and Political Success* (New York: Basic Books, 1992).

Hashimoto, Masanori, *The Japanese Labor Market in a Comparative Perspective with the U. S.: A Transaction-Cost Interpretation* (Kalamazoo, Mich.: W.E.Upjohn Institute for Employment Research, 1990).

Heller, Robert, "How the Chinese Manage to Keep It All in the Family," *Management Today* (1991): 31–34.

Herrigel, Eugen, *Zen in the Art of Archery* (New York: Pantheon Books, 1953).

Hexham, Irving, "Dutch Calvinism and the Development of Afrikaner Nationalism," *African Affairs* 79 (1980): 197–202.

Hickson, Charles and Thompson, Earl E., "A New Theory of Guilds and European Economic Development," *Explorations in Economic History* 28 (1991): 127–168

Hirschman, Albert O., *The Passions and the Interests : Political Arguments for Capitalism before its Triumph* (Princeton: Princeton University Press, 1977).

Hirschmeier, Johannes, *The Origins of Entrepreneurship in Meiji Japan* (Cambridge: Harvard University Press, 1964).

Hirszowicz, Maria, *Industrial Sociology: An Introduction* (New York: St. Martin's Press, 1982).

Ho, Samuel P. S., *Small-Scale Enterprises in Korea and Taiwan* (Washington, D.C.: World Bank, Staff Research Working Paper 384, April 1980).

Hoffmann, Stanley, *Decline or Renewal? France since the 1930s* (New York: Viking Press, 1974).

Hoffmann, Stanley, Kindleberger, Charles et. al., *In Search of France* (Cambridge, MA: Harvard University Press, 1963).

Hofheinz, Roy Jr. and Calder, Kent E., *The Eastasia Edge* (New York: Basic Books, 1982).

Hofstede, Geert and Bond, Michael H., "The Confucius Connection: From Cultural Roots to Economic Growth," *Organizational Dynamics* (1988): 5–21.

Horie, Yasuzo, "Business Pioneers in Modern Japan," *Kyoto University Economic Review* 30 (1961): 1–16.

_____, "Confucian Concept of State in Tokugawa Japan," *Kyoto University Economic Review* 32 (1962): 26–38.

Hounshell, David A., *From the American System to Mass Production 1800–1932* (Baltimore: Johns Hopkins University Press, 1984).

Howard, Ann and Wilson, James A., "Leadership in a Declining Work Ethic," *California Management Review* 24 (1982): 33–46.

Hsu, Francis L. K., *Iemoto: The Heart of Japan* (New York: Schenkman Publishing Co., 1975).

Hsu, Francis L. K., *Under the Ancestors' Shadow: Kinship, Personality and Social Mobility in China* (Stanford, Ca.: Stanford University Press, 1971).

_____, *Kinship and Culture* (Chicago: Aldine Publishing Co., 1971).

Huber, Peter, *Orwell's Revenge: The 1984 Palimpsest* (New York: Free Press, 1994).

Huber, Peter, Kellogg, Michael et. al., *The Geodesic Network II: 1993 Report on Competition in the Telephone Industry* (Washington, D.C.: The Geodesic Company, 1994).

Huntington, Samuel P., *The Third Wave: Democratization in the Late Twentieth Century* (Oklahoma City: University of Oklahoma Press, 1991).

_____, "The Clash of Civilizations?" *Foreign Affairs* 72 (1993): 22–49.

Huntington, Samuel P. and Weiner, Myron, eds., *Understanding Political Development* (Boston: Little, Brown and Co., 1987).

Hutcheon, Robin, *First Sea Lord: The Life and Work of Sir Y. K. Pao* (Hong Kong: Chinese University Press, 1990).

Imai, Ken'ichi, "The Corporate Network in Japan," *Japanese Economic Studies* 16 (1986): 3–37.

Jacobs, Jane, *The Death and Life of Great American Cities* (New York: Random House, 1961).

Jacobs, Norman, *The Origins of Modern Capitalism in Eastern Asia* (Hong Kong: Hong Kong University Press, 1958).

Jacoby, Sanford, "The Origins of Internal Labor Markets in Japan," *Industrial Relations* 18 (1979): 184–196.

Jamieson, Ian, *Capitalism and Culture: A Comparative Analysis of British and American Manufacturing Organizations* (London: Gower, 1980).

_____, "Some Observations on Socio-Cultural Explanations of Economic Behaviour," *Sociological Review* 26 (1978): 777–805.

Janelli, Roger L., *Making Capitalism: The Social and Cultural Construction of a South Korean Conglomorate* (Stanford: Stanford University Press, 1993).

Janelli, Roger L. and Janelli, Dawn-hee Yim, "Lineage Organization and Social Differentiation in Korea," *Man* 13 (1978): 272–289.

Jenner, W. J. F., *The Tyranny of History. The Roots of China's Crisis* (London: Allen Lane/The Penguin Press, 1992).

Johnson, Chalmers, *MITI and the Japanese Miracle* (Stanford: Stanford University Press, 1982).

_____, "Keiretsu: An Outsider's View," *Economic Insights* 1 (1990): 15–17.

_____, "The People Who Invented the Mechanical Nightingale," *Daedalus* 119 (1990): 71–90.

Johnson, Chalmers, and Keehn, E. B., "A Disaster in the Making: Rational Choice and Asian Studies," *National Interest* no. 36 (1994): 14–22.

Johnson, Chalmers, Tyson, Laura D'Andrea et. al., *The Politics of Productivity* (Cambridge: Ballinger Books, 1989).

Jones, Leroy P. and Sakong, I., *Government, Business, and Entrepreneurship in Economic Development: The Korean Case* (Cambridge: Harvard University Press, 1980).

Julius, DeAnne, *Global Companies and Public Policy: The Growing Challenge of Foreign Direct Investment* (London: Royal Institute of Intl Affairs, 1990).

Kao, John, "The Worldwide Web of Chinese Business," *Harvard Business Review* 71 (1993): 24–34.

Kaplan, Robert, "The Anarchy," *Atlantic* 273 (February, 1994): 44–81.

Katz, Harry and Sabel, Charles, "Industrial Relations and Industrial Adjustment in the Car Industry," *Industrial Relations* 24 (1984): 295–315.

Katz, Harry, *Shifting Gears: Changing Labor Relations in the US Automobile Industry* (Cambridge: MIT Press, 1985).

Keeble, David and Wever, E., eds., *New Firms and Regional Development in Europe* (London: Croom Helm, 1982).

Kelman, Steven, "'Public Choice' and Public Spirit," *Public Interest* (1987): 80–94.

Kenney, Charles C., "Fall of the House of Wang," *Computerworld* 26 (1992): 67–68.

Kerr, Clark, Dunlop, John et. al., *Industrialism and Industrial Man: The Problems of Labor and Management in Economic Growth* (Cambridge: Harvard University Press, 1960).

Kertzer, David I., ed., *Family Life in Central Italy, 1880–1910: Sharecropping, Wage Labor, and Coresidence* (New Brunswick, N.J.: Rutgers University Press, 1984).

Kertzer, David I. and Saller, Richard P., *The Family in Italy from Antiquity to the Present* (New Haven: Yale University Press, 1991).

Kim, Choong Soon, *The Culture of Korean Industry: An Ethnography of Poongsan Corporation* (Tucson: The University of Arizona Press, 1992).

Kim, Eun Mee, "From Dominance to Symbiosis: State and Chaebol in Korea," *Pacific Focus* 3 (1988): 105–121.

Kim, Kwang Chung and Kim, Shin, "Kinship Group and Patrimonial Executives in a Developing Nation: A Case Study of Korea," *Journal of Developing Areas* 24 (1989): 27–45.

Kim, Myung-hye, "Transformation of Family Ideology in Upper-Middle-Class Families in Urban South Korea," *Ethnology* 32 (1993): 69–85.

King, Winston L., "A Christian and a Japanese-Buddhist Work-Ethic Compared," *Religion* 11 (1981): 207–226.

Kinzer, Robert H. and Sagarin, Edward, *The Negro in American Business: The Conflict Between Separation and Integration* (New York: Greenberg, 1950).

Kitagawa, Joseph M., *Religion in Japanese History* (New York: Columbia University Press, 1966).

Kitaoji, Hironobu, "The Structure of the Japanese Family," *American Anthropologist* 73 (1971): 1036–57.

Klitgaard, Robert E., *Tropical Gangsters* (New York: Basic Books, 1990).

Kotkin, Joel, *Tribes: How Race, Religion, and Identity Determine Success in the New Global Economy* (New York: Random House, 1993).

Krugman, Paul, "The Myth of Asia's Miracle," *Foreign Affairs* 73 (1994): 28–44.

Kumagai, Fumie, "Modernization and the Family in Japan," *Journal of Family History* 11 (1986): 371–382.

Kumon, Shumpei and Rosovsky, Henry, eds., *The Political Economy of Japan. Vol. 3: Cultural and Social Dynamics* (Stanford: Stanford University Press, 1992).

Kwon, Jene K., *Korean Economic Development* (Westport, Conn.: Greenwood Press, 1989).

Landes, David S., "French Entrepreneurship and Industrial Growth in the Nineteenth Century," *Journal of Economic History* 9 (1949): 45–61.

Landes, David S., "New-Model Entrepreneurship in France and Problems of Historical Explanation," *Explorations in Entrepreneurial History,* Second Series 1 (1963): 56–75.

Laslett, Peter N., and Wall, Richard, eds., *Household and Family in Past Time* (Cambridge: Cambridge University Press, 1972).

Lau, Lawrence J., *Models of Development: A Comparative Study of Economic Growth in South Korea and Taiwan* (San Francisco: Institute for Contemporary Studies, 1986).

Lazonick, William, *Competitive Advantage on the Shop Floor* (Cambridge: Harvard University Press, 1990).

Lebra, Takie Sugiyama, "Adoption Among the Hereditary Elite of Japan: Status Preservation Through Mobility," *Ethnology* 28 (1989): 185–218.

Lee, Sang M. and Yoo, S., "The K-Type Management: A Driving Force behind Korean Prosperity," *Managment International Review* 27 (1987): 68–77.

Lee, Shu-Ching, "China's Traditional Family, Its Characteristics and Disintigration," *American Sociological Review* 18 (1953): 272–280.

Lee, W. R. and Rosenhaft, Eve, *The State and Social Change in Germany, 1880–1980* (New York, and Oxford, Berg, 1990).

Leff, Nathaniel H., "Industrial Organization and Entrepreneurship in the Developing Countries: The Economic Groups," *Economic Development and Cultural Change* 26 (1978): 661–675.

Levine, Solomon B., *Industrial Relations in Postwar Japan* (Urbana, Ill.: University of Illinois Press, 1958).

Levy, Marion J., *The Family Revolution in Modern China* (Cambridge: Harvard University Press, 1949).

Levy, Marion J., *The Rise of the Modern Chinese Business Class* (New York: Institute of Pacific Relations, 1949).

Light, Ivan H., *Ethnic Enterprise in America* (Berkeley: University of California Press, 1972).

Light, Ivan H. and Bonacich, Edna, *Immigrant Entrepreneurs: Koreans in Los Angeles, 1965–1982* (Berekeley: The University of California Press, 1988).

Lincoln, James R., Olson, Jon et. al., "Cultural Effects on Organizational Structure: The Case of Japanese Firms in the United States," *American Sociological Review* 43 (1978): 829–847.

Lincoln, James R., Gerlach, Michael L. et. al.,, "Keiretsu Networks in the Japanese Economy: A Dyad Analysis of Intercorporate Ties," *American Sociological Review* 57 (1992): 561–585.

Lindblom, Charles, *Politics and Markets: The World's Political-Economic Systems* (New York: Basic Books, 1977).

Lipset, Seymour Martin, *Continental Divide: The Values and Institutions of the United States and Canada* (New York & London: Routledge, 1990).

———, "Culture and Economic Behavior: A Commentary," *Journal of Labor Economics* 11 (1993): S330–347.

———, *Revolution and Counterrevolution* (New York: Basic Books, 1968).

———, "Pacific Divide: American Exceptionalism—Japanese Uniqueness," in *Power Shifts and Value Changes in the Post Cold War World*, Proceedings of The Joint Symposium of the International Sociological Association's Research Committees: Comparative Sociology and Sociology of Organizations (Japan: Kibi International University, Institute of International Relations of Sophia University, and Social Science Research Institute of International Christian University, 1992)

———, "Some Social Requisites of Democracy: Economic Development and Pol Legitimacy," *American Political Science Review* 53 (1959): 69–105.

———, "The Work Ethic, Then and Now," *Journal of Labor Research* 13 (1992): 45–54.

Lipset, Seymour Martin and Hayes, Jeff, "Individualism: A Double-Edged Sword," *Responsive Community* 4 (1993): 69–81.

Locke, John, *The Second Treatise of Government* (Indianapolis: Bobbs-Merrill, 1952).

Lockwood, William W., *The Economic Development of Japan: Growth and Structural Change, 1868–1938* (Princeton: Princeton University Press, 1954).

Macaulay, Stewart, "Non-Contractual Relations in Business: A Preliminary Study," *American Sociological Review* 28 (1963): 55–69.

Mahler, Vincent A. and Katz, Claudio, "Social Benefits in Advanced Capitalist Countries," *Comparative Politics* 21 (1988): 38–59.

Martin, David, *Tongues of Fire. The Explosion of Protestantism in Latin America* (Oxford: Basil Blackwell, 1990).

Marty, Martin E. and Appleby, R. Scott, eds., *Accounting for Fundamentalisms: The Dynamic Character of Movements* (Chicago: University of Chicago Press, 1994).

———, eds., *Fundamentalisms and Society. Reclaiming the Sciences, the Family, and Education* (Chicago: University of Chicago Press, 1993).

Mason, Edward S., *The Economic and Social Modernization of the Republic of Korea* (Cambridge: Harvard University Press, 1980).

Mason, Mark, *American Multinationals and Japan: The Political Economy of Japanese Capital Controls, 1899–1980* (Cambridge: Harvard University Press, 1992).

Mathias, Peter and Postan, M. M., eds., *The Cambridge Economic History of Europe, Vol. VII: The Industrial Economies: Capital, Labour, and Enterprise. Part I: Britain, France, Germany, and Scandinavia* (London: Cambridge University Press, 1978).

Maurice, Marc, Sellier, Francois et. al., *The Social Foundations of Industrial Power: A Comparison of France and Germany* (Cambridge: MIT Press, 1986).

Mayo, Elton, *The Human Problems of an Industrial Civilization* (New York: Macmillan, 1933).

Mayo, Elton, *The Social Problems of an Industrial Civilization* (London: Routledge and Kegan Paul, 1962).

McFarquhar, Roderick, "The Post-Confucian Challenge," *Economist* (1980): 67–72.

McMullen, I. J., "Rulers or Fathers? A Casuistical Problem in Early Modern Japanese Thought," *Past and Present* 116 (1987): 56–97.

McNamara, Dennis L., *The Colonial Origins of Korean Enterprise, 1910–1945* (Cambridge: Cambridge University Press, 1990).

_____, "Entrepreneurship in Colonial Korea: Kim Yon-su," *Modern Asian Studies* 22 (1988): 165–177.

Mead, Margaret and Metraux, Rhoda, *Themes in French Culture: A Preface to a Study of French Community* (Stanford: Stanford University Press, 1954).

Mearsheimer, John J., "Back to the Future: Instability in Europe after the Cold War," *International Security* 15 (1990): 5–56.

Merton, Robert K., "Science, Religion, and Technology in Seventeenth Century England," *Osiris* 4 (1938): 360–632.

Miller, Michael B., *The Bon Marché: Bourgeois Culture and the Department Store, 1869–1920* (Princeton: Princeton University Press, 1981).

Milward, Alan S. and Saul, S. B., *The Development of the Economies of Continental Europe 1780–1870* (London: George Allen and Unwin, 1977).

Min, Pyong Gap and Jaret, Charles, "Ethnic Business Success: The Case of Korean Small Business in Atlanta," *Sociology and Social Research* 69 (1985): 412–435.

Miyanaga, Kuniko, *The Creative Edge: Emerging Individualism in Japan* (New Brunswick, NJ: Transaction Publishers, 1991).

Montagu-Pollack, Matthew, "Stocks: Hong Kong, Indonesia, Japan, Malaysia, Philippines, Singapore, South Korea, Taiwan, Thailand," *Asian Business* 28 (1992): 56–65.

Moore, Barrington Jr., *Social Origins of Dictatorship and Democracy* (Boston: Beacon Press, 1966).

Moore, R. A., "Adoption and Samurai Mobility in Tokugawa Japan," *Journal of Asian Studies* 29 (1970): 617–632.

Morgan, S. Philip and Hiroshima, Kiyoshi, "The Persistence of Extended Family Residence in Japan: Anachronism or Alternative Strategy?" *American Sociological Review* 48 (1983): 269–281.

Morioka, Kiyomi, "Demographic Family Changes in Contemporary Japan," *International Social Science Journal* 126 (1990): 511–522.

Morishima, Michio, "Confucius and Capitalism," *UNESCO Courier* (1987): 34–37.

Morishima, Michio, *Why Has Japan Succeeded? Western Technology and the Japanese Ethos* (Cambridge: Cambridge University Press, 1982).

Moynihan, Daniel P. and Glazer, Nathan, *Beyond the Melting Pot: The Negroes, Puerto Ricans, Italians, and Irish of New York City* (Cambridge: MIT Press, 1963).

Muller, Jerry Z., *Adam Smith in His Time and Ours: Designing the Decent Society* (New York: Free Press, 1992).

Myers, Ramon H., "The Economic Transformation of the Republic of China on Taiwan," *China Quarterly* 99 (1984): 500–528.

Myrdal, Gunnar, *Asian Drama. An Inquiry into the Poverty of Nations.* 3 vols. (New York: Twentieth Century Fund, 1968).

Nakamura, James I. and Miyamoto, Matao, "Social Structure and Population Change: A Comparative Study of Tokugawa Japan and Ch'ing China," *Economic Development and Cultural Change* 30 (1982): 229–269.

Nakane, Chie, *Japanese Society* (Berkeley: University of California Press, 1970).

Nakane, Chie, *Kinship and Economic Organization in Rural Japan* (London: Althone Press, 1967).

Nee, Victor, "The Peasant Household Economy and Decollectivization in China," *Journal of Asian & African Studies* 21 (1986): 185–203.

Nee, Victor and Sijin, Su, "Institutional Change and Economic Growth in China: The View From the Villages," *Journal of Asian Studies* 49 (1990): 3–25.

Nee, Victor and Stark, David, eds., *Remaking the Economic Institutions of Socialism: China and Eastern Europe* (Stanford: Stanford University Press, 1989).

Nee, Victor and Wong, Herbert Y., "Asian American Socioeconomic Achievement: The Strength of the Family Bond," *Sociological Perspectives* 28 (1985): 281–306.

Nee, Victor and Young, Frank W., "Peasant Entrepreneurs in China's "Second Economy": An Institutional Analysis," *Economic Development and Cultural Change* 39 (1991): 293–310.

Needham, Joseph, *Science and Civilization in China. Vol. I: Introductory Orientations* (Cambridge: Cambridge University Press, 1954).

Negandhi, A. R. and Estafen, B. D., "A Research Model to Determine the Applicability of American Management Know-How in Differing Cultures," *Academy of Management Journal* 8 (1965): 309–318 .

Nelson, Bryce, "The Mormon Way," *Geo* 4 (1982): 79–80 .

Nevins, Allan and Hill, Frank E., Ford: *Decline and Rebirth 1933–1962* (New York: Charles Scribner's Sons, 1962).

Nevins, Allan and Hill, Frank E., Ford: *Expansion and Challenge 1915–1933* (New York: Charles Scribner's Sons, 1954).

Nevins, Allan and Hill, Frank E., Ford: *The Times, the Man, the Company* (New York: Charles Scribner's Sons, 1954).

Nichols, James. and Wright, Colin, eds., *From Political Economy to Economics . . . and Back?* (San Francisco: Institute for Contemporary Studies, 1990).

Niehoff, Justin D., "The Villager as Industrialist: Ideologies of Household Manufacturing in Rural Taiwan," *Modern China* 13 (1987): 278–309.

Nivison, David S. and Wright, Arthur F., eds., *Confucianism in Action* (Stanford: Stanford University Press, 1959).

Noam, Eli, *Telecommunications in Europe* (New York and Oxford: Oxford University Press, 1992).

North, Douglass C. and Thomas, Robert P., *The Rise of the Western World: A New Economic History* (Cambridge: Cambridge University Press, 1973).

Novak, Michael, *The Catholic Ethic and the Spirit of Capitalism* (New York: Free Press, 1993).

O'Brian, Patrick and Keyder, Caglar, *Economic Growth in Britain and France*

1780–1914: Two Paths to the Twentieth Century (London: George Allen and Unwin, 1978).

O'Dea, Thomas F., *The Mormons* (Chicago: University of Chicago Press, 1957).

Okochi, Akio and Yasuoka, Shigeaki, eds., *Family Business in the Era of Industrial Growth* (Tokyo: University of Tokyo Press, 1984).

Olson, Mancur, *The Logic of Collective Action. Public Goods and the Theory of Groups* (Cambridge: Harvard University Press, 1965).

_____, *The Rise and Decline of Nations* (New Haven: Yale University Press, 1982).

Orrù, Marco, Hamilton, Gary et. al., "Patterns of Inter-Firm Control in Japanese Business," *Organization Studies* 10 (1989): 549–574.

Parish, William L., ed., *Chinese Rural Development: The Great Transformation* (Armonk, N.Y.: M.E. Sharpe, 1985).

Pelikan, Jaroslav J., Kitagawa, Joseph et. al., *Comparative Work Ethics: Christian, Buddhist, Islamic* (Washington, D.C.: Library of Congress, 1985).

Piore, Michael J. and Berger, Suzanne, *Dualism and Discontinuity in Industrial Societies* (Cambridge: Cambridge University Press, 1980).

Poole, Gary A., "'Never Play Poker With This Man'," *UnixWorld* 10 (1993): 46–54.

Porter, Bruce, *War and the Rise of the Nation-State* (New York: Free Press, 1993).

Postan, M. M., Rich, E. E., and Miller, Edward, eds., *Cambridge Economic History of Europe,* Vol. 3 (Cambridge: Cambridge University Press, 1963).

Potter, Jack M., *Capitalism and the Chinese Peasant* (Berkeley: University of California Press, 1968).

Preston, Richard, *American Steel* (New York: Avon Books, 1991).

Prestowitz, Clyde V., Jr., *Trading Places: How We Allowed Japan to Take the Lead* (New York: Basic Books, 1988).

Putnam, Robert D., *Making Democracy Work: Civic Traditions in Modern Italy* (Princeton: Princeton University Press, 1993).

_____, "Bowling Alone: America's Declining Social Capital," *Journal of Democracy* 6 (1995): 65–78.

_____, "The Prosperous Community," *American Prospect* (1993): 35–42.

Pye, Lucian W., *Asian Power and Politics: The Cultural Dimensions of Authority* (Cambridge: Harvard University Press, 1985).

Rauch, Jonathan, *Demosclerosis: The Silent Killer of American Government* (New York: Times Books, 1994).

Redding, S. Gordon, *The Spirit of Chinese Capitalism* (Berlin: De Gruyter, 1990).

Rhoads, Steven E., *The Economist's View of the World: Government, Markets, and Public Policy* (Cambridge: Cambridge University Press, 1985).

_____, "Do Economists Overemphasize Monetary Benefits?," *Public Administration Review* (1985): 815–820.

Rich, E. E., and Wilson, C. H., eds., *The Economic Organization of Early Modern Europe,* in *The Cambridge Economic History of Europe,* Vol. 5 (Cambridge: Cambridge University Press, 1977).

Richter, Rudolf, ed., *Zeitschrift für die gesamte Staatswissenschaft* 135 (1979): 455–473.

Riesman, David, Glazer, Nathan et. al., *The Lonely Crowd* (New Haven: Yale University Press, 1950).

Riha, Thomas, "German Political Economy: History of an Alternative Economics," *International Journal of Social Economics* 12 (1985).

Roberts, Bryan R., "Protestant Groups and Coping with Urban Life in Guatemala," *American Journal of Sociology* 6 (1968): 753–767

Robertson, H. H., *Aspects of the Rise of Economic Individualism* (Cambridge: Cambridge University Press, 1933).

Rose, Michael, *Re-working the Work Ethic: Economic Values and Socio-Cultural Politics* (New York: Schocken Books, 1985).

Rosen, Bernard, "The Achievement Syndrome and Economic Growth in Brazil," *Social Forces* 42 (1964): 341–354

Rosenberg, Nathan and Birdzell, L. E., *How the West Grew Rich* (New York: Basic Books, 1986).

Rozman, Gilbert, ed., *The East Asian Region: Confucian Heritage and Its Modern Adaptation* (Princeton: Princeton University Press, 1991).

Ruthven, Malise, "The Mormon's Progress," *Wilson Quarterly* 15 (1991): 23–47.

Sabel, Charles and Zeitlin, Jonathan, "Historical Alternatives to Mass Production: Politics, Markets and Technology in Nineteenth-Century," *Past and Present* 108 (1985): 133–176.

Sabel, Charles and Piore, Michael J., *The Second Industrial Divide* (New York: Basic Books, 1984).

Sabel, Charles, *Work and Politics* (Cambridge: Cambridge University Press, 1981).

Saith, Ashwani, ed., *The Re-Emergence of the Chinese Peasantry: Aspects of Rural Decollectivation* (London: Croom Helm, 1987).

Sakai, Kuniyasu, "The Feudal World of Japanese Manufacturing," *Harvard Business Review* 68 (1990): 38–47.

Salaff, Janet W., *Working Daughters of Hong Kong: Filial Piety or Power in the Family?* (Cambridge: Cambridge University Press, 1981).

Samuelsson, Kurt, *Religion and Economic Action* (Stockholm: Svenska Bokforlaget, 1961).

Sandler, Todd, *Collective Action: Theory and Applications* (Ann Arbor: University of Michigan Press, 1992).

Sangren, P. Steven, "Traditional Chinese Corporations: Beyond Kinship," *Journal of Asian Studies* 43 (1984): 391–415.

Scherer, Frederick M. and Ross, David, *Industrial Market Structure and Economic Performance.* Third Edition (Boston: Houghton Mifflin Co., 1990).

Schmalensee, Richard and Willig, Robert D., eds., *Handbook of Industrial Organization* (Amsterdam: Elsevier Science Publishers, 1989).

Schmidt, Vivien, "Industrial Management under the Socialists in France: Decentralized Dirigisme at the National and Local Levels," *Comparative Politics* 21 (1988): 53–72.

Schumpeter, Joseph A., *The Theory of Economic Development* (Cambridge: Harvard University Press, 1951).

Schwartz, Barry, *The Costs of Living: How Market Freedom Erodes the Best Things of Life* (New York: Norton, 1994).

Scott, Richard, "British Immigrants and the American Work Ethic in the Mid-Nineteenth Century," *Labor History* 26 (1985): 87–102.

Scranton, Philip, "Understanding the Strategies and Dynamics of Long-lived Family Firms," *Business and Economic History* 21 (1992): 219–227.

Sen, Amartya K., "Behavior and the Concept of Preference," *Economics* 40 (1973): 214–259.

_____, "Rational Fools: A Critique of the Behavioral Foundations of Economic Theory," *Philosophy and Public Affairs* 6 (1977): 317–344.

Sexton, James, "Protestantism and Modernization in Two Guatemalan Towns," *American Ethnologist* 5 (1978): 280–302.

Shane, Scott, *Dismantling Utopia: How Information Ended the Soviet Union* (Chicago: Ivan Dee, 1994).

Shima, Mutsuhiko, "In Quest of Social Recognition: A Retrospective View on the Development of Korean Lineage Organization," *Harvard Journal of Asiatic Studies* 50 (1990): 30–78.

Shimokawa, Koichi, "Japan's Keiretsu System: The Case of the Automobile Industry," *Japanese Economic Studies* 13 (1985): 3–31.

Shin, Eui-Hang and Han, Shin-Kap, "Korean Immigrant Small Business in Chicago: An Analysis of the Resource Mobilization Processes," *Amerasia* 16 (1990): 39–60.

Shiroyama, Saburo, "A Tribute to Honda Soichiro," *Japan Echo* (1991): 82–85.

Silin, Robert H., *Leadership and Values: The Organization of Large Scale Taiwanese Enterprises* (Cambridge: Harvard University Press, 1976).

Skocpol, Theda, Evans, Peter B. et. al., eds., *Bringing the State Back In* (Cambridge: Cambridge University Press, 1985).

Skully, Michael T., ed., *Financial Institutions and Markets in the Far East. A Study of China, Hong Kong, Japan, South Korea* (New York: St. Martin's Press, 1982).

Smelser, Neil J. and Swedberg, Richard, eds., *The Handbook of Economic Sociology* (Princeton: Princeton University Press, 1994).

Smith, Adam, *An Inquiry into the Nature and Causes of the Wealth of Nations* (Indianapolis: Liberty Classics, 1981).

Smith, Adam, *The Theory of Moral Sentiments* (Indianapolis: Liberty Classics, 1982).

Smith, Warren W., *Confucianism in Modern Japan* (Tokyo: Hokuseido Press, 1959).

Sombart, Werner, *The Jews and Modern Capitalism* (New York: E.P. Dutton, 1913).

_____, *The Quintessence of Capitalism* (New York: Dutton and Co., 1915).

Song, Byong-Nak, *Rise of the Korean Economy* (Hong Kong: Oxford University Press, 1990).

Sorenson, Clark, "Farm Labor and Family Cycle in Traditional Korea and Japan," *Journal of Anthropological Research* 40 (1984): 306–323.

Sorge, Arndt and Warner, Malcolm, *Comparative Factory Organizatin: An Anglo-German Comparison on Manufacturing, Management, and Manpower* (Aldershot: Gower, 1986).

Soskice, David, "Reconciling Markets and Institutions: The German Apprenticeship System," Wissenschaftszentrum Berlin and Oxford University, Institute of Economics and Statistics, 1992.

Sowell, Thomas, *Essays and Data on American Ethnic Groups* (Washington, D.C.: Urban Institute, 1978).

_____, *Ethnic America: A History* (New York: Basic Books, 1981).

_____, Thomas, *Race and Culture: A World View* (New York: Basic Books, 1994).

_____, Thomas, "Three Black Histories," *Wilson Quarterly* (Winter 1979): 96–106.

Stark, Rodney and Finke, Roger, "How the Upstart Sects Won America: 1776–1850," *Journal for the Scientific Study of Religion* 28 (1989): 27–44.

Steers, Richard, Shin, Y. et. al., *The Chaebol: Korea's New Industrial Might* (New York: Harper Business, 1989).

Steinberg, David, "Sociopolitical Factors and Korea's Future Economic Policies," *World Development* 16 (1988): 19–34.

Stern, Fritz, *The Politics of Cultural Despair: A Study in the Rise of German Ideology* (Berkeley: University of California Press, 1974).

Stigler, George and Becker, Gary S., "De Gustibus Non Est Disputandum," *American Economic Review* 67 (1977): 76–90.

Stix, Gary, and Wallich, Paul, "Is Bigger Still Better?" *Scientific American* 271 (March 1994): 109.

Stokes, Randall G., "The Afrikaner Industrial Entrepreneur and Afrikaner Nationalism," *Economic Development and Cultural Change* 22 (1975): 557–559.

Stoll, David, *Is Latin America Turning Protestant? The Politics of Evangelical Growth* (Berkeley: University of California Press, 1990).

Strauss, Leo, *The Political Philosophy of Thomas Hobbes: Its Basis and Genesis* (Chicago: University of Chicago Press, 1952).

Tang, Thomas Li-ping and Tzeng, J. Y., "Demographic Correlates of the Protestant Work Ethic," *Journal of Psychology* 126 (1991): 163–170.

Tawney, R. H., *Religion and the Rise of Capitalism* (New York: Harcourt, Brace and World, 1962).

Taylor, A. J. P., *Bismarck: The Man and Statesman* (New York: Vintage Books, 1967).

Taylor, Frederick Winslow, *The Principles of Scientific Management* (New York: Harper Brothers, 1911).

Thurow, Lester, *Head to Head: The Coming Economic Battle Among Japan, Europe, and America* (New York: Warner Books, 1993).

Tocqueville, Alexis de, *Democracy in America*. 2 vols. (New York: Vintage Books, 1945).

_____, *The Old Regime and the French Revolution* (New York: Doubleday Anchor, 1955).

Toffler, Alvin and Toffler, Heidi, *War and Anti-War: Survival at the Dawn of the 21st Century* (Boston: Little, Brown and Co., 1993).

Troeltsch, Ernst, *The Social Teaching of the Christian Churches* (New York: Macmillan, 1950).

Tsui, Ming, "Changes in Chinese Urban Family Structure," *Journal of Marriage and the Family* 51 (1989): 737–747.

Tu, Wei-Ming, *Confucian Ethics Today* (Singapore: Curriculum Development Institute of Singapore, 1984).

Tully, Shawn, "Raiding a Company's Hidden Cash," *Fortune* 130 (1994): 82–89.

Turner, Jonathan H. and Bonacich, Edna, "Toward a Composite Therory of Middle-man Minorities," *Ethnicity* 7 (1): 144–158.

Turner, Paul, "Religious Conversions and Community Development," *Journal for the Scientific Study of Religion* 18 (1979): 252–260

Turpin, Dominique, "The Strategic Persistence of the Japanese Firm," *Journal of Business Strategy* (1992): 49–52.

Tyson, Laura D'Andrea, *Who's Bashing Whom? Trade Conflicts in High-Technology Industries* (Washington, D.C.: Institute for International Economics, 1993).

Umesao, Tadao, Befu, Harumi et. al., eds., "Japanese Civilization in the Modern World: Life and Society," *Senri Ethnological Studies* 16 (1984): 51–58.

U.S. Bureau of the Census, *Changes in American Family Life,* P-23, no. 163, (Washington: U.S. Government Printing Office, 1991).

_____, *Family Disruption and Economic Hardship: The Short-Run Picture for Children (Survey of Income and Program Participation),* p-70, no. 23 (Washington: U.S. Government Printing Office, 1991).

_____, *Poverty in the United States,* P-60, no. 163 (Washington: U.S. Government Printing Office, 1991).

_____, *Studies in Marriage and the Family,* P-23, no. 162 (Washington: U.S. Government Printing Office, 1991).

van Wolferen, Karel, *The Enigma of Japanese Power: People and Politics in a Stateless Nation* (London: Macmillan, 1989).

Vogel, Ezra F. and Lodge, George C., eds., *Ideology and National Competitiveness* (Boston: Harvard Business School Press, 1987).

Wade, Robert, "East Asian Financial Systems as a Challenge to Economics: Lessons from Taiwan," *California Management Review* 27 (1985): 106–127.

Walraven, B.C.A., "Symbolic Expressions of Family Cohesion in Korean Tradition," *Korea Journal* 29 (1989): 4–11.

Watson, James L., "Agnates and Outsiders: Adoption in a Chinese Lineage," *Man* 10 (1975): 293–306.

Watson, James L., "Chinese Kinship Reconsidered: Anthropological Perspectives on Historical Research," *China Quarterly* 92 (1982): 589–627.

Weber, Max, *From Max Weber: Essays in Sociology* (New York: Oxford University Press, 1946).

_____, *General Economic History* (New Brunswick, N.J.: Transaction Books, 1981).

_____, *The Protestant Ethic and the Spirit of Capitalism* (London: Allen and Unwin, 1930).

_____, *The Religion of China: Confucianism and Taoism* (New York: Free Press, 1951).

Whitley, Richard D., "Eastern Asian Enterprise Structures and the Comparative Analysis of Forms of Business Organization," *Organization Studies* 11 (1990): 47–74.

_____, Richard D., "The Social Construction of Business Systems in East Asia," *Organization Studies* 12 (1991): 47–74.

Whyte, Martin King, "Rural Economic Reforms and Chinese Family Patterns," *China Quarterly* No. 130 (1992): 316–322.

Whyte, William H., *The Organization Man* (New York: Simon and Schuster, 1956).

Wiener, Martin J., *English Culture and the Decline of the Industrial Spirit, 1850–1980* (Cambridge: Cambridge University Press, 1981).

Wildavsky, Aaron, "Choosing Preferences by Constructing Institutions: A Cultural Theory of Preference Formation," *American Political Science Review* 81 (1987): 3–21.

Wildavsky, Aaron and Drake, Karl, "Theories of Risk Perception: Who Fears What and Why?" *Daedalus* 119 (1990): 41–60.

Willems, Emilio, *Followers of the New Faiths: Culture, Change and the Rise of Protestantism in Brazil and Chile* (Nashville: Vanderbilt University Press, 1967).

_____, "Protestantism as a Factor of Culture Change in Brazil," *Economic Development and Cultural Change* 3 (1955): 321–333.

Williamson, Oliver E., *Corporate Control and Business Behavior* (Englewood Cliffs, N.J.: Prentice-Hall, 1970).

_____, Oliver E., "The Economics of Organization: The Transaction Cost Approach," *American Journal of Sociology* 87 (1981): 548–577.

_____, "The Modern Corporation: Origins, Evolution, Attributes," *Journal of Economic Literature* 19 (1981): 1537–156.

_____, *The Nature of the Firm: Origins, Evolution and Development* (Oxford: Oxford University Press, 1993).

_____, "The Vertical Integration of Production: Market Failure Considerations," *American Economic Review* 61 (1971): 112–123.

Wilson, James Q., "The Family-Values Debate," *Commentary* 95 (1992): 24–31.

_____, *The Moral Sense* (New York: Free Press, 1993).

_____, *Negro Politics: the Search for Leadership* (Glencoe, Ill.: Free Press, 1960).

Wilson, Kenneth L. and Martin, W. A., "Ethnic Enclaves: A Comparison of the Cuban and Black Economies in Miami," *American Journal of Sociology* 88 (1982): 138–159.

Wilson, Kenneth L. and Portes, Alejandro, "Immigrant Enclaves: An Analysis of the Labor Market Experiences of Cubans in Miami," *American Journal of Sociology* 86 (1980): 295–319.

Winter, J. Alan, *The Poor: A Culture of Poverty, or a Poverty of Culture?* (Grand Rapids, Mich.: William B. Eerdmans, 1971).

Wolf, Margery, *The House of Lim* (New York: Appleton, Century, Crofts, 1968).

Womack, James P., Jones, D. et. al., *The Machine that Changed the World: The Story of Lean Production* (New York: Harper Perennial, 1991).

Wong, Siu-lun, "The Chinese Family Firm: A Model," *British Journal of Sociology* 36 (1985): 58–72.

World Bank, *The East Asian Economic Miracle* (Oxford: Oxford University Press, 1993).

Yamamoto, Shichihei, *The Spirit of Japanese Capitalism and Selected Essays* (Lanham, Md.: Madison Books, 1992).

Yanagi, Soetsu, *The Unknown Craftsman. A Japanese Insight into Beauty* (Tokyo and New York: Kodansha International, 1989).

Yang, C. K., *Religion in Chinese Society: A Study of Contemporary Social Functions of*

Religion and Some of Their Historical Factors (Berkeley: University of California Press, 1961).

Yoshimori, Masaru, "Sources of Japanese Competitiveness. Part I," *Management Japan* 25 (1992): 18–23.

Yoshinari, Maruyama, "The Big Six Horizontal Keiretsu," *Japan Quarterly* 39 (1992): 186–199.

Yoshitomi, Masaru, "Keiretsu: An Insider's Guide to Japan's Conglomerates," *Economic Insights* 1 (1990): 15–17.

Zhangling, Wei, "The Family and Family Research in Contemporary China," *International Social Science Journal* 126 (1986): 493–509.

INDEX